Digital Finance and Metaverse in Banking

RELIGION, SPIRITUALITY AND PUBLIC HEALTH

Since 1905, the *Proceedings of the British Academy* series has provided a unique record of British scholarship in the humanities and social sciences. Each themed volume drives scholarship forward and is a landmark in its field. For more information about the series, please visit www.thebritishacademy.ac.uk/proceedings

PROCEEDINGS OF THE BRITISH ACADEMY • 278

RELIGION, SPIRITUALITY AND PUBLIC HEALTH

COMPETING AND COMPLEMENTARY EPISTEMES

Edited by
KAREN O'BRIEN-KOP AND
SUZANNE NEWCOMBE

Published by THE BRITISH ACADEMY
Marketed and distributed by Liverpool University Press

Published by The British Academy
10–11 Carlton House Terrace, London SW1Y 5AH

Marketed and distributed by Liverpool University Press
4 Cambridge Street, Liverpool L69 7ZU

First edition published in 2025

The open access publication of this volume is supported by the Wellcome Trust

British Library Cataloguing in Publication Data
Data available

Library of Congress Cataloguing in Publication Data
Data available

Typeset by Newgen Publishing UK
Printed in Great Britain by CMP, Poole, Dorset

ISBN 978-1-83-624564-3 (print)
ISBN 978-1-83-624925-2 (pdf)
ISBN 978-1-83-624944-3 (epub)

ISSN 0068-1202

The manufacturer's authorised representative in the EU for product safety is:
Easy Access System Europe, Mustamäe tee 50, 10621 Tallinn, Estonia
https://easproject.com (gpsr.requests@easproject.com)

Contents

List of Figures

Notes on Contributors

Joana Bahia is Professor of Sociology and Anthropology at the State University of Rio de Janeiro and Associate Researcher at the Interdisciplinary Center for Migration Studies (NIEM) at the Rio de Janeiro Institute for Urban Research and Planning (IPPUR/UFRJ). She coordinates the religion studies centre (Nuer-Uerj) at Conselho Nacional de Desenvolvimento Científico e Tecnológico (CNPQ). Her main research topics are religious transnationalisation, Afro-Brazilian religions, religious and political conservatism in Latin America, ethnic identities and migration. She co-edited (with M. Oosterbahn and L. Van de Kamp) *Lusospheres: Global Trajectories of Brazilian Religion*, published by Bloomsbury in 2020. She has also written a range of journal articles: 'If You Have Faith, Eshus Responds On-line: The Day to Day Life of Quimbanda' (*Open Theology*, 2023); 'Multiple Space Time of the Transnational Mediumship: Case Studies in Afro-Brazilian Religions' (*Shaman: Journal of the International Society for Shamanistic Research*, 2021); (with Renata Siuda Ambroziak) 'Religious Leaders in Politics Rio de Janeiro Under the Mayor-Bishop in the Times of the Pandemic' (*International Journal of Latin American Religions*, 2020); 'Dancing with the Orixás: Music, Body and the Circulation of African Candomblé Symbols in Germany African Diaspora' (Special issue on 'Religious Circulation in Transatlantic Africa', *African Diaspora*, 2016); 'Under the Berlin Sky: Candomblé on German Shores' (*Vibrant – Virtual Brazilian Anthropology*, 2014).

Kin Cheung is Associate Professor of East and South Asian Religions at Moravian University, where he is Chair of the Global Religions and Philosophy Departments. His research focuses on how contemporary agents use Buddhist doctrine and ritual practices in Chinese and American contexts as well as transnational networks. His interests include Buddhists engaging with healing, meditation, ethical dilemmas, secularism, science, technology, economics and capitalism. He is co-editor of *Buddhism and Healing in the Modern World* (University of Hawai'i Press, 2024) and has authored articles that have appeared in *The Journal of the American Academy of Religion*; *Religion, State and Society*; 마음공부 [*Mindful Practice*]; *Studies in Chinese Religions*; and *The Journal of Buddhist Ethics*. Kin is a steering committee member of the American Academy of Religion's Buddhist Philosophy Unit and Buddhist Critical-Constructive Reflection Unit, as well as a former steering committee member of the Economics and Capitalism in the Study of Buddhism Unit and Transnational Religious Expression: Between Asia and North America Unit. He serves in various roles for the *Journal of Global Buddhism*, the *Journal of Dharma Studies: Asian and Transcultural Religion, Philosophy, & Ethics* and the *Religious Studies Review*. Kin is a Public Intellectuals Program Fellow (Cohort VIII) of The National Committee on United States-China Relations.

Quinton Deeley is a senior lecturer at the Institute of Psychiatry, Psychology, and Neuroscience (IOPPN), Kings College London and an honorary consultant neuropsychiatrist at South London and Maudsley NHS Foundation Trust. He chairs the Maudsley Philosophy Group and co-chairs the Social and Cultural Neuroscience Group at the IOPPN. He has researched the relations between culture, cognition and brain function since studying theology and religious studies at Cambridge University, medicine at Guys and St Thomas' and psychiatry at the Maudsley Hospital. Quinton's work brings cognitive neuroscience research into dialogue with the humanities to improve understanding of cultural variation in mental health and religious cognition, experience and behaviour. His current research topics include using suggestions to alter self-experience, understanding experiences of spirit communication and accompanying brain activity in spiritualist mediums, investigating how religious practices modulate cognition using a virtual reality reconstruction of an ancient Greek religious ritual, and influencing threat perception in healthy individuals with medications that influence dopamine transmission.

Hormoz Ebrahimnejad is the Wellcome Trust Lecturer in History at the University of Southampton's School of Humanities, with a focus on the history of Iran. He completed his Ph.D. at the Sorbonne, where his dissertation explored succession under the Qajars (18th–19th centuries) as a lens through which to examine the structure of the Qajar state. His subsequent research has focused primarily on the history of medicine and epidemics in Iran, examining in particular the importance of institutional modernisation of traditional medicine in the process of medical modernisation in Iran. He has published extensively on the impact of epidemics on the transformation of traditional medicine in 19th-century Iran, as well as the institutional and theoretical shifts that shaped this transformation. He has emphasised the pivotal role that traditionally trained physicians played in the development of anatomical pathology and even biomedicine in Iran. In addition to his work on medical history, Hormoz has also studied modern waqf (Islamic charitable endowments), investigating how waqf institutions operate either alongside or independent of Sharia law. His approach examines the practice of waqf and how its dynamics influence legal frameworks across different countries. His current research revisits Iran's modern historiography, offering new insights into the country's political and social evolution.

Suzanne Newcombe studies religion with the tools of a sociologist and social historian. She is Senior Lecturer in Religious Studies at the Open University (UK) and the director of Inform, which is based in the Department of Theology and Religious Studies at King's College London. Much of her work has focused on investigating the popularisation of yoga in the modern period, such as *Yoga in Britain: Stretching Spirituality and Educating Yogis* (Equinox, 2019) and the *Routledge Handbook of Yoga and Meditation Studies* (2020), which she co-edited with Karen O'Brien-Kop. From 2015 to 2020 she was a post-doctoral researcher on the

European Research Council funded project 'AYURYOG: Entangled Histories of Yoga, Ayurveda and Alchemy in South Asia'. Since 2001, she has also explored different aspects of new and minority religions through her work with Inform. From 2025 to 2027, she is the co-principal investigator (with Stephen Christopher) on a John Templeton Foundation-funded project (63357) entitled 'New Religiosity and the Digital Study of Eudaimonia', a collaboration between the Open University, the Database of Religious History based at the University of British Columbia and Inform based at King's College London.

Karen O'Brien-Kop is Lecturer in Asian Religions at King's College London. She works on Hindu and Buddhist mind–body philosophies in South Asian Sanskrit texts; topics in health and nature ontology; and critical perspectives on contemporary religious cultures. She has published *Rethinking 'Classical' Yoga and Buddhism: Meditation, Metaphors and Materiality* (Bloomsbury, 2021) and articles in peer-reviewed journals such as the *Journal of Indian Philosophy*, *Journal of the British Academy* and *Religious Studies*. She is co-editor of the journal *Religions of South Asia* (Equinox Publishing) and served as co-chair of the Indian and Chinese Religions in Dialogue research unit at the American Academy of Religion from 2020 to 2025.

Chakravarthi Ram-Prasad is Distinguished Professor of Comparative Religion and Philosophy at Lancaster University and Fellow of the British Academy. He is the author of over 60 papers on a wide range of topics and of some seven books. His most recent book is *Human Being, Bodily Being: Phenomenology from Classical India* (Oxford University Press, 2018). He is currently working on a project concerning the philosophical anthropology of emotions based on a close study of both theoretical analysis in Sanskrit aesthetics and the rich representations of Sanskrit literature.

Eugenia Roussou is Assistant Professor of Social Anthropology at the Department of Social Anthropology and History, University of the Aegean, Mytilene, Greece. She is also a senior researcher at the Centre for Research in Anthropology (CRIA-Iscte), Lisbon, Portugal, as the principal investigator of the project 'ReSpell: Religion, Spirituality and Wellbeing. A Comparative Approach of Transreligiosity and Crisis in Southern Europe' (https://respell.cria.org.pt), funded by the Portuguese Foundation for Science and Technology (FCT) and hosted by CRIA. She is the author of *Orthodox Christianity, New Age Spirituality and Vernacular Religion: The Evil Eye in Greece* (Bloomsbury, 2021) and the co-editor of *Expressions of Religion: Ethnography, Performance and the Senses* (Lit-Verlag, 2019). Her research interests include, and she has published extensively on, religion and spirituality, vernacular and lived religion, religious pluralism, ritual healing practices, Complementary and Alternative Medicine (CAM), transreligiosity and spiritual elasticity, among others, with comparative ethnographic reference to Greece and Portugal.

Liora Sarfati is an anthropologist and folklorist specialising in religion, society, culture and media. She holds a Ph.D. from Indiana University and is currently a senior lecturer (associate professor) and head of the Department of East Asian Studies at Tel Aviv University. Since 2005, she has conducted extensive fieldwork with shamans in Korea, exploring the material, social and cultural aspects of this living tradition. Her research focuses on the production and representations of vernacular rituals in contemporary South Korea and the recent protests in downtown Seoul. She employs a range of research methods, including ethnography in urban settings, media analysis, folklore research and digital humanities. Her recent work on Korean shamanism has been published in the journals *Urbanities*, *Religions* and *The Drama Review.* Other articles appeared in the *Journal of American Folklore*, *Journal of Korean Studies*, *Asian Studies Review*, *Journal of Folklore Research*, and as book chapters. Her book, *Contemporary Korean Shamanism: From Ritual to Digital* was published by Indiana University Press in 2021.

Dominic Steavu is a historian of religion and medicine. He focuses on therapeutic, healing and self-cultivation practices in historical Daoism and Buddhism, considering their imbrication with classical Asian medical traditions. He is presently working on a monograph-length cultural history of mushrooms in medieval China, especially those of the sacramental and medicinal varieties. He is the author of *The Writ of the Three Sovereigns: From Local Lore to Institutional Daoism* (University of Hawaiʻi Press, 2019) and the co-editor (with Anna Andreeva) of *Transforming the Void: Embryological Discourse and Reproductive Symbolism in East Asian Religions* (Brill, 2016). More recently, he has completed a study and critical annotated translation of *The Incapable Master* (*Wunengzi*), a medieval Daoist utopian treatise that represents an untapped source for contemporary environmental ethics, and has edited a volume on current trends in Daoist studies. Dominic is Associate Professor at the University of California Santa Barbara. He previously taught at Heidelberg University in Germany and has completed multi-year research stints in Japan, Taiwan and China. He holds graduate degrees from Harvard University and Stanford University.

V. Sujatha is Professor at the Centre for the Study of Social Systems, School of Social Sciences, Jawaharlal Nehru University, New Delhi. She specialises in the fields of sociology of knowledge and sociology of health and medicine. Her research focuses on the dynamic interface between knowledge, social structure and institutions. Her books *Health by the People* (Rawat Publications, 2003), *Medical Pluralism in Contemporary India* (co-editor Leena Abraham; Orient BlackSwan, 2012) and *Sociology of Health and Medicine: New Perspectives* (Oxford University Press, 2014) brought medical pluralism into the theoretical ambit of sociology. Her subsequent work on globalisation led to two publications: an edited volume, *Global Capital and Social Difference* (Routledge, 2020) and an exclusive research paper on European practitioners of Ayurveda based on her fieldwork in four European countries, ‘Globalisation of South Asian Medicines:

Knowledge, Structure and Sustainability', which was published in a special journal issue of *Society and Culture in South Asia*. As well as research articles in refereed journals in English, she has written articles in the Tamil language for intellectual journals. She received the UGC-DAAD fellowship for fieldwork in Germany and the ICSSR-NIHSS fellowship for research at the University of Cape Town, South Africa. She has completed book-length reports on neoliberalism and nutritional status in South Africa and India (2018) and on social inequality and access to medicine in rural Madhya Pradesh (2021) for the ICSSR, linking conceptual studies in health with policy initiatives. Sujatha's ongoing work on experience, knowledge and expertise in traditional Indian medicine seeks to go beyond binaries of tradition and modernity and develop a processual framework for the study of innovations and transformations in Ayurveda and Siddha.

Abel Ugba is an associate professor in the School of Sociology and Social Policy at the University of Leeds. His research and pedagogical interests cover the sociology of religion, migration and media. For two decades, he has studied the transnational religions of African diasporic groups and everyday religiosity in immigration contexts. This has included an empirically based investigation of transnational Pentecostalism among Europe's new African diasporas, focusing on the implications of religiosity for self-understanding and for the construction of social boundaries and commonalities in a precarious immigration context. The outcomes of this research are documented in *Shades of Belonging…*, a monograph published by Africa World Press in Trenton, USA. More recently, Abel has been researching the innovative adoption and adaptation of divine healing practices by Pentecostal Africans in 'secular' Britain and some of the conflicts and negotiations that have characterised the interface between immigrant-led minority religions and the dominant cultures and religions. He has participated in multinational migration and religion-related projects and written country reports for Ireland and the United Kingdom. In his capacity as the current vice president of the African Association for the Study of Religion, Abel is advising a multinational project on 'The Religious and Spiritual Lives of Transnational Young People of African Migrant Background'. The project is funded by the Economic and Social Research Council in the UK and based at the University of Glasgow. He is also one of the conveners and a co-investigator of a research and writing project sponsored by the British Academy. Abel's most recent publications include an overview of the history and dynamics of Europe's megachurches for a Routledge *Handbook* on this theme (2024) and an analysis of the Irish state and immigrant religions, a contribution to *The Study of Religions in Ireland: Past, Present and Future* (Bloomsbury Publishing, 2022).

Acknowledgements

This volume would not have been possible without the financial support of the British Academy and the Wellcome Trust, who supported the conference from which this work derived in May 2023. We were able to hold the conference at King's College London thanks to support from the Head of the Department of Theology and Religious Studies, Professor Linda Woodhead. In the process of securing the British Academy Conferences Grant, the help and support of Eileen Barker, John Maiden, David G. Robertson and Linda Woodhead were invaluable. The grant management and administrative staff were essential in both the management of the grant and the organisation of the conference. Key support staff included Justyna Ladosz at King's College London, who assisted with the event organisation, and Wendy DeVille and Lizzy Clark, who administered the grant and managed the budget at the Open University.

We would like to thank all of those who participated in the discussion at the conference and to the many audience members who raised valuable insights and questions. The conference would not have run smoothly without the help of our volunteers on the day: Matthew Aldridge, Lucy May Constantini, Ruby Forrester, Ruth MacNeil and particularly Ruth Westoby, who went above and beyond in her assistance on the day for which we are extremely grateful. Silke Steidinger assisted with further film editing. We also gratefully acknowledge the support of Inform's trustees for allowing Inform resources to be used for the event. A special thank you goes to the chairs and conference presenters who contributed to the thinking and development of this volume but are not represented with chapters. These individuals include Eileen Barker, Azita Chellappoo, Erminia Colucci, Benson Igboin, David G. Robertson, Pierce Salguero (and Priya Mathiy who contributed to the research), Mark Sinclair and Dominik Wujastyk.

Our discussions were much enriched by a screening of Professor Erminia Colucci's film *Breaking the Chains* (2015), an ethnographic photo/film-documentary. The penetrating discussions following this film were chaired by Simon Dein and included Anto Agus Sugianto as well as Ursula Read and a number of other mental health professionals who were collaborators on the British Academy project 'Qualitative and Visual Mental Health Research in Ghana and Indonesia'.

We would like to extend our gratitude to Professor Chakravarthi Ram-Prasad for his assiduous reading of the entire volume in order to offer synthesising closing reflections. Thanks are also due to all of the anonymous peer reviewers who offered generous feedback on each chapter and our two anonymous proposal reviewers at the British Academy. We also want to thank the editorial team at the British Academy, including Portia Taylor and Yas Afshar.

Suzanne: I would like to thank Helen Barnett for her enthusiastic conversations around this topic; my husband, Alaric, for his interest, insightful inputs and wonderful support; and my daughter for putting up with me gracefully. I am also grateful to my parents for their unfailing support and encouragement.

Karen: I would like to thank the late philosopher Dr Anand Jayprakash Vaidya for a helpful and inspiring conversation on epistemology that supported the writing of my chapter. I am also grateful to my family and friends for support during the completion of this volume but especially for the patience of my son, Z.

Preface

This volume arises from a conference titled 'Public Health After COVID: Beliefs, Religion and Competing Epistemologies' funded by the British Academy and Wellcome Trust. The conference was co-hosted by The Open University and King's College London and was held at King's College London, 26–27 May 2023. Additional funding and support for the event was provided by The Open University, King's College London and the educational charity Inform.

Karen O'Brien-Kop and Suzanne Newcombe
April 2025

Part I

Nuancing Concepts in Health Epistemology

In the opening chapter, Newcombe and O'Brien-Kop introduce the key concepts, theories and frameworks that scaffold the specific case studies and examples analysed in this volume. Drawing out distinctions between epistemology and epistemes, they establish parameters for discussing religion, spirituality and epistemic concerns in varied contexts of public health. Moreover, they highlight key themes such as the vexed division between religion and science paradigms, the material realities of epistemic injustice in healthcare and the importance of the experiential dimension in knowledge-making.

In Chapter 2, O'Brien-Kop takes a philosophy of religion approach to consider social science analyses of lived religion. She argues for engaging pluriversal understandings of knowledge formation, such as South Asian epistemologies.

This section is complemented by the closing chapter of the volume (Ram-Prasad, Chapter 13) which identifies how the themes and case studies of this volume are underpinned by the cultural complexities of global health challenges and offers us fresh ways to think about minority and majority epistemes.

1

Introduction: Competing Epistemes – Religion, Science and Truth in a Healthcare Crisis

SUZANNE NEWCOMBE AND KAREN O'BRIEN-KOP

Introduction

POINTS OF CRISIS are revealing. When ordinary routines are disrupted, assumptions can be more easily re-evaluated. When what is normal has been irrevocably disturbed, it is sometimes possible to more easily see previously overlooked fault lines. This volume takes the tragedy of the Covid-19 pandemic as a prism through which to focus more clearly on how knowledge is created and how decisions are made in contemporary global society. Specifically, this volume explores the ways in which individuals and groups navigated different means of acquiring knowledge, narrating 'truth' and deciding on courses of action amid this crisis. In these pages we foreground the competing and complementary epistemes (i.e. the situated practice of a knowledge system) that produce and permeate individual and collective discourses and choices around health and healing. Focusing on religion and spirituality within the context of the pandemic highlights some of the deepest and most enduring conflicts in our dominant epistemic frameworks. The central question of this book is: How can we best address the critical and dangerous tensions between competing epistemologies when making utilitarian choices about public health?[1]

During the global Covid-19 pandemic crisis period (2020–2), contradictions in working assumptions in both politics and health became more clearly apparent,

[1] This volume arises from a conference titled 'Public Health After COVID: Beliefs, Religion and Competing Epistemologies' held at King's College London, 26–27 May 2023, and funded by the British Academy and Wellcome Trust. Additional funding and support was provided by The Open University, King's College London and Inform at King's College London.

causing concern for social order in many national contexts. The novel virus of Covid-19 was identified in January 2020 and the World Health Organization declared a global pandemic on 11 March of the same year. In the months that followed, both individuals and governments struggled to determine the best courses of action. There were many unknowns in this early period: Just how deadly was this virus? How exactly was it spread? Who was most at risk? How should governments best protect their populations and economies? What were the best actions an individual could undertake for their own health and wellbeing? Communities of trust, expert knowledge, reliability of evidence and competing rationalities became central issues in public health. The epidemiological crisis of the global pandemic coalesced with a growing awareness that there was a concurrent epistemological crisis most visible in political contexts (e.g. Beer and Hariman 2020; Špecián 2022; Crockford 2023; Friedman 2023).

The complexity and urgency of determining what was true during the pandemic highlighted other social transformations that had been developing for decades. Rapid technological transformations of mass media, the omnipresence of social media, generative artificial intelligence, the capacity for creating 'deep fakes' and misinformation have transformed the information landscape for individual and collective decision-making. A concise articulation of an epistemological crisis was prominently expressed by the former President of the United States, Barack Obama. In an interview focused on the information and political landscape that was conducted at the height of the Covid-19 lockdowns, Obama reflected: 'If we do not have the capacity to distinguish what's true from what's false, then by definition the marketplace of ideas doesn't work. And by definition our democracy doesn't work. We are entering into an epistemological crisis' (Obama in Goldberg 2020). Many contemporary issues – from decolonisation to identity politics, religious conflicts to conspiracy theories, 'post-truth' global media to the climate crisis – revolve around questions of what counts as legitimate knowledge and ways of knowing.

Of course, this apparent crisis has deeper roots, and from a historical perspective there is little new about many of the dilemmas we are facing. It is also true that this moment in time is unique: there are new technologies and potential capacities to find solutions to material problems, and perhaps the human species' propensity to cause catastrophic damage on the other-than-human world is occurring at an unprecedented scale. The nexus of power and the production of what is socially validated as knowledge is not new, but capacity to articulate these concerns is developing and destabilising the certainties of knowledge construction that were developed as part of the European Enlightenment (Hall [1992] 2019). In a time of global precarity, it serves humanity to have access to as many cultural epistemes as possible for material problem-solving. The issue of competing forms of knowledge, with dominant and counter-ideologies – based on different ways of knowing and experiencing the world – is a theme that we can find being grappled with, for instance, in ancient texts in India, China and elsewhere in the world. Many chapters in this volume draw on diverse global epistemes to discuss contemporary knowledge communities in relation to religion, spirituality and public health. Some global epistemes are better reflected in this volume than others, and we wish that we had been able to include a broader range of cultural and historical framings and insights. However, we hope that the chapters in this volume will be able to advance the discussion and encourage further contextualisation and awareness of the multiple ways humans seek to know and to effect experiences of health and healing.

Epistemes in religion, science and health

Epistemology is the theory or study of systemic knowledge formation, underpinned by criteria such as reasoning and evidence. Epistemes are the cultural/regional/community expressions of those knowledge systems. We might consider epistemology to be the theory of knowledge and an episteme to be the situated practice of that knowledge. Epistemic frameworks are, perhaps, the intersection of these two aspects of knowledge. In exploring how theoretical and practical knowledge about health informed individual and group choices during the Covid-19 pandemic, this book puts religious epistemes and epistemology in the foreground as a significant factor that has been largely underexposed in analyses of the post-Covid public health landscape.

In the context of public health, the facts on the ground are often held to be incontrovertible. However, global public health is also engaged in broader projects of actively consulting with marginalised communities and seeking to better understand how religious or cultural beliefs may impact on public health goals.[2] These dual imperatives in themselves lead to epistemic competition. On the one hand, within the framework of the empirical research of science, factuality is asserted to be the primary criterion that counts towards valid knowledge about health. However, as many authors in this volume demonstrate, any perceived opposition of facts and experience is not tenable, and experience is not only deeply factual but can also provide a valid basis for truth. Yet, while employing the category of 'experience' as epistemically valid in religio cultural understandings of health, this volume seeks to avoid the inadvertent reification or relocation of religion back into the

[2] For example, the British Academy/Wellcome Trust conference from which this book stems was able to showcase the pioneering work of Professor Erminia Colucci, who uses arts-based and visual methodologies to promote, support and ignite action and change, particularly in the areas of mental health and suicide prevention, and women/child/human rights. The conference hosted a film screening and discussion of *Breaking the Chains* (2015), an ethnographic photo/film-documentary project about human rights violations against people with mental illness and which shows how co-working between biomedical and traditional cultural and religious leaders enables more compassionate and coordinated treatment of people with mental illness in remote communities in Indonesia (Anto and Colucci 2015; Colucci 2015 and 2016). See also the United Nations Population Fund technical report 'Religion, Women's Health and Rights: Points of Contention and Paths of Opportunities' (2016), which analyses the roles of religion and culture in global women's health.

'non-rational' camp (in the now outmoded binary wherein science=rational and religion=irrational). Instead, this book seeks to expand ideas about how epistemes function and what rationality can encompass. Therefore, this discussion about systematised health knowledge, religion and spirituality seeks to avoid any extreme position which automatically positions individual embodied health as being at odds with public and verifiable facts. For example, vaccine choices in a pandemic were an evaluation of the conditions of probability in a context of acute uncertainty. Even when scrutinising the epistemic tendencies of vaccine hesitancy, there is no need to reach for stereotypes of deficient intelligence or education, and in certain cases even cognitive bias may be a 'trivial' factor (Navin 2016: 61).[3]

Therefore, this book is not about valorising the rationality of vaccine accepters over the irrationality of the vaccine hesitant – the case studies, analyses and conclusions are more nuanced and textured than this. Rather, we are offering an active exploration of the grey areas of minoritised epistemes and how they interact with public health domains. Advocating for epistemic dialogue in public health is not about showcasing medical pluralism, and neither is it an issue of political liberalism (Nussbaum 2011) in which differing religious worldviews may be proposed to co-exist respectfully. Moreover, is it not about prioritising religious over secular objections (Navin 2016: 208). Beyond issues of respect, a religious worldview which determines that a community collectively refuses vaccine uptake during a pandemic may be a matter of life or death.

Rather, this book explores religious epistemology but not the form that is well recognised in systematic theology and philosophical theology, which engage debates on proofs of God or other matters of doctrine. This volume encompasses a different project that investigates lived religious epistemes in a range of global contexts. Intentionally, it does not focus on the attitudes or responses of religious institutions during the Covid-19 pandemic (well covered by Chryssides and Cohn-Sherbok 2023), the way that religious communities were able to continue to foster community and develop ritual innovation during pandemic lockdowns (Edelman *et al.* 2021; Borkataky-Varma, Eberhart and Bjelland Kartzow 2023; Hertzman *et al.* 2023) or the angle of how actions taken in response to the pandemic impinged upon religious freedom (e.g. Wisdom 2023).

The authors in this volume give focus to case studies that consider ontologies and epistemes in an epidemic crisis, with space purposefully carved out for non-dominant ideologies and epistemologies. This work centres epistemes that are marginalised in specific regional contexts, such as *musok* in Korea, divine healing in African Pentecostalism in Britain or the potential of Daoist visualisation for psychedelic 'trips' in the US, as well as considering the epistemes that governed dominant public health decisions made in pandemic-era Iran and Tamil Nadu, India.

[3] It is important to note here that Navin is discussing the pre-pandemic context and the specific instance of vaccine denial in relation to children and parental choices. Nonetheless, it is a highly relevant epistemological analysis of vaccine hesitancy and public health.

The included chapters are based on case studies and qualitative research, allowing the authors to look in depth at outlying cases and contextual details to analyse what these marginalised examples can reveal about the social construction of the world and the conceptual and epistemological assumptions. The motivating beliefs, embodied experiences and social contexts are all important to consider when we are dealing with people in health crises and in periods of more widespread uncertainty such as we lived through during the recent pandemic.

Our focus on how knowledge about health and healing is created in religious communities is informed by the decolonial turn in the humanities in the past two decades, disrupting projects of inclusion (such as pluralism) for a more deep-rooted questioning of how knowledge is formed, taking into account particular power relationships (Bhambra, Gebrial and Nişancıoğlu 2018). In focusing on the lived knowledge of communities, specifically marginalised religious communities, we argue that knowledge claims should be properly evaluated in epistemic terms rather than summarily dismissed in public debates, and we suggest that this provides a key means of strengthening public health outcomes. One of the benefits of considering minoritised epistemology is that it can offer new perspectives on dominant modes of biomedical/political/philosophical epistemologies which are often still rooted in a modernist worldview. Despite their relegation to the margins (of social, economic or political power), a better understanding of sidelined epistemes can strengthen understandings of health and healing in the public domain as well as, potentially, public health outcomes.

There are several divides to be navigated from the epistemic margins to the centre: first there is a need to bridge dominant epistemes with culturally marginalised epistemes that include religio-ethical dimensions; and second, there is a need to bridge health epistemologies from the dominant biomedical to the marginalised, which can include the religious. This shift has already been underway in, for example, scholarship on Asian medicine. Garrett notices how in the early 21st century the 'conflict thesis' between religion and science gave way to a 'complexity thesis', noting of Tibetan Buddhist medicine and science in particular the fresh claim that 'the definitions of science and religion and the relationships between them are in flux and inherently contextual' (Garrett 2008: 5). Yet, since that assessment, the global landscape has changed, altered by the Covid-19 pandemic and an intense and intimate encounter between religious epistemes and biomedicine in a way never seen before in such a concentrated time span. In this volume, we seek to go beyond the 'complexity of encounters' (Adams, Schrempf and Craig 2010: 16) between religious medicine and biomedicine in order to engage in a shift towards productive solutions/encounters. Although there is much complexity to acknowledge, the studies in this volume often orient to a pragmatism that was a fast outcome of makeshift epistemic reconciliation during the crisis of Covid-19. Thus we see in the following chapters examples of how Afro-Brazilian moral cosmology was located in a hospital ward in São Paulo (Bahia, Chapter 9) or how a fully vaccinated Portuguese scientist could nonetheless adopt some 'conspiritual' beliefs (Roussou, Chapter 3).

However, even this acknowledgement of pragmatism, epistemic complexity and competition/friction between biomedicine and religion should not be reduced to a unproblematic model of pragmatic parallelism. If we resist 'cognitive imperialism' (Roth 2008) and acknowledge local epistemologies, we also accept that all understandings of health and healing are 'historically grown, culturally specific and intersubjective in nature' (Meinert and Seeberg 2022: 10) and that local beliefs can remain difficult to reconcile with the standardised measures of global public health discourse and practice. The epistemic competition or friction of this volume's title occurs most acutely when local healing systems are 'challenged by interactions with biomedicine … as part of modernization and the politics of secularization occurring in different locales' (Adams, Schrempf and Craig 2010: 6).

In their analysis of ways to reduce epistemic friction, Adams, Schrempf and Craig undermine the competition of 'religion' and 'science' in the context of Tibetan medicine by simply collapsing the distinction between the two categories. In translating the Tibetan term for religious healing (*sowa rigpa*) as a 'science of healing' (Adams, Schrempf and Craig 2010: 3), the authors highlight that '[a]s a classificatory concept, then, [translation] makes no distinction between scientific and religious knowledge' (Adams, Schrempf and Craig 2010: 4).[4] Indeed, this argument is extended to propose 'translation' as an overarching but complex framework for how medicine (specifically Tibetan medicine) is produced *between* religion and science: 'Fundamentally, translation is defined as an act of encounter and conversation, but in its nuances can mean assimilation, correlation, insertion, syncretism, replacement, antagonism, complementarity and more' (Adams, Schrempf and Craig 2010: 19).

It is difficult to get the balance right between taking local healing paradigms seriously on their own terms, which includes accepting their empirically verifiable validity, while avoiding the anachronistic dangers of labelling historical medical developments as 'scientific'. Yet as we see in many chapters of this volume, the applied tools of religious epistemology are more robust than might be expected, and also more flexible. As many chapters demonstrate, not all epistemologies under discussion are competing nor do they exist in 'battle zones' between traditions (Adams, Schrempf and Craig 2010: 3). Rather, they can be partly competing while also overlapping, interlocking or even integrated – the both/and approach of epistemic pragmatism. Sarfati's chapter illustrates how Korean *manchin*s (ritual healing specialists) accepted the Covid-19 vaccine without hesitation, rationalising that while the cause of the disease may be neglect of veneration of the gods, the cure can only be dispensed by the vaccine (Sarfati, Chapter 8). Likewise, Sarfati details that when Korean public health regulations around death were not being observed during the pandemic (due to the perception of impure death atmospheres), *manchin*s were brought in by public health officials to 'clear'

[4] Something also seen in many presentations of yoga and meditation as 'Indian sciences' in many Indian state-sponsored contexts.

the space, acknowledging that these practitioners can deal with things that modern medicine cannot and engaging pragmatic solutions to facilitate the rollout of public health measures.

Competing knowledge paradigms between public health and religion are worth focusing on because, as the case studies in this volume show, epistemic competition not only leads to 'dead ends' and walls of irreconcilable differences but can also produce pragmatic ways to handle competing truth claims. However, we need to put aside the expectation that consensus can be reached between religious and public health epistemologies, because it will not. Rather, the objective in this discussion is to better understand how knowledge disagreements and differences are treated, engaged and acted upon – not only by communities but also by public health bodies. Medina terms these productive points of contact as 'beneficial epistemic frictions' that can be transformative in intersubjective epistemes (Medina 2013: 3).[5] What we call epistemic pragmatism is what Adams, Schrempf and Craig refer to as 'grounded and practical engagement with biomedicine' (Adams, Schrempf and Craig 2010: 17) on the part of Tibetan Buddhist healers or an 'epistemological and practical constancy' in engaging with biomedicine (Adams, Schrempf and Craig 2010: 19). The Covid-19 crisis brought such medical choices into more visible and dramatic relief in the public health landscape. We can now reconceive how epistemic pragmatism might look in a future of well-funded public health: the admittance of certain marginalised experiential epistemes of patients into biomedicine alongside the normative public health requirements.

Epistemic injustice in religion, spirituality and health

Miranda Fricker (2007) has articulated two main forms of what she terms 'epistemic injustice' which are fruitful in considering the overlapping space between religion and health and how knowledge is constructed. The first is testimonial injustice, which is when someone's experience is dismissed or marginalised because of their position of social inequality. In European societies, we have seen increasing acknowledgement of the importance of standpoint epistemology in public health research and practice. This has involved the inclusion of perspectives grounded in the lived experiences of those experiencing health conditions in advisory committees around public health interventions, largely due to the activism of those with disabilities and long-term illnesses. Attention to minoritised religious perspectives on Covid-19 in this volume highlight alternative experiences and

[5] Medina proposes that the regulative principles that should be used to evaluate different forms of cognitive friction are: 'the principle of acknowledgement and engagement, and the principle of epistemic equilibrium' (Medina 2013: 70), with both having a clear intersubjective dimension. These epistemological concepts are different from the more ontological concepts of lived religion (see the 'eclectic combinations', 'personal syntheses', 'pragmatic experimentation', 'bricolage', 'assembled amalgam' and 'creative blending', all associated with practice in McGuire's 2008 discussion: 145–51).

ways of knowing to the more expected (yet also important) reflections of 'religious responses to Covid-19'. The embodied experiences of health and healing among the global majority have had only partial and sporadic attention from those operating from dominant biomedical epistemologies. This issue needs further, more intelligent attention.

When it comes to health and healing, we are all pragmatic pluralists to some extent. Most humans look for simple, practical and accessible ways to alleviate suffering and increase happiness. However, if lived experiences of suffering are left unaddressed or dismissed by medical professionals, it is rational to turn to other places to alleviate the discomfort (which might have overlaps between physical, psychological, ecological and spiritual aspects). However, there is often a significant duplicity in how we frame and narrate the ideological, epistemological and healthcare pluralism found in global majority contexts, compared to how we narrate and describe WEIRD (that is, Western/White, Educated, Industrialised, Rich and Democratic (Henrich, Heine and Norenzayan 2010)) populations where the biomedical epistemologies are more dominant. The extent to which we have choice is largely context-dependent on our social power, wealth and privilege. Choice and access to plural epistemologies are more tolerated in discourses of the global elite where there is wealth and privilege. During the Covid-19 crisis there were many occasions when an 'us' was pitted against a 'them' – and in talking about competing epistemologies we should not assume that this unsettling state of internally competing epistemologies belongs solely to an imagined 'them'. We each live in an ecology of truth experiences, and we may do harm to ourselves or others by denying this fact. Therefore, these 'competing and marginalised knowledges' are not just 'someone else's truth'. By marginalising particular groups, beliefs and practices without exploring the processes by which they have come to their embodied truths, we deny intrinsic aspects of *all* approaches to health and healing.

Fricker's second form of epistemic injustice is termed 'hermeneutical injustice'; this occurs when we lack the language to even identify a particular harmful behaviour. This is another reason why many people sought out alternative communities in response to the uncertainty, suffering and panic experienced during the pandemic. People often find ways in which they can explore their experiences and have them named and validated, sometimes in more skilful ways than others. One such example is the fad of ingesting MMM (Miracle Mineral Supplement or Master Mineral Solution), which was marketed as a cure for Covid-19 and autism (Harvey, forthcoming). This product has been shown to contain high concentrations of sodium chlorite (essentially bleach), which is a known toxin and can cause kidney failure when ingested. Many people, including the President of the United States, Donald Trump, found the idea of injecting bleach as a potential Covid-19 treatment to have an intuitive appeal (BBC 2020). This speaks to a need for miracles and purification, powerful and important ideas that are often addressed in religious contexts and which *can* play a role in promoting health and wellbeing (and do not require actions that are known to cause the body harm) (e.g. see Duffin 2009, Scott 2010 and Stolz 2011).

Mainstream discussions around appropriate behaviour in the epidemiological crisis of Covid-19 were largely reduced to encouraging conformity with political authorities and consensus opinion. However, there was a call for public health to actively engage with populations who did not or could not easily conform to the social mandates of lockdown orders and vaccine receptivity (Burgess *et al.* 2021; Mylan and Hardman 2021). An over-reliance on conformity to institutional authorities is no longer a straightforward expectation in the 21st century, given the plethora of information channels that populations can regularly access. Pushing legal authority behind a scientific consensus statement will not bring alienated people on board with public health messaging and does not necessarily support the reduction of harm.

In recent years there has been a turn in sociology towards studying the social construction of ignorance, that is, 'agnotology' as coined by Robert Proctor (2008: 27–8), as well as the social construction of knowledge. The articulation of this concept has highlighted that sometimes an attitude of ignorance is wilfully manufactured as propaganda; the canonical example is of health research funded by tobacco companies that question associations between smoking and cancer (Michaels 2008; Proctor 2008). Other studies have suggested that it is critical to address the state of 'informed ignorance' revealed by the pandemic, characterised by cognitive overload and frustration in 'interpreting and assessing the quality and reliability of information' as well as 'skepticism towards expert authority, pursuit of alternative information sources, and a propensity to question established norms of rationale and justification' (Cohen and Garasic 2024). This volume proposes that a position of open inquiry towards the epistemological methods employed in the contemporary world is a key first step towards being able to identify, engage in dialogue with and effectively evaluate potential courses for future action towards public benefit. In this, we advocate a position not dissimilar to epistemic virtue theory where qualities like open-mindedness and humility are understood as being essential to enhancing critical thinking and reducing ignorance (e.g. Bevan 2009).[6]

What should practically be done to improve public health outcomes is neither clear nor easy but the aim of this book is to highlight the role of reflexive epistemology in relation to the health goals of reducing harm and suffering. It is this area of epistemic and hermeneutical injustice that we hope this volume will contribute to advancing. In many of the case studies discussed across the chapters, experiential knowledge and the importance of social belonging predominate. We all draw upon a range of different ways of knowing in different contexts. Sometimes a lack of a common vocabulary and ability to nuance our operative epistemologies in personal and political conversations create dismissive reactions of 'liar' and claims of 'fake news'. If we dismiss the articulations of others with disdain, we risk further

[6] The complexities of acting with 'epistemic virtue' in the contemporary environment is well captured in Nguyen (2020) and in religious and conspiratorial contexts pre-Covid in Duymaer van Twist and Newcombe (2018).

isolating, alienating and marginalising people and populations with whom we need to live and converse. We are arguing for a deeper and more systematic engagement with alternative epistemes as a way forward for better evaluating the nature of truth and the basis of decision-making in global society at a point of epistemological re-evaluation.

By starting such a conversation, the aim is to better develop the capacity – both in vocabulary and hermeneutical acumen – to distinguish and value different kinds of truths and ways of knowing. This includes the ability to identify, value, describe and better evaluate the extent to which any 'truth' should be weighed in each specific context. As a society, we are grappling to find the vocabulary and ways of communicating which can take this evaluative conversation forward skilfully. And if academics are struggling with the vocabulary to describe the contemporary landscape of what Michael Stanley-Baker (2023: 2) has termed the 'epistemological borderlands' – then it is hard to expect the media and minimally regulated online social discourse spaces to behave with any subtlety. Several authors in this volume explore how the dominance of European modernist epistemology is in crisis (O'Brien-Kop, Chapter 2; Cheung, Chapter 10; Ram-Prasad, Chapter 13). However, we are not yet at the point where we can envision the ways in which globally dominant conceptual structures and ways of knowing (such as biomedicine) – which all were formed over the last few hundred years of modernity – will shift. Before we can discern a path forward, we need to know where we are. And the major objective of this volume is to analyse the current landscape – to advance the conversation by developing the awareness and vocabulary to identify how knowledge and truth claims operate in contemporary health contexts. Nuanced engagement with epistemology cannot dictate specific policy outcomes. However, it can help us imagine how best practice might look in a future of public health. We invite a future where there is more epistemic honesty about areas of ignorance. We advocate for an active negotiation with the experiential epistemes of patients (which often include overlapping secular and religious ontological assumptions). We hope that a more gradated awareness of the nature and varieties of contemporary worldviews and experiences can enter the medical treatment purview alongside empirical, evidence-based best practice and epidemiological public health analysis.

References

Adams, V., Schrempf, M. and Craig, S. R. (eds) (2010), *Medicine Between Science and Religion: Explorations on Tibetan Grounds* (Oxford: Berghahn Books).

Anto, S. G. and Colucci, E. (2015), 'Free from *pasung*: A Story of Chaining and Freedom in Indonesia Told Through Painting'. *World Cultural Psychiatry Research Review*, September–December 2015: 149–67. https://www.worldculturalpsychiatry.org/wp-content/uploads/2019/08/5-Free-V10N3-4.pdf

BBC. (2020), 'Coronavirus: Outcry After Trump Suggests Injecting Disinfectant as Treatment', 24 April. Available at: https://www.bbc.co.uk/news/world-us-canada-52407177. Accessed 17 June 2025.

Beer, F. A. and Hariman, R. (2020), 'Learning from the Pandemic: Catastrophic Epistemology'. *Social Epistemology Review and Reply Collective*, 9(5): 19–28. https://wp.me/P1Bfg0-4Wa

Bevan, R. (2009), 'Expanding Rationality: The Relation Between Epistemic Virtue and Critical Thinking'. *Educational Theory*, 59(2): 167–79. https://doi.org/10.1111/j.1741-5446.2009.00312.x

Bhambra, G. K., Gebrial, D. and Nişancıoğlu, K. (2018), *Decolonizing the University* (London: Pluto Press).

Borkataky-Varma, S., Eberhart, C. and Bjelland Kartzow, M. (2023), *Religious Responses to Pandemics and Crises: Isolation, Survival, and #Covidchaos*. 1st ed. (Oxford: Taylor & Francis Group).

Burgess, R. A., Osborne, R. H., Yongabi, K. A., Greenhalgh, T., Gurdasani, D., Kang, G., *et al.* (2021), 'The COVID-19 Vaccines Rush: Participatory Community Engagement Matters More Than Ever'. *The Lancet*, 397(10268): 8–10. https://www.thelancet.com/journals/lancet/article/PIIS0140-6736(20)32642-8

Chryssides, G. and Cohn-Sherbok, D. (eds) (2023), *The Covid Pandemic and the World's Religions: Challenges and Responses* (London: Bloomsbury Academic).

Cohen, N. and Garasic, M. D. (2024), 'Informed Ignorance as a Form of Epistemic Injustice'. *Philosophies*, 9(3): 59. https://doi.org/10.3390/philosophies9030059

Colucci, E. (2015), *Breaking the Chains: Human Rights in Mental Health.* Directed, produced and edited by Erminia Colucci.

Colucci, E. (2016), 'Breaking the Chains: Ethnographic Film-making in Mental Health'. *The Lancet Psychiatry*, 3(6): 509–10. https://doi.org/10.1016/S2215-0366(16)30034-7

Crockford, S. (2023), 'That Which They Will Not See: Climate Denial as a Vector of Epistemological Crisis in the Contemporary United States'. *Ethnos*, 8 August. https://doi.org/10.1080/00141844.2023.2242599

Duffin, J. (2009), *Medical Miracles: Doctors, Saints, and Healing in the Modern World* (Oxford: Oxford University Press).

Edelman, J., Vincent, A., O'Keeffe, E., Kolata, P., Minott, M. A., Steurzenhofecker, K., *et al.* (2021), 'British Ritual Innovation under COVID-19', Manchester Metropolitan University. Available at: https://indd.adobe.com/view/6fe8a0a2-a121-4ca4-bd46-5cf4c2a7575f. Accessed 16 June 2025.

Friedman, J. (2023), 'Post-Truth and the Epistemological Crisis'. *Critical Review*, 35(1–2): 1–21. https://doi.org/10.1080/08913811.2023.2221502

Garrett, F. (2008), *Religion, Medicine and the Human Embryo in Tibet* (London: Routledge).

Goldberg, J. (2020), 'Why Obama Fears for Our Democracy', *The Atlantic Magazine*, 16 November. Available at: https://www.theatlantic.com/ideas/archive/2020/11/why-obama-fears-for-our-democracy/617087/. Accessed 16 June 2025.

Hall, S. (2019), 'Five. The West and the Rest: Discourse and Power [1992]' in D. Morely (ed.) *Essential Essays, Volume 2: Identity and Diaspora* (Charlotte, NC: Duke University Press), 141–84.

Harvey, S. (forthcoming), 'Illness as Impurity: Practices for Cleansing and Purifying the Body' in S. Harvey and E. Barker (eds) *Health and Healing in Minority Religions* (London: Routledge).

Henrich, J, Heine, S. J. and Norenzayan, A. (2010), 'The Weirdest People in the World?'. *Behavioral Brain Science*, 33(2–3): 61–83.

Hertzman, E., Lang, N., Larson, E. and Lorea, C. (2023). *CoronAsur: Asian Religions in the Covidian Age* (Honolulu. HI: University of Hawai'i Press).

Medina, J. (2013), *The Epistemology of Resistance: Gender and Racial Oppression, Epistemic Injustice, and the Social Imagination* (New York: Oxford University Press).

Meinert, L. and Seeberg, J. (eds) (2022), *Configuring Contagion: Ethnographies of Biosocial Epidemics* (London: Berghahn Books).

Michaels, D. (2008), 'Manufactured Uncertainty: Contested Science and the Protection of the Public's Health and Environment' in R. N. Proctor and L. Schiebinger (eds) *Agnotology: The Making and Unmaking of Ignorance* (Stanford: Stanford University Press), 90–107.

Mylan, S. and Hardman, C. (2021), 'COVID-19, Cults, and the Anti-vax Movement'. *The Lancet*, 397(10280): 1181. https://www.thelancet.com/journals/lancet/article/PIIS0140-6736(21)00443-8/

Navin, M. (2016), *Values and Vaccine Refusal: Hard Questions in Ethics, Epistemology and Healthcare* (London: Routledge).

Nguyen, C. T. (2020), 'Echo Chambers and Epistemic Bubbles'. *Episteme*, 17(2): 141–61. https://doi.org/10.1017/epi.2018.32

Nussbaum, M. (2011), 'Perfectionist Liberalism and Political Liberalism'. *Philosophy and Public Affairs*, 39(1): 3–45. https://www.jstor.org/stable/41301860

Proctor, R. N. (2008), 'Agnotology: A Missing Term to Describe the Cultural Production of Ignorance (and Its Study)' in R. N. Proctor and L. Schiebinger (eds) *Agnotology: The Making and Unmaking of Ignorance* (Stanford, CA: Stanford University Press), 1–36.

Roth, H. (2008), 'Against Cognitive Imperialism: A Call for a Non-Ethnocentric Approach to Cognitive Science and Religious Studies'. *Religion East and West*, 8: 1–26. https://doi.org/10.1007/978-1-4614-6086-2_9079

Scott, R. A. (2010), *Miracle Cures: Saints, Pilgrimage, and the Healing Powers of Belief.* 1st ed. (Berkeley, CA: University of California Press). https://doi.org/10.1525/9780520946200

Stanley-Baker, M. (ed.) (2023), *Situating Religion and Medicine in Asia: Methodological Insights and Innovations* (Manchester: Manchester University Press).

Stolz, J. (2011), '"All Things Are Possible": Towards a Sociological Explanation of Pentecostal Miracles and Healings'. *Sociology of Religion*, 72(4): 456–82. https://doi.org/10.1093/socrel/srr019

Špecián, P. (2022), 'Epistemology and the Pandemic: Lessons from an Epistemic Crisis'. *Social Epistemology*, 36(3): 167–79. https://doi.org/10.1080/02691728.2021.2009931

United Nations Population Fund. (2016), 'Religion, Women's Health and Rights: Points of Contention and Paths of Opportunities'. New York: UNFPA.

Wisdom, K. (ed) (2023), 'The Impact of the COVID-19 Pandemic on Religious Minorities'. *Special Issue of the International Journal for Religious Freedom*, 16(1). https://secgen.thomasschirrmacher.net/wp-content/uploads/2023/06/20-57-PB.pdf

2

Health Beliefs and Embodied Rationalities: A Pluriversal Philosophy of Lived Religion

KAREN O'BRIEN-KOP

Introduction

WHEN IT COMES to debates about epistemology, public health and religion, the systemic approach of philosophy provides clear concepts for analysing how knowledge is made and how truth is arrived at. This chapter aims to show that when the tools of epistemology are focused on lived religion, its truth-making practices, and its beliefs about health, the analytical yields are high. Combining a philosophical epistemology with a social scientific analysis of situated knowledge leads to fresh insights about how religiously grounded beliefs and embodiment interact to shape healthcare choices. The yields for philosophy of religion are also considerable in that an embrace of lived religion and its concerns makes philosophy relevant as an approach to studying contemporary religion and its social and global challenges (Knepper 2021; Griffioen 2022[1]) in order to 'to better address the tears in our social fabric' (Sherman 2023b: 424). This chapter also explores the pragmatic integration of differing epistemes from a 'pluriversal' perspective (Mbembe 2016, 2021), building towards an inclusive consensus on how truth is arrived at between public health and religious domains.

[1] Griffioen complains that analytic philosophy of religion (APR) has outsourced 'the practical and cultural aspects of religion, not to mention the very definition of religion itself' to social sciences and religious studies (Griffioen 2022: 22–3). The result is that APR has remained 'too detached from lived religion in ways that have insulated it from outside criticism and have inhibited its potential to become a more inclusive, relevant and ambitious discipline' (Griffioen 2022: 23).

Proceedings of the British Academy, **278**, 15–38, © Authors 2025.

Belief and rationality in a lived religion approach

Theoretically, it might seem that a (re)focus on 'belief' goes against the recent grain in religious studies, which has been to foreground lived religion (or everyday religion) as social practice beyond an outmoded 'texts and beliefs' definition of religion (e.g. Hall 1997; Orsi 1997; McGuire 2008; Ammerman 2016). However, this chapter argues that we cannot discuss 'epistemology' without some consideration of 'belief', while also insisting that 'belief' refers to the dynamics of materially embodied belief that is socially situated, that is, an episteme.[2] Such an understanding of embodiment as the site or interface of meaning-making draws on concepts from material culture and material religion in which the body is a living material entity in space which is constantly engaged in transactions.[3] This framing of belief expands it beyond any narrow definition as solely cognitive, eschews mind–body dualism and proposes an episteme as more than a set of conditions for the possibility of knowledge (in the Foucauldian sense) such that epistemic practices are always materially embodied. As Kirloskar-Steinbach (2022: 92–3) puts it: 'Philosophical activity cannot be meaningfully separated from the historical and corporeal particularity of its epistemic subjects. It is not carried out by disembodied minds but by concrete bodies placed in specific, spatiotemporal and socio-material contexts'. Moreover, beyond classical, social and critical accounts of how knowledge is formed, this chapter seeks out materially embodied epistemes *at the community level* in which there are distinct knowledge formation patterns that we can term 'religious epistemology'.[4] The aim of exploring this aspect of religious epistemology is to better understand how 'health knowledge' is produced and practised in the interface between communities and public health.[5]

[2] This understanding combines the more ontological understanding of a 'material body' from material religion with the situated and contingent nature of the episteme (as discursive formation) as presented by Foucault (1989). Material religion, which grows out of the study of material culture (Miller 2005), includes the study of embodiment and physicality as well as how bodies interact with material surroundings. Foucault defines an episteme as 'the total set of relations that unite, at a given period, the discursive practices that give rise to epistemological figures, sciences, and possibly formalized systems' (Foucault 1989: 191).

[3] Plate's definition of material religion is useful here: 'Material religion refers to (1) an investigation of the interactions between human bodies and physical objects, both natural and human-made; (2) with much of the interaction taking place through sense perception; (3) in special and specified spaces and times; (4) in order to orient, and sometimes disorient, communities and individuals; (5) toward the formal strictures and structures of religious traditions' (Plate 2015: 4).

[4] This notion of a community episteme is more localised than Foucault's. Whereas Foucault still worked with universal norms such as 'the Renaissance' or 'science', this chapter suggests an array of pluriversal epistemes, specific to time and space in more localised ways.

[5] Epistemologically speaking, this chapter uses meta-reflection to examine epistemic processes and is focused on the systemic aspects of argumentative truth-making. However, a pluriversal lived epistemology might equally take many other research directions and integrate much more closely with social scientific qualitative methods, actual subjects and specifically localised communities.

First, a key distinction needs to be made between faith beliefs and reasoned or justified beliefs (religious epistemology).[6] This is not to say that faith beliefs are not epistemological, but simply that faith beliefs (in the sense of systematic theology) are not central to this chapter's focus. Rather than discussing adherence to specific doctrines (faith beliefs), this chapter examines the systematised underpinning of religious beliefs about health by processes of reasoning, evidence, validity, authority, certification and so forth. Accepting that there are many *lived* ways of forming knowledge and exercising rationality undermines any perceived gap between everyday 'reason-giving' (Knepper 2021: 63) and 'philosophical rationality'. Accepting that *all* beliefs (including religious) are necessarily embodied and experientially grounded entails a definition of rationality as not only an intellectual practice (which often rests on assumptions of mind–body dualism) but a lived practice (which I propose as mind–body integration).[7] Lived reasoning is extended beyond a merely cognitive or mental process to include embodied knowledge and experience of the world. The basis on which valid claims may be made can include experience, feeling or bodily truths – acknowledging the embodied basis of reasoning.[8] Therefore, embodied subjectivity will be the context for all understandings of rationality and belief formation.

It is hoped that this insertion of philosophical approaches into lived religion will also enhance the latter. For example, in some critical and social scientific use of 'epistemic' there can be a behavioural leaning towards attitudes, dispositions, and sensibilities (Medina 2013), which, while necessary for the purpose of analysing structural bias, can be too general for looking at specific truth-making processes. The turn to lived religion can also be critiqued for suggesting a kind of dualism between mind and body approaches to studying religion, with lived religion over-emphasising the body as the site of practice while sidelining rationality (which is implied to be mental-only): 'Because religion-as-lived is based more on such religious practices than on religious ideas or beliefs, it is not necessarily logically coherent. Rather it requires a practical coherence' (McGuire 2008: 15).[9] On the whole, therefore, a critically aware philosophy of religion can enhance our understanding of lived processes of truth formation at the social or community level.

[6] While examining reasoned belief within epistemology, I acknowledge that there are other types of justified belief – such as memory, introspection, *a priori* or sensation-based – which I do not have space to discuss here in detail.

[7] Of course, philosophy of religion discusses embodiment in a range of ways, although the ideas are expressed differently to social science understandings, e.g. Sherman's global-critical philosophy of religion assertion 'we know the world only through integral, imaginal acts of personal participation or indwelling' (Sherman 2023b: 424).

[8] 'Basing is a relation of *epistemic* dependence and does not imply explicit inference, although particular theories might hold that the relation is satisfied only when inference occurs' (Lyons 2023; emphasis in the original).

[9] McGuire goes on to argue, however, that that the category of spirituality has the potential capacity to offer a more holistic analysis of minds, bodies and spirits (McGuire 2008: 97).

Pluriversal epistemologies

The decolonial turn in the humanities and social sciences has been clear in the rejection of Eurocentric categories of the universal, both in the content and frame of knowledge: 'any serious effort to decolonise philosophy cannot be satisfied with simply adding new areas to an existing arrangement of power/knowledge' (Maldonado-Torres et al. 2018: 55). Decolonising knowledge requires a radical re-understanding of epistemology itself and the acknowledgement that is there is no singular understanding of reason, reasoning or rationality but rather many 'geographies of reason' (Maldonado-Torres et al. 2018: 67).

Within decolonial theory, Mbembe (2016) uses the concept of the pluriversal to deconstruct the hegemony of the universal, so that diverse ways of knowing are equally considered, following Chakrabarty's directive towards provincialising Europe (Chakrabarty 2000). Using Mbembe's concept of the pluriversal is to assert that practices of 'rationality' are necessarily culturally diverse because any 'monological constructions of reason are politically, geographically and historically contingent' (Sherman 2023a: 36). The limits of the Western episteme that has shaped global biomedicine thus becomes clear: 'epistemic categories that emerge from modern-Western scientific and philosophical traditions may be inadequate and even destructive when it comes to the analysis of knowledge claims from other cultures, other periods, diverse ways of knowing and domains of reality unacknowledged by dominant modern ontologies' (Sherman 2023a: 27). In contrast, pluriversal epistemologies, such as South Asian epistemology, discussed below, illuminate that any analysis of embodied rationality does not entail a diminished place for logic. Moreover, recognising 'that practices of rationality are tradition- and culture-specific, need not force one into a subjective or nonrealist account of rationality' (Sherman 2023a: 27). This chapter seeks a pluriversal approach by employing tools from Buddhist and Hindu epistemology as well as analytic philosophy of religion to make sense of the critical questions at hand. Such an approach means steering religious epistemology away from the twin imperatives of 'avoiding epistemic blame and defending the rational permissibility of realist theistic belief' (Griffioen 2022: 23). It also means steering it away from hegemonic mechanistic analysis that assumes that disagreement is a true/false binary: either someone has a 'performance error in her evaluation of the evidence' or 'the disagreement stems from the application of distinct models of how to interpret the evidence' (Vaidya 2013: 542). Such binaries may be valid in a single and particular kind of epistemology, such as modernist, but not in a landscape of pluriversal epistemologies.

Modernist epistemology can be defined as 'the hegemonic Eurocentric knowledge system, which originated in 16th-century Europe and together with industrial capitalism produced a specific kind of knowledge that is embodied in modern science' and which produced an 'exclusion and Othering of other epistemologies' (Breidlid 2013: 1). 'It is one of the characteristic traits of colonialism that it denied diversity, epistemic diversity, and created instead inferiority. The production of the hegemonic epistemology necessitated the Other, which was characterised as uncivilized, irrational, superstitious' (Breidlid 2013: 7). Yet despite the oppressive and flawed legacy of modernist epistemology, there is value in addressing its emphasis on rationality because the two primary and intersecting social groups discussed in this chapter – non-mainstream religious communities and 'alternative' health groups including vaccine refusers – are often dismissed as 'irrational', drawing on hegemonic ideas about the superiority of Eurocentric epistemic norms, such as culture or science. There is also strategic value in addressing rationality as one of the main grounds on which public health is willing to 'legitimately' engage with marginalised epistemes for better health outcomes, given that public health itself is an exemplar of modernist epistemology.

Even before the Covid-19 pandemic, some of the popular or media criticism of vaccine refusers was made on the grounds of 'irrationality' or 'hysteria' (Navin 2016: 21). Even though academics such as Navin challenged such discourses (in relation to childhood vaccines), he nonetheless concluded that 'vaccine denialists are insufficiently committed to truth-oriented inquiry. The poor epistemic practices prevalent in vaccine denialist communities prevent vaccine denialists from endorsing the well-established results of vaccine science' (Navin 2016: 22). In many mainstream popular forums, post-Covid characterisations of vaccine hesitancy as irrational (or unconcerned with truth) have only hardened, but to relegate the concerns of minority groups, non-mainstream health practitioners or vaccine refusers as 'irrational' signals a missed opportunity for epistemic and practical engagement between these groups and public health.[10]

A pluriversal lived approach

The need for a pluriversal philosophy of religion and for a philosophy of lived religion are two connected projects that eschew universal norms.[11] The endeavour of cultivating a global-critical philosophy of religion is gathering pace (Knepper 2021; Loewen and Rostalska 2023),[12] with philosophers of religion asking how their research might be better reconciled with religious studies and its 'thick, regional descriptions of religious communities' (Sherman 2023b: 424).[13] Yet a philosophy of lived religion is still in its early stages (Knepper 2021). In his exploratory

[10] Several recent public health studies emphasise the importance of understanding hesitancy in local contexts – hesitancy is often rational and specific to a particular vaccine product (Driedger *et al.* 2023) or reflects a lack of trust in specific governmental and public health organisations based on lived experience (Kekana 2024).

[11] For a thorough critique of hegemonic epistemology and a strategy of epistemic resistance, see Medina (2013), and for a call for alternative epistemologies, see Mills (1997).

[12] This label derives from a research seminar held at the American Academy of religion since 2015.

[13] See also Schilbrack (2014); Burley (2020); Sherman (2023a).

essay, Knepper advocates for a broader approach to knowledge formation: 'Such a philosophy of lived religion considers all acts of religious reason-giving, not just those of the literate elite' and it includes 'discourses and practices' of 'ordinary people' in contemporary communities (Knepper 2021: 63–4). Developing this approach theoretically and using it as a lens to discuss community belief formation can bring critical clarity to discussions about health epistemology and strengthen the efficacy of public health to engage with particular religious epistemes. By combining a 'ground-up' approach of lived religion with a systemic approach of philosophy of religion, we may advance understanding of how communities operate as a mediating space between individual health and institutionalised healthcare, including the policies, practices and physical sites of public health. However, I will not discuss religion at an institutional level, since the focus here is on community religion and marginalised religion, both of which tend to operate in spaces outside or adjacent to hegemonic religion.[14]

What is religious health epistemology?

Religious epistemology and health epistemology are both focused on the question of how we can prove that claims are true and how the proof is demonstrated – a vital process employed by global citizens to evaluate competing community and public health claims during the Covid-19 pandemic. Here I argue that a combined examination of how religious and health beliefs (which underpin healthcare choices) are formed at community level constitutes 'religious health epistemology'.

An appeal for embodied rationality rests on a non-dual understanding of mind–body, such as we see in certain South Asian ontologies (discussed below). Embodied rationality, based on prior knowledge or proofs (e.g. of health or healing), can inform well-reasoned choices. Indeed, experiential tools can include presuppositions, criteria, verification, concepts, debate and dialectical beliefs, all employed by a dynamically embodied subject in the world. Most importantly, religious health epistemology is not at odds with valid justification, be it through reasoning or intrinsic validity (such as authority), and neither is it at odds with principles of coherence,[15] since 'distinct cultures display their own living coherence' (Sherman 2023a: 24).

Epistemological tools rely on different forms of reasoning to produce the justification for truth, but meta-reflection also enables us to understand the ways

[14] My understanding of community religion is community formations, often defined as local populations but also increasingly instantiated as international networks. These community identities may be shaped by institutional religion but are also independent of it. For example, a community of the Pentecostal Redeemed Christian Church of God (RCCG) in London, UK, may adopt different shared ideas and practices on health to communities of the same church organisation in Lagos, Nigeria.

[15] Coherence is a probabilistic relation that produces a justified belief (i.e. being justified in believing something to be true).

in which religious practitioners *justify* their engagement with traditional healing practices and the ways in which they *justify* the exclusion or integration of public health messaging with those religious health practices (such as belief in divine healing).[16] Epistemic competition occurs when justification is amplified above all else, such as when religious reasons for health choices are considered sufficient, even if proven not true by biomedicine. Therefore, we have to separate out justification from truth: one may hold a justified belief, but it may not be true – and an over-emphasis on justification can lead to an entrenched distance from public health policy or the spread of misinformation. In the following sections I will focus on processes of justification adopted by marginalised communities (such as those discussed elsewhere in this volume) in evaluating the truth of health beliefs, analysing both reliable and unreliable determinations. It is only by accepting community beliefs as rationalised that public health professionals can improve the grounding for communication, exchange and intervention in community knowledge healthscapes.

Empiricist foundationalism: learning from pluriversal epistemologies

How might we bring different epistemologies – that is, religious, health, and regional – into a productive conversation? When global models of public health, dispersed through governing bodies such as the World Health Organization (WHO), come into contact with regional epistemologies, there can be competition between the global and the local. Nonetheless, the picture is changing, and public health projects such as the 'WHO International Standard Terminologies on Ayurveda' (WHO 2022) or the academic 'Decolonizing Health and Medicine' podcasts by the *British Medical Journal* (*British Medical Journal* 2023) demonstrate that leading-edge research is already opening up frontiers of knowledge in productively glocal ways.[17] A further relevant example in recent UK public health is the set of principles used to construct the 'Public Involvement Impact Assessment Framework' funded by the Medical Research Council in 2019,[18] which seeks to set up public–institutional partnerships to co-produce health research, building on a longstanding commitment to patient and public involvement (PPI) in healthcare.[19] The already existent awareness in UK public health of the need to incorporate community

[16] The emphasis here is not so much on causal grounding of beliefs but on justification processes within the larger epistemic frameworks for knowing.

[17] WHO: https://iris.who.int/bitstream/handle/10665/365543/9789240064935-eng.pdf (accessed 12 June 2024); BMJ: https://www.bmj.com/podcasts/decolonising (accessed 12 June 2024).

[18] This was part of a broader project titled 'UK Standards for Public Involvement in Research', backed by the National Institute for Health and Care Research (NIHR), Chief Scientist Office (CSO) Scotland, Health and Care Research Wales, and the Public Health Agency (Northern Ireland).

[19] For more on the background to PPI since its inception in 1996, see Rose (2014) and the programme of work called INVOLVE (www.invo.org.uk).

knowledge is reflected in one of the eight guiding principles of the health research framework document 'Valuing Different Kinds of Knowledge':

> One guideline called for lay and professional knowledge to be valued equally (31). At the very least research teams should respect the differing skills, knowledge and experience of public representatives (2, 23) and *be committed to listen to the experiences of a range of people, including those whose voices are not often heard* (8, 9).
>
> (Medical Research Council 2019; emphasis added)

However, there are further steps to be taken in reimagining a global architecture of public health based on pluriversal epistemologies rather than universal.[20] For example, epistemology from South Asia can make relevant contributions to our discussion, allowing a rehearsal of what it might look like to responsibly question or decentre the dominance of a global biomedical hegemony which still largely rests on Western reasoning about how health beliefs should be formed (i.e. on the basis of certain types of scientific evidence that form part of modernist epistemology).

Reason and experience

A first point is the relation between reason and experience. It is important to note that a Descartian-style mind–body split is rare in South Asian religion and philosophy – in most Hindu, Buddhist and Jain ontologies the mind and body are one unit (Ram-Prasad 2018).[21] Such ontology can therefore challenge dominant biomedical assumptions about health and clarify that epistemology includes embodied rationality (e.g. bodily reasoning, bodily certainty or bodily validity). Moreover, the early Hindu Nyāya school of logic presents syllogistic reasoning (in five stages) that always includes the stage of experience. ('I can infer that there is fire where there is smoke, because *in every example where I have seen smoke in the kitchen*, it has been produced by fire').[22] This experiential stage is known as the principle of invariable concomitance, pervasion or universal co-presence (*vyāpti*).[23] Therefore, inferential reasoning in Indian traditions is not abstract or disembodied: prior experience always informs logical conclusions and counts as adequate evidence.

This contrasts somewhat with Western theories of inference where there is often a divide between logic and epistemology: 'From the Western perspective, logic does not deal with things that go on in the mind but with abstract structures of implication' (Westerhoff 2018: 228). What are the considerations here for religious

[20] With increasing patterns of global migration, any national health system in the Global North may reasonably be expected to come into contact with the religious health beliefs of patients from a wide range of cultural backgrounds.

[21] See also the early Indian medical compendium *Carakasaṃhitā*, circa 3rd to 5th century CE, which states that 'mind, self and body' are a 'disciplining triple staff' and a 'unified combination' (Ram-Prasad 2018: 29).

[22] The five stages are: (1) the thesis (e.g. where there is smoke there is fire); (2) the reason; (3) the experience-based example; (4) the application of the rule/example; (5) the conclusion.

[23] It indicates that the subject of an inference (e.g. fire) has a property (e.g. smoke) that is always co-present.

health epistemology? This example illuminates that within certain religious communities, inference may be intrinsically linked to experience in establishing a subjectively embodied reason for making a health choice, one that is logically underpinned and far from 'irrational' (I am taking as a given here the claim that all religious meaning-making is underpinned by 'reason-giving').[24] Moreover, in a non-dualist ontology in which minds and bodies are continuous, looping extensions of each other, we are engaging an epistemology that not only investigates belief as mental and bodily but also existent in material interactions between bodies and environments, including intersubjective and social interactions. Beliefs are thus dispersed beyond individual cognition, formed in community interspaces and exist in non-linguistic (material) as well as linguistic modes.

Perception, inference and conspiracy theorising

A second contribution from South Asian epistemology is a nuanced theorising of the relation between perception and inference. In early South Asia, varieties of realism are found in many schools in both Hindu and Buddhist traditions. According to direct realism (which is more aligned with scientific direct realism than with recent innovations in naïve realism),[25] philosophers adhered to 'the claim that perception yields altogether uninterpreted data' (Arnold 2005: 31) and employed various techniques[26] to 'leave untrammeled perception free to register things as they really are' (Arnold 2005: 25).[27] According to this principle, perception leads to direct knowledge and any form of linguistic-conceptual elaboration that is overlaid on the particulars (that are directly perceived) carries the risk of introducing cognitive error. Reliable warrants or epistemic instruments (*pramāṇas*) were historically ranked in South Asia from among a range of instruments. The early Buddhist philosophers Dignāga (5th–6th century CE) and Dharmakīrti (6th–7th century CE) of the logico-epistemological school asserted that there were only two valid epistemic instruments that could form a basis for truth: perception (*pratyakṣa*) and inference (*anumāna*).[28] For them, perception did not necessarily produce knowledge, and they reserved this function for inferential reasoning (with perception of raw sense data constituting the prompt for the knowledge-generation

[24] Here, I concur with Knepper's 'working hypothesis' that 'religious reason-giving is present in all religious traditions and communities' (Knepper 2021: 66).

[25] In naïve realism, it is key that the object is constitutive of experience, such that the conscious phenomenal character of that experience is *shaped* by the objects of perception and their features (see e.g. Fish 2010 or Logue 2012).

[26] Such techniques ranged from removing cognitive impairments to moral cultivation.

[27] Arnold here is discussing the Buddhist philosophers, Dignāga and Dharmakīrti.

[28] These are broadly in line with Buddhist epistemology generally and are selected from a longer list of valid bases in Indian philosophy, also including authority (or testimony), comparison, postulation and non-perception. As Westerhoff points out, 'in the Indian context perception is always understood to include the cognition of mental events in a manner that is as direct and immediate as the sensory cognition of external objects' (Westerhoff 2018: 225).

process).[29] Indeed, these philosophers were so dedicated to foregrounding the rules of inference that in their lifetimes 'the study of inferential patterns occupied centre-stage in the Buddhist philosophical world' (Westerhoff 2018: 225). The outcome for certain Buddhist schools of epistemology was that, as Arnold argues, 'if there is any final court of appeals in thinking' (Arnold 2005: 208) then it is not perception but rather inference which is the most reliable means of assessing truth claims. Dignāga's logico-epistemological approach asserted that valid inferences have to be characterised by three conditions, known as the evidential triple mark (*trairūpya*): (1) A characteristic connection between the subject of the inference and the reason; (2) one prior existing similar entity or example; and (3) no prior existing dissimilar entity or example (Westerhoff 2018: 226). Within the ontologies of Buddhist philosophy, the generalities produced by concepts are less 'real' than the particularities produced by perception, but this does not prohibit the capacity to produce knowledge. And for the purposes of this chapter's focus on contemporary belief-making, the pragmatic success of being able to produce well-reasoned generalisations in the public domain is a key concern in its own right.

In any community, there are of course limits as to what can be admitted into an epistemic frame as valid and limits to the way in which justification can support truth. In order to understand how knowledge claims are certified in religion, we must further consider justification and coherence. It is necessary, in some measure, to discuss conspiracy theorising because there can be an overlap between some minoritised religious communities and conspiracy theorising (see Roussou, Chapter 3; Deeley, Chapter 4; Newcombe, Chapter 12 in this volume). I am not interested in specific 'conspiracy theories' here, that is, beliefs but in patterns of truth-making that may underpin community formations of theorising truth, that is, conspiracy *theorising*. Conspiracy theorising is not devoid of systematic reasoning (i.e. justified by evidence or premises), but the success of such arguments often falls apart in terms of coherence. An analysis of how conspiracy theorising works demonstrates that the most reliable warrant (or justification for holding a true belief) is not as we might expect the cognitive instrument of direct perception (seeing with one's own eyes) but rather inference (making rationally constructed arguments).[30] When inference is applied, the lack of coherence in conspiracy theories is often exposed.[31]

To connect this point to our social media age: a citizen can hold any number of unmediated beliefs that are based on perception (e.g. 'I believe there is a health conspiracy, based on videos that I have watched online'), yet one can only

[29] A further distinction is that perception (with conception) leads to direct knowledge, while inference leads to indirect knowledge.

[30] As Griffioen points out, epistemic warrants actually refer to a broader notion than justified true belief: 'whatever it is that would, in a particular instance make a true belief into knowledge' (Griffioen 2022: 22 fn1).

[31] Of course, sometimes sound forms of 'conspiracy theorising', such as activism-based challenges to hegemonic narratives or campaigns driven by social justice aims, can lead to truth on the basis of both perceptual evidence and inference. This chapter is, however, interested in 'conspiracy theorising' based on flawed epistemic bases.

reasonably know if those beliefs are true knowledge based on inference, that is, 'by virtue of reflection on *what else* one might know in virtue of knowing one thing, and on whether it *coheres* with other beliefs' (Arnold 2005: 208; added emphasis). For conspiracy theorists, coherence breaks down (e.g. trust in public health is violated) because inference is no longer sufficiently applied (or no longer appears to work) in the very cases where inference is most needed – those circumstances where phenomena cannot be directly perceived by the senses and where there is likely to be less certainty and more dispute about the truth of a matter. Hence, without the stabilising effect of inference in determining truth, there is often an absence of coherence in conspiracy theorising.

The importance of reinstating inference back into a global public health episteme was evident in the European Commission/UNESCO guidelines on identifying conspiracy theories during Covid-19. These guidelines often directed readers to ask, 'How does this belief relate to other beliefs I hold'?, prompting inferential investigation (European Commission/UNESCO n.d.). Interestingly, as the EC/UNESCO guidelines pointed out, the very purpose of conspiracy theories is 'to seek clarity' during times of acute uncertainty, such as Covid-19 – and an often-observed trait of conspiracy theorising is the push towards the inviolability of knowledge based on perception to the detriment of inference in order to promote certainty. The foregrounding of inference in Buddhist epistemology aids us in seeing this relation. Birchall, Knight and Knight (2024: 13) describe the epistemic pattern of conspiracy theorising as a 'feedback loop' which is a 'dysfunctional pattern of amplification, weaponisation and denunciation' that starts with grassroots conspiracy communities and then moves to influencers, political figures and later researchers, factcheckers and media figures. The cycle is one of generation of non-truth to gradual debunking and re-establishment of truth norms (Birchall, Knight and Knight 2024: 13) – but it is only when inferential reasoning is reintroduced in the loop (driven initially by claims of perception) that truth norms can be re-established.[32]

Empiricist foundationalism

A further relevant feature of South Asian epistemology is the foregrounding of foundationalism in certain Buddhist schools.[33] Foundationalism is the view that some beliefs are epistemologically basic, that is, that they are based on, or are dependent on, other beliefs. Foundationalism is also central to Western epistemology:

[32] However, it should be remembered that 'conspiracy theorising' is complex; sometimes conspiracy narratives reflect evidence-based conspiracies of those in power and in many other cases these theories could be argued to function *as* a religion and as serving to define in-groups and out-groups (alongside several other socially contextual functions) rather than being primarily an error of theorising. For a more sophisticated framework on theorising on the nature of conspiracy theories in contemporary society, see Dyrendal, Robertson and Asprem (2019) and Robertson (2025).

[33] The Hindu Nyāya school also upholds foundationalist epistemology.

> In order for perception to give us genuine knowledge of the external world, perceptual knowledge must be grounded in direct acquaintance with something; we are not directly acquainted with physical objects but only with our experiences, so beliefs about these experiences must serve as the foundations of perceptual knowledge.
> (Lyons 2023)

While basic beliefs are often derived from sense experience (which can be mistakenly classed as infallible, such as perception), foundationalism also operates according to inferential justification. There is a tension here because foundationalism is at odds with the theory that all knowledge claims are socially situated or contextual. So it is only when we combine foundationalism with empiricism that we can accommodate the situated and contingent nature of knowledge.

This is what Arnold achieves in his discussion of empiricist foundationalism as reflected in the Buddhist epistemology of Dignāga and Dharmakīrti in the first millennium CE. One of Dignāga's landmark works was the *Compendium of Epistemic Instruments* (*Pramāṇasamuccaya*) and Dharmakīrti's was the related *Commentary on Epistemic Instruments* (*Pramāṇavārttika*). Because empiricism entails that knowledge of truth is derived from experience, empiricist foundationalism credits 'real existence to the objects disclosed in ordinary, precritical experience' (Arnold 2005: 6). To draw the discussion back to religious health epistemology, the frame of empiricist foundationalism can help us to better understand the religious convictions of marginalised epistemic subjects, such as Afro-Brazilian medical patients on the truth of their other-dimensional healing experiences while lying in a public hospital bed receiving biomedical treatment (Bahia, Chapter 9). Some of these patients' truth claims may be hard for observers to believe. But early Buddhist thinkers like Dignāga and Dharmakīrti help us to think through any potential clash between propositional truth and experiential truth.[34] If, as Dignāga and Dharmakīrti asserted, propositional truth is difficult to claim (or impossible to know) then it might be said that all we can be certain of is the phenomenological content of our experience. In philosophical terms, these arguments can stray into concerns that all that we can know is that we have mental contents and experience. An obvious critique of these concerns in a pragmatic context is that while they are sufficient for judging whether or not a self exists, or for producing self-awareness, they are not suited for any judgements about the external world.

But again, the early empiricist foundationalism of Buddhist philosophy guards against such interiority by insisting that inference exists not only 'for oneself' (i.e. internal cognition that is certain) but should also exist 'for others',[35] such that any inference is always subject to 'the underlying facts in the world' and can be communicated intersubjectively through speech acts or other means to a convincing degree (Westerhoff 2018: 228). Hence, successful inference is never only about the formal validity of an argument but also about its soundness (i.e. its truth value),

[34] Propositional truth is determined by the meanings and inferential relationships between sentences.

[35] This theory was developed by Dignāga.

again marking a significant difference from Western logic in which validity and soundness can be separated (such that an argument can be valid without being true). This emphasis on empirical reality is partly resultant from the grounding of inference in perception and, by extension, embodiment. We are inevitably led back to embodied context – society and culture – because critical judgements can only exist in a social web of beliefs that lend coherence to any one conclusion. In practice, religious health epistemology can be aligned with empiricist foundationalism in that the experiential episteme (or embodied rationality) is always operating according to beliefs that are epistemologically basic. And judgements about health often follow those basic beliefs, forming justifications for health choices. Therefore, an understanding of the episteme of a religious community is key to analysing the basis on which collective health beliefs and choices are formed and exercised in the public sphere.

The insights from early South Asian epistemology, temporally remote though they might be from the context of Covid-19, help us to identify parameters for religiously grounded forms or patterns of knowing. And although a key mark of conspiracy theorising is its *lack* of inferential capability – in which justification contains no probabilistic connection (inference) to causes – in contrast, religious reasoning can be strongly grounded in inference. Even if systematic reasoning is not always evidently at work in community religion, the capacity and tendency for it to underpin health choices should at least signal to healthcare professionals that religious health epistemology can be a reliable way of producing evidence-based knowledge.

Credulity, scepticism and critical thinking: the value of expert knowledge

This section builds further on the argument for the rationally motivated nature of religious health epistemology by employing tools from analytic philosophy of religion. In the post-pandemic health landscape, two themes are especially important to consider: the collectively agreed value of health expertise and the presence or absence of critical thinking in healthcare choices.

As Barua outlines in his analysis of critical thinking, there are basic ways in which the public '[c]onsider any controversial, publicly discussed issue' (Barua 2021: 286). Let's consider Covid-19 and public health responses as controversial events. In analytic philosophy of religion, the three main approaches to accepting truth claims in the public domain are (1) credulity, which involves gathering expert views; (2) withholding a judgement (scepticism); or (3) critical thinking, which involves not only assessing expert statements on all sides but also assessing the reasons for those statements (looking for the norms that might shape those statements) (Barua 2021: 286).[36] Although critical thinking is often presented as

[36] Barua is here discussing Huemer's (2005) arguments. See also Vaidya (2013: 535).

the gold standard in epistemology and public debate, philosophers such as Huemer (2005) have argued that critical thinking is not always the most epistemically responsible way to form knowledge. In a landmark paper, he argued that when there is consensus, then *credulity* is a safer approach, but when there is a lack of consensus, then *scepticism*, or withholding, may be better in terms of forming true beliefs and avoiding false ones (Huemer 2005). From a decolonial and pluriversal perspective we might spot a tension here in the general dangers of what is termed 'credibility excess' (Kirloskar-Steinbach 2022) or 'epistemic arrogance' (Medina 2013) in hegemonic epistemology. But my discussion focuses narrowly on the credibility of public health information about Covid-19 vaccines rather than the broader topic of credibility excess and structural bias in certain modes of institutionalised knowledge (discussed in many chapters of this volume).

To pick up on Huemer's foregrounding of credulity and scepticism over and above critical thinking, the Covid-19 pandemic demonstrated that many members of the public lacked the skills, knowledge or confidence to critically challenge science-based health claims, and that in the face of mainstream biomedical consensus, credulity (or deference to the expert view) was the often the choice made. WHO data shows that a majority of the world's population had a Covid-19 vaccination.[37] Of course, many citizens did engage in significant research of scientific literature and, as this section elaborates, the positions of credulity and critical thinking were not always so separate. Some citizens adopted sceptical positions on a spectrum for different reasons: this included opting to delay vaccinations until there was more information about the success and side effects of specific new vaccines, and at the harder end of scepticism was vaccine refusal on the basis of conspiracy theorising.[38]

Epistemological analyses of vaccine hesitancy existed before the Covid-19 pandemic, often in relation to parental vaccine hesitancy.[39] Such childhood vaccine choices continue to be topics of public debate today in new ways, as has been

[37] The World Health Organization Covid Dashboard, which shows global data for Covid-19 vaccination, states that as of 31 December 2023, 67 per cent of the world's population were 'vaccinated with a complete primary series of COVID-19 vaccine', while 32 per cent were 'vaccinated with at least one booster dose of a COVID-19 vaccine'. https://data.who.int/dashboards/covid19/vaccines (accessed 18 April 2025).

[38] There are a wide variety of sceptical positions for vaccine refusal from the rational concerns about the novelty and rapid production of the new Covid vaccinees during the pandemic (e.g. Driedger *et al.* 2023) to the rumours circulating about the vaccines containing microchips controlled by Bill Gates, that the vaccine would permanently alter the recipient's DNA, or that it contained lung tissue of an aborted foetuses (BBC 2020).

[39] Writing in 2016, Navin evaluated the 'poor epistemic practices' of '[v]accine denialist communities' as the 'pursuit of an uncritical affirmation of their existing beliefs and a failure to show appropriate regard for differences in expertise or competence' (Navin 2016: 38). In the case of 'epistemically vicious' (Navin 2016: 38) cycles of conspiracy theorising, Navin identified a reliance on causal narratives that confirm pre-existing beliefs and offer relatively simple stories (Navin 2016: 66). Nonetheless, this chapter will not follow the route of social psychology with concepts like groupishness, motivated reasoning, confirmation bias, implicit bias, affect bias, framing bias and so forth. See e.g. Navin (2016: 72–9).

evidenced in the 2025 measles outbreak in the US.[40] However, there are fresh layers of complexity for the post-Covid-19 epistemic communities we are discussing, not only due to the present-day rise of scepticism through conspiracy theorising but also due to the interlocking concerns of religious epistemes. Vaidya discusses dilemmas in public debate, and we may apply some of his insights to religious epistemes in the age of Covid-19, in which expertise refers not only to health science but also to religious knowledge, producing epistemic competition:

> the dilemma argument is that when one is attempting to form a belief in a domain where there are experts and one is epistemically inferior to those experts, it is not *epistemically responsible* to take the judgement formed by the output of one's own process of critical thinking as being more important than that of the experts.
>
> (Vaidya 2013: 537; emphasis in the original)

Such dilemmas regarding one's own critical conclusions can apply equally to challenging authority in public health and in religious contexts. Interestingly, Huemer's argument on critical thinking discussed medical health as *the* benchmark for how to approach *all* 'controversial, publicly discussed issues' (Huemer 2005: 523–4).[41] However, in the public domain, lived religious truth-making is often characterised as a low-status epistemology in relation to scientific-based reasoning on health because of lived religion's *perceived* commitment to credulity (deference) over critical thinking.[42] However, as Barua points out, the two are not so distinct: 'in any case where credulity and [critical thinking] CT are available, it is possible to implement credulity without any CT … (but) identifying genuine sources of information and determining majority view would count as application of CT' (Barua 2021: 290).[43] As Barua, Huemer and Vaidya argue, responsible credulity necessarily requires some critical thinking. In the case of information on Covid-19 and vaccines, all citizens, religious or otherwise, encountered challenges in identifying sources of accurate information due to the spread of misinformation, and they encountered difficulty in determining the majority view following the spread of counter-narratives online. Therefore, to even engage credulity (to follow biomedical expert opinion), citizens during the Covid-19 pandemic had to first

[40] See the WHO statement from 27 March 2025 on the measles outbreak in the US. The advisory notes: 'As of 14 March, the New Mexico Department of Health reported 35 cases of measles. Of the 35 cases, 28 were unvaccinated, two were vaccinated, and five had unknown vaccination status.' The WHO risk assessment included 'an increase in the susceptible population due to persistently low vaccination coverage related to factors such as the COVID-19 pandemic, increased vaccine hesitancy in some communities and sectors of the population, and limited access to health services, particularly for vulnerable populations'. https://www.who.int/emergencies/disease-outbreak-news/item/2025-DON561 (accessed 18 April 2025).

[41] Where, however, such pre-Covid philosophical arguments are now outdated is in the wide acceptance of the claim that 'medical diagnosis is largely a matter of factual analysis' (Vaidya 2013: 544). As the pandemic demonstrated, not all global citizens agreed with the facts of vaccine necessity and efficacy, no matter how empirically proven.

[42] Excluding the case of theology.

[43] Barua is, again, discussing Huemer's (2005) arguments.

employ critical thinking (identify and weigh all sides of each 'expert statement'). Therefore, we cannot assume that credulity leads to 'uncritical, dogmatic acceptance of the experts' views' (Barua 2021: 293), since we have established that appropriate credulity, including that within religious epistemes, requires some measure of critical thinking.

Situated critical thinking and emic epistemologies

As the Covid-19 pandemic showed, some religious communities did not accept the reliability of science-based evidence regarding health choices such as vaccines (see in this volume Roussou, Chapter 3; Deeley, Chapter 4; Newcombe, Chapter 12). It is important to note here that: 'There are multiple goals of belief formation, and one may choose to forgo a more reliable process of belief formation in order to further some other end' (Barua 2021: 290). In belief formation, truth is not the only epistemic goal, since there are other epistemic values that are considered, from the virtuous to an empirically active interrogation of one's environment (Barua 2021: 294). However, there are limits to employing virtue epistemology in the context of healthcare, unless we want to shift from rationality to ethics. As Navin explains: 'Virtue epistemologists are less interested in identifying "necessary and sufficient conditions" for knowledge than in describing the dispositions that better orient knowers towards knowledge' (Navin 2016: 22). While such an approach can lead to a carving up of medical and non-medical knowledge along the lines of morality, epistemic virtue can also be understood more pragmatically:

> These virtues include trustworthiness, credibility, and accuracy, among many others. Accordingly, an 'epistemic virtue' relative to inquiry about medicine is a disposition which facilitates the acquisition of empirically grounded medical knowledge. In contrast, an 'epistemic vice', relative to inquiry about medicine, is a disposition which inhibits the acquisition of empirically grounded medical knowledge.
>
> (Navin 2016: 23)

Of course, ethics and ontology often inform the goals of religious health epistemology, not just a concern for truth.[44] Indeed, any health episteme is always underpinned by ontological goals since it is geared towards preserving or promoting health and healing. The practice of health therefore always has an instrumental goal, in which truth is only a means to an ontological or ethical end. If we suspend true belief as the only goal of epistemic choices, then we can see that when faced with competing epistemes, religious subjects can justify particular health choices through various coherence-making processes. This can lead to the

[44] In an acute and desperate pandemic, scientists and public health experts were not always able to address religio-ethical issues, e.g. whether vaccines were halal, contain GMO components or contravene foundational ethical beliefs on animal products. For that certainty on moral truth, subjects often turn to religious experts and back to credulity.

avoidance of *either/or* choices in favour of pragmatic *both/and* choices between public health and traditional religious healing. Hence, experience remains a key explanatory basis for truth-making: 'An empirically adequate theory is one that will never be refuted by the course of experience, and one makes sense of the course of experience by developing a classification system of experiences together with a theory of explanation of how various categories are explanatorily related' (Barua 2021: 297). However, even if epistemic competition can be reduced at an individual or community level, the institutional biomedical episteme is bound to evaluate many religious health claims as lacking, flawed or wrong. A standard public health approach is to privilege the 'etic' value of biomedical expertise over the 'emic' value of lived experience.[45]

On a practical level, then, how can pragmatically integrated systems of religio-biomedical health (at personal or community levels) be valued or utilised in public health? Moreover, how can epistemic hierarchies of health expertise be maintained alongside a growing public health commitment to epistemic egalitarianism and patient-centred approaches?[46] As Vaidya points out, in practice, 'nonexperts trained in critical thinking have the ability to contribute to capturing the mistakes of experts or providing insights that are not within the frame through which the expert conceives the issue' (Vaidya 2013: 541). Nonetheless, while a 'lived religion' approach acknowledges the everyday expertise of subjects when it comes to their own individual and community realities, this epistemic ground still has to be responsibly questioned and contested in the face of a global public health crisis such as a pandemic.

As we have established, religious health epistemology, even if often based on credulity (deference to expert view), still employs aspects of critical thinking. And, as Vaidya highlights, critical thinking is never neutrally situated but is always about occupying a '*critical point of view* or perspective and identification with a concern of a certain kind' (Vaidya 2013: 551; emphasis in the original). Among the various examples of situated critical thinking that Vaidya cites (such as Marxist, feminist or postcolonial) is the 'religious-ethical'. Situated critical thinking, then, might be understood to be a part of a broader category that has recently been labelled 'emic epistemology' (Sherman 2023a). Seen to characterise the fundamental approach of a global-critical philosophy of religion that addresses postcolonial critique through acts of deprovincialisation,[47] emic epistemology is concerned with upending normative and Eurocentric assumptions about epistemology.[48]

[45] For a discussion of gender-based power imbalances in the medical profession, see Navin (2016) and for a discussion of race-based power imbalances, see Medina (2013).

[46] There are severe limits to many of these analytic philosophical arguments, especially Huemer's, about the reliability of critical thinking when the points are framed in terms of 'average intelligence' and 'superior intelligence' – this suggests an elitist approach and also posits intelligence as mental rationality (Huemer 2005).

[47] Referring here to Chakrabarty (2000).

[48] E.g. (1) normative understandings of rationality and justification and (2) the assumption that proving theism is the central concern of religious epistemology (Sherman 2023a: 24).

Here, again, we can see a vital link to the emergence of the lived religion paradigm in the social sciences:

> An emic epistemology is an account not of the knowledge that a subject claims, but of the way in which the subject seeks to attain knowledge. Such epistemologies may be reflexively articulated in sophisticated systems or they may be implicit. Emic epistemologies do not determine what a subject takes to be true, but rather govern what a subject can regard as intelligible, the plausibility conditions under which a claim's truth might become a compelling candidate for consideration.
>
> (Sherman 2023a: 25)

In contrast to emic epistemology, public health provides an example of an 'epistemically advantaged' discourse in that the etic understanding (medical expertise) is privileged over the emic for utilitarian ends (maintaining public health). While biomedical professionals are employing greater reflexivity in how emic epistemologies such as 'spirituality' might be gainfully used in public health,[49] there are still a plethora of fact-based indicators as to why one health choice is right and another wrong. Therefore, philosophy of religion must tread carefully in any engagement with the rationality of public health discourse – the truth claims under examination are not about abstract arguments or long-term patterns of social and cultural perception, but are often about acute issues of life and death, in which the referent is a body and its ability to cope/thrive/survive as a result of ill health. In pandemic conditions, the epistemological concerns of philosophy may seem a luxury to public health officials. Indeed, if, as Sherman says, 'philosophy has no neutral "cool place" from which to assess the claims of others' (Sherman 2023a: 36), the same is markedly *not* true of public health, which claims scientific evidence, such as randomised controlled trials, as its neutral place from which to assess the efficacy of healthcare claims.

But the question remains: what can a serious consideration of marginalised religious views on health and healing bring to the table of public health? The answer is that it can bring an epistemic advantage of its own. Some of the theoretical basis of situated critical thinking is drawing on feminist standpoint epistemology, which argued that marginalised subjects and groups often have an epistemic advantage in that they can obtain a collective viewing vantage point from the margins that cannot be obtained in the mainstream position (e.g. Hartsock 2004; Hill Collins 2004). Standpoint epistemology also has a strong empiricist tendency that foregrounds the value of lived experience and observation from the standpoint of the margins: 'Standpoint theories map how a social and political disadvantage can be turned into an epistemic, scientific and political advantage' (Harding 2004: 7–8). But in evaluating how some religious subjects may pragmatically integrate orthodox public health choices with orthodox religious health beliefs, we are not

[49] For a recent round-up of literature on spiritual care in clinical practice, see Palmisano and Pannofino (2022).

only considering the interest value of the 'double vision' (or 'double objectivity' in Harding's terms) of specific groups in their religious health epistemology. There are broader institutional changes that can be made in healthcare if the mainstream biomedical system is able to cultivate a pluriversal vision (or polyvisuality) when it comes to health epistemology – being able to detect and take into account multiple epistemic frames (including marginalised religious) for research, policy and practice innovations that lead to greater public health efficacy.

Acceptance, understanding, assent and inconsistency in truth-making?

This chapter has sought to provide a technical scaffolding to the discussion of epistemic disagreement and argued that 'competition' (competing truth claims) can lead to fuzzy overlaps in embodied health beliefs, for better and for worse. There are clear dangers in any project of this kind of nuancing 'truth' too far by decentreing its absolute value (biomedical or otherwise) – and the danger exists in relation to post-truth regimes, conspiracy theorising and their intersections with religions. An argument designed to support coherence-making processes over the absolute value of truth – such as Griffioen's assertion that 'even if truth remains an important epistemic value, it is not the end-all-be-all of our epistemic activities' (Griffioen 2022: 28) – can give dangerous ammunition to those who disregard truth and expert knowledge in favour of populist power. Nonetheless, in her effort to broaden the reach of analytic epistemology Griffioen asserts that we should eschew the primacy of 'justified true belief' in favour of an 'attitude of *acceptance*' which should be subject to 'rational assessment' (Griffioen 2022: 28; emphasis in the original). Griffioen proposes this model as a way to get out of the deadlock of truth/non-truth that is entailed in models of 'justified true belief', and although she foregrounds the pragmatic value of this approach in relation to science, we can see its applicability to understanding pluriversal religious epistemes (or indeed to polarised culture wars). Accordingly, a proposition (e.g. 'Religion produces healing') can be accepted as 'obtaining' or 'feeling' to be true outside of cognitive measures: 'two practitioners in the same field operating with the same model need only agree in their *acceptance* and *use* of the relevant propositions and objects to do "good" science and math, even if they may ultimately disagree on their truth or ontological status' (Griffioen 2022: 29; emphasis in the original). We can transpose the two practitioners from 'science' and 'math' to 'religious health epistemology' and 'biomedical health epistemology' – with both groups overlapping in commitments to health and healing. A religious practitioner and public health official may *disagree* on the truth or ontological status of a healing practice from a religious tradition, but by bracketing the truth value and *accepting* or *using* the relevant proposition, each may be able to engage epistemic dialogue as a basis for intersubjective health practice (engaging collaboratively with knowledge claims about the body and health), which may lead to better patient care for an individual or greater shared ground between communities of practice. Griffioen also proposes an epistemic shift from acceptance to understanding, which takes place on three bases: understanding 'need not be propositional', 'does not always require truth' and 'involves acceptance but not necessarily belief' (Griffioen 2022: 29). Whereas knowledge is 'a static, all-or-nothing state that one either has or does not', understanding is a '*dynamic, discursive process* that can admit of degrees' (Griffioen 2022: 29; original emphasis). The project becomes one of intersubjective understanding between differing truth regimes – as long as we have agreed benchmarks, such as the presence of an inferential basis of reasoning, alongside other valid bases of truth formation, such as coherence or empiricist foundationalism.

Yet one important difference or source of friction remains between science-based truth and religious reasoning: that of causality. Medical diagnosticism is based on causal explanation (symptom, illness, cure). However, as Griffioen asserts, religious understanding can also involve collective hermeneutical approaches: 'whereas causal explanations are discovered, existential meaning is something religious subjects *make* (and make together!)' (Griffioen 2022: 34; emphasis in the original). Religious understanding, then, emerges from experience and interaction as a way for subjects to 'locate themselves in relation to each other and the universe' (Griffioen 2022: 34). Understandably, cash-strapped, time-poor public health officials do not have the resources for localised hermeneutic encounters on an individual or even community basis, but such hermeneutic considerations should at least be prioritised for how public health engages particular communities, religious traditions or local populations – if not directly on issues of health/healing then at least on issues of coping with ill health.

To what extent should we seek to reduce epistemic competition in relation to public health? And can we reach for a more certain position than Griffioen's 'acceptance and understanding?' Vaidya proposes 'dialectical engagement' as necessary to arrive at agreement or assent, noting that the two outcomes are not the same (Vaidya 2013: 555). Whereas agreement can be arrived at through coercion, involuntary adoption or even misunderstanding, assent is only reached through choosing to believe a conclusion and through correct understanding of the validity of an argument (Vaidya 2013: 555). Therefore, in Vaidya's view, we should 'seek assent because social cohesion with respect to belief is brought about through assent and not through agreement' (Vaidya 2013: 555).[50] This returns us to the social context in that critical thinking is part of the formation of one's critical identity and rational assent can only be arrived at through critical thinking. So critical thinking is key to social cohesion (Vaidya 2013: 551–4).

[50] Vaidya distinguishes between agreeing and assenting for a theoretical reason concerning identity as a reasoner.

However, this chapter has argued that in the tense post-Covid landscape of public health, assent is unlikely to be arrived at in a majoritarian way globally or even locally. Agreement or as Griffioen puts it, acceptance, may be the best we can hope for. Even if agreement only brings about 'adoption' and not 'corroboration' or 'alignment' of systems of belief (Vaidya 2013: 555), during times of crisis this may be a good enough target in public health. Similarly, we cannot expect consistency. As Navin asks: 'How could democratic allocations of epistemic authority be consistent with the recognition of differences of expertise and competence?' (Navin 2016: 44). The response here is that it does not have to be consistent. Epistemic hierarchies will inevitably exist, but religious practitioners can navigate their way through regimes of truth (such as science-based biomedical expertise) as well as through their own embodied rationality, drawing complex paths of truth-making that are not exclusive either/or choices, nor ones that are fully compatible or consistent with public health messaging, but which may offer some useful applications through pragmatic integration of religious and biomedical healthcare.

Conclusion

In her 2014 appraisal of the deficiencies of patient and public involvement (PPI) in health research in the UK, Rose pointed out that, although many descriptive case studies could be found, there was a lack of conceptual work that could contribute to 'an overarching framework' to 'allow for more general statements about knowledge generation' (Rose 2014: 150–1). This observation converges with that of South Asian epistemology, which advises that while perception generates particular truths, it is only through inferential reasoning that we can make general statements about the world. Without the systemic means to extract generalisations, inclusive advances in healthcare and health research remain hampered. It is hoped that this chapter can contribute towards a conceptual framework, a pluriversal philosophy of lived religion, that could be used to further consider religious epistemology in the context of health or other public domains. From pluriversal epistemologies, such as South Asian, we can draw many keen insights about truth-making processes (from the importance of inference in debunking conspiracy theorising, to the value of keeping a tight link between validity and soundness in arguments, to the entailment of embodied-experiential evidence in determining truth). We also garner an armoury of epistemic tools for identifying, analysing and exposing false narratives, pseudo-reasoning and dangerous counterfactual claims in the public sphere, strengthening the base of a religious health epistemology that can be practically engaged in public health.

In Mbembe's view, the future of rationality itself has a short shelf life (Mbembe 2021). First, he asserts, due to the rise of technology and artificial intelligence, reason is being decentred from its human-made throne (dethroning humans with it) and, second, in a decolonising age other forms of 'human being' are increasingly valued, such as 'affect and emotions', 'passion' or 'feeling and acting with one's guts, viscerally rather than reasoning', particularly in matters of politics (Mbembe 2021: 25–6). Yet, as Mbembe (2021) also states, integrating pluriversal knowledge systems is the only way forward to deal with the current environmental crisis, and this is as true for the architecture of public health as it is for politics, education, the economy or other anthropocentric knowledge infrastructures.

References

Ammerman, N. T. (2016), 'Lived Religion as an Emerging Field: An Assessment of Its Contours and Frontiers'. *Nordic Journal of Religion and Society*, 29(2): 83–99.

Arnold, D. (2005), *Buddhists, Brahmins and Belief: Epistemology in South Asian Philosophy of Religion* (New York: Columbia University Press).

Barua, S. (2021), 'Critical Thinking and Epistemic Responsibility Revisited'. *Journal of Indian Council of Philosophical Research*, 38, 285–99.

Birchall, C., Knight, P. and Knight, S. (2024), *Distrust to Conspiracy to Culture Wars*. Report. (London: King's College London). Available at: https://demos.co.uk/wp-content/uploads/2024/04/Conspiracy-Loops_Report.pdf. Accessed 17 June 2025.

Breidlid, A. (2013), *Education, Indigenous Knowledges and Development in the Global South: Contesting Knowledges for a Sustainable Future* (New York: Routledge).

British Medical Journal. (2023), 'Decolonizing Health and Medicine' podcast series. Available at: https://thebmjpodcast.podbean.com/e/decolonising-health-and-medicine-episode-6-getting-our-house-in-order-decolonising-the-british-medical-association/. Accessed 12 June 2023.

Burley, M. (2020), *A Radical Pluralist Philosophy of Religion: Cross-cultural, Multireligious, Interdisciplinary* (London and New York: Bloomsbury Academic).

Chakrabarty, D. (2000), *Provincialising Europe: Postcolonial Thought and Historical Difference* (Princeton, NJ: Princeton University Press).

Driedger, M. S. Capurro, G., Tustin, J. and Jardine, C. G. (2023), '"I Won't Be a Guinea Pig": Rethinking Public Health Communication and Vaccine Hesitancy in the Context of COVID-19'. *Vaccine*, 41(1): 1–4. https://doi.org/10.1016/j.vaccine.2022.11.056

Dyrendal, A., Robertson, D. G. and Asprem, E. (eds) (2019), *Handbook of Conspiracy Theory and Contemporary Religion* (Leiden: Brill).

European Commission and UNESCO. (n.d.), 'Identifying Conspiracy Theories'. Available at: https://commission.europa.eu/strategy-and-policy/coronavirus-response/fighting-disinformation/identifying-conspiracy-theories_en. Accessed 5 June 2024.

Fish, W. (2010), *Philosophy of Perception: A Contemporary Introduction* (New York: Routledge).

Foucault, M. (1989), *Archaeology of Knowledge* (London: Routledge).

Gadamer, H. ([1960] 1975), *Truth and Method* (English translation) (New York: Seabury Press).

Griffioen, A. L. (2022), 'Rethinking Religious Epistemology'. *European Journal for Philosophy of Religion*, 14(1): 21–47.

Hall, D. D. (ed.) (1997), *Lived Religion in America: Toward a History of Practice* (Princeton, NJ: Princeton University Press).

Harding, S. (ed.) (2004), *The Feminist Standpoint Theory Reader* (New York and London: Routledge).

Hartsock, N. (2004), 'The Feminist Standpoint: Developing the Ground for a Specifically Feminist Historical Materialism' in S. Harding (ed.) *The Feminist Standpoint Theory Reader* (New York and London: Routledge), 283–310.

Hill Collins, P. (2004), 'Learning from the Outsider Within: The Sociological Significance of Black Feminist Thought' in S. Harding (ed.) *The Feminist Standpoint Theory Reader* (New York and London: Routledge), 103–26.

Huemer, M. (2005), 'Is Critical Thinking Epistemically Responsible?' *Metaphilosophy*, 36: 52.

Kekana, L. (2024), 'Beyond the "Single Story" of Vaccine Hesitancy: "Studying Up" a Public Health Response to Vaccine-Associated Polio in South Africa'. *Anthropology Southern Africa*, 47(1): 73–84. https://doi.org/10.1080/23323256.2023.2265968

Kirloskar-Steinbach, M. (2022), 'Paving the Way for World Philosophies Through a Philosophy of Practice'. *Educational Studies in Japan: International Yearbook*, 16: 91–102.

Knepper, T. (2021), 'Philosophy of Lived Religion: The Next Revolution?' in M. D Eckel, C. A. Speight and T. DuJardin (eds) *The Future of the Philosophy of Religion* (Cham: Springer), 61–72.

Loewen, N. R. B. and Rostalska, A. (eds) (2023), *Diversifying Philosophy of Religion: Critiques, Methods and Case Studies* (London: Bloomsbury).

Logue, H. (2012), 'Why Naïve Realism?' *Proceedings of the Aristotelian Society*, 112(2): 211–37.

Lyons, J. (2023), 'Epistemological Problems of Perception' in E. N. Zalta and U. Nodelman (eds) *The Stanford Encyclopedia of Philosophy* (Summer 2023 edition). Available at: https://plato.stanford.edu/archives/sum2023/entries/perception-episprob/. Accessed 12 August 2024.

Maldonado-Torres, N., Vizcaíno, R., Wallace, J. and We, J. E. A. (2018), 'Decolonising Philosophy' in G. K. Bhambra, D. Gebrial and K. Nişancıoğlu (eds) *Decolonising the University* (London: Pluto Press), 64–90.

Mbembe, A. (2016), 'Decolonizing the University: New Directions'. *Arts and Humanities in Higher Education*, 15(1): 29–45.

Mbembe, A. (2021), 'Futures of Life and Futures of Reason'. *Public Culture*, 33(1): 11–33.

McGuire, M. (2008), *Lived Religion: Faith and Practice in Everyday Life* (Oxford: Oxford University Press).

Medical Research Council. (2019), 'Public Involvement Impact Assessment Framework'. Available at: http://piiaf.org.uk/documents/piiaf_draft_standards.pdf. Accessed 12 August 2024.

Medina, J. (2013), *The Epistemology of Resistance: Gender and Racial Oppression, Epistemic Injustice, and the Social Imagination* (Oxford: Oxford University Press).

Meinert, L. and Seeberg, J. (eds) (2022), *Configuring Contagion: Ethnographies of Biosocial Epidemics* (London and New York: Berghahn Books).

Miller, D. (2005), 'Materiality: An Introduction' in D. Miller (ed.) *Materiality*. (Durham, NC and London: Duke University Press), 1–50.

Mills, C. W. (1997), *Blackness Visible: Essays on Philosophy and Race*. (Ithaca, NY: Cornell University Press).

Navin, M. (2016), *Values and Vaccine Refusal: Hard Questions in Ethics, Epistemology and Healthcare* (London and New York: Routledge).

Orsi, R. (1997), 'Everyday Miracles: The Study of Lived Religion' in D. D. Hall (ed.) *Lived Religion in America: Toward a History of Practice* (Princeton, NJ: Princeton University Press), 3–21.

Palmisano, S. and Pannofino, N. (2022), 'The (Un)expected Gift: Implicated Religion in the Kidney Transplant Experience'. *Implicit Religion: Journal for the Critical Study of Religion*, 25(1–2): 175–91.

Ram-Prasad, C. (2018), *Human Being, Bodily Being: Phenomenology from Classical India* (Oxford: Oxford University Press).

Robertson, D. G. (2025), *Religion and Conspiracy Theories* (London: Routledge).

Rose, D. (2014), 'Patient and Public Involvement in Health Research: Ethical Imperative and/or Radical Challenge?' *Journal of Health Psychology*, 19(1): 149–58.

Schilbrack, K. (2014), *Philosophy and the Study of Religions: A Manifesto* (Chichester: John Wiley & Sons).

Sherman, J. H. (2023a), 'Deprovincializing Philosophy of Religion: From "Faith and Reason" to the Postcolonial Revaluation of Religious Epistemologies' in N. R. B. Loewen and A. Rostalska (eds) *Diversifying Philosophy of Religion: Critiques, Methods and Case Studies* (London: Bloomsbury), 23–39.

Sherman, J. H. (2023b), 'Philosophy of Religion in a Fragmented Age: Practice and Participatory Realism'. *Religions*, 14: 424.

Vaidya, A. (2013), 'Epistemic Responsibility and Critical Thinking'. *Metaphilosophy*, 44(4): 533–56.

Westerhoff, J. (2018), *The Golden Age of Buddhist Philosophy*. The Oxford History of Philosophy (Oxford: Oxford University Press).

World Health Organization (WHO). (2022), 'WHO International Standard Terminologies on Ayurveda'. Available at: https://iris.who.int/bitstream/handle/10665/365543/9789240064935-eng.pdf?sequence=1. Accessed 12 June 2022.

Part II

Competing Ontologies: Elasticity of Truth and Meaning

THESE TWO CHAPTERS examine different ways of thinking about elasticity and truth. On the one hand, Roussou (Chapter 3) proposes elasticity as a way to talk about beliefs that are culturally porous and borderless, leading to experiences that defy easy categorisation in any single episteme. This can lead to a positive valuing of truth-making at an individual level where coherence can be rationalised in a limited, personal domain that is dominated by the value of 'choice'. In contrast, Deeley (Chapter 4) points out that such elasticity of truth can be a dangerous phenomenon at scale, leading to a lack of accountability for truth claims in society and patterns of blame that shore up false claims in various forms of 'scapegoating' and 'othering'. He proposes a cultural schema model for understanding the culturally distinctive and socially shared interpretations of beliefs in 'secret plots by evil and malevolent groups' that have been documented to appear in times of acute stress, specifically considering the 'QAnon beliefs' which were amplified by the Covid-19 pandemic.

Both chapters highlight the critical tension that this volume seeks to explore: what happens when competing epistemes and ontologies collide in regard to health, creating seemingly incompatable belief constellations and intractable problems for public policy.

3

Religion, Spirituality, Episteme: Transreligious Epistemologies for Health, Wellbeing and Covid-19 in Southern Europe

EUGENIA ROUSSOU

Introduction

EPISTEME, IN THE Greek language, signifies 'science'. At the same time, it denotes the epistemological knowledge one can acquire through implementing a scientific methodology on a research topic, approach or question. As a Greek anthropologist who has conducted half of her research in a sociocultural Greek context, it is important to begin with the observation that the discourses of and on 'episteme', epistemological approaches and knowledge production in relation to religion, spirituality and medicine are usually complex and multidimensional. Consequently, it seems useful to clarify from the beginning the central significance of 'episteme' as I use it in the present analysis, namely as a conceptual tool that encompasses both science and epistemology in its core, with its multiple connotations and conceptual associations, from an emic and etic perspective.

Science is equated usually with the Western conceptualisation of positivist forms of episteme, which can be regarded as 'a quintessence of rationality' (Tambiah 1990: 140). Western biomedicine constitutes part of this equation in southern Europe and is generally regarded as the official public healthcare system, which is rationalised and thus legitimised accordingly (Almeida and Gabe 2016). Throughout this chapter I approach holistic spirituality and healing practices as 'those forms of practice involving the body ... which have as their goal the attainment of wholeness and wellbeing of "body, mind, and spirit". Such practices shade into the realm of complementary and alternative health care practices (CAM)' (Sointu and Woodhead 2008: 259; cf. Bowman 1999). They have stereotypically been considered to be outside the epistemological social construction of rational and medical safeguarding, and have been by far less legitimised publicly. This is also due

Proceedings of the British Academy, **278**, 41–58, © Authors 2025.

to the fact that holistic practices of healing carry religio-spiritual connotations, which make them, again according to the strict Western epistemological paradigm, less falsifiable and publicly verifiable and more emotive (see Lett 1997).

The aim of this chapter is to place a broader analytical emphasis on the notion of 'episteme', as a formation of knowledge that informs practice, in relation to epistemology, approached here as more open and reflexively concerned with principles, systems and theories. Both are considered within the transreligious context of contemporary religiosity and healthcare. Through my ethnography, I explore questions, such as: What kind of epistemic discourses are produced when religion, spirituality and healthcare mutually interact in the context of the pandemic? Should religious and health epistemologies be approached as contested or collaborating, and what kind of conceptual as well as empirical implications would such affinities and/or ruptures entail? What is the role of complementary and alternative medicine in a pandemic and post-pandemic landscape, and what kind of dynamic shifts could it potentially introduce to both private healthcare and public health policies? In what ways can the old, stereotypically antithetical, interrelation between science and religion/religiosity be approached, challenged and reinterpreted? How can the notion of transreligiosity (Panagiotopoulos and Roussou 2022) contribute to a more thorough exploration of the elastic – or inelastic, at times – boundaries between religion and spirituality, religiosity and episteme, alternative healing and biomedicine, ontology and epistemology?

Using an anthropological lens, I have studied the intersection between transnational religiosity, contemporary spirituality and holistic healing in the capital cities of Lisbon, Portugal and Athens, Greece, since 2012. My research methodology has been ethnographic, in an empathetic and collaborative way, by observing but at the same time also participating actively in the everyday life of my interlocutors and practising alongside them, so as to feel, embody and understand more profoundly their holistic spirituality and healing. During the pandemic, my research was interrupted, and I gradually had to move it online and slowly rebuild it under the novel circumstances, introducing the theme of Covid-19 into my focus of contemporary spirituality and CAM healing. In this context, I continued my ethnographic research predominantly with a small(er) group of holistic healing practitioners, both spiritual healers and healing recipients, which consisted of older interlocutors and newly gained research collaborators in Lisbon, Athens and the virtual space in between. The criteria of including them in my ethnographic fieldwork were independent of gender, age and social class, to name a few basic ones – which I chose to leave open – but were mostly based on those individuals' continuous involvement with holistic spirituality and healing, during the pandemic and to date. Comparatively, I also talked with a small number of Christian priests and adherents about their attitudes and beliefs with regard to the pandemic and the(ir) relationship between episteme, religion and public health.

With my previous research as a basis, my analysis here reflects upon questions regarding spirituality, health and wellbeing in relation to Covid-19 as part of the research project 'ReSpell. Religion, Spirituality and Wellbeing: A Comparative Approach of Transreligiosity and Crisis in Southern Europe'.[1] The project employs the novel term of 'transreligiosity' as a tool to study the transgression of frontiers of contemporary religiosity, in relation to but mostly beyond more established forms of religion and healthcare. Transreligiosity is viewed 'as a religiosity that is characterised by elasticity, creativity and fluidity when it comes to the negotiation, transgression, and transformation of religio-spiritual identities and frontiers, while being directly connected with transnationalism, alternative healing and holistic spirituality' (Panagiotopoulos and Roussou 2022: 621). It is, moreover, a concept that points to the elasticity of contemporary religio-spiritual practices, the transreligious spaces such elasticity creates from both theoretical and empirical viewpoints and in the context of institutionalised religions, holistic spiritualities and vernacular religiosity, as well as their complex zones of negotiation in between (Roussou, Rivadossi and Panagiotopoulos 2023; see also Roussou and Panagiotopoulos 2023). One of the project's central focuses is the dimension of spiritual healthcare, through the critical lens of the Covid-19 pandemic, and how therapeutic transreligious practices influenced the way people experienced, reacted towards and viewed the pandemic itself. This included everyday beliefs, ideologies and responses to vaccination and their relation to religion, spirituality and wellbeing, as well as attitudes in relation to episteme, epistemology and/through vernacular religiosity.

What follows is an ethnographic account of the pluralistic and competing epistemologies of contemporary religiosity and health in Portugal and Greece, in an attempt to demonstrate, more particularly, the transreligious, complex, transformative and elastic field of so-called holistic spirituality and healing, as defined above, and the non-biomedical, CAM therapeutic practices with which it is connected. Emphasis is placed on practices of spiritual healing in relation to Covid-19 from two perspectives that have become pertinent and thus require special attention: first, from the point of practising and working for a pluralistic, inclusive healthcare system, which is thought to be complementary to biomedical healthcare, with relevant attitudes towards the pandemic; second, from the perspective of beliefs that share a greater affinity to 'conspirituality' (Ward and Voas 2011) and vaccination refusal among individuals and groups that are spiritual but not religious (Kosarkova *et al.* 2021).

[1] 'ReSpell' is a three-year anthropological research project (2023–6), which is funded by the Portuguese Foundation for Science and Technology (FCT, grant reference: 2022.01229.PTDC), and hosted by the Centre for Research in Anthropology (CRIA), where I am the Principal Investigator (PI). Our team members focus their research attention on three southern European countries, Portugal, Greece and Spain, working on the transreligious practices relating to religion, spirituality and wellbeing in direct relation to crisis. In terms of methodology, ReSpell is ethnographically based, following the ethical guidelines of the EU and of the ethical committee of CRIA.

Episteme, religiosity and medicine in contemporary Portugal and Greece

In present-day southern Europe, where Christianity appears to prevail as the dominant religion, it is also recognised, generally speaking, as a largely rational belief system, enjoying many social privileges equal to that of biomedicine. The long debate, however, regarding '[magic,] science, religion and the scope of rationality' (Tambiah 1990) remains. On the one hand, then, there is Christianity in Portugal and Greece, which is considered rationalised and legitimised, with a somewhat ambivalent status in relation to the categories of episteme and epistemology. On the other hand, there is holistic spirituality, which is legitimised through more unofficial routes while nonetheless claiming an increasingly strong position in the public healthcare system of the two countries, having already been established, to an extensive degree, in people's everyday lives and performances of healing. Holistic spirituality and healing also 'steals' in a way part of its epistemological recognition and popularity from occupying an elastic position within but also beyond the boundaries of (Christian) religion and (bio)medicine.

In southern European countries, such as Portugal and Greece, which are the ethnographic focus of this chapter, holistic spiritualities have been very popular for some time (see, among others: Fedele 2012, 2016; Palmisano and Pannofino 2017, 2020; Roussou 2018, 2021; Saraiva 2023). Despite not being directly connected to 'science', the ongoing popularity of such spiritualities, in both private practice and public performance, has resulted in their perhaps less official yet nowadays 'quintessential' legitimised position in the Portuguese and Greek healthcare systems, at least from below. At the same time, the concept of 'wellbeing' (Manderson 2005; Atkinson, Fuller and Painter 2012) has gained new research and analytical ground and has become even more pertinent in the global context of the recent pandemic.[2] Subsequently, the single-faith stereotype that accompanies the European South, namely that southern European religious identity equals Christianity (Mapril and Blanes 2013), has been challenged, while the belief in and practice of 'alternative' forms of healing have become an active and legitimate part of everyday Portuguese and Greek life. Furthermore, the pandemic has renovated the popularity of transreligious practices of a holistic spiritual character.

Southern Europe is indeed stereotypically associated with a particular institutionalised religion (Christianity) and healthcare system (biomedicine). However, recent decades have seen this space significantly permeated and transformed by the socioeconomic and political challenges and transnational flows, and very recently by a critical healthcare crisis, the Covid-19 pandemic. The research focus is two-fold: first, the aim is to look into the official statements and guidelines of the institutionalised religion, namely Portuguese Catholic and

[2] From here onwards, when I mention the pandemic, I refer specifically to the pandemic of Covid-19.

Greek Orthodox Christianity, towards the pandemic. Second, I intend to shed some light on the individual beliefs and practices of holistic spirituality and 'alternative' healing, including 'conspiritual' discourses and diverse and pluralistic attitudes about Covid-19.

When Covid-19 entered the epistemological and ontological picture, as will be shown with more ethnographic detail in the following sections, the sociocultural and symbolic strings between episteme, religiosity and medicine were tangled once again. Suddenly, the focus was cast on public health and how science could and should resolve a global pandemic that was affecting people's wellbeing, individual health but also religious faith. Scepticism was raised with regard to scientific knowledge and, as a consequence, conspiracy theory movements appeared, many of which were religious based. In this context, political and economic afflictions became even more relevant to the public discussions with regard to implementing policies to control the pandemic. It was these strategies of public control, mainly through the lockdowns and vaccination state-imposed obligations, which globally created a variety of conflicting responses towards epistemological questions of health and wellbeing but also faith, religion and spirituality.

To offer a more specific framework with regard to Portugal and Greece, multiple attitudes were adopted towards Covid-19 from the scope of religiosity and medicine, including holistic spirituality and healing, which, widely speaking, were quite similar in both countries. In the context of institutionalised religion, namely Christianity, and from the perspective of its official representatives as well as lay practitioners, there were two main stances towards Covid-19. First, there was compliance with the scientific biomedical regulations, indications and healthcare preventive measures; in this case, religious and medical discourses followed a parallel, non-conflictive pathway, being elastic in their mutual counter-interpretations and epistemological interactions. Second, there was denial of scientific efficacy, of episteme, of scientific empirical knowledge creation, incorporating discourses that ranged from denying the existence of the pandemic to exhibiting behaviours against vaccination and any kind of protective measures while offering strict religious belief and performance as an alternative to explain Covid-19, both ontologically and epistemologically. In this context, the boundaries between religion and episteme were much more rigid, incompatible and almost uncrossed. The epistemological perspective of biomedicine was much clearer, and its boundaries were defined within the discourses of an official healthcare system that is scientifically recognised and adopted globally – yet not always socioculturally adapted – namely, within the quintessential, rational, stereotypical, discourses of episteme.

Holistic spirituality and healing falls somewhere in between all the above: as a popular aspect of contemporary religiosity as well as contemporary healthcare and wellbeing, the attitudes that surrounded it fluctuated from collaboration to rupture. Sometimes holistic spiritual and healing practitioners chose the route of negation of an episteme, and at other times they adopted it; sometimes they were closer in perspective to institutionalised religion, and at other times they chose intentionally or more indirectly to deviate from it. It seems, therefore, that this last category of contemporary religiosity, medicine and wellbeing followed a much more elastic, or at least a much more fluid, pathway. In the two sections that follow, all the above attitudes will be demonstrated within a more particular ethnographic scope, exploring, at the same time, their transreligious character or their relationship to 'transreligiosity'.

Religious beliefs, pandemic convictions

The Portuguese religious landscape is pluralised to a great degree, due primarily but not exclusively to the transnational migratory interactions with Portugal's former colonies (Saraiva 2008). However, Catholic Christianity continues, according to the 2021 Portuguese national census, to be the predominant religion of the country, with 80.2 per cent of the population declaring Catholicism as their religious identity. As Dix (2008: 80) has observed, there has been a tendency in recent decades to practise 'homemade religion' extensively, while contemporary Portuguese religiosity has gone through a process of individualisation and transformation (Roussou 2015). In Greece, equivalently, about 97 per cent of the total population are thought to belong to the Orthodox Christian Church, even if nominally. Yet, Greek religious pluralism has a long historical presence (Prodromou 2004: 477), and, as Roudometof (2014, 2015) has argued, Orthodox Christianity has been highly affected by processes of globalisation and transnationalisation, leading to religious pluralism, diversity and a 'Greek spiritual revolution' in everyday practice (Roussou 2013). Within these two pluralised religious contexts, where Christianity continues to remain the institutionalised religion of the two countries, beliefs and religious attitudes in relation to Covid-19 have varied with regard to both official and vernacular, public and private standpoints.

When the highest representative of the Catholic Church, Pope Francis, called vaccination against Covid-19 a 'moral obligation' and the vaccines 'an act of love' while addressing Catholic believers worldwide within the pandemic, he certainly created a forceful impact, challenging the supposed antithesis between two of the most important socialisation systems: the religious and the biomedical one (Vatican News 2021). By publicly announcing his support for biomedicine and 'science', he highlighted the classical debates concerning the interrelation between science, religion and rationality (Tambiah 1990), only to overturn them. In Portugal, the majority of priests chose to follow their religious leader, judging at least from those I managed to speak with, urging their congregation to wear masks in mass and follow the regulations about Covid-19 set by the government as well as the Pope. My Portuguese religiously observant interlocutors also followed, as a majority, those general religious guidelines regarding public health and private healthcare, choosing to be vaccinated and use all preventive measures against

Covid-19; religious praying and attending mass frequently went hand in hand with getting vaccinated and wearing masks in public spaces.

In Greece, the Orthodox Church held a less forceful yet still friendly attitude towards biomedicine: the Archbishop of Greece was more moderate than the Pope, calling for general support for all medical doctors and nurses, for respect to fellow Christians with serious healthcare issues, and to stay at home out of an act of love, inviting people to 'make every home a small church' (Ekathimerini 2020). Many bishops strengthened the argument of the leader of the Greek Orthodox Church, arguing openly that they supported vaccination and a public healthcare system where religion would complement medicine in these critical times of a global healthcare crisis (see Michailidis, Vlasidis and Karekla 2021; Makrides and Sotiriou 2024). There were also many popular bishops, however, who equally openly expressed theories of conspiracy, strongly advised Orthodox believers to boycott vaccination and mask wearing, and even proposed the use of holy water as a better alternative to disinfectants (Ta Nea 2021). This divided public stance of Greek Orthodox Christianity created equivalent divisions in attitudes within vernacular religious practice. From my ethnographic observations and conversations, many local priests and religious adherents were vaccinated, wore masks in church liturgies and followed the public healthcare Covid-19 rules. However, other priests refused to wear masks as it would 'insult God'; supported the idea that the vaccines are 'acts of the devil' that implanted the 666 into people's bodies, thus turning them into atheists and sinners; and insisted that the collective holy communion would save people from being afflicted by Covid-19 (cf. Michailidis, Vlasidis and Karekla 2021; Makrides and Sotiriou 2024).[3]

From a strictly institutionalised religious – and more specifically Christian – perspective, therefore, there were competing and conflicting beliefs with regard to public health, epistemologies of medical knowledge and 'truth', and the relation between religion and science itself. On the one hand, there was a willingness and openness by the Catholic and Orthodox Church to bend their boundaries, be more socioculturally elastic and subsequently to adopt a more transreligious position, arguing for a personal and collective healthcare and wellbeing that blends religious and biomedical discourses together. On the other hand, one could observe a complete rigidness in terms of Covid-related beliefs, leading to an attempt to create and claim an epistemology of religious 'authenticity' and authority as a legitimate therapeutic means against Covid-19. This resulted in unconventional and religiously innovative –albeit dangerous to public health – protective measures, such as the use of holy water and communion as personal and social disinfectants and 'anti-pandemic medicines', to use a phrase of a local Greek priest.

[3] In the Christian Orthodox Church, the religious adherents receive holy communion through a shared single spoon, which the priest dips for each person in a chalice filled with a special kind of sweet wine and bread, both of which (are supposed to) have become sacralised during the liturgy.

CAM and holistic healing in vernacular practice: spiritual and conspiritual attitudes towards healing and wellbeing

Within this wider contextualisation of institutionalised religion and its attitudes and influences, and the practice of vernacular religiosity (Primiano 1995; Bowman and Valk 2012) as it is 'lived' (McGuire 2008) transreligiously, the popularity of contemporary spirituality, Complementary and Alternative Medicine (CAM) and holistic healing appears to have increased during the pandemic crisis and beyond. In Lisbon and Athens, holistic healing practices have become popularised over the last decades (Fedele 2016; Roussou 2021; Saraiva 2023). In both cities, there are a plethora of 'alternative' therapeutic offers, which range from yoga, reiki, energy healing, mindfulness, shamanic therapies, wellbeing studios and retreats to a multiplicity of primarily non-biomedical discourses and healing adaptations through different religio-spiritual traditions.

CAM can be considered as an active part of the Portuguese and Greek healthcare systems. In Portugal, in accordance with official legislation – which, after a long process, was finalised in 2013 – CAM practices that are considered more 'scientific', like homeopathy, acupuncture and osteopathy, have become officially legitimised. Despite such attempts to embrace a more open public health agenda that goes beyond the field of biomedicine and places CAM officially in the National Healthcare System (see Almeida and Gabe 2016), the more 'alternative' therapeutic practices of CAM, of a holistic spiritual character, continue to be ignored. In Greece, homeopathy is one of the very few practices so far that can be practised by medical professionals and is thus legitimised through the Greek state. The Greek biomedical system is inelastic in terms of incorporating alternative healing in its core. Despite their officially equivocal status, however, alternative forms of healing continue to gain ground in both the public and private healthcare field of Lisbon and Athens, creating – at the level of vernacular, everyday practice – a transreligious space where holistic spirituality and healing can be sought after and performed, not just in parallel but in combination with biomedicine, promoting a genre of wellbeing culture that is both personal and collective.

During the pandemic, the practitioners of holistic health in Lisbon and Athens adapted to the new reality creatively, by moving most of their therapeutic performances and attendance online or to outdoor spaces where Covid-19 transmission would be more difficult. Post-Covid, such practitioners returned to direct contact and communication, which is, as they reported, one of the most crucial characteristics of healing: it is primarily the face-to-face interaction between healers and the recipients of alternative therapy, the energy exchange between them and the sensorial co-inhabitancy of sacred spaces that leads to an efficacious therapeutic performance. Yet, most of the practitioners have since kept their virtual seminars, online meditations and therapeutic interactions active, adding a novel aspect to the more generalised and integrated healthcare system in the post-Covid era. This healthcare system now appears to encompass both public and private health practices, including virtual therapies, following – as practitioners have asserted – the paradigm of biomedicine, which continues to offer online consultancy with medical doctors and nurses.

Lisa,[4] a Greek woman in her late forties, is a recipient and practitioner of holistic spirituality and other therapies, who has been 'trying out', as she expressed it, 'various types of healing that many people would recognise or characterise as alternative, which may be a good thing or a bad thing, but I don't care, it is my health, my body, my wellbeing, and I will practise whatever I want to'. Lisa is very athletic and goes to the gym every week, where she was introduced to yoga, which she began primarily as a form of exercise there. Slowly, she began to warm up to the meditative aspects of it and, in her own words, 'explore a more spiritual side of myself that I didn't know I had. I was born Christian Orthodox, I am not a churchgoer, but I believed. But now I have become more spiritual. I still consider myself as Christian, but my mind, my belief, are open to other religious, let's say, traditions.'

Having suffered from some immune-related health issues, which trouble her to date, her first go-to therapeutic path was always the biomedical one, which she trusted. When she got ill with Covid-19 some of her symptoms returned more intensively and her chronic illness was manifested differently. Despite believing initially in the power of the vaccines, receiving two doses of the vaccine and following all of her doctors' recommendations, these days she is more doubtful as to whether she should have been vaccinated in the first place. She has connected the timeline of her current symptoms with her being vaccinated, and she told me she will no longer trust any globalised scientific approach completely, but she will take care of her personal wellbeing herself, as 'I know better what my body needs.' She currently continues with a combination of biomedical and homeopathic treatments, keeps up with her yoga and meditation classes, and lights incense in her house for the spiritual connection and its benefits. As she told me, she cannot clearly characterise whether her practices have a religious or medical basis, given that what is most important is her wellbeing, which includes both, in a varied, fluid, sometimes even unexpected way. Lisa follows a transreligious path which combines freely her background religious identity – that of Orthodox Christianity – and her institutional healthcare background – that of biomedicine – with spiritual, more alternative means, as she characterises them, thereby expressing and practising her religiosity and wellbeing in everyday life. Her openness to believing in and combining different and at times stereotypically conflicting practices, which can be religious, spiritual, scientific and/or CAM-alternative, creates an elastic field of transreligious epistemes that fluctuates and moves according to Lisa's individual needs and religio-spiritual and therapeutic belonging.

Matilde is a Portuguese woman in her fifties, who is a spiritual healer of a transreligious character: she incorporates Asian therapeutic practices, such as

[4] The names of all my interlocutors used in this chapter are pseudonyms, in order to protect their real identity.

qi gong, with 'multidimensional therapy', a form of energetic therapy that is considered as 'complementary' and 'integrative' and is based on the heart chakra, energy exchange, spiritual canalisation and mediation between the material and the spiritual world.[5] This latter therapy was invented by a French-born female healer, whose travels to Africa and around the world influenced her practice; she is popular in Portugal and organises retreats, especially in Brazil and Peru. Matilde also lived in Mozambique, where she learned African divination therapies, such as spiritual readings through seashells, as well as in Brazil, where she gained further spiritual healing experience. During the pandemic, she continued to organise in-person group classes of qi gong at a Lisbon park, which were well attended, with the only request that the people should not wear masks: 'I didn't want to be responsible for them having a heart attack or something, with all the deep respiration exercises we have been practising', as she put it. She also continued to run her individual therapeutic sessions of multidimensional therapy and divination virtually because, as she explained to me, she preferred this format as a therapeutic method because of the risks of Covid-19. Matilde received all three doses of vaccination against Covid-19 and during the pandemic she refrained from personal touch between her and her healing recipients, 'to respect their bodies and mine' and thus minimise any danger of infection. When the pandemic subsided, she decided to put her qi gong classes on hold and travel to Brazil again, in order to renew her pluralistic therapeutic learning while working on a transnational online basis between Brazil and Portugal.

In addition to my interlocutors who have followed a transreligious itinerary with regard to their religion, spirituality and wellbeing, I also met some who were inclined towards a more complex, and perhaps more rigid, transreligious itinerary, adopting instead a conspiritual belief, practice and ideology. 'Conspirituality', namely the 'hybrid of conspiracy theory and alternative spirituality' (Ward and Voas 2011: 103), is an attitude I began to ethnographically encounter during the strict lockdowns. Since social media platforms, such as Facebook and Instagram, had become one of the most popular means of communication and ethnographic observation during the full force of the pandemic, I used them both as a personal and as a professional vehicle of socialisation and ethnographic interaction. From both personalised ethnographic interactions and virtual ones, conspiritual beliefs, especially anti-vaccination attitudes, proved to be popular.

Daniela is a Portuguese positivist scientist in her late thirties. She defines herself as mostly agnostic but with Christian roots, a result of her Catholic upbringing and socialisation. At the same time, she incorporates holistic spirituality and healing, which is a non-biomedical, spiritual and CAM therapeutic pathway, into her everyday life. She practises yoga and meditation, believes in spiritual and natural energy and has tried various energetic therapies. She sometimes follows feng shui

[5] https://terapiamultidimensional.com/ (accessed 24 February 2022).

home regulations and occasionally seeks advice from homeopathic professionals as well as from physicians. She mentioned to me that she is not dedicated to one or another form of religiosity and medicine: 'I just go with the flow, of whatever feels right at that particular moment when my body suffers, or my mind cannot relax, or I feel an annoyance, that something disturbs me, and that has to do with my general wellbeing.' When the pandemic began, Daniela's flexible religio-spiritual and medical identity became firmer.

Despite being a 'scientist', which stereotypically would be associated with adopting an epistemological understanding of and knowledge about the pandemic that would be closer to biomedicine, Daniela expressed discomfort and reservations about the generalised scientific implementations and measures against Covid-19. She was unconvinced about either the efficacy of the vaccines or about the public and global discourse of the Portuguese public health department, stating that in her view there was a large probability that Covid-19 was:

> created just for the pharmaceutical companies to become richer, but, you know, that is not the science I want to be part of, nor do I believe in the lockdowns, the vaccines, etc. I do believe we now have a virus around us. I am not saying we don't. But I also think we should all be free, what's the point of being locked inside? We should all be in contact with one another, and let our bodies deal with their epidemiological response individually.

Daniela received two doses of vaccination, not out of personal choice but because it was obligatory in her workplace. Otherwise, she would have to face the risk of getting fired. Her perception of science was subjectively constructed but also legitimised due to her professional status. After the pandemic, she has continued her holistic itinerary of spirituality and healing, but she has also continued to show traces of conspiritual beliefs, which she considers 'epistemologically true and valid' from her own point of view.

Sotiris is a Greek man in his mid-forties, who had been involved with 'alternative' culture and spirituality for many years, practising mindfulness, meditation, spiritual travelling and receiving energetic therapies, along with many other performances of spirituality and healing. Carrying a long history of hospitalisation due to mental health issues and substance abuse, holistic healing helped him considerably to stabilise himself bodily, mentally and spiritually. When I met him, back in 2014, through a common spiritual healer whose therapeutic sessions we were both attending, Sotiris proclaimed his belief immediately that we shared a karmic spiritual connection. Knowledgeable about the theme of my research and my attending our common healer's sessions from both a personal and a professional positioning, he chose to trust me with his therapeutic past and story. He was candid about his mental health issues and how holistic healing and alternative spirituality helped him move forward. When I met him and in the few years that followed, he was perceptive to the spiritual world, engaging frequently with a variety of spirits, from angels and Greek Orthodox saints to Buddhist monks and Peruvian shamans. In the periods in which he was drawn more to Buddhism, he would find Buddhist teachers in Athens and invite me to go to park walks, where we would meditate and practise mindfulness while reciting Buddhist mantras. When he would drift more towards shamanism, he would ask me to join him at the healer's place, where he would call his shaman teachers, and we would go on shamanic journeys together.

Just before the beginning of the pandemic, Sotiris stopped going to our common healer's therapeutic sessions. He began to behave strangely and ended up joining, as he later confessed to me, a group of extreme right-wing religious believers. In our last meeting, he told me that he was now following Jesus, regarded all the holistic spiritual influences as dangerous, and believed that the new group he belonged to would reinstate the exclusivity of Christianity globally, even if it was through violent terms. He reassured me though that I would be spared, as I was his close spiritual companion, even if I still followed, in his own words, a 'blasphemous spiritual path'. This is how his 'conspiritual' path began and continued through the pandemic. However, as his mental health began to deteriorate because of Covid-19, he was hospitalised again, moving back into trusting and committing to his biomedical healthcare path. In 2023, he also got back in touch with the spiritual healer and reconnected with his Buddhist and alternative medicine practices. Sotiris has displayed a full spectrum of trusting and distrusting, adopting and rejecting, being radical and being elastic, creating a unique transreligious biography of constantly mobilised, unpredictable and fluid epistemologies.

As it has been claimed in a very useful article concerning the theme of vaccine refusal in the Czech Republic among spiritual practitioners, spirituality has greatly influenced people's attitudes towards conceptions of their health and their body, and in many cases has led them to anti-vaccination behaviour (Kosarkova *et al.* 2021). In Portugal and Greece, a common thread has been observed between everyday attitudes and beliefs against the vaccine and spiritual practitioners. From the more personalised interviews I conducted with my interlocutors to more generalised participant observation online, scepticism exists among people who belong to the holistic spiritual scene of Lisbon and Athens about whether they should allow a foreign substance to enter their physical body or not. Most of the people I have spoken with and observed virtually, through their posts on Facebook, Instagram and their websites, are not against the scientific intentionality of the vaccination process *per se*; they have been, however, worried that the vaccine might affect their mind, body, and spirit energetically, in a negative and invasive manner. Consequently, there has been an increasing number of holistic health practitioners who have refused to get vaccinated, without, nevertheless, necessarily tuning into conspiritual discourses and life stances.

My above-mentioned interlocutors are a few characteristic ethnographic examples of a number of holistic healers and healing recipients who, during the pandemic, adopted a pluralistic itinerary when it came to their personal choices about not endangering or improving their wellbeing. This was also the case regarding the adoption of more radical beliefs, attitudes and practices according to their personal needs, social influences and collective mobilities of religio-spiritual and healthcare belonging. Their itinerary was and still is sometimes transnational, certainly more elastic and open, albeit sceptical at times. It incorporates a multiplicity of healthcare choices, ideologies and beliefs, which encounter each other in vernacular practice and create a distinctive spiritual route to health, healing and wellbeing that is socioculturally diverse and therapeutically consistent, leading to innovative and integrative transreligious healthcare epistemologies.

Towards a transreligious epistemology of holistic healing

As David Graeber points out, the word 'epistemology', similarly to that of 'ontology', is 'of relatively recent coinage', yet the 'conceptual divisions they represent can be traced back to the very origins of Greek philosophy' (Graeber 2015: 15). He furthermore argues that in order to understand a local culture it is crucial that we also understand its epistemology, offering the example of his own ethnographic work on Malagasy, where 'ideas about spirits were themselves a form of epistemology – that is, they are reflections on the possibility of knowledge' (Graeber 2015: 28–9). In agreement with Graeber, what I have attempted above is to offer an ethnographic perspective of the most popular, or prevalent, epistemologies in the two southern European countries where I conducted my research. These are epistemologies that (re)present knowledge with regard to contemporary religiosity, healing and wellbeing from both an emic and etic perspective. Sometimes it is even difficult to distinguish between epistemological and ontological beliefs, viewpoints and panoramas, as they become entangled in observing, ethnographically participating in and analysing local cultural phenomena and attitudes. According to Christina Toren, 'epistemology and ontology always implicate one another and are best understood, therefore, in terms of a figure-ground relation … the trick is to hold onto the awareness that what exists for us and how we know what we know are, for any one of us, lived as inextricable from one another' (Toren and Pina-Cabral 2009: 2). Moreover, as Toren and Pina-Cabral (2009: 2) put it: 'We want an acknowledgment … of the necessity for an engagement with "what it is to know" (epistemology) and "what exists" (ontology) … with respect not only to others but also to ourselves, since the analyst's tendency is to take so very, very much for granted.'

When it comes to religious epistemology, more precisely, which most commonly refers to the study of how epistemological concepts – such as rationality, falsification and reason, among others – could potentially be applied to religious beliefs and practices in order to produce knowledge, the frontiers between epistemology and ontology become even more blurred. Questions such as whether religious belief is rational, if God exists or whether spiritual convictions incorporate any form of scientific truth are among those often asked in the context of epistemological discussions about religion. What is more important, however, is not to question the rationality, scientificity or objectivity of religion and belief but rather to explore the sociocultural, epistemological and anthropological value of the metaphysical, somewhat mystical and spiritual perspective of contemporary religiosity – considering what it can teach us about the world, both natural and supernatural, that we live in and engage with empirically as well as transcendentally, and in which we feel, experience and believe.

During Covid-19 and afterwards, institutionalised religion, namely Christianity, in the two countries under study had to enter a more direct dialogue with scientific – or to be more accurate, biomedical epistemology – adapting and readapting its public discourse about knowledge production (about the pandemic, belief, ritualism, religious authority, as well as lived and vernacular religion) accordingly. At most times, it adopted public health epistemological itineraries, contributing to knowledge production that incorporated religious epistemology while placing emphasis on the rationality and 'truth' of 'episteme' as the principal carrier of knowledge and reason, creating a sociocultural bridge between a 'religious episteme' and a 'medical episteme'. At other times – less frequent, more dispersed and more individually triggered by local religious representatives – it went against the public health epistemology of biomedical knowledge, creating its own epistemology based on strict and dogmatic criteria, albeit arbitrary, to safeguard – supposedly – religious belief and knowledge. Both of these religious epistemologies entered into an explicit interaction with public health epistemologies – to either walk along together or build extra borders in between.

At this point it is also crucial to shift attention to the epistemological impact of studying religious epistemology and its potential consequences, influences and afflictions. In the field of sociocultural anthropology, more particularly, there has been a well-known long debate, almost ever since the birth of the discipline, with regard to the degree of its methodological 'scientificity' and rationalisation, since its predominantly ethnographic methodology is not based on objectification and falsification criteria but on empiricism and personal and collective experience. For the anthropologists who study religious phenomena, such criticism appears at times even stronger due to the more transcendental nature of their research – which is still often stereotyped as non-scientific and lacking epistemological legitimacy. However, from Turner's (1993) 'reality of spirits' to the extensive amount of recent works (see, for example, Pierini, Groisman and Espírito Santo 2023), anthropology has a long history of dealing with questions of religious epistemology while highlighting the relationship between religiosity and health. Such anthropological works respect local epistemologies, studying their reality – whether we speak about the reality of spirits, of believers and disbelievers, (spi)ritual practitioners, religious healers and/or holistic spiritual therapists.

Considering all the above, what I want to propose here is the idea of 'transreligious epistemology' as a conceptual tool and framework of analysis for the academic study of knowledge formation, as well as a way of understanding sociocultural debates that may or may not relate to episteme, religiosity, medicine and healthcare. Furthermore, it serves as a methodological approach for studying religion, spirituality, healing, wellbeing, episteme, public health and Covid-19 and their elastic, fluid, often unpredictable boundaries. Holistic spirituality and healing offer a rich ethnographic example with reference to the multiple and possibly complex, yet always creative, modes to which to apply this transreligious epistemology as a way to produce knowledge. This epistemology should be understood as more empirical and as a tool to approach religious, public health, biomedical and Covid-19 epistemologies not from a contrasting perspective but from the perspective of collaborative interactions where knowledge can be co-created. Sometimes, of course, ruptures can occur. But transreligious epistemology has an elastic character that creatively incorporates a variety of different epistemologies depending on the research context, including, crucially, that of anthropology. Ultimately, the most important aspect of transreligious epistemology is creating knowledge through the production of elastic religio-spiritual, therapeutic, biomedical, epistemic pathways, and of a wellbeing that relates creatively to both public and private healthcare.

Conclusion

In very recent years, CAM practices have been criticised publicly, with opinion articles written in highly popular newspapers online by positivist scientists, as occurred in Portugal, and with official biomedical associations reacting against their legitimation, as happened in Greece (see Roussou 2021). During the pandemic, such public voices denouncing and claiming the inefficacy of 'alternative' forms of therapy in fighting against Covid-19 were multiplied. My interlocutors, and holistic practitioners in general – especially those who approached their therapeutic practices as complementary and not alternative to biomedicine – felt offended. As spiritual healers shared with me, since the beginning of the pandemic and now that we supposedly live in a post-pandemic epoch – 'supposedly' because, as they clarified, Covid-19 still remains active among us – they have been helping a lot of individuals address their mental health and psychosomatic symptoms caused by Covid-19 related stress and illness. They narrated how important their therapeutic role has been for people's personal wellbeing and pathway to healing in the course of their everyday life.

What the holistic healers, healing recipients and practitioners at a more general level have envisioned and proposed to the anthropologist as a solution for the current institutionalised healthcare system – and perhaps here is where the most important contribution of my chapter lies – is a transformation of the (bio)medical system from below. With the exception of a few individuals that I spoke to, most of the Portuguese and Greek CAM and/or alternative and holistic practitioners consider the therapies they offer and/or receive as complementary to the main biomedical-based healthcare system. Covid-19 has raised many questions concerning the efficacy of biomedicine as the only legitimate system. It managed to cope with a global healthcare crisis as far as the general social and pharmaceutical mechanisms and public healthcare were concerned, but it ignored, as many of my interlocutors put it, people's vernacular needs and beliefs around health, healing and wellbeing, as well as the sensorial and empathetic everyday aspects of individual health histories, challenges and crises. What my research among the holistic practitioners in Lisbon and Athens has demonstrated, especially now that masks and any other preventive measures against Covid-19 have ceased to be obligatory, is the necessity for an inclusive healthcare system with post-Covid-19 policies that are transreligious. This would be a system that is focused on individual therapeutic needs and beyond the physicality of one's body. Such a system would encompass, legitimise and provide easy access to CAM therapies, which have become even more popular during the pandemic and in what is considered as the current post-pandemic era; it would also integrate a spiritual elasticity and elastic epistemologies that can transgress religious and medical boundaries.

Acknowledgements

I am truly grateful to the Portuguese Foundation for Science and Technology (FCT) for funding the project 'ReSpell' (FCT grant reference: 2022.01229.PTDC). I am also thankful to the Centre for Research in Anthropology (CRIA/ISCTE-IUL, IN2PAST) for hosting the project and for making possible the writing up of this chapter, through my current position as a CRIA researcher. My gratitude goes to the anonymous reviewers for reading the text and offering such encouraging comments; to Karen O'Brien-Kop and Suzanne Newcombe for all their effort, excellent communication and insightful comments; and to all the participants of the conference 'Public Health after COVID: Beliefs, Religion and Competing Epistemologies' for providing a fruitful environment to think further about the ideas and analysis presented in this chapter. Last but not least, I am greatly appreciative of the time, empirical narratives and experiences that my interlocutors in Lisbon and Athens generously shared with me, both virtually and in person, whose help made this research possible.

References

Almeida, J. and Gabe, J. (2016), 'CAM within a Field Force of Countervailing Powers: The Case of Portugal'. *Social Science & Medicine*, 155: 73–81. https://doi.org/10.1016/j.socscimed.2016.02.044

Atkinson, S., Fuller, S. and Painter, J. (eds) (2012), *Wellbeing and Place* (Farnham: Ashgate).

Bowman, M. (1999), 'Healing in the Spiritual Marketplace: Consumers, Courses and Credentialism'. *Social Compass*, 46(2): 181–9. https://doi.org/10.1177/003776899046002007

Bowman, M. and Valk, Ü (eds) (2012), *Vernacular Religion in Everyday Life: Expressions of Belief* (Sheffield: Equinox).

Dix, S. (2008), 'Roman Catholicism and Religious Pluralities in Portuguese (Iberian) History'. *Journal of Religion in Europe*, 1: 60–84. https://doi/org/10.1163/187489208X285477

Ekathimerini. (2020), 'Ieronymos Urges Faithful to Stay at Home as Act of Love', 21 March. Available at: https://www.ekathimerini.com/news/250875/ieronymos-urges-faithful-to-stay-at-home-as-act-of-love/. Accessed 21 May 2024.

Fedele, A. (2012), *Looking for Mary Magdalene: Alternative Pilgrimage and Ritual Creativity at Catholic Shrines in France* (Oxford: Oxford University Press).

Fedele, A. (2016), '"Holistic Mothers" or "Bad Mothers"? Challenging Biomedical Models of the Body in Portugal'. *Religion and Gender*, 6(1): 95–111. https://doi.org/10.18352/rg.10128

Graeber, D. (2015), 'Radical Alterity Is Just Another Way of Saying "Reality": A Reply to Eduardo Viveiros de Castro'. *Hau: Journal of Ethnographic Theory*, 5(2): 1–41. https://doi.org/10.14318/hau5.2.003

Kosarkova, A., Malinakova, K., van Dijk, J. P. and Tavel, P. (2021), 'Vaccine Refusal in the Czech Republic Is Associated with Being Spiritual but Not Religiously Affiliate'. *Vaccines*, 9 (1157): 1–12. https://doi.org/10.3390/vaccines9101157

Lett, J. (1997), 'Science, Religion, and Anthropology' in S. D. Glazier (ed.) *Anthropology of Religion: A Handbook* (Westport, CT: Greenwood Press), 103–19.

Makrides, N. V. and Sotiriou, E. (2024), 'Conspiracies, Anxieties, and Ritual Arrhythmia: Exploring Orthodox Discourses and Practices in Greece and Cyprus During the Coronavirus Pandemic' in T. Metreveli (ed.) *Orthodox Christianity and the COVID-19 Pandemic* (London and New York: Routledge), 65–101.

Manderson, L. H. (2005), 'The Social Context of Wellbeing' in L. Manderson (ed.) *Rethinking Wellbeing* (Perth: Network Books), 1–26.

Mapril, J. and Blanes, R. (2013), 'Introduction: Sites and Politics of Religious Diversity in Southern Europe' in J. Mapril and R. Blanes (eds) *Sites and Politics of Religious Diversity in Southern Europe: The Best of All Gods* (Leiden: Brill), 1–15.

McGuire, M. (2008), *Lived Religion: Faith and Practice in Everyday Life* (Oxford: Oxford University Press).

Michailidis, R., Vlasidis, V. and Karekla, S. (2021), 'An Exploratory Study on the Attitudes of the Greek Believers Towards the State's Measures During the First Wave of Coronavirus Pandemic'. *Social Sciences*, 10(2): 67. https://doi.org/10.3390/socsci10020067

Palmisano, S. and Pannofino, N. (eds) (2017), *Invention of Tradition and Syncretism in Contemporary Religions: Sacred Creativity* (London: Palgrave Macmillan).

Palmisano, S. and Pannofino, N. (2020), *Contemporary Spiritualities: Enchanted Worlds of Nature, Wellbeing and Mystery in Italy* (London: Routledge).

Panagiotopoulos, A. and Roussou, E. (2022), 'We Have Always Been Transreligious: An Introduction to Transreligiosity'. *Social Compass*, 69(4): 614–30. https://doi.org/10.1177/00377686221103713

Pierini, E., Groisman, A. and Espírito Santo, D. (eds) (2023), *Other Worlds, Other Bodies: Embodied Epistemologies and Ethnographies of Healing* (Oxford: Berghahn Books).

Primiano, L. N. (1995), 'Vernacular Religion and the Search for Method in Religious Folklife'. *Western Folklore*, 54(1): 37–56. https://doi.org/10.2307/1499910

Prodromou, E. (2004), 'Negotiating Pluralism and Specifying Modernity in Greece: Reading Church–State Relations in the Christodoulos Period'. *Social Compass*, 51(4): 471–85. https://doi.org/10.1177/0037768604047870

Roudometof, V. (2014), *Globalization and Orthodox Christianity. The Transformations of a Religious Tradition* (New York: Routledge).

Roudometof, V. (2015), 'Orthodox Christianity as a Transnational Religion: Theoretical, Historical and Comparative Considerations'. *Religion, State and Society*, 43(3): 211–27. https://doi.org/10.1080/09637494.2015.1092230

Roussou, E. (2013), 'Spirituality within Religion: Gendered Responses to a Greek "Spiritual Revolution"' in A. Fedele and K. Knibbe (eds) *Gender and Power in Contemporary Spirituality: Ethnographic Approaches* (London: Routledge), 46–61.

Roussou, E. (2015), 'From Socialization to Individualization: A New Challenge for Portuguese Religiosity'. *Italian Journal of Sociology of Education*, 7(3): 89–112. https://doi.org/10.14658/PUPJ-IJSE-2015-3-4

Roussou, E. (2018), 'Spiritual Movements in Times of Crisis: An Anthropological Account of Alternative Spirituality in Portugal and Greece' in G. Chryssides (ed.) *Minority Religions in Europe and the Middle East: Mapping and Monitoring* (London: Routledge), 52–64.

Roussou, E. (2021), 'Transnational Spirituality and Healing: An Ethnographic Exploration of Alternative Medicine in Lisbon and Athens'. *Anthropology and Medicine*, 28(4): 493–507. https://doi.org/10.1080/13648470.2021.1888870

Roussou, E. and Panagiotopoulos, A. (2023), 'Encountering Other Worlds Through "Transreligiosity": A Comparative Account of Healing, Embodiment and Transformation in the Field' in E. Pierini, A. Groisman and D. Espírito Santo (eds) *Other Worlds, Other Bodies: Embodied Epistemologies and Ethnographies of Healing* (Oxford: Berghahn Books), 133–52.

Roussou, E., Rivadossi, S. and Panagiotopoulos, A. (2023), Special Issue 'Spiritual Elasticity and Crisis: From Non-religiosity to Transreligiosity'. *Religions*, 14. https://doi.org/10.3390/rel15030373

Saraiva, C. (2008), 'Transnational Migrants and Transnational Spirits: An African Religion in Lisbon'. *Journal of Ethnic and Migration Studies*, 34(2): 253–69. https://doi.org/10.1080/13691830701823921

Saraiva, C. (2023), 'A Sacred Place, an Enchanted Space: Crisis and Spiritual Elasticity in the Mountain of the Moon'. *Religions*, 14(9): 1153. https://doi.org/10.3390/rel14091153

Sointu, E. and Woodhead, L. (2008), 'Spirituality, Gender, and Expressive Selfhood'. *Journal for the Scientific Study of Religion*, 47(2): 259–76. https://doi.org/10.1111/j.1468-5906.2008.00406.x

Ta Nea. (2021), 'Ambrosios – Sanctification Is the Weapon Against Coronavirus'. Available at: https://www.tanea.gr/2021/09/01/greece/amvrosios-o-agiasmos-einai-to-oplo-kata-tou-koronaiou/. Accessed 28 July 2024.

Tambiah, S. (1990), *Magic, Science, Religion and the Scope of Rationality* (Cambridge: Cambridge University Press).

Toren, C. and de Pina-Cabral, J. (2009), 'Introduction: What Is Happening to Epistemology?'. *Social Analysis*, 53(2): 1–18. https://doi.org/10.3167/sa.2009.530201

Turner, E. (1993), 'The Reality of Spirits: A Tabooed or Permitted Field of Study?' *Anthropology of Consciousness*, 4(1): 9–12. https://doi.org/10.1525/ac.1993.4.1.9

Vatican News. (2021), 'Pope Francis Urges People to Get Vaccinated Against Covid-19', 18 August. Available at: https://www.vaticannews.va/en/pope/news/2021-08/pope-francis-appeal-covid-19-vaccines-act-of-love.html. Accessed October 2024.

Ward, C. and Voas, D. (2011), 'The Emergence of Conspirituality'. *Journal of Contemporary Religion*, 26(1): 103–21. https://doi.org/10.1080/13537903.2011.539846

4

Trust and Doubt in the Internet Age: QAnon, Vaccine Hesitancy and the Politics of Belief

QUINTON DEELEY

Introduction: judgments of truth

CONSIDER THE FOLLOWING statements:

> *Covid is caused by a virus.*
>
> (UK Health and Security Agency 2022)
>
> *Serious side effects of Covid vaccines do occur but are very rare.*
>
> (NHS 2024)
>
> *The Covid virus does not exist.*
>
> *The Covid virus was created by the 'Deep State'.*
>
> *The Covid virus is a cover-up for child sex trafficking.*
>
> *The Covid virus is caused by 5G.*
>
> *The Covid virus is a population control scheme created by former Microsoft CEO Bill Gates.*
>
> *Industrial bleach is a cure for Covid.*

All of these statements have been expressed in relation to the Covid-19 virus and pandemic. Statements like this tend to elicit rapid judgments about their truth or plausibility. Responses may be immediate and unambiguous or more ambivalent and subject to further reflection. They are appraised as propositions which to varying extents are believed or disbelieved, where belief is understood in Sperber's terms as a 'disposition to assent to and otherwise act in accordance with some proposition' (Sperber 1996: 86). Judgements of truth or plausibility have a distinctive phenomenology involving our sense of reality. As Hume put it, 'an idea assented

Proceedings of the British Academy, **278**, 59–83, © Authors 2025.

to feels different from a fictitious idea, that the fancy alone presents to us' (Hume [1738] 2000).

These kinds of rapid judgements about ontology (what exists) and epistemology (what we know and how we know it) are made possible by the extensive internalisation of related concepts and supportive assumptions which form what Quine and Ullian (1970) termed 'webs of belief'. These 'webs of belief' are internalised from many sources of information. The statements about Covid-19 above come from different sources. Some are from the British government reflecting medical research and public health advice. Others are from viral conspiracy theories largely communicated through social media, text messaging and mass media. During the pandemic, Covid-19 and anti-vaccination conspiracy theories increasingly merged with the QAnon conspiracy theory, the core tenet of which is that the world is run by a cabal of Satan-worshipping paedophiles that President Trump is fighting against (Spring and Wendling 2020).[1]

This chapter considers the QAnon conspiracy theory, and in particular the reasons for its rapid propagation and entwinement with Covid-19 and anti-vax conspiracy theories. This involves consideration of the nature of belief and its emergence from interactions between the different levels at which human lives are organised – from political, religious and other cultural processes to neurobiology. This approach draws on my clinical experience as a neuropsychiatrist, as well as cultural neuroscience research on the relations between culture, cognition and the brain in normal human variation and psychopathology (e.g. Deeley 2018, 2019, 2023).

To begin we will consider some of the features of QAnon itself, before considering how ethnographic studies of witchcraft belief and the neuropsychiatry of paranoia provide insights into social cognition at times of crisis at different levels of human organisation. QAnon and its motivation of vaccine scepticism during a global health crisis invite us to consider how the fragility and malleability of epistemologies under conditions of stress have been greatly amplified in the internet age.

QAnon

QAnon began with an October 2017 post on the anonymous imageboard website 4chan, by 'Q Clearance Patriot' (or 'QAnon'). This username implied that 'Q' was a high-level government official with Q clearance, a United States Department of Energy security designation giving access to classified information on nuclear

[1] This chapter covers the first presidency of Donald Trump (2016–20) and the period of the presidency of Joseph Biden (2020–4), during which many QAnon supporters believed that the November 2020 election was 'stolen' and that Donald Trump remained the rightful President of the United States, continuing to refer to him as President Trump. The second presidency of Donald Trump commenced in January 2025 when this chapter was undergoing final revisions.

weapons and materials. Followers of QAnon came to believe that Q was a team of US government and military insiders revealing secret information about the Trump administration and its opponents in the United States. The imageboard website 8chan (rebranded to 8kun in 2019) became QAnon's online home as it was the only place Q posted messages after migration from 4chan (Rothschild 2022). Q fell silent after the attack on the United States Capitol on 6 January 2021 by rioters attempting to overturn the election defeat of President Trump, although a small number of posts resumed from 24 June 2022 (Thompson 2022).

QAnon's posts elaborated several interlocking conspiracy theories. The core idea was that the world is run by the 'Deep State', a cabal of Satan-worshipping paedophiles that President Trump is confronting. The Deep State and its collaborators will be arrested on a day of reckoning called 'the Storm', when they will face military tribunals and execution for their crimes (Rothschild 2021).

The notion that elites are involved in the trafficking, sexual abuse and murder of children was present in the Pizzagate internet conspiracy theory, a progenitor of QAnon ideas that went viral in 2016. It alleged that Mr Trump's opponent in the Presidential election, Hilary Clinton, and her associates were operating a child sex-trafficking ring out of the basement of a Washington, DC pizza restaurant. QAnon followers developed these ideas, alleging a worldwide conspiracy in which elites sexually abuse children in Satanic rituals, before extracting the life-extending drug adrenochrome from their adrenal glands while they are still alive (Rothschild 2021: 52).

The rapidity of QAnon's spread is striking. In March 2020 a Pew Research Center survey reported that 76 per cent of Americans said they had never heard of QAnon, 20 per cent had heard 'a little' and 3 per cent said they had heard a lot (Pew Research Center 2020). In March 2021 a poll of the Public Religion Research Institute (PRRI) and Interfaith Youth Core fielded three questions containing a tenet of the QAnon movement. Fifteen per cent of Americans agreed with the statement 'the government, media, and financial worlds in the U.S. are controlled by a group of Satan-worshipping pedophiles who run a global child sex trafficking operation' (PRRI 2021). One in five Americans (20 per cent) agreed that 'there is a storm coming soon that will sweep away the elites in power and restore the rightful leaders'. Fifteen per cent of Americans as a whole agreed that 'because things have gotten so far off track, true American patriots may have to resort to violence in order to save our country'.

To assess overall belief in QAnon, PRRI created a composite measure from these three questions to identify the following groups: QAnon believers, who completely or mostly agreed with the statements; QAnon doubters, who mostly disagreed with them; and QAnon rejecters, who completely disagreed with all three statements. In March 2021, 14 per cent of Americans were QAnon believers, which rose to roughly one in four Republicans. Forty-six per cent of Americans (and 55 per cent of Republicans) fell into the more ambivalent category of QAnon doubters, while 40 per cent of Americans (but only 21 per cent of Republicans) were QAnon rejecters. Those who endorsed QAnon core beliefs were also far more likely than others to say that they believed in other conspiracy theories, including those involving Covid-19. For example, 39 per cent of this group said they thought that 'the Covid-19 vaccine contains a surveillance microchip that is the sign of the beast in biblical prophecy'. This compared to 9 per cent of all Americans who endorsed this belief (PPRI 2021).

At one level the cultural influence of QAnon can be linked to the scale of its dissemination across a range of platforms. Q made thousands of posts on 4chan and 8chan/8kun, and the cryptic language of the posts required users to decode clues and solve puzzles. Followers were also encouraged to do their own 'research' with the phrase 'Follow the White Rabbit' (a homage to the film *The Matrix*, 1999), used as a hashtag but also inspiring a Facebook group of the same name, which had 90,000 users by June 2020 (Wong 2020). These ideas filtered out of the more obscure chan sites; images and memes based on this Q-inspired research entered into mainstream social media feeds. In 2018 Q-drop aggregator sites started to emerge; QMap, for example, was a site which catalogued Q drops and gave followers a place to find and research Q content 'without having to wade through the anarchy of 8chan' (Rothschild 2021: 41). QAnon-related accounts and influencers on popular social media sites disseminated and elaborated Q messaging until all were progressively removed in 2020 in the run-up to the November 2020 election and taken off completely after the Capitol Riot of 6 January 2021. Many members of the movement then migrated to alt-tech platforms such as Gab, Parler and Telegram. QAnon-related accounts were reinstated on Twitter/X after Elon Musk bought the site in October 2022, with an increase of Q-related messaging on X. The volume of Q-related messaging across all platforms since the first drop in October 2017 has been immense. A study of Q-related messaging on Telegram alone found around 700 Telegram channels and groups created by QAnon influencers and supporters, which contained a total of approximately 42 million posts between March 2016 and July 2021 (Robertson and Amarasingam 2022).

While Q drops are the core of QAnon messaging, the Q movement also elaborated ideas that went beyond the drops themselves (Rothschild 2021: 52). Indeed, QAnon has been described as a 'big tent' conspiracy movement holding together a constantly evolving set of conspiracist ideas (PRRI 2021). For example, adrenochrome was not mentioned in Q drops, nor were common ideas in the Q movement such as John F. Kennedy Jr. still being alive or prominent politicians being secretly executed and replaced by clones (Rothschild 2021). As Robertson and Amarasingam (2022) observe:

> QAnon is not a neatly boundaried movement in a strict sense … In Europe, where Trumpism was less of a factor, QAnon was more associated with the idea of 'elite paedophiles', essentially becoming a new name for an already long-running conspiratorial Satanic Ritual Abuse narrative that goes back to at least the 1960s.

This coalitionary character of Q-related followers and ideas extends to the entwinement of QAnon with Covid-19 and anti-vax conspiracy theories. As Rothschild (2021: 125) notes:

> QAnon believers played a major role in creating and spreading conspiracy theories about the pandemic. Everywhere that fringe plots and theories emerged, whether it was about the effectiveness of wearing masks, videos of seemingly empty hospitals that theoretically should have been overrun, or the true cause of the outbreak, Q believers were making memes and sharing hoaxes.

Within this context, former US President Donald Trump and his allies emerged as major propagators of QAnon, along with other conspiracy theories. A *New York Times* article of 2 November 2019 – 'In Trump's Twitter Feed: Conspiracy-Mongers, Racists, and Spies' – analysed Trump's interactions with Twitter since he took office, at that point comprising 11,000 tweets and hundreds of accounts he had retweeted, including numerous QAnon accounts (McIntire, Yourish and Buchanan 2019).

By October 2020, 'Trump's conspiracy theories were now indistinguishable from QAnon's. The president kept tweeting about fraud and rigging' (Rothschild 2021: 169). He shared a conspiracy theory being promoted by Q followers 'that as vice president, Biden had helped organise the mass killing of the Navy SEAL team that had killed Osama bin Laden – just one of the 315 separate times Trump would retweet or boost content from a QAnon believer before his eventual banning from Twitter' (Rothschild 2021: 169). By the time of his Twitter ban on 9 January 2021, his handle @realDonaldTrump had over 88.9 million followers (Küfner and Martin 2021).

Trump was reinstated on X (the rebrand of Twitter after its purchase by Elon Musk) in August 2023, and also communicated QAnon content on his own Truth Social platform, including a post in September 2022 showing an image of himself wearing a Q pin on his suit jacket above the 'Storm' caption and the QAnon slogan 'WWG1WGA' ('Where We Go One, We Go All') (Klepper and Swenson 2022). Trump's relationship with QAnon was symbiotic. He amplified QAnon messaging, and QAnon followers came to refer to him as 'Q+'.

Why, we might ask, did the QAnon conspiracy theory become so widespread so quickly and in the process become entwined with Covid-19 conspiracy theories? And why do politicians such as Trump, and other interest groups, disseminate conspiracy theories so vigorously?

Beliefs and belief systems

The interconnectedness of conspiracy theories suggest that they form a 'web of beliefs', with underlying assumptions that make them plausible to their adherents (Quine and Ullian 1970). As such some general considerations about the nature of beliefs are relevant before considering the characteristics of conspiracy theories in more detail.

The notion that there are 'webs of belief' fits with a shift away from earlier views of cultures as homogeneous sets of concepts and beliefs uniformly shared within a bounded social group (Deeley 2006). Cognitive anthropologists introduced the notion of cultural models or schemata to describe how cultural knowledge is organised and learned. Schemata are 'learned, internalized patterns of thought-feeling that mediate both the interpretation of ongoing experience and the reconstruction of memories' (Strauss 1997: 3); they comprise 'networks of strongly connected cognitive elements that represent the generic concepts stored in memory' (Strauss and Quinn 1997: 6). Cultural schemata (or cultural models) are those schemata that are widely distributed in a population, such that a 'cultural meaning is the typical (frequently recurring and widely shared aspects of the) interpretation of some object or event evoked in people as a result of their similar life experiences' (Strauss and Quinn 1997: 6).

In addition to informal enculturation in routine social interaction and wider media consumption, cultural institutions and systems have been developed to intensively impart knowledge – such as medical schools and religions (Bowker 1987; Good 1995). Culture is not merely ideational but encompasses a wider patterning of roles, relationships, practices and sensory environments which transmit concepts and imbue them with a sense of reality and motivational force. Enculturation engages symbolic, social and emotional cognition, in which immersion in stable, repetitive conjunctions of meanings and social-emotional signals in the social environment from infancy onwards promotes the formation of cognitive-affective schemata (Deeley 2004). As Strauss and Quinn put it, ' "culture" is merely a name for all of the learned schemas that are shared by some people, as well as all of the diverse things from which these schemas are learned' (Strauss and Quinn 1997: 38). Cultural schemata, when internalised, inform and constrain both agency and subjectivity.

People navigate the world drawing on a range of cultural models. Indeed, the range of approaches in the UK which make some claim to be able to explain, prevent and treat (or cause) various kinds of illness and misfortune is probably impossible to list exhaustively. In addition to the dominant forms of biomedicine, examples might include evangelical Christianity, acupuncture, homeopathy, aromatherapy, witchcraft, spirit possession, Ayurveda, macrobiotic diets, TM, scientology, and voodoo (noting that to list them as such is not to imply equivalence between them but to illustrate their diversity) (Littlewood and Lipsedge 1989; Littlewood 2002; Deeley 2006). Each invokes a distinct ontology and epistemology which underpin a different intuition or sense of what counts as a plausible cause of symptoms or distress, and an appropriate remedy. They employ different approaches to epistemic justification. All conceptual systems involve coherence approaches to justification which test the conceptual fit of new concepts or interpretations with foundational concepts of the model. In religions these foundational concepts are typically revealed. However, other areas of knowledge, and the sciences in particular, also involve correspondence approaches to justification, which hold that propositions are justified when they correspond to what they purport to be about as determined by empirical observation (Bowker 2005). Criteria for what counts as valid observation vary with the methods of the science in question. In the case of Covid-19 this might be observations of laboratory virology research or the fit between epidemiological simulations of the spread of the virus and observed data as it becomes available.

Apparent incompatibilities between health models may be ignored or suppressed when concepts and actions are opposed, such as the co-prescription of allopathic medicines and homeopathy. Off-loading the cognitive challenge of resolving apparent incompatibilities to higher agencies – whether human specialists or supernatural agents – may allow a fuzzy compatibility to be achieved or at least for incompatibilities to be ignored in practice. Equally, one model may be deemed to account for events better than another – such as on the psychiatry ward at the All India Institute of Medical Sciences in New Delhi when a young woman with aphonia (inability to speak) attributed to spirit possession did not recover following a *puja* ceremony, meaning that the family came to accept a psychiatric explanation of 'conversion hysteria' for her difficulties (Deeley 1999). In other situations, conflict between models becomes highly accentuated at a personal, cultural and political level. What Charles Taylor described as 'cross-pressures' when discussing the tensions between different world views erupt into open conflict, occasioning a sense of crisis and social division (Taylor 2007). This occurred during Covid-19 and was the context within which Covid-19 conspiracy theories emerged and rapidly spread.

The Covid-19 pandemic as a social and epistemological crisis

The Covid-19 pandemic motivated governments to mandate emergency public health interventions. In the UK this took the form of national lockdowns, social distancing, mask wearing and an accelerated vaccine programme whereby new vaccines were developed and administered at scale.

The pandemic imposed unique societal and individual epistemological pressures. Public health policy had to be developed with limited epidemiological data. Policy was informed by statistical modelling of different policy decisions updated with evolving data, with health and other stakeholders appraising the costs and benefits. A Scientific Advisory Group for Emergencies (SAGE) was convened to advise the government. Its decisions, and government policy more generally, were subject to widespread analysis by scientific peers and others. Its impartiality and transparency were questioned, particularly when it became known that political advisors attended. Trust in the scientific and political basis for public health policy and messaging emerged as a key issue – even from scientific peers. For example, in early May 2020 a group of scientists created Independent SAGE, chaired by Sir David Anthony King, a former Government Chief Scientific Advisor, to 'provide a clear structure on which an effective policy should be based given the inevitability that the virus will continue to cross borders' (Independent SAGE 2020). Later that month, for example, Independent SAGE warned against ending lockdown prematurely in places like schools.

Within this context it was not, in reality, possible for non-experts to form a fully informed view of how they should act in relation to public health policy. The correspondence mode of epistemic justification was a central concern for a relatively small number of expert epidemiologists, research scientists and senior medical personnel, rather than the wider population. Covid-19 brought together an extreme combination of uniquely disruptive and stressful state interventions, with high levels of scientific uncertainty and a conspicuous running commentary of expert and other critique. The provisionality and corrigibility of medical understanding – always present – became particularly acute and salient. This extended to the accelerated development of novel vaccines, some involving new technologies. For many the RNA vaccine evoked anxiety about an unnatural, chimeric mixing of species elements with unknown consequences. State encouragement (but not compulsion) to take vaccines elicited anxiety. Under these circumstances, doubt and mistrust became a critical impediment to acceptance of vaccines or indeed any other pandemic-related government policy.

From doubt to conspiracism

Doubt about the safety and effectiveness of vaccines may lead to vaccine hesitancy but without attributing malign intent to the government, scientists or manufacturers. The vaccine policy may simply be wrong or uncertain. Conspiracy theories about the vaccine involve, along with other conspiracy theories, the additional notion that important events include secret plots by powerful and malevolent groups (Bell, Raihani and Wilkinson 2021). Conspiracy theories are salient and motivating because they simultaneously evoke a sense of threat and reinforce group identity – the group that is threatened by the conspiracy.

In paranoid delusions, conspiracy thinking becomes self-focused: delusions commonly involve the perception of organised attempts to harm the individual, rather than malign explanations for public events that affect large numbers of people (Bell, Raihani and Wilkinson 2021). Conspiracist beliefs shared by large numbers of people are not delusional in the psychiatric sense precisely because they are normative for a group. Nevertheless, they share features with paranoid delusions, in the detection of meaningful patterns in events and the attribution of hostile intent. In 1958 the German psychiatrist Klaus Conrad used the word 'apophenia' to describe this cognitive mode of pattern detection in psychosis, defined as an 'unmotivated seeing of connections' accompanied by 'a specific experience of abnormal meaningfulness' (quoted in Brugger 2001: 208). This apophenic 'denial of chance' (Brugger 2001: 14, quoting Glatzel's phrase) is characteristic of psychosis (for example, in interpreting unrelated events as forming part of a conspiracy), which in turn is linked to psychosocial stress. Similarly, conspiracy theories in the general population increase at times of psychosocial stress (Swami *et al.* 2016).

Cognition at times of crisis

Psychosocial stress increases emotional arousal, which influences cognition. The dopamine system is an important arousal system in this respect – for example, many lines of evidence link dysregulation of dopamine transmission to the formation of paranoid delusions and hallucinations in psychosis (Howes, Bukala and Beck 2024). The role of dopamine in threat detection in healthy individuals has been studied using a Sharing Game, in which an experimental participant plays a partner who divides money fairly or unfairly (Barnby *et al.* 2020a). The participant has to judge whether player actions are motivated by self-interest or harmful intent. People with high-trait paranoia, for example, are more likely to interpret actions as motivated by harmful intent. Administering the dopamine blocker haloperidol reduces the tendency to interpret ambiguous actions as motivated by harmful intent. Notably, haloperidol also reduces the influence of prior beliefs on attributions about ambiguous actions. Attributions are instead more responsive to the observed behaviour of the player – there is greater 'belief flexibility'. This helps to explain how haloperidol may work in people with psychosis but also by implication shows how emotional arousal under conditions of stress, acting via increased dopamine transmission, can bias cognition to greater detection of threat and also increase cognitive rigidity (whereby prior beliefs have a greater influence on interpreting events) (Barnby *et al.* 2020b, 2024).

How, then, might individual cognitive and neurobiological processes such as hyperdopminergia (increased dopamine transmission) in relation to perceived threat and mistrust be linked to social and cultural processes? A key point here is that psychosocial stresses are appraised in terms of available cultural schemata and the social relations and practices within which they are communicated and reinforced (Deeley 2019). This creates the possibility of self-reinforcing feedback loops, contributing to culturally distinctive and socially shared interpretations of perceived stresses.

Anthropological studies of witchcraft beliefs provide insights into how notions that others intend harm conform to schemata shared by a social group, which are activated under conditions of social stress and perceived threat. Here, an example of the relationship between culture and the dynamics of belief from a small-scale 'traditional' society is relevant. This provides a relatively bounded example which by analogy – and with relevant adjustments – can help us to interpret the dynamics of belief in large-scale industrial and post-industrial societies. The example concerns the *nyongo* phenomenon, a particularly dreaded form of witchcraft among the Bakweri people of western Cameroon studied by the Oxford social anthropologist Edwin Ardener in the 1950s and 1960s. Ardener's account of the relationship of *nyongo* to social and psychological tensions is striking because he was able to track the emergence and fluctuation of this set of beliefs within the colonial and postcolonial situation of the Bakweri over many decades. The belief itself involved the following key ideas:

> A person with *nyongo* was always prosperous, for he was a member of the witch association that had the power of causing its closest relatives, even its children, to appear to die. But in truth they were taken away to work for their witch-masters on another mountain sixty or seventy miles to the north: Mount Kupe in the territory of the Bakossi people. On Mount Kupe, the *nyongo* people were believed to have a town and all modern conveniences … *Nyongo* people could best be recognized by their tin houses which they had been able to build with the zombie labour force of their dead relatives. How this belief grew up, and by what processes the association of dying children and the ownership of tin houses became so firmly fixed, cannot easily be traced. But by 1953 the belief had taken such a hold that no one would build a modern house for fear of being accused of possessing *nyongo*.
>
> (Ardener 1970: 147)

Indeed, Ardener commented that at this point in time 'there is no doubt that all "economic" initiative was much affected by the climate of that belief' (Ardener 1970: 148). In other words, shared beliefs affected 'real-world' behaviour. The *nyongo* phenomenon eventually resolved with the use of an expensive ritual remedy for *nyongo* witchcraft performed by witch-finding specialists of the remote Banyang tribe (Ardener 1970). This in turn allowed the Bakweri to take advantage of the prosperity made possible by the banana boom of the 1950s by being able to accumulate wealth without being accused of possessing *nyongo*.

However, by 1960 for a variety of reasons the banana market weakened and the village co-operatives started to lose money, which was accompanied by more adverse political and economic conditions for the Bakweri. Ardener observed how in 1963 a rumour spread from Bakweri villages on the mountains that the elders had forbidden money to be picked up from the ground since it was placed there to entice men to the waterside: 'There, "Frenchmen" would use them to work as zombies on a new deep sea harbor, or use them to appease the water spirits' (Ardener 1970: 154). In other words, economic downturn and increased social stress were accompanied by reactivation of *nyongo*-like ideas, even though the Bakweri maintained that the old *nyongo* spirits continued to be exorcised.

Ardener discussed the relationship between social stress and the witchcraft beliefs of the Bakweri in his paper 'Some Outstanding Problems in the Analysis of Events'. Ardener ([1978] 1989: 88f) noted:

> Certain kinds of zombie manifestations were correlated with low economic performance of the mass of the population. Yet that which correlated on each occasion was not the symbolic content of the behaviour. This was separately 'assembled' at the different periods of manifestation, or so I hypothesised, through new symbols, or newly arranged old symbols. Thus, at one period, zombie manifestations were caused by persons who had built corrugated iron houses. They were thought to kill their younger relatives and to use them as zombie labour. At another period, the zombie phenomena were thought to be caused by 'Frenchmen.'[2] The content was not continuous over time, but something else was: a repetitive, distinctive, structuring tendency that I then called a template.

[2] In the colonial context.

In fact, Ardener speculated that there may even have been an earlier, now forgotten manifestation of the zombie witchcraft template in the 19th century or before, given the use of the Bakweri term *somba*, most likely cognate with the Caribbean term 'zombie', to designate pledging a relative to *nyongo* (Ardener 1970).

Ardener was researching *nyongo* in the 1950s and 1960s. The contingent details through which the underlying template of zombie witchcraft is expressed have continued to evolve. For example, the social anthropologist Peter Geschiere (2013) notes how in *kong*, a form of zombie witchcraft similar to *nyongo*, Mount Kupe is now imagined as a staging post where zombie relatives are sold to the mafia as part of global circuits of labour exploitation (Figure 4.1).

In his initial account of the *nyongo* phenomenon, Ardener distinguished between template structures and structures of realisation, the conceptual content through which a template structure is expressed. He later used the distinction between paradigm and syntagm in linguistics to describe them as p-structures and s-structures, respectively. The s-structures are the particular versions of zombie witchcraft realised in the stream of events. The p-structures, by contrast, are

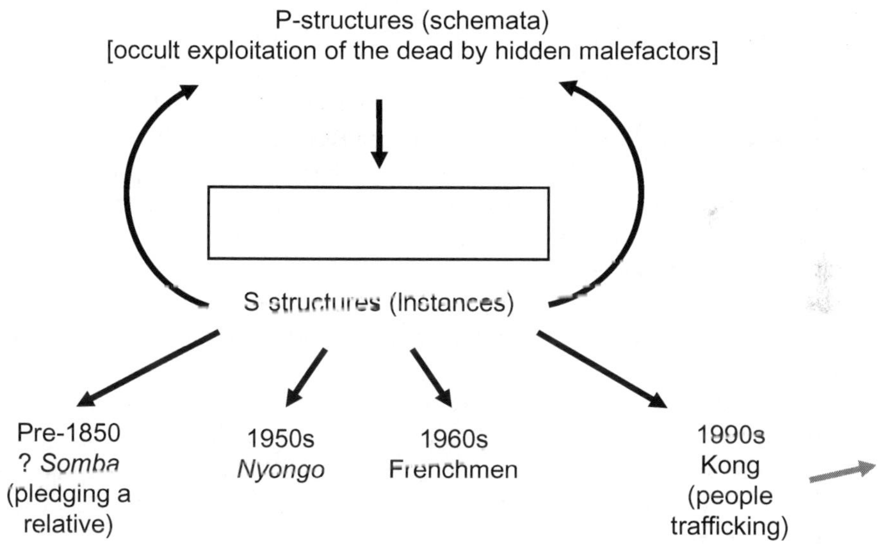

Figure 4.1 Nyongo-like phenomena. Generation of nyongo-like zombie witchcraft beliefs among the Bakweri and other Cameroonian peoples under conditions of communal stress in the work of Edwin Ardener (1970, [1978] 1989). An underlying conceptual template or p-structure forms the basis for differing specific expressions of zombie witchcraft through time, from the 19th century, 1950s, 60s and 90s, to the present day. Ardener's p-structure would now be termed a cultural model or schema in cognitive anthropology. At the deepest and most general level the p-structure entails that hidden agents cause or intend harm and misfortune, which acquires greater specificity as zombie witchcraft with the notion of occult exploitation of the dead through ritual powers. This underlies varying concrete expressions as s-structures. Specific expressions reinforce but also potentially modify the underlying template as it is reproduced across generations.

inferred from the contingent manifestations of s-structures. In Ardener's terms, the s-structures were generated from p-structures by a mode of specification – implicit rules through which the underlying system of ideas of the p-structure are expressed in concrete terms under specific circumstances.

What Ardener described as a template or p-structure as distinct from a structure of realisation or s-structure would now, in cognitive anthropology, be termed a cultural schema underpinning specific expressions of zombie witchcraft beliefs (Deeley 2019). Cognitive anthropologists have emphasised the hierarchical organisation of schemata, from the high-level and general (Ardener's p-structure) to their specific expressions (the s-structure). In this case of zombie witchcraft, the deepest and most general level of the p-structure is the assumption that hidden agents cause or intend harm and misfortune. This acquires greater specificity with the conceptual template of occult exploitation of the dead through ritual powers, which then acquires further specificity in particular beliefs relating to *nyongo*, Frenchmen and the mafia. The deep assumption – the p-structure – of hidden malefaction is shared with conspiracism as it manifests in the West and indeed many other attributions about misfortune across cultures, but the schemata become more differentiated and culture specific at each step towards their expression in more concrete and locally distinctive ideas.

Coalitional cognition and virtual cognitive enclaves

How, then, does this help us to understand the rapid propagation and entwinement of QAnon and Covid-19 conspiracy theories, and their promotion by President Trump and his allies as a political strategy?

The type of traditional society represented by the Bakweri is so different from the modern, complex societies within which virtual communities form that it might be thought that little can be learned from the comparison. Yet applications of the concept of 'coalitional cognition' to understanding paranoia and conspiracy theories in the work of Vaughan Bell, Nicola Raihani and Sam Wilkinson (2021) help show how virtual communities can reproduce important characteristics of shared identity, social influence and belief acquisition in traditional societies – although there are important differences.

As they put it,

> An important feature of human social groups is the presence of coalitions: any situation where two or more individuals unite in competition against a third party or parties. Coalitionary conflict in human groups can manifest in the form of lethal aggression … but can also include non-lethal and non-aggressive conflict, such as stigmatization, ostracism, exclusion, and derogation. For example, witchcraft accusations have been (and still are) used to identify individuals or groups for ostracism, persecution or even death … In modern industrialised societies, similar forms of indirect aggression are used by coalitions to damage the reputation of (often higher-ranking) rivals, for example via gossip or derogation …
>
> (Bell, Raihani and Wilkinson 2021: 5)

Coalitions are, in fact, easily formed:

> coalition boundaries in human groups are themselves highly fluid and flexible and can be formed in the absence of any stable group identifiers. The fact that coalitions can be formed on the basis of minimal cues or markers of similarity in turn selects for cognitive machinery that readily and flexibly categorizes people into groups on the basis of such 'minimal' cues. Indeed, humans readily form and detect minimal groups, even from a young age and the perception of these groups fundamentally alters expectations about the intentions and behaviour of individuals within them.
>
> (Bell, Raihani and Wilkinson 2021: 5)

From this perspective, online communities of the internet can be viewed as virtual coalitions, with low entry requirements and a rapidly acquired sense of group membership and identity – particularly where identity markers are grounded on prior notions of identity. Within this context, stimuli which are cognitively and emotionally salient 'win' and are more likely to propagate. Among the most salient of stimuli are those evoking a sense of shared threat – as in the case of conspiracy theories.

Conspiracy thinking is common in the general population and is defined as a tendency to provide 'explanations for important events that involve secret plots by powerful and malevolent groups' (Bell, Raihani and Wilkinson 2021). The QAnon conspiracy theory is distinct from, but resembles, the underlying conceptual template of zombie witchcraft. The secret ritualised sexual abuse and murder of children by an elite of wealthy, powerful Satan worshippers to extract life-extending adrenochrome parallels the occult extraction of labour from dead relatives by unaccountably prosperous people in *nyongo*. Both phenomena are accompanied by a profound sense of unthinkable depravity. In *nyongo* the notion that witches would kill their own relatives – particularly children – and turn them into *yekongi* (zombies) to work for new masters inspires terror (Geschiere 2013). In the QAnon-related Frazzledrip conspiracy story of 2018, it was claimed that an extreme snuff film was recovered from ex-Congressman Anthony Wiener's stolen laptop which showed Hilary Clinton and her aide Huma Abedin raping and murdering a young girl, drinking her adrenochrome-rich blood in a Satanic ritual, and taking turns wearing the little girl's face like a mask. The video was said to be so sick that the NYPD officers who saw it immediately killed themselves (Rothschild 2021: 53f.). The similarity of both sets of beliefs and their propagation and cognitive traction under conditions of perceived crisis suggest that QAnon can be thought of as our *nyongo*.

As Ardener was able to discern, there is long-running, if periodic, evidence for *nyongo*-like beliefs among the Bakweri, suggesting a conceptual fit with a larger network of enduring cultural models (Ardener 1970, [1978] 1989). The large-scale uptake of QAnon beliefs is ostensibly surprising, although there are cultural precedents for many of its ideas. These would include not only its immediate internet conspiracy precursors such as Pizzagate but the Satanic ritual abuse narrative that dates back at least to the 1960s, the Biblical Storm and End Times of the Left Behind series, the spiritual warfare genre of Christian fiction, allegations about the Rothschilds controlling world banking, and the anti-Semitic blood libel originating in the 12th century in England – among many other related ideas, imagery and tropes (Robertson and Amarasingam 2022; Rothschild 2021). In this sense QAnon can be regarded as an example of the 'remixing' of familiar cultural elements in religio-political and spiritual movements that is characteristic of contemporary – and increasingly online – society (Burton 2020).

The issue of cultural precedent and 'fit' for conspiracy theories is relevant in debates about whether or not external actors originate conspiracy theories. As Rothschild observes, 'Russian trolls and domestic political operatives will amplify what's already out there, but … only Americans can create conspiracy theories that will sucker in Americans' (Rothschild 2021: 194). Nevertheless, the scale and pace of QAnon's cultural penetration raises the question of whether social media, under conditions of perceived social crisis and political encouragement, is particularly effective in reshaping beliefs, and whether this is key to understanding both the coupling and rapid propagation of QAnon and Covid-19 conspiracy theories.

Propagating conspiracism through social media

In their book *The Web of Belief*, the philosophers Willard Van Orman Quine and Joseph Ullian wrote: 'Just about any hypothesis … can be held unrefuted no matter what, by making enough adjustments in other beliefs – though sometimes doing so requires madness' (Quine and Ullian 1970: 79).

Social media can – in Quine and Ullian's terms – introduce new beliefs and adjust background beliefs to maintain them, such as those relating to conspiracism as a general orientation and specific conspiracist beliefs in particular. Social media has 'discovered' a cognitive sweet spot, with a convergence of social, cognitive and neurobiological processes that synergically interact to incubate and canalise cognition in uniquely effective ways. The proof of this is the astonishing pace at which the political imaginaries of Americans changed before and during the Trump presidency and Covid-19 – the uncoupling of millions of Americans from what might otherwise be regarded as reality. It is not psychosis in the psychiatric sense because the beliefs are widely shared, and within their coalitional communities are normative – and, indeed, based on the engagement of normal cognitive processes which nevertheless produce extreme and rapidly evolving outcomes. This is by not only reproducing but also intensifying the cognitive dynamics of highly bounded social groups online to produce what might be termed 'cognitive enclaves' (Table 4.1).

Important questions for a cognitive anthropology or sociology of virtually constructed group identities are the extent to which their perpetuation requires ongoing virtual immersion, and whether the sense of identity they promote obscures social differences that might be more evident in real-world encounters. Nevertheless, the motivational potential of social media has been exploited by politicians and interest groups. Conspiracism as a specific political strategy has been relentlessly promoted in particular by President Donald Trump and his followers to foment a mistrust of 'elites' and galvanise support for Trump as an insurgent strongman fighting for 'the people'.

Table 4.1 Runaway evolution of cognitive enclaves through social media

Cognitive-symbolic and sensory-affective processes

- Conspiracism
- Cognitive precursors – vaccine scepticism, mistrust of elites
- Grievant thinking
- Imagery / salient sensory stimuli
- Relentless algorithmic reinforcement of key assumptions
- Immunity to contradiction / totalising vision

Neurocognitive

- Kindling of arousal systems – e.g. mesolimbic dopamine system
- Attentional capture, associative learning, pattern detection
- Heightened sense of meaning, significance and threat
- Affective rewards of coalitional bonding / exclusionary identities

Social cognitive

- Coalitional identity and social approval
- Absence of challenge / consensus effects
- Perceived agency, participation, choice, empowerment

Political

- Authoritative endorsement for political advantage by elected officials
- Role of hostile powers/ troll farms / internal dissident actors

The results

- Strongly weighted priors producing 'evidence'
- Positive feedback loops = 'runaway evolution'
- Uncoupling from verifiable reality / 'alternative facts'
- Cognitive immersion at scale
- Vaccine hesitancy
- Crisis of democratic legitimacy and political violence

Consider the examples in Figure 4.2, which have been variously endorsed by Trump in his Twitter account (with related themes since his reinstatement on X in August 2023).

Conspiracism is self-perpetuating, allowing reattribution of any contradictory evidence as proof of conspiracy by the fake news media and the elites. Individuals

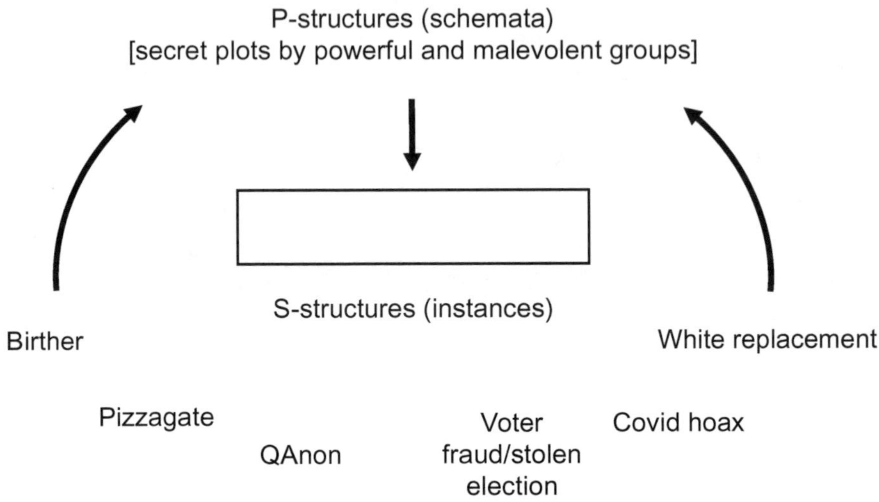

Figure 4.2 Trump and conspiracism. President Trump's use of conspiracism as a political strategy to foment mistrust of 'elites' and galvanise support for him as an insurgent strongman fighting for 'the people'. Following Ardener ([1978] 1989) the p-structure or core schema of conspiracism involves secret plots by powerful and malevolent groups. President Trump has promoted numerous specific conspiracy theories (s-structures in Ardener's terms) which share the assumptions of conspiracism, although specific types of theory (e.g. relating to health or Satanic paedophilia) are differentiated by additional features. Specific conspiracy theories feed back to reinforce the general schema of conspiracism, which is potentially open to change. In Western societies, for example, belief in ritual action at a distance by hidden malefactors was once widely accepted but not since the growth of secularism (Thomas 2003).

reach a cognitive tipping point at which they come to organise their view of the world in terms of its ideas. In this model, the acceptance of QAnon-related ideas is a runaway virtual phenomenon driven by iterative feedback loops of information in virtual enclaves. The algorithms driving this constantly intensify and refresh the confluence of thematically related conspiracist ideas. The ideas are different expressions of related underlying assumptions, analogous to Ardener's identification of a family of *nyongo*-like ideas among the Bakweri which fit an underlying conceptual template. Within this context Covid-19 conspiracy theories are only one example of interconnected and mutually influential beliefs which are congruent with the core schema of conspiracism. This is the case even if distinguishing features of specific conspiracist ideas (Satanic paedophilia, the Covid-19 hoax, vaccine chips) mean that any given individual who accepts one may not necessarily accept another.

These proposals raise the question, though, of the cognitive status of QAnon-related ideas among those who propagate them. To what extent are they actually *believed*, in Sperber's sense of belief as a 'disposition to assent to and otherwise act in accordance with some proposition' (Sperber 1996: 86). One study used a 'feeling thermometer' to measure favourable feeling towards QAnon on a 0–100 scale (0–49 unfavourable, 50–100 favourable). In national samples the study found broadly unfavourable ratings for QAnon: 21 in August 2019, 25 in March 2020, 24 in June 2020 and 16 in October 2020 – in other words, during a period of increasing public awareness and internet traffic relating to QAnon (Enders *et al.* 2022). Yet the average rating of 16 in the October 2020 poll corresponded with 7 per cent of individuals agreeing or strongly agreeing with the statement 'I am a believer in QAnon' – about 18 million of the adult American population of *c.* 258 million in 2020. The proportion of 'QAnon believers' – those who completely or mostly agree with core tenets of QAnon – increased in 2021 according to four successive surveys in 2021 by PRRI. There was in fact a slight upward trend from 14 per cent in March, compared to 16 per cent in July, 17 per cent in September and 17 per cent in October – the latter percentage corresponding to almost 44 million adults (PRRI 2022). As noted above, the PRRI surveys distinguished QAnon believers, doubters and rejecters. The doubters, who mostly disagree with QAnon statements, amounted to 20 per cent, 29 per cent and 25 per cent over the survey period. The doubters are an important group in their own right because their ambivalence indicates some persisting influence of the ideas which prevents their outright rejection. The most recent survey by PRRI in August to September 2024 showed an increase in QAnon believers to 19 per cent of the individuals, corresponding to over 49 million adults, with 49 per cent doubters and 32 per cent rejecters (PRRI 2024a). It would seem, then, that the cognitive traction of QAnon-related ideas in the American population is considerable and has trended upward as awareness of it has increased since the first Q drop of October 2017.

Nevertheless, this trend of increasing endorsement of QAnon tenets revealed by successive PRRI surveys has continued in the absence of posting by Q since the attack on the United States Capitol on 6 January 2021 (with the possible exception of a small number of posts from 25 June 2022) (Thompson 2022). In an article entitled 'Four Years After the Capitol Riot, Why QAnon Hasn't Gone Away' (Joffe-Block 2024), the journalist and author Mark Rothschild observes that while 'there haven't been new Q drops in years and there appears to to be less interest in online content analyzing those drops in the way there once was … ideas QAnon helped popularize, like the idea of a battle against an evil Deep State, and anti-vaccine conspiracy theories, have become common ideas on the right'. He states: 'QAnon as a movement based around secret codes and clues and riddles doesn't so much exist anymore … But it doesn't need to exist anymore because its tenets have become such a major part of mainstream conservatism and such a big part of the base of people that reelected Donald Trump' (Joffe-Block 2024). This view is borne out by PRRI's post-election survey of December 2024, which showed that 81 per cent of QAnon believers reported voting for Donald Trump (PRRI 2024b), within the context of a pre-election survey showing that 28 per cent of Republicans qualified as QAnon believers (PRRI 2024a).

While questionnaire surveys allow estimates of the prevalence of attitudes to QAnon ideas and their relationship to demographic, political, personality and other variables, they provide little insight into individual trajectories regarding identification with the QAnon movement and agreement with its ideas. The status of 'QAnon believer' is a heterogeneous category, most likely encompassing subgroups such as those with a pre-existing tendency to endorse conspiracy beliefs and those whose adoption of the movement is perceived as 'cult-like' by family and friends. Many examples of the latter are included in journalistic accounts, with Rothschild's book on QAnon opening with an anonymised comment: 'I vividly remember the first time he asked me to watch one of the QAnon videos. He mocked it and laughed at the idea that anyone would fall for it. Then, over the next couple of months, something changed.' The book concludes with a chapter on 'how to help people who want to get out of Q' (Rothschild 2021: ix).

Conclusion: conspiracism and epistemology

In an article entitled 'Reality Rebellion' of 1 July 2021 concerning the attempted US coup of 6 January 2021, the journalist Mark Danner notes that 'Nearly half of Republicans tell pollsters Trump was "called by God to lead". Seven in ten say the election was stolen and the current president is illegitimate' (Danner 2021). Danner takes the phrase 'reality rebellion' from the former FBI special agent and terrorism expert Clinton Watts. This is a reflection not only on the disconnection from reality by followers of conspiracy theories but how the insistence that conspiracies are true feeds back into actions in the world we all share – Pizzagate, the Capitol riot, as well as related clusters of ideas relating to Covid-19 and other matters – such as protesters outside St Thomas' Hospital in London claiming that Covid-19 is a hoax (Howie 2021). The consequentiality of beliefs compels consideration of epistemology – of how truth and untruth can be distinguished.

The present analysis is indebted to a tradition in social anthropology originating with Durkheim which analyses how cultural concepts – 'collective representations' – are imbued with a sense of reality and motivational force by ritual, understood as emotive symbolic action (Deeley 2004). Nevertheless, the diverse concepts that may come to be accentuated by ritual and other cultural contexts and practices, including social media, also influence cognition in their own right. The properties of existing cultural models or webs of belief act as priors which influence responses to Covid-19 – for example, ideas of health and nature which often oppose themselves to biomedicine (homeopathy, humoral medical systems). There is scope for deeper consideration of the many models of health which distinguish themselves from biomedicine and what motivates the seeming intuitiveness of their cognitive appeal (Leslie and Young 1992). This would include the pre-Covid movement of vaccine scepticism. By contrast, as noted, biomedicine can often seem counterintuitive. Its mechanistic underpinnings are abstruse and technical, and the epidemiological reasoning at a population level governing Covid-19 policy and vaccination strategy is not only difficult to fully personalise but is also provisional and corrigible. Within the context of contradictory truth claims of different health models in relation to vaccination it may seem that epistemology is a zero-sum game – one set of beliefs is correct, the other false – or at least one set comes to prevail as action. One cannot both have, and not have, a vaccine.

At a political level, the strategic cultivation of falsehoods by authoritative figures demotes truth, facts or more broadly 'realism' as an aspiration and value. It implicitly promotes a meta-attitude to beliefs about reality closer to Nietzsche's perspectivism, whereby what counts as reality is solely a product of human interests – the will to power – in a permanent contest of shouting down rival interpretations with no agreed means of adjudicating disputes about what is true or real (Craig 1987). For those with a performative approach to truth, there is no pivotal moment in which facts could be revealed which would cause them to acknowledge that opposed views were correct – because this is not what the performance of truth is for.

Against this background the promotion of conspiracism as a political strategy can be read as calculated disinformation. So, for example, when President Trump retweeted in October 2020 that as vice president Joseph Biden had helped organise the mass killing of the Navy SEAL team that had killed Osama bin Laden, many would assume that he maintains a private distinction between expedient narrative and what is 'really real' – noting that when challenged about it in a 'town hall' event, 'Trump defended the post by arguing it was simply "a retweet" of someone's "opinion." He added, "I'll put it out there, and people can decide for themselves" ' (Fichera and Spencer 2020). It is, however, unclear to what extent President Trump believes some of the conspiracy theories he propagates; whether, for example, a constitutional aversion to the idea of losing led him to persuade himself that the 2020 election was indeed stolen.

Nevertheless, in the case of scientifically led fields such as public health and vaccination policy what is 'really real' would conventionally be considered to be determined by experts such as epidemiologists, microbiologists and public health physicians. By contrast, a salient feature of the second Trump presidency is the readiness to cede critical policy-making to political allies who are committed to what conventional expertise would consider to be conspiracist, unscientific views. A prominent example would be the appointment of Robert F. Kennedy Jr. as Health Secretary, given his established and well-publicised vaccine scepticism and endorsement of anti-vax conspiracy theories (McCausland 2025). To repeat the point, one cannot both have and not have a vaccine, so the vaccination policy that prevails – for example, in presenting misinformation about vaccination and promoting unevidenced 'cures' during a measles epidemic in Texas in 2025 (Rosenbluth 2025) – reflects a political decision about what counts as authoritative knowledge for society as a whole. In other words, the second Trump presidency has pursued a far-reaching and fundamental reset of epistemic authority in which scientific knowledge in areas such as public health and climate science is demoted in the service of political aims, to the extent of deleting health and climate-related databases on government websites (Guardian Editorial 2025; Milman 2025). The 'alternative facts' justifying these rival policy agendas are run through with conspiracist views of conventional science and the motivations of those who promote it. This forms part of a broader strategy of information control which, for example, uses political, legal and financial pressure to influence the behaviour of institutions such as universities, corporations and law firms.

Yet the readiness with which conspiracy beliefs are adopted in wider society also raises questions about whether they are always completely uncoupled from reality, or whether in some cases at least they act as concretely understood metaphors, a distorted refraction of genuine causes of suffering and reasons for mistrusting powerful people. The ecological anthropologist Roy Rappaport distinguished cognised and operational environments, the former being the world as it is locally experienced and understood, and the latter the world as defined by scientific observers (Rappaport [1968] 2000). If the cognised environment is the level of *nyongo* and QAnon attributions, what might the operational environment be?

The social anthropologist Peter Geschiere and others have speculated about whether *nyongo*-type beliefs originated at the time of the transatlantic slave trade, when a person might be betrayed by kin (pledged, *somba*) into slavery, in which labour was extracted in a kind of death (Fisiy and Geschiere 1991; Geschiere 2020; see also Oyugi 2016). The *nyongo*-like idea of *kong* imagines the dead as people trafficked by the mafia. *Nyongo* is also now used as a term to refer to the condition of migrant labourers from Cameroon working long hours in unskilled jobs in Europe, remitting money home, sometimes to distant relatives who pressurise them with occult threats from afar (Nyamnjoh 2005; Geschiere 2013). In QAnon the extraction of life-extending adrenochrome from what is most precious and full of life and potential – children – could be read as a metaphor for a more general exploitation of people by the rich and powerful, although as a right-wing trope it substitutes moral for economic exploitation in a political culture which treats open recognition of the latter as a taboo. QAnon-related ideas can be understood as causal attribution errors based on concretely understood metaphors within the context of widespread social suffering in American society, marked by conditions such as insecure employment, widespread waged and unwaged poverty, homelessness and the opioid crisis (Kristoff and WuDunn 2020). Equally, other reinforcements of QAnon-related conspiracy ideas can be traced across American culture – such as the arrest and reported suicide of the high society paedophile Jeffrey Epstein and his connections with the rich and powerful or stories about wealthy individuals receiving blood transfusions from the young to prolong life (Simonpillai 2025).

Nevertheless, unlike the *nyongo* phenomenon, for many the uptake of conspiracist ideas does not correlate with economic distress. Government policies to mitigate economic distress would, therefore, not make much difference to the already wealthy who endorse these ideas. Given the premise of mistrust and the scale of misattributions, governments would not be credited much for any improvements. In a sense, the 'crisis' which correlates with identification with QAnon by the already wealthy is formed by conspiracist ideas themselves, which are mutually predisposing. If these beliefs are linked to underlying stressors, they would not be so much economic as a range of prior beliefs that motivate mistrust of elites and receptiveness to QAnon ideas. These beliefs are likely to be varied, providing different bases for a readiness to accept QAnon and related ideas. They might range from religious ideas (such as Christian belief in the End Times and a prior conviction that Godless cultural and political elites are sinful) to feelings of victimisation and loss of social standing in the contested arena of cultural politics (Nagle 2017). Again, the perceived 'crisis' is amplified on social media and as a political strategy (Applebaum and Pomerantsev 2021). Yet from a government perspective, policy cannot address problems that do not exist. You cannot liberate children from the basement of a Washington pizzeria if there are no children there, and you cannot remedy a stolen election if it was not stolen.

An irony of Rappaport's distinction between cognised and operational environment is that it places experts in the role of determining what counts as reality as opposed to its indirect representation in the cognised environments of everyone else. In conspiracism the status of official (government or university) expertise disqualifies the expert from speaking the truth, to the extent that the attempts of experts to counter conspiracism itself become evidence for conspiracism.

This points back to the digital information environment and how it works. There is scope for a wider debate about policies and strategies to regulate the feedback dynamics of social media that are uncoupling large numbers of people from a verifiable, shareable world – even where people continue to disagree about reality – which they will (Applebaum and Pomerantsev 2021). No system is infinitely buffered, and the distortions of communal identity and belief sweeping through digital communities pose a fundamental threat not only to public health but to the viability of democracies. As Sara Lipton wrote in a review of works on the anti-Semitic blood libel, 'Seven Centuries of Slander' (Lipton 2021), 'in any era truth sits on a precarious perch, and … a slight shift in political or social winds can send reason and fact toppling into a conspiratorial void'.

Acknowledgement

With thanks to Dr Elisa Brann for preparing the figures.

References

Applebaum, A. and Pomerantsev, P. (2021), 'How to Put Out Democracy's Dumpster Fire', *The Atlantic*, April. Available at: https://www.theatlantic.com/magazine/archive/2021/04/the-internet-doesnt-have-to-be-awful/618079/. Accessed October 2024.

Ardener, E. (1970), 'Witchcraft, Economics, and the Continuity of Belief' in M. Douglas (ed.) *Witchcraft Confessions and Accusations* (London: Routledge), 141–60.

Ardener, E. ([1978] 1989), 'Some Outstanding Problems in the Analysis of Events' in M. Chapman (ed.) *The Voice of Prophecy and Other Essays* (Oxford: Oxford University Press), 86–104.

Barnby, J. M., Bell, V., Deeley, Q., Mehta, M. A. and Moutoussis, M. (2024), 'D2/D3 Dopamine Supports the Precision of Mental State Inferences and Self-relevance of Joint Social Outcomes'. *Nature Mental Health*, 2(5): 562–73. https://doi.org/10.1038/s44220-024-00220-6

Barnby, J. M., Deeley, Q., Robinson, O., Raihani, N., Bell, V. and Mehta, M. A. (2020a), 'Paranoia, Sensitization and Social Inference: Findings from Two Large-scale, Multi-round Behavioural Experiments'. *Royal Society Open Science*, 7(3): 191525. https://doi.org/10.1098/rsos.191525

Barnby, J. M., Bell, V., Deeley, Q. and Mehta, M. A. (2020b), 'Dopamine Manipulations Modulate Paranoid Social Inferences in Healthy People'. *Translational Psychiatry*, 10(1): 214.

Bell, V., Raihani, N. and Wilkinson, S. (2021), 'Derationalizing Delusions'. *Clinical Psychological Science*, 9(1): 24–37. https://doi.org/10.1177/2167702620951553

Bowker, J. (1987), 'Religions as Systems' in *Licensed Insanities: Religions and Belief in God in the Contemporary World* (London: Dartman, Longman, and Todd), 9–14.

Bowker, J. (2005), *The Sacred Neuron* (London: IB Tauris).

Brugger, P. (2001), 'From Haunted Brain to Haunted Science: A Cognitive Neuroscience View of Paranormal and Pseudoscientific Thought' in J. L. Houran and R. Lange (eds) *Hauntings and Poltergeists: Multidisciplinary Perspectives* (Jefferson, NC: McFarland), 195–213.

Burton, T. I. (2020), *Strange Rites: New Religions for a Godless World* (London: Hachette UK).

Craig, E. (1987), *The Mind of God and the Works of Man* (Oxford: Clarendon Press).

Danner, M. (2021), 'Reality Rebellion'. *The New York Review of Books*, 1 July.

Deeley, P. Q. (1999), 'Medicine, Psychiatry, and the Ecology of Mind'. *Philosophy, Psychiatry, and Psychology*, 6(2): 109–24.

Deeley, Q. (2004), 'The Religious Brain: Turning Ideas into Convictions'. *Anthropology & Medicine*, 11(3): 245–67.

Deeley, Q. (2006), 'The Cognitive Anthropology of Belief' in P. W. Halligan and M. Aylward (eds) *The Power of Belief* (Oxford: Oxford University Press), 33–54.

Deeley, Q. (2018), 'Neuroanthropology: Exploring Relations Between Brain, Cognition, and Culture' in I. S. Gilhus and A. K. Petersen (eds) *Evolution, Cognition, and the History of Religion: A New Synthesis* (Leiden: Brill), 380–96.

Deeley, Q. (2019), 'Witchcraft and Psychosis: Perspectives from Psychopathology and Cultural Neuroscience'. *Magic, Ritual, and Witchcraft*, 14(1): 86–113. https://dx.doi.org/10.1353/mrw.2019.0002

Deeley, Q. (2023), 'Experiencing and Believing in Invisible Others: Anthropological and Neurocognitive Perspectives'. *Religion, Brain & Behavior*, 13(1): 49–61. https://doi.org/10.1080/2153599X.2022.2050795

Enders, A. M., Uscinski, J. E., Klofstad, C. A., Wuchty, S., Seelig, M. I., Funchion, J. R., *et al.* (2022), 'Who Supports QAnon? A Case Study in Political Extremism'. *The Journal of Politics*, 84(3): 1844–9.

Fichera, A, and Spencer, S. A (2020), 'Trump's Long History with Conspiracy Theories', Factcheck.org, 20 October. Available at: https://www.factcheck.org/2020/10/trumps-long-history-with-conspiracy-theories. Accessed 26 March 2025.

Fisiy, C. F. and Geschiere, P. (1991), 'Sorcery, Witchcraft and Accumulation: Regional Variations in South and West Cameroon'. *Critique of Anthropology*, 11(3): 251–78. https://doi.org/10.1177/0308275X9101100304

Geschiere, P. (2013), *Witchcraft, Intimacy, and Trust: Africa in Comparison* (Chicago, IL: University of Chicago Press).

Geschiere, P. (2020), 'Capitalism and "Witchcraft". Everyday Convergences in Africa – and Elsewhere'. *Lares*, 86(2): 227–46. https://lares.cfs.unipi.it/archivio/2020-2/geschiere-abstract/

Good, B. (1995), *Medicine, Rationality and Experience: An Anthropological Perspective* (Cambridge: Cambridge University Press).

Guardian Editorial. (2025), 'The Guardian View on Trump and Reality: From Promoting Alternative Facts to Erasing Truths', 27 March. Available at: https://www.theguardian.com/commentisfree/2025/mar/27/the-guardian-view-on-trump-and-reality-from-promoting-alternative-facts-to-erasing-truths. Accessed 27 March 2025.

Howes, O. D., Bukala, B. R. and Beck, K. (2024), 'Schizophrenia: From Neurochemistry to Circuits, Symptoms and Treatments'. *Nature Reviews Neurology*, 20(1): 22–35. https://doi.org/10.1038/s41582-023-00904-0

Howie, M. (2021), 'Doctor Tells of "Heartbreak" as Crowd Shouted "Covid Is a Hoax" Outside St Thomas' Hospital', *Evening Standard*, 2 January. Available at: https://www.standard.co.uk/news/london/doctor-covid-hoax-crowd-outside-st-thomas-hospital-b633377.html. Accessed 3 April 2024.

Hume, D. ([1738] 2000), *A Treatise of Human Nature: Being an Attempt to Introduce the Experimental Method of Reasoning into Moral Subjects* (Oxford: Oxford University Press).

Independent SAGE. (2020), 'COVID-19: What Are the Options for the UK? Recommendations for Government Based on an Open and Transparent Examination of the Scientific Evidence', The Independent Scientific Advisory Group for Emergencies (SAGE), 12 May. Available at: https://www.independentsage.org/wp-content/uploads/2020/05/The-Independent-SAGE-Report.pdf. Accessed 3 April 2024.

Joffe-Block, J (2024), 'Four Years After the Capitol Riot, Why QAnon Hasn't Gone Away', *NPR*, 30 December. Available at: https://www.npr.org/transcripts/nx-s1-5230801. Accessed 26 March 2025.

Klepper, D. and Swenson, A. (2022), 'Trump Begins Openly Embracing and Amplifying False Fringe QAnon Conspiracy Theory', Public Broadcasting Service, 16 September. Available at: https://www.pbs.org/newshour/politics/trump-begins-openly-embracing-and-amplifying-false-fringe-qanon-conspiracy-theory. Accessed 3 April 2024.

Kristoff, N. and WuDunn, S. (2020), 'Who Killed the Knapp Family?', *New York Times*, 9 January. Available at: https://www.nytimes.com/2020/01/09/opinion/sunday/deaths-despair-poverty.html. Accessed 27 March 2025.

Küfner, M. and Martin, T. (2021), 'Donald Trump Loses Social Media Megaphone', *Deutsche Welle*, 7 January. Available at: https://www.dw.com/en/donald-trump-loses-social-media-megaphone/a-56158414. Accessed October 2024.

Leslie, C. and Young, A. (1992), *Paths to Asian Medical Knowledge* (Berkeley, CA: University of California Press).

Lipton, S. (2021), 'Seven Centuries of Slander', *New York Review of Books*, 23 September. Available at: https://www.nybooks.com/articles/2021/09/23/blood-libel-seven-centuries-slander/. Accessed October 2024.

Littlewood, R. (2002), *Pathologies of the West: An Anthropology of Mental Illness in Europe and America* (London: Continuum).

Littlewood, R. and Lipsedge, M. (1989), *Aliens and Alienists: Ethnic Minorities and Psychiatrists* (London: Unwin-Hyman).

McCausland, P (2025), 'What RFK Jr Could Do on US Vaccines, Fluoride, and Drugs', *BBC News*, 15 November 2024, updated 28 January 2025. Available at: https://www.bbc.co.uk/news/articles/c4gx3kkz8z3o. Accessed 24 March 2025.

McIntire, M., Yourish, K. and Buchanan, L. (2019), 'In Trump's Twitter Feed: Conspiracy-Mongers, Racists and Spies', *New York Times*, 2 November. Available at: https://www.nytimes.com/interactive/2019/11/02/us/politics/trump-twitter-disinformation.html. Accessed 3 April 2024.

Milman, O (2025), 'Scientists Brace "for the Worst" as Trump Purges Climate Mentions from Websites', *Guardian*, 4 February. Available at: https://www.theguardian.com/us-news/2025/feb/04/trump-climate-change-federal-websites. Accessed 26 March 2025.

Nagle, A. (2017), *Kill all Normies: Online Culture Wars from 4chan and Tumblr to Trump and the Alt-right* (London: John Hunt Publishing).

NHS. (2024), 'Covid-19 Vaccine'. Last reviewed 2 September. https://www.nhs.uk/vaccinations/covid-19-vaccine. Accessed October 2024.

Nyamnjoh, F. B. (2005), 'Images of Nyongo Amongst Bamenda Grassfielders in Whiteman Kontri'. *Citizenship Studies*, 9(3): 241–69. https://doi.org/10.1080/13621020500147319

Oyugi, O. W. (2016), 'Historicizing Ethnicity and Slave-trade Memories in Colonial Africa: The Cases for Rwanda and Northern Cameroon'. *Ufahamu: A Journal of African Studies*, 39(1): 66–86. https://doi.org/10.5070/F7391029818.

Pew Research Center. (2020). 'QAnon's Conspiracy Theories Have Seeped into U.S. Politics, but Most Don't Know What It Is', *Pew Research Center*, 30 March. Available at: https://www.pewresearch.org/short-reads/2020/03/30/qanons-conspiracy-theories-have-seeped-into-u-s-politics-but-most-dont-know-what-it-is. Accessed 3 April 2024.

PRRI. (2021), 'Understanding QAnon's Connection to American Politics, Religion, and Media Consumption', *The Public Religion Research Institute*, 27 May. Available at: https://www.prri.org/research/qanon-conspiracy-american-politics-report. Accessed 3 April 2024.

PRRI. (2022), 'The Persistence of QAnon in the Post-Trump Era: An Analysis of Who Believes the Conspiracies', *The Public Religion Research Institute*, 24 February. Available at: https://www.prri.org/research/the-persistence-of-qanon-in-the-post-trump-era-an-analysis-of-who-believes-the-conspiracies. Accessed 19 September 2024.

PRRI. (2024a), 'The Rise and Impact of Q: The 2024 Election from the View of QAnon Believers', *The Public Religion Research Institute*, 4 November. Available at: https://www.prri.org/spotlight/the-rise-and-impact-of-q-the-2024-election-from-the-view-of-qanon-believers. Accessed 26 March 2025.

PRRI. (2024b), 'Analyzing the 2024 Presidential Vote: PRRI's Post-Election Survey', *The Public Religion Research Institute*, 13 December. Available at: https://www.prri.org/research/analyzing-the-2024-presidential-vote-prris-post-election-survey. Accessed 26 March 2025.

Quine, W. V. and Ullian, J. S. (1970), *The Web of Belief* (New York: Random House).

Rappaport, R. A. ([1968] 2000), *Pigs for the Ancestors: Ritual in the Ecology of a New Guinea People* (Long Grove, IL: Waveland Press).

Robertson, D. G. and Amarasingam, A. (2022), 'How Conspiracy Theorists Argue: Epistemic Capital in the QAnon Social Media Sphere'. *Popular Communication*, 20(3): 193–207. https://doi.org/10.1080/15405702.2022.2050238

Rosenbluth, T. (2025), 'Kennedy Links Measles Outbreak to Poor Diet and Health, citing fringe theories', *New York Times*, 10 March. Available at: https://www.nytimes.com/2025/03/10/health/measles-texas-kennedy-fox.html. Accessed 26 March 2025.

Rothschild, M. (2021), *The Storm Is Upon Us: How QAnon Became a Movement, Cult, and Conspiracy Theory of Everything* (Brooklyn, NY: Melville House).

Simonpillai, R. (2025), 'Are We the First Generation That Won't Die?': Bryan Johnson on His Controversial Lifestyle', *Guardian*, 2 January. Available at: https://www.theguardian.com/film/2025/jan/02/bryan-johnson-documentary-dont-die-netflix?utm_source=chatgpt.com. Accessed 26 March 2025.

Sperber, D. (1996), *Explaining Culture* (London: Blackwell).

Spring, M. and Wendling, M. (2020), 'How Covid-19 Myths Are Merging with the QAnon Conspiracy Theory', *BBC News*, 3 May. Available at: https://www.bbc.co.uk/news/blogs-trending-53997203. Accessed 4 April 2024.

Strauss, C. (1997), 'Models and Motives' in R. D'Andrade and C. Strauss (eds) *Human Motives and Cultural Models* (Cambridge: Cambridge University Press), 45–58.

Strauss, C. and Quinn, N. (1997), *A Cognitive Theory of Cultural Meaning* (Cambridge: Cambridge University Press).

Swami, V., Furnham, A., Smyth, N., Weis, L., Lay, A. and Clow, A. (2016), 'Putting the Stress on Conspiracy Theories: Examining Associations Between Psychological Stress, Anxiety, and Belief in Conspiracy Theories'. *Personality and Individual Differences*, 99: 72–6. https://doi.org/10.1016/j.paid.2016.04.084

Taylor, C. (2007), *A Secular Age* (Cambridge, MA: Harvard University Press).

Thomas, K. [1971] 2003), *Religion and the Decline of Magic: Studies in Popular Beliefs in Sixteenth and Seventeenth-Century England* (London: Penguin UK).

Thompson, S. A. (2022), 'The Leader of the QAnon Conspiracy Theory Returns', *New York Times*, 25 June. Available at: https://www.nytimes.com/2022/06/25/technology/qanon-leader-returns.html. Accessed 3 April 2024.

UK Health and Security Agency. (2022), 'Guidance: COVID-19: Epidemiology, Virology and Clinical Features', updated 12 May. Available at: https://www.gov.uk/government/publications/wuhan-novel-coronavirus-background-information/wuhan-novel-coronavirus-epidemiology-virology-and-clinical-features. Accessed October 2024.

Wong, J. C. (2020), 'Down the Rabbit Hole: How QAnon Conspiracies Thrive on Facebook', *Guardian*, 25 June. https://www.theguardian.com/technology/2020/jun/25/qanon-facebook-conspiracy-theories-algorithm. Accessed 3 April 2024.

Part III

Power, Authority and Contested Truths: Belief and Public Health

THE WAYS IN which the nation-state takes responsibility for the provision of medical care for its citizens were engendered in the modern era and via the 'imagined communities' central to nationalism. As we saw in the Covid-19 crisis, nation-states sometimes use their interpretations of health in tradition and history to regulate public behaviour and public health.

This section considers the response to the pandemic crises in two distinct political contexts. In the case of Tamil Nadu in South India, Sujatha (Chapter 5) explores a political division of labour between various disciplines dealing with human life and suffering in the social organisation of knowledge and informed practice. This chapter looks at how the state attempts to balance the interests of a highly developed pharmacology of traditional remedies, alongside biomedical models and an approach to the human body that is fundamentally less dualistic than European models.

Turning to Iran, Ebrahimnejad (Chapter 6) considers a differential analysis of the rationale for healthcare decisions in Iran during the height of the pandemic, exploring the way the social context within Iran shaped perception of and responses to disease and illness during the Covid-19 pandemic. The government's response is analysed to be motivated primarily by an exercise of power through the clerical regime, that is, the professional religious traditionalists and by considerations of ontological integrity, while the majority of the population's decisions were a personal response to a complex combination of cultural, religious, financial and political factors.

Together these chapters highlight the entanglements of power, knowledge and healthcare decisions in the national context.

5

Experience, Knowledge and Expertise: Traditional Medicine and Infectious Fevers in Contemporary India

V. SUJATHA

udambār aliyil uyirār alivar
tidambada meyjnām cēravum māttār
udambai valarkum ubayām arindē
udambaivalarttēn uyir valarttēnē

— *Tirumantiram*, 724[1]

(When the body is ruined, life is also ruined
Nor can the certainty of true knowledge be reached
Learning the way to nurture the body
I nurtured the body and, so doing, nurtured life)[2]

Lived experience, the core concept of phenomenology, has profound significance for the philosophical and anthropological study of medical knowledge owing to its inextricable connection to the human body.

> In general, the classical phenomenologists begin their reflections from the distinction they draw between two aspects of the body – between *Leib* and *Körper* – between the living, animate, organic 'lived body' (what Merleau-Ponty calls '*le corps vecu*'), the body as it is personally experienced, and the body understood as a purely physical, corporeal thing, extended in space, the material body, the body as an object of science, or as 'corpse' – as Sartre puts it ... The term physical body (*Körper*) is used by Husserl primarily to refer to the physical body which occupies space and is subject to causal laws as described by physics and the natural and biological sciences ... In one sense

[1] *Tirumantiram* is a set of 8,000 verses attributed to Tirumular, who is one of the principal saints associated with the Siddha tradition. He is also one of the 63 prime Saiva devotees whose story appears in the Saivite epic poetry of the 8th century CE. His time period is roughly estimated to be 5–6th century CE (Ganapathy, Arumugam and Anand 2006).

[2] Translations of the Tamil verses and terms presented in this chapter are by the author.

Proceedings of the British Academy, **278**, 87–111, © Authors 2025.

> the body is a physical thing like other physical things; it is governed by gravity, has the character of weight, impenetrability, having 'parts outside of parts', is affected by cold and heat, can be cut or damaged, is affected by disease and so on. In another sense, the body is the animate body I possess or which more accurately I am. The lived body is much more difficult to describe, precisely because it is experienced so close to me it is indeed, as Husserl puts it, the living centre of my experience.
>
> (Jensen and Moran 2013: viii)

The binary between the lived experience 'of' the body on the part of the subject and medical knowledge 'about' the human body as an object has been a persistent theme in the philosophical, sociological and anthropological study of medicine. Michel Foucault also drew attention to the process by which the dissection of the corpse became the basis for knowledge of life and the living patient. This very theme is reflected in Drew Leyder's work (1992) on the metaphor of the corpse that looms in the dyadic encounter of the biomedical doctor with the patient lying flat on the table like an 'animated corpse' reproducing the images of dissection of corpses in the lab.

The dichotomy between disease and sickness in Parsonian sociology's concept of the sick role was roughly based on an extension of this understanding of the divide between the biological and social aspects of health – disease as a lesion in the corporeal body which biomedical doctors diagnose and treat is opposed to sickness as the patient's behavioural adaptation to disease, namely, the sick role. In his study of the healing practices of Taiwan, Arthur Kleinman (1980) refined this division between the biological and socio-psychological aspects of affliction, assigning the former to the jurisdiction of the psychiatrist and the latter to that of the healer/patient/caregiver. In short, he argued that disease is the clinical reality, whereas illness is the private experience of the patient, lacking in objective validity yet crucial to the patient's wellbeing.

The phenomenological and anthropological critique of biomedical reductionism reinforced the very same reductionism by positioning illness experience as the opposite of disease (conceived as an objective fact based on lesions in the organic body that could be recorded) (Sujatha 2009). In Kleinman's view (1980), Taiwanese healers worked on mental stress through ritual, prayer, music and medicine, dealing with the patient's subjective response to the mental disease, namely, illness. He, however, concluded that the traditional healers left the mental 'disease' untreated. Kleinman's cross-cultural psychiatry/anthropology proposed to the biomedical fraternity that enhancing communicative modalities with the patient is likely to enrich the humane aspect of the biomedical system, which is already efficacious in dealing with the body. Thus, in the social sciences, 'the disease-illness dichotomy was intended to show the inadequacy of the singular hegemonic explanatory model on disease, namely, that of the physician. The term illness was, therefore, designed to highlight the centrality of the patient's experience of the disease condition' (Sujatha 2009: 77).

This chapter aims to present the dichotomies stemming from the phenomenological approach to experience and knowledge, drawing attention to the way fundamental divisions – such as between body and mind, nature and culture, curing and healing – are addressed in the traditional medical systems of India, namely Ayurveda and Siddha. Based on the literature review, this chapter tries to tie together the author's arguments on the characteristics of non-dualist medical theories. Non-dualistic and holistic medical epistemes need not necessarily emphasise the mind over the body, as in the customary opposition between allopathy and homeopathy. Highlighting the case of traditional Indian medicine, this chapter argues that there could be other approaches within a corporeal medical episteme. Later sections examine the interesting question of how a delicate balance between the principles of holism and non-dualism is maintained alongside a corporeal approach to the body and a highly developed pharmacology in the Indian setting. The answer lies in the division of labour between various disciplines dealing with human life and suffering in the social organisation of knowledge and informed practice.

This chapter hence avoids being a pure theoretical exegesis on the medical body; rather, it tries to show how non-dualist medical knowledge is enacted within conditions of medical pluralism in which old unities have been dismantled. Using fieldwork data on the role of Siddha medicine in the management of infectious fevers in Tamil Nadu from the author's previous research, it seeks to examine the dynamic of experience, knowledge and expertise as it plays out in the context of Siddha medicine's response to infectious fevers.

The knowledge and experience distinction is echoed in the body–mind binary and in the division between the material and the non-material, which is intrinsic to the dualist thinking of the modern West in several ways. While rich insights have been generated on the behavioural and social responses to the experience of disease, I would argue that the anthropology/sociology of medicine has remained 'the alter ego' of biomedicine, accepting the binaries of biology–sociology, disease–illness, body–mind and experience–knowledge (Sujatha 2013) and trying to fill in the gaps left by biomedicine without challenging the anatomical understanding of the body that is the fulcrum of biomedical knowledge. Religious healing and shamanistic practices have often been understood as representing non-biomedical or alternative approaches to biomedicine. They readily fitted into the dichotomous pattern in which biomedicine dealt with and 'cured' disease, while shamanistic and alternative practices 'healed' the patient (Sujatha 2013), thus bringing another dimension of curing and healing to the basic schism between the body and mind. The schism runs so deep that anything in between cannot exist and has to be classified on either side. Pain is a case in point.

In his insightful analysis of the secular body, Talal Asad (2011) argues that the binary model of biomedicine that separates the material body from the non-material mind has yielded a host of ailments like hypochondria. Here, the pain experienced by the subject for which there is no corresponding lesion in the body that is detectable by diagnostic tests is designated as a psychiatric condition.

> Although the pain, anxiety, and fear are genuinely experienced by someone labelled a hypochondriac, in ordinary life these feelings tend to be dismissed as 'imaginary' and, therefore, as not worthy of being taken seriously … The authoritative medical view

> (which today even 'religious' people in a secular state may accept) is that the pain and fear experienced by the hypochondriac are not 'healthy'.
>
> (Asad 2011: 659)

The labels 'chronic pain syndrome', 'persistent somatoform disorder' or 'pain disorder' signal the conviction that the pain, lacking any biomedical basis, is part of a psychiatric condition (Morris 2013: 168). Pain is an especially intriguing phenomenon for medicine because of its 'ambiguous position between the "material" and the "ideal," or the "secular" and "the religious"', and if it is not confirmed by diagnostic tests on the material body it is relegated to the realm of the psychogenic (Asad 2011: 658). Phenomenology and medical anthropology, despite a long tradition of inquiry, also struggle to overcome the material and non-material dualism, seeking to study the experience of chronic pain through narratives as something that is opposed to the positivist approach of quantifying pain.

Again, the quantitative versus qualitative approach is further differentiated – within the qualitative/narrative legacy, phenomenology foregrounds sensory 'narratives' of pain, while medical anthropology attends to cultural 'idioms of distress' (cf. Morris 2013: 170), dissatisfied with the 'scant attention' paid by phenomenology to the role of culture in the experience and expression of pain (Morris 2013: 167). The nature and culture division is also thus subtly implicated in the dichotomy of the body and mind in which phenomenology explores the sensations of pain, while anthropology focuses on the linguistic and cultural context of the recognition of pain.

In every respect, we are left with schisms that run deep. Here, experience is sensory, emotional and devoid of cognition. Patients' narratives are ethically necessary to improve their sense of wellbeing and to cope with their subjective experience of illness, but the patient's narrative of their lived experience no longer has any epistemic centrality in the curing process. Such interventions have certainly enhanced the patient's right to good care, though not necessarily their cognitive role in the clinical process.

In fact, the division between experience and knowledge has so deepened within biomedicine due to the advent of sophisticated technologies of diagnosis and treatment that the physician's judgement and skill in treatment have been displaced for the sake of standardisation. In addition to the first dimension in the dyadic relation between the physician and the patient – marked by the division between the experience 'of' the disease by the patient and the knowledge 'about' the disease located in the physician, which manifests itself in the division between illness (patient's experience and subjective narrative) and disease (the objective reality of biomedicine) – there is a second dimension to the experience and knowledge dichotomy. This pertains to the relation between the clinical experience and acumen of the trained physician and the expertise that comes from the application of diagnostic tools that standardise and quantify clinical judgement. Philosophy of medicine views the scientific aspect of causal reasoning in diagnosis and treatment by the physician to be as important as the artistic acumen to draw information from various sources to address the given clinical case. 'Medicine seemed to us like a technique of art at the crossroads of several sciences, rather than, strictly speaking, like one science' (Canguilhem 1989: 34). The gap between the clinical assessment of a patient's bodily signs by the physician and the objective parameters of laboratory-based medical science theories are brought to relief in the second dimension, and the more the physicians rely on the latter, the art of medicine becomes compromised at the altar of positivist medical science. The shift from the whole body to subclinical entities like cell pathology, along with the increasing technological prowess of biomedicine in diagnosis, visualisation of internal organs and the standardisation of numerical parameters of physiology, has been seen not only as distancing the lived experience of the patient from the knowledge of the physician but also as alienating the physician's lived clinical expertise and medical judgement from the objective corpus of biomedicine driven by heavy capital investment and the laboratory parameters of disease.

The anthropology of medicine has contributed a variety of rich studies on the institutional sites where medical knowledge is generated, such as the laboratories of pharmaceutical companies, research institutes, classrooms, medical journals and clinics. Today, the physician and patient dyad is at the receiving end in the network of hospitals and the medical care industry, which are the key institutions generating medically relevant knowledge. While this has been the ground for fertile social science research, there is little research on how other epistemes address the question of experience and knowledge, body and being. Despite decades of studies on medical pluralism, the study of non-biomedical therapies has not gone far enough to draw insights from non-dualist medical approaches to the body and mind complex. The following section will examine the central problem of this chapter, namely the relation between bodily experience, knowledge and expertise in medicine as it is set out in Āyurveda and Siddhamedicine.[3]

Bodily experience, knowledge and expertise in traditional Indian medicine

In the statement 'the patient is a knower in Siddha medicine' (Sujatha 2009: 76), I previously outlined my argument with regard to bodily experience and knowledge in Siddha medicine. If we consider the structure of knowledge in the dyadic relation between the patient and the physician, the patient has 'experience of' the disease, while the physician has 'knowledge about' the disease, notwithstanding the different possible connotations of the English terms 'experience' and 'knowledge' across

[3] For more information on Siddha medicine, see Ministry of AYUSH, 2019, *Siddha System of Medicine: The Science of Holistic Health* (New Delhi: Ministry of AYUSH, Govt. of India), http://Siddhacouncil.com/ccrs/wp-content/uploads/2020/08/Siddha-Dossier_CCRS_Chennai-1.pdf (accessed 4 May 2023).

medical epistemes and intellectual cultures. We saw above that in the Cartesian dualism reinforced by phenomenology, experience is sensory and emotional, and it is attributed to the pre-reflective or unreflective consciousness of laypeople. Knowledge requires retention and reflection acquired by training that can be claimed by the expert. The physician's objective knowledge of the body is superior because it can pronounce judgement on the bodily suffering experienced by the patient, while the patient cannot lay claim to knowledge about the body from their subjective experience. However, in the Indigenous systems of medicine (ISMs) in general and Siddha in particular, the anomaly of a radical disjuncture between the patient's experience and physician's knowledge is unlikely. 'That is, a situation in which a patient's discomfort is deemed illegitimate or psychological/imagined because there is no corresponding, measurable organic lesion in the body will not occur in Siddha medicine' (Sujatha 2009: 78). The reasons for this position can be seen in the non-dualist understanding of the human body and being, the theories of the microcosm and macrocosm, and the theories of the knowing subject contained in Ayurveda and Siddha texts.

Ironically, systems of medicine are both strengthened and limited by their conceptual and methodological characteristics in dealing with the complexity of life; this is true as much of biomedicine as it is of Ayurveda and Siddha. We saw how pathological anatomy – that is, the dissection of dead bodies of sick people and lifeless cross-sections of tissues – was the cornerstone of biomedical knowledge, which was then applied to the understanding of living bodies (Foucault 1975). Biomedicine gains its precision from the fact that it hones its expertise by working on lifeless fragments of bodily tissues, curtailing the variability in living bodies and thus creating a standardised template.

Like most Asian systems of medicine, Ayurveda and Siddha are directed to the study of life, that is, living bodies as microcosms of a larger macrocosm of terrestrial nature. Their view of the body includes the mind by its very definition, and the functional approach to pathology presents mental and corporeal symptoms together. 'The *nadi*[4] method of diagnosis and the *varma*[5] method in Indian medicine that consists in applying pressure to the vital meridians in the body could not have evolved by studying dead bodies that do not have *prana*[6] *or* life' (Sujatha 2021a: 21). Acquiring the skill to diagnose with *nadi* and correlate symptoms with functional pathology is a long, drawn-out process and requires several years of personal training under a senior *vaidya* (traditional Ayurvedic or Siddha physician). The non-dualist

[4] *Nadi nidanam*, roughly translated as pulse diagnosis, refers to the study of rhythmic variations in the pulse as a diagnostic tool. It has been perfected into a specialised science in both Siddha and Ayurveda, supported by texts, commentaries and separate training.

[5] *Varma Cikitcai* is a branch of body practice in which stimulation or pressure is applied to vital points of the body based on a comprehensive anatomical understanding of the pathways of wind, similar to acupressure in Chinese medicine.

[6] *Pranan* as it is called in Siddha is wind/*vali*/*vayu* which circulates through hollow channels in the body and sustains the breath that is fundamental to life.

approach has restrictions in terms of replicability and standardised model building, relying on real-life training and acquiring clinical acumen under lived conditions. This, however, does not imply that traditional medicines have nothing to say about modern anatomy and are therefore narrative centred (Zimmermann 1987). Such statements try to fit non-dualist epistemes into the binary notion of anatomy as constituting the core of medicine versus non-anatomical approaches as constituting narrative medicine, such as the binary drawn between allopathy and homeopathy. In other words, the binary division between the corporealism of biomedicine and the vitalism of homeopathy – into which other non-biomedical systems of medicine are framed – has to be replaced by a pluralism in which other kinds of corporeal medical epistemes like the Asian systems of medicine can be understood on their own terms. Ayurveda and Siddha are medical epistemes whose approach to the body is non-dualistic, yet systematic and scientific with a fully developed pharmacology of thousands of ingredients; this contrasts with the vitalism of homeopathy, which does not rely on pharmacological intervention.

We next turn to examine the key themes in Ayurveda and Siddha that are of interest to this discussion. Let us begin with the idea of the relation between the macrocosm and microcosm, which proposes the fundamentals of the world and the knowing subject in one stroke.

Panchabhutas and sensory modes of knowing

The theory of *panchabhutas* (the five forms of matter) and the methods of gaining knowledge about them highlight the significance of a basic form of cognition as a universal starting point.[7] There is no arbitrary or speculative assumption about a pure state of consciousness devoid of cognition. In Indian systems of medicine, all substances (*dravya*) in the world are made up of the five *bhutas* which can be apprehended through the five sense organs – skin, tongue, eye, nose and ears, and their respective functions that include feeling, tasting, seeing, smelling and hearing, which are basic to the process of knowledge formation. The properties of substances and their actions are known only through the sensory mechanism. All living beings possess the ability to cognise through their sense organs, which is a basic requirement for their survival. Plants also gain knowledge by sensing the *bhutas* in terms of light, moisture and warmth and respond by directing their roots and stems accordingly. Animals constantly sense data from their environment for their defence and survival (Sathaye 1986). Humans ascertain the *panchabhautic* properties of substances by observing their colour, smell, taste and sound, and by feeling their effect on the body system.

[7] The *panchabhutas* are *prithvi*, *ap*, *tejas*, *vayu* and *akasa* in Sanskrit; *mann*, *neer*, *azhal*, *vali* and *veli* in Tamil, in that order, crudely translated as earth, water, fire, wind and ether in English. The *bhutas* are principles of matter apprehensible by the five sensory organs.

But sense organs in themselves cannot gain knowledge because they are just instruments or equipment in the process of knowledge. The mind is responsible for connecting the sense organ to its object in order to discern the data, and this is true of animals as well. 'Living beings are thus endowed with basic cognitive abilities to sense and interpret inputs from their habitat' (Sujatha 2009: 79). According to medical texts, '[o]rgans in themselves do not experience any pain as they are inconscient (*Acit*). The experience of pain or pleasure from the sensory inputs is by the self as a "knower"' (Sathaye in Sujatha 2009: 79). Information from the gross elements of the body is collated and interpreted by a subtle substratum: the knower inside the corporeal body. Without this subtle substratum, the knower, the anatomical or structural sense organs cannot attain knowledge. The patient is thus a knower and not merely an object of the physician's investigation through diagnostic equipment. Cognition, in terms of the ability to grasp variations in one's metabolism – intake, excretion and sleep – is the precondition for a knower, whether this is a layperson or expert.

Thus, it can be argued that experience as sheer sensations devoid of cognition is not engendered in Indian medical thought. More appropriate terminology would be cognition and knowledge, and the basic tools of cognition are available to both the patient and the physician. Even plants and animals cognise what is suitable for their survival. So, the idea of a body amenable to sensation without any cognition does not hold much significance.

'Bodily being' in Ayurveda

In his ingenious analysis of the *Caraka Samhita*'s characterisation of the body in illness and health,[8] Chakravarthi Ram-Prasad (2021) rejects the phenomenological idea of 'embodiment' that treats the body as an isolated and material entity, instead proposing that Ayurveda advocates the conception of a 'bodily being' – composed of the body, senses and the mind – as constituting the definition of life. Instead of beginning with certainties about our bodily subjectivity, he suggests that 'we should begin to see that what permits us to feel ourselves to be enworlded bodily subjects is also what renders the body what it is' (Ram-Prasad 2021: 21). As mentioned earlier, Ayurveda begins not with the corpse as the emblem of medicine but with the living body. 'The unified combination (*samyoga*) of body, sense, mind, and self is called "longevity" and is synonymous with "bearing up," "living", "perpetuation" and "mutual attachment" (of the combinatory factors)' (ibid.: 27).

[8] *Caraka Samhita* is one of the three great classical texts of Ayurveda belonging to a period between the 3rd and 2nd century BCE and is considered to be a compilation of previously existing work that could date back to 1500 BCE. There are 43 commentaries on this text, and it has been redacted several times over the centuries until the 19th century. The other two of the three great medical texts are *Susruta Samhita* and *Astanga Hrdaya* (Sharma 1992).

Ram-Prasad (2021: 40) examines the philosophical anthropology of the *Caraka Samhita* to explore 'how consciousness is to be located as an occurrence in the natural world?' The feeling of pain that demands medical attention is a bodily state, but 'the possibility for such states to occur at all seems to require something which is not reducible to a bodily component'. In order to present 'the subject as a bodily being – not as occupying a body, and not reducible to the body, but as being subject that is bodily, Caraka shows how the subject is not wholly a bodily being yet not totally divorced from it'. This is achieved through three moves – first, by positing a self/*purusa* as the limit to the material body; second, by situating the patient/subject in relation to the intersubjective relationality with the physician; and third, by elaborating the social environment that provides the meaning and context to the subject. According to the *Caraka Samhita,* the knowing subject or *purusa* is not reducible to bodily states but goes beyond them in that it is constituted by many kinds of elements such as the mind, the ten sensory and motor organs, five objects of the senses, the functional entities of the body that are made up of the five forms of matter, the 'I' sense, the faculty of judgement and the primordial base of all these constituents (Ram-Prasad 2021: 36). Unlike the transcendental subject of Husserlian phenomenology, *Caraka Samhita*'s subject does not require a phenomenological reduction of experience but remains as a limit to the diagnostic capacities of the physician which cannot go beyond all the constitutive elements of the *purusa.* The enigmatic suggestion made by the *Caraka Samhita* that the *purusa* is 'beyond' the bodily states though located in them is thus a reminder to the limits of medicine.

> It is just a way of saying that the self is not what is manifest in the investigative procedures of the physician … It is beyond the physician's ken … Self in this sense lies outside the realm of the science of health, i.e., the symptoms that the physician handles, and whose aetiology he traces back to causes.
>
> (Ram-Prasad 2021: 42)

Notwithstanding the statement that the self is beyond the physician's investigation, *Caraka Samhita,* drawing on other contiguous philosophies of its time, nevertheless seeks to discuss the signs by which the self could be inferred. But instead of proposing a transcendental self, as in metaphysical schools, it locates this self within each and every bodily being – this is the core of the medical relationship, which is posited as the limit to the physician's expertise (ibid.).

The four pillars of the therapeutic relationship outlined by the *Caraka Samhita* include the physician, medicine, the patient and the caregiver. Not only are key qualities like mastery over texts, extensive practical experience, dexterity and purity required of a physician, but four qualities are also required of the patient – good memory, compliance with instructions, courage and being informative. The patient thus is not the passive recipient of medical expertise but has a cognitive and social role in the treatment. Among those factors beyond bodily states are included 'the world of the patient/subject and the practices of social discipline' (Ram-Prasad 2021: 51). The *Caraka Samhita* 'talks about what it is to live well and how to avoid being a patient'. Wellness is thus a joint 'function of the organic body and the agentive subject' (Ram-Prasad 2021: 51). Ram-Prasad concludes that the 'ecological phenomenology' of the *Caraka Samhita* 'offers us an alternative to the terminology of "embodiment," with its uneasy dependence on a dualist vocabulary of a human subject and its body, without letting its naturalistic treatment of the human subject becoming reductive' (Ram-Prasad 2021: 56).

Body and being in Siddha medicine

According to the Siddha episteme, the body is not just an organ system and disease cannot be accounted for by the organs alone. The body is constituted by different substrata on the basis of substances that nourish them. Material substances such as food and water nourish the seven tissues (*dhatus*) that constitute the gross body (*stula udampu*), but it is only one among other substrata/sheaths. Subtle substances like breath and thoughts nourish the subtle body or *suksma udampu*. Thus, *prana*, commonly translated as life-sustaining breath, nourishes the *vali udampu* (body of wind/air); thoughts and memories nourish the *mana udampu* (the body of mind/ thoughts), *ariv udampu* (the body of the intellect) and *inba udampu* (the body of bliss) (Sujatha 2009).

It is not just that there are many substrata of the body, as mentioned earlier; the internal organs are also understood to be layered and cannot be denoted by the singular term 'mind'. 'The human knower is endowed with *agakaruvigal* (internal apparatus), namely, *manam* (thought), *puthi* (reason), *aganthai* (will) and *arivu* (intellect) are part of the first level of the 96 principles in Siddha medicine' (Uttamaroyan 1968 in Sujatha 2009: 79). Of these, the *manam* (in Siddha) or *manas* (in Ayurveda) is an internal substratum which, though not visible, is essentially an organ that mediates between the senses and other faculties like reasoning and intellect. This is further manifested in the very conception of disease or pathology in Siddha medicine: 'A change in the indications of the seven *dhatus*[9] of the gross body produced by a *dosha*[10] is experienced as a disease by the knower' (Uttamaroyan 1983: 79). *Dosha* is an alteration in various bodily parameters triggered by changes in metabolism, namely, the process of digestion and distribution of food essence to

[9] The seven *dhatus* or tissues in traditional medicine are the seven material/gross constituents of the body nourished by food. They are undigested food juice (*rasa*), blood (*rakta*), muscle (*mamsa*), fat (*medas*), bone (*asti*), brain (*majja*) and semen (*sukra*). The seven *dhatus* are the same for Ayurveda and Siddha, though the words used may vary. Dr JS, a Siddha doctor, stated in 2024 during a phone interview that 'the seven *dhatūs* are our anatomy, and *agni* or digestive fire is our physiology and the *tridoshas* are our pathology. Even the Ancient Tamil poet Avvaiyār has written about the seven *dhatūs* that constitute the body.'

[10] *Doshas* are three internal functions (commonly referred to as *tridosha*) which, when vitiated can produce disease: *vali/vatam* refers to movements and channels within the body, roughly translated as the wind; *azhal/pitham* refers to digestion, metabolism and transformation, translated as fire; and *iyam/ kapam* refers to vitiation in control, cohesion and respiratory mechanisms, translated as phlegm/water.

various tissues (*dhatus*), conditioned by a combination of gross factors like food and subtle factors like stress. Among other things, *doshas* could be ascertained by observation of bodily patterns and by examination of excrement. The entities of the body identified by Siddha medicine such as *doshas* are not the organs themselves but their functions. The Siddha conception of the body includes the mind by its very definition. The mind, as the repository of thoughts and memories, is a subtle substratum constituted by food and lifestyle as much as the other bodily tissues (*dhatus*) (Obeyesekere 1977) and is subject to the *tridosha* principles.[11] As suggested earlier, it is a key factor in the very recognition of the sensation of pain and illness by the patient (Sujatha 2009: 79).

In Ayurveda and Siddha, pain is treated as a valid disease category requiring clinical intervention because the bodily vitiation/*dosha* which causes the pain could produce both psychic and somatic symptoms simultaneously irrespective of whether the pain is psychogenic or somatogenic. The widespread use of numerous fomentations, massages and douches in Ayurveda is directed towards the management of symptomatic disorders that linger between bodily states and mental vitiation. Examining Siddha medical texts that are used by practising *vaidyas* revealed that 'they are compendia of diseases organised under a well-defined system of classification' (Sujatha 2009: 80). It is interesting to note that in many of the texts, the description of diseases is in terms of symptoms experienced by the sufferer/patient. Importantly, aches and pains are a valid disease category in Siddha. There are standard terms in the texts to denote kinds of pain in relation to their causes and tested methods of treating them. 'In the classification of diseases, subclasses often have as a prefix the kind of pain they produce' (ibid.).

'Actionable experiential reasoning' of Ayurveda

Explicating the connotation of experience in Ayurveda, Anuradha Singh (2007) argues that Ayurveda deals with what she refers to as '*actionable experiential reasoning*' (Singh 2007: 28–9; emphasis in the original) as it explores the causal efficacy of secondary sensory qualities (hearing, smell and taste) along with primary sensory qualities, whereas biomedical science focuses only on the causal efficacy of primary sensory qualities (vision and touch), which is independent of all aspects of sensory experience. Hence, experience and knowledge appear as opposites leading to a gap between theory and practice or what Aristotle referred to as episteme (theoretical reason) and phronesis (practical reason).

Life or *ayus* (commonly understood as lifespan) is a primary subject matter of Ayurveda. Life is a *locus* of experience (*anubhava*), action (*prayatna*) and disposition (*samskara*). It is dispositions that influence experience, which in turn leads to action. In reverse, actions and experience determine dispositions (Singh 2007: 30).

[11] This refers to the three internal functions mentioned above.

Instead of postulating a mechanical universalism of the consciousness or the body, the suggestion is that experiences and actions are temporally ephemeral but dispositions are trans-temporal, though not atemporal as they are subject to change. 'Experiences and actions are differentially determined by dispositions that characterise any organism; otherwise, all living organisms will be identical' (ibid.).

Thus, experience is not the sheer sensory experience of the corporeal body and in the theory of traditional Indian medicine, an unbridgeable gap between experience and knowledge of the patient and doctor is not possible, though expertise could be a prerogative of the trained physician. Beginning with the symptoms of disease narrated by the patient and its interpretation in terms of clinical signs of underlying vitiation/pathology is core to the interaction between the doctor and patient. Medical texts in India suggest that the categorisation and names of diseases may change over time, but the focus should be on specifics such as presentation, site of manifestation and the like. Ayurvedic texts instruct the physician who is trying to apply old textual classifications to the diseases of another period to follow this principle. As Rammanohar *et al.* put it:

> In recent times, Gananatha Sen in his work *Siddhantanidāna* discusses about changes in the clinical presentation of diseases due to the influence of place and time as well as the influence of varied etiological factors [Sid.Nid] [40].[12] He points out that textual descriptions of diseases may not match with clinical presentations seen today. In fact classical Ayurvedic texts provide guidelines for analysis of diseases not listed in the literature. *Astāngahrdaya* points out that analytical understanding of a disease in terms of its finer constituents like *samprāpti*, site of manifestation, and specific *nidānas* is more important than identifying it by its name [As.Hr.Su.St.12.64–66] [36].[13] A new disease (*anuktavyadhi*) can be understood by the study of *nidāna, dosa sthāna* [33] and other factors involved in the disease causation, progress, and clinical outcomes as evidenced in texts like [Ma.Ni..25 and 51] [34].[14]
>
> (Rammanohar *et al.* 2022: 5)

In the following section, I would like to focus on how such a non-dualist aetiology can be applied to the understanding of infectious fevers in Siddha medicine, with special reference to Covid-19.

Infectious fevers in traditional Indian medicine

In my previous writings on the role of traditional medicine in the management of Covid-19 in India, I dealt with questions about how traditional medicine

[12] *Siddhanta Nidana* (textbook of aetiology) was composed in two parts in 1926 and 1931 by Kaviraj Gananath Sen, the renowned Bengali Ayurvedic physician.

[13] *Astanga Hrdaya* is one of the 'three great trio' of Ayurvedic classical texts. It is attributed to Vagbahata I, belonging to 500 CE (Sharma 1992).

[14] *Madhavanidana* is a renowned work also known as *Nidana Rogaviniscaya*, and is attributed to Madhavakara who belonged to the period between the 7th and 8th century CE. It could be the earliest detailed description of the diseases based on '*Nidăna Pancăkam* (Five groups of subjects concerned with aetio-pathogenesis)' (Subhose, Srinivas and Narayana 2005).

approached infectious fevers through a host-based perspective and without a theory of microorganisms (Sujatha and Payyappallimana 2022; Sujatha 2024). In the host-based approach of Ayurveda and Siddha, fevers are classified on the basis of the vitiated *doshas* in the body of the afflicted human being; this is considered to be the proximate and particular cause for the onset of fever (Sujatha 2024: 248) because microorganisms exist everywhere and at all times. Irrespective of the kinds of microorganisms involved, fevers are clinically understood on the basis of the affected bodily parameters and impaired functions. Thus, the body of the host, not the infectious agent, is the crux of Siddha pathology of fever. The physiological processes set off by the onset of the disease are understood through 'symptoms, signs and properties (*kuri-kunam*) of the vitiated organ system/functions that are primarily affected' (Sujatha 2024: 250).

The aphorism that fever is the 'King of Diseases' is found in Siddha texts, and they engage with its aetiology and classification in great detail.[15] Fever (*curam)* is considered to be a disease in Siddha and not a symptom as in biomedicine. Etymologically, *curam* refers to a 'disease in which there is the appearance of heating the body' (Sujatha 2024: 248). '*Cura nilam*' is a term that is also applied to the dry and hot '*palai*' landscape, which is one of the five basic ecoclimatic cultural zones listed in the ancient Tamil classic *Tolkapiyam.*[16] *Palai* is land or a region that becomes a sandy desert due to repetitive drought ending in scorching heat. The didactic use of the hydraulic physiology of the *palai* land to explain fever pathology in the body illustrates that this is not an analogy but an extension of the macrocosm–microcosm principle to decipher the contiguity of natural processes in ecology that includes the human body (Mudaliar 1936).[17]

A 20th-century Siddha text categorises fevers into 64 types, with information on the incubation phase, progression, symptomatic presentation in various stages of progression and interventions relevant to those stages.[18] Fifty-two out of the 64 types of fever are attributed to 'own route' (*tan vazhi curam*),[19] or what I would

[15] See the text *Vaitiyasintāmani*, attributed to the Siddha saint *Yugimuni*, manuscript prepared by pandit *Māргalinga Nāyanar* and printed in 1898 at Chennai.

[16] *Tolkāpiyam* is an ancient Tamil text of grammar written by Tolkāpiyar in the 3rd century BCE which refers to previous works of grammar in Tamil (Varadarasan 1972).

[17] During a phone interview on 12 May 2024 in connection to this chapter, I asked Dr JS, a government Siddha doctor, the question as to how Siddha pharmacology understood the metabolism of medicines and their effects on the body without viewing the internal organs of the body. He replied: 'by a systematic and analytical study of the universe and every aspect of nature ... For instance, the morphological properties of plants that flower in different seasons manifest the *tridoshas* mechanisms in nature and give us the cue to understand their pharmaceutical properties. Examining these mechanisms in great detail and theorising plant physiology could have been a crucial step in the study of their metabolic effects on the living body.'

[18] Mudaliar Kuppuswamy's *Siddha Medicine (General) (Siddha Marutuvam (Potu)* is a compilation of several ancient Siddha texts and is the textbook for the Bachelor's course in Siddha Medicine and Surgery (BSMS) in Tamil Nadu.

[19] 'Own route' (*tan vazhi*) refers to the corporeal process by which undigested and fermented food juice clog the hair root in the skin, leading to rise in body heat, which is the cause for the onset of fever. Starting with this generic cause, 52 kinds of 'own route' fevers are then subclassified based on affected body tissues. The 'outside route' (*pira vazhi*) are those like poisoning, fear, injury and so on, in which the fever does not originate from undigested food juice in the intestine (Mudaliar 1936).

refer to as 'corporeal factors', and 12 types to 'outside route' (*pira vazhi curam*) such as toxic substances, effects of medicines, anger, fear, injury, unfulfilled sexual urge, black magic and other entities that cannot be seen. The 'own route' fevers are divided based on the 'three aberrations' (*mukutram*) – vitiations in movement within the organ systems, commonly referred to as 'wind' (*vali/vatam*) which produces 20 kinds of fever; vitiation in digestion, metabolism and transformation, commonly referred to as 'bile/fire' (*azhal/pitham)* which causes 24 kinds; and vitiation in control, cohesion and respiratory mechanisms, commonly referred to as 'phlegm/water' (*iyam/kapam*), which causes 20 kinds of fever. These vitiations affect the seven body tissues – food juice, blood, muscle, fat, bone, marrow and semen – differentially.

Interestingly, the compendiums on the treatment of these many kinds of fevers, including regional and locality-specific Siddha texts,[20] prescribe a battery of medicaments and treatments even for the 'outside route' fevers attributed to fear, anxiety, excessive sexual urge and the like, while no 'psychotherapy' is mentioned. Whereas the aetiology of fever in non-dualist traditional medicine includes both psychic and somatic causes which are listed separately, its therapeutics consists only in pharmacological interventions, dietary and lifestyle prescriptions; this indicates that the medical texts position themselves within the medical domain. In fact, it is surprising to note that such a somatic approach characterises the treatment of mental illness as well.

Local palm-leaf manuscripts dating to a period between the 18th and 20th centuries from the Kanyakumari region on 18 kinds of mental diseases and their treatment begin with a mythical story that is rich in insight and symbolism on the origin of mental diseases: a war breaks out in public between the gods themselves.[21] Lord Vishnu and Lord Brahma, both of whom were powerful, waged a war to establish their supremacy against each other. They deployed many dangerous weapons, which led to dreadful tremors in the terrestrial world. Lord Shiva, disturbed in his penance, sought to stop the war. He decided to cause frailty and loss of courage within both the parties to the war and unleashed a host of diseases which led to weakness, fatigue, emaciation and suffering in the fighting gods, Vishnu and Brahma, such that they left the war front and returned to their abode. They worshipped Lord Shiva, pleading for relief from their suffering, who ordered them to go to the terrestrial world and unleash diseases on those who betray friends, disobey the teacher and the father, rape women, murder children and abort fetuses, destroy legal documents, provide false witness and others who engage in such

[20] See *Cura nōi toguti*, which is the print version in three parts of a palm-leaf manuscript titled *Agateesar kaviya Cura nool* discovered in the Kanyakumari district and published by Siddha book publications: Kanyakumari Munsirai, with commentary by Dr. T Mohanraj and Dr P Prema (https://eap.bl.uk/collection/EAP810-1).

[21] The palm-leaf manuscripts said to belong to a period between the 18th and 20th centuries have been retrieved by Dr Mohanraj (see listings under the Endangered Archives Programme of the French Institute of Pondicherry – https://eap.bl.uk/project/EAP810).

acts of betrayal and horror.[22] Thus, a set of 54 diseases of the mind is engendered, specific to human beings, separate from the 4,448 diseases common to four-legged creatures and birds. Of these 54 diseases that the animal world is spared of are the diseases of the mind classified under three categories of 18 each. Despite such a meaningful narrative on mental illness as a moral affliction that characterises a lawless society, the very same text goes on to describe the aetiology of the 18 specific forms of mental illness in terms of the *tridoshas* or bodily pathology. It also goes on to list a host of pharmacological formulae for each category of mental diseases, including those caused by fear and excessive thirst for knowledge. Prescriptions for restoring moral norms of society are not elaborated in the local compendiums. The somatisation of mental illness here is quite striking, a point which the renowned psychoanalyst Sudhir Kakar (1990) highlighted while differentiating the therapeutic approach to mental ailments that is adopted by shamans and mystics from that of the traditional doctors in India.

A non-dualist approach to bodily being and pathology that places the somatic and psychic on a continuum should not be taken to mean that Ayurveda and Siddha would foreground some kind of healing practice/psychotherapy for every disease or that the Ayurvedic and Siddha physicians necessarily spend more time in counselling the patient on emotional adjustment. Such a position would only be the logical consequence of the disease–illness dichotomy of medical anthropology in which non-biomedical treatments do not cure but serve in healing and as palliatives.

What we find in Ayurveda and Siddha medicine is that they take a somato-psychic approach even to mental illness. They address the underlying vitiation/*dosha* through pharmaceutical interventions – both through internal medicines and external applications – supplemented by massages, dietary prescription and lifestyle changes as may be relevant, which is the prerogative of the physician. The moral concerns of the cause, timing and prognosis of the ailment are dealt with mostly by the branch of astrology. While Ayurvedic and Siddha training does include familiarity with knowledge of astrology: in the social organisation of medicine, a large group of medical physicians generally had one member trained exclusively in astrology (Sujatha 2011).[23] The non-dualist approach in actual practice was reflected in the social division of expertise and was not always resolved within the clinical encounter.

The argument that I seek to advance here is that the holistic conception of the mind and body, experience and knowledge in actual practice, is exemplified through the division of labour within social and cultural institutions. This yields mutually non-exclusive specialisations of clinical medicine, literature, astrology, mysticism and healing in which medicine as a body of knowledge and expertise

[22] The translation of this mythical story from verse form in the printed text is a free translation by the author of this chapter.

[23] In my fieldwork in Tamil Nadu during 2007–8, the cousins of the 11th generation *Kan vaitiyar* (eye doctor) were specialising in astrology and he mentioned that it has been so for many generations.

does not disenfranchise the other allied fields of knowledge seeking to address human suffering. Instead, it guards the integrity of its own purpose to treat the bodily being whose corporeal body is its object of intervention.

Thus, we find that Siddha medicine returns to its mandate by focusing on pharmacological and corporeal interventions for fever of all kinds, even as its holistic cosmology and complex aetiologies include a broader vision of human life as part of the universe of nature and culture. There is a certain pragmatism in the 14th to 15th-century compendiums of Siddha medicine that separates complicated theory and metaphysics from everyday life requirements. It adopts what I refer to as a praxeological approach (Sujatha 2024: 245). Practically relevant therapeutic knowledge for the layperson is disseminated in the form of formularies, compendiums in simple verse form accessible to all and reserving expertise on theories of the *nadi*, for the trained. The higher yogic and spiritual practices of the initiated are expressed in 'twilight language', which is apparently simple but coded with concealed metaphysical meaning (Ganapathy 2006: 297). A huge number of medical texts, compendiums and formularies were written in the Tamil language during the 12th–19th centuries. These works were transmitted by wandering mendicants through verses and proverbs across the Tamil region, who were collecting home remedies from households for further refinement in a way that did not have a parallel of this magnitude in the Ayurvedic belt of North India.

This praxeological orientation of Siddha medicine, which penetrated deeply into the health culture of the Tamil region, could be a reason why the college-educated Siddha doctors could put together a mass-distribution scheme of a herbal-spice mineral water during the outbreak of Covid-19. This leaves us with the following questions: What happens to a non-dualist approach when it enters 21st-century Tamil society characterised by a strong biomedical health bureaucracy? And what gets selectively exemplified under the vastly transformed circumstances in which traditional medicine is practised in contemporary India?

21st-century form of non-dualist medical epistemes

Transformation is not new to traditional medicine in South Asia, which has survived for over two millennia. If we start with the colonial period in India, three major phases in the transformation of traditional Indian systems of medicine are discernible over a period of two centuries: the first phase from the late 19th to the early 20th century was led by the *vaidyas* and *hakims*; the phase after independence in the 1950s was directed by the state, though in an ambivalent manner; and the phase after the 1990s has been driven by the global market for natural health therapies, which in turn has alerted the Indian state to take stock of its therapeutic heritage in yoga and Ayurveda (Sujatha 2011). There is an overwhelmingly large body of historical and anthropological work on specific moments in each of these phases (Sujatha 2013). Suffice it to point out that today we have fewer hereditary

Ayurveda and Siddha practitioners; the college-educated doctors of these systems are going to constitute the medical workforce of traditional systems in the health bureaucracy of the future. The college-educated Ayurveda and Siddha doctors are very different from the generation of *vaidyas*; they do not inherit an unbroken medical tradition but instead are diverse social actors who enrol for an AYUSH medical degree as a last-resort career option after other choices such as dentistry and veterinary medicine have eluded them.[24] Besides, they are not like the *vaidya*s and *hakim*s (Ayurvedic and Unani physicians) who saw themselves as the guardians of an ancient medical tradition; instead, they resemble biomedical doctors working in the health bureaucracy or in the private sector, who are minor nodes in the health machinery dominated by the state or market forces in healthcare and the pharmaceutical industry. Interestingly, however, studies do show that young interns from Ayurveda and Siddha colleges turn to charismatic *vaidyas* to work with as apprentices to obtain in-depth medical knowledge of the texts and skills in *nadi* reading (Abraham 2013). How far this can counteract the bureaucratic reduction of these systems remains to be seen.

The current state of Ayurveda and Siddha in contemporary India, however, should not be viewed just as an epistemological transformation but as an ontological shift, in which the traditional class of Ayurveda and Siddha medicine practitioners has been overturned over the decades by the introduction of college-based education in traditional medicine coupled with the influence of market forces in pharmaceutical industry. Medical knowledge and practices mutate with the social constituency of people who carry them forward. I have hence argued that medicine should be viewed as a social institution and not as a text, and that such an ontological perspective is crucial to gain insight into the way experience and knowledge of health and disease meander through political and social imperatives (Sujatha 2019a).

The trajectory of traditional medicine in 21st-century India is intriguing and difficult to grasp from a linear perspective. If we consider the massive transformation in the social background of physicians and patients and in the institutions of medical education and healthcare delivery, an epistemological approach will not suffice. The question, therefore, should not be why Ayurveda and Siddha are deviating from their *shastric* tradition and getting biomedicalised, but rather how the present class of practitioners – trained in modern life sciences – pick up the threads of traditional medicine knowledge from the partial, fragmented information and the skill sets imparted in their Bachelor's degree. How do they create or fail to create 'epistemological bridges' (Abraham 2013) with the tradition in the face of the huge gaps in training and knowledge? To what extent does non-dualist medical knowledge sustain itself in the face of the disjuncture in the economic and social institutions

[24] AYUSH is the acronym given to the five non-biomedical therapies of Ayurveda, yoga, Unani, Siddha and homeopathy that have been placed under the Ministry of AYUSH, Government of India.

of traditional medicine in contemporary India? What are the counteracting forces? How are experience, knowledge and expertise articulated in the pluralist health arrangements of contemporary India where biomedical vocabulary and parameters have become intrinsic to health culture along with traditional medical knowledge?

The phases of change, however, are not similar for Ayurveda, Siddha and Unani, as the regional historical, political and social contexts vary. The trajectory of Unani and Siddha medicine has been quite different from that of Ayurveda, which has been in the limelight and has also entered the global health market along with yoga. In this section, I will focus on the situation of Siddha medicine in Tamil Nadu and its response to infectious diseases.

Two factors differentiate Siddha medicine from the situation of Ayurveda and Unani medicine in other regions. First, Siddha has had to co-exist with a well-developed biomedical professional network and flourishing infrastructure in Tamil Nadu, and therefore cross-practice is limited.[25] Siddha doctors are resorted to for their systems' reputation in the treatment of a few chronic ailments. Second, Siddha medicine has been deeply embedded in the political and linguistic history of the Tamil region. It has suffered similar ruptures to Ayurveda, but its moorings in the health culture of the Tamil region enabled by the praxeological approach of the texts has made everyday therapeutics accessible to the common person. The fact that the language of the texts is Tamil has also facilitated greater dissemination of medical knowledge.

Let us examine the role of Siddha medicine in the management of infectious fevers in the public healthcare system in Tamil Nadu to see how the principles of Siddha medicine are adapted by college-educated Siddha doctors. Three questions will guide us through this brief account that has been elaborated elsewhere (Sujatha and Payyappallimana 2022; Sujatha 2024).

Symptom matching as a cognitive process

The first question is how do college-educated Siddha doctors today decipher the old texts and connect them to the biomedical nosology of fever, which is the current norm?

Even under a pluralistic public healthcare system, Ayurveda and Siddha doctors are generally not allowed direct access to treat patients suffering from infectious fevers in biomedical hospitals. Their understanding therefore can only be derived from refereed biomedical publications describing the symptoms of these diseases, from discussions with colleagues in biomedicine and the clinical experience of

[25] Department of Economics and Statistics (2022), *Statistical Handbook of Tamil Nadu 2020–21* (Chennai: Government of Tamil Nadu). https://www.tn.gov.in/deptst/medicalandhealth.pdf; World Bank (2019), *Health, Nutrition & Population Global Practice: South Asia Region*. https://documents1.worldbank.org/curated/en/311171553306470266/pdf/INDIA-TAMIL-NADU-newPAD-02282019-636888888466936316.pdf (accessed 24 April 2023).

private practitioners of traditional medicine. Since 2006, the government of Tamil Nadu has included Siddha medicine in its integrative approach to the management of infectious fevers like swine flu and dengue, under the supervision of biomedical doctors. As mentioned earlier, Siddha texts and compilations from the original Siddha texts by 20th-century Siddha physicians provide a comprehensive description of each type of fever. When there is an outbreak of swine flu, bird flu, chikungunya, dengue, or Covid-19, Siddha doctors study the standard clinical symptoms of the fevers as expressed by the World Health Organization (WHO) and in other international publications in great detail and 'correlate' the symptoms with the Siddha textual classification of fevers. Siddha texts give several symptoms for each category of fever with variations, delineating the symptoms in terms of stage. 'The name of the disease is not important; it is the "signs and symptoms" (*Kuri-kunam)* that matter to us the most', clarified Dr. B, a private Siddha doctor.[26]

Dengue was identified by the Siddha doctors as a kind of 'fever caused by vitiation of fire' (*Pitha Curam*) based on a 'matching of symptoms' listed by the WHO on its website (severe headache, nausea, vomiting, skin rashes and pain behind the eyes), other pathological characteristics and the incubation period with those listed in the Siddha texts. Derangements of fire (*Pitha*) are said to be mediated by blood and so the vector-borne character of dengue was correlated with this description. Fever caused by vitiation of bile (*Pitha Curam*) causes intermittent fever and mild shivering with minor reduction in appetite. On the other hand, Covid-19 symptoms like mild fever, total lack of appetite, weakening sense of smell, sore throat, cough, cold, breathing difficulty, thirst and fatigue matches the Siddha classification of 'fever caused by the vitiation of phlegm' (*Kapa Curam*). In the spring season, *Kapa Curam* is the most frequent type of fever, recovery from which is long drawn. *Kapa Curam* is also linked to long incubation and mild fever progressing to delirium in the final stages and resulting in death on around the 14th day. Phlegm (*Iyam*/*Kapam*) is said to have the characteristic of bonding of mucous fluids on surfaces and is not something that is airborne. In fact, a Siddha doctor explained that about 40 symptoms of *Kapa Curam* are given in the texts, including symptoms of the advanced stages such as pallor of tongue and face associated with oxygen saturation and muscle pain (Sujatha 2024).

There are a number of Siddha articles published by qualified Siddha doctors that undertake such 'symptom matching' (Rathinam *et al.* 2021) in tabular form based on a literature survey. Thus, by adopting what I refer to as 'symptom matching' and 'sign correlation', government Siddha doctors in Tamil Nadu devised an integrative strategy to deal with infectious fevers – including what the WHO termed Covid-19 – and this cognitive process of correlation is an attempt to build epistemological bridges between disparate parameters.

[26] Interestingly, this very statement is expressed in Ayurvedic texts that instruct the physician who is trying to apply old textual classifications to the diseases of another period. See Rammanohar *et al.* (2022: 5 for details).

From folk medicine to public health care delivery

The second question is how a medical aetiology like that of Ayurveda and Siddha, which is based on personalised therapy suited to the body constitution of the patient, could be used to devise a strategy for public health. As mentioned earlier, Ayurveda and Siddha have a stratified pharmacology in which for the same ailment, formulations for everyday use as home remedies and complicated formulations that require medical supervision are both available. So, the Siddha expert team (Siddha Pharmacoepia of India) chose simpler formulations such as *Nilavembu kutinīr* and *Kapa cura kutinīr* for public distribution during the dengue outbreak of 2007 and the Covid 19 outbreak of 2020–1 because these formulations were known to be safe for mass public consumption and because the Siddha texts recommend medicated *kutinīr* in watery form for fever as it hydrates the body (Sujatha and Payyappallimana 2022: 4).

There are 32 dosage forms of medicines for internal consumption mentioned in the Siddha texts, such as fresh juice, decoction, extracts, distillates, powders, pastes, chewables, syrups, medicated ghee, and oils, each classified on the basis of their shelf life. Specific adjuvants for internal medications are also clearly indicated in Siddha pharmacology. Herbal decoctions have a life of three hours, and the advanced drugs can last up to hundred years. 'Medicated water' (*Kutinīr*) (literally, drinking water) is one such instant medicated water in which a dried and powdered herb and spice mix is boiled in water to be consumed within three hours. On the other hand, the dosage form called 'fired water' (*Tinīr*) is a distillate from the herbs which has a shelf life of one year (Sujatha 2024: 253).

The third question is: how could this be built into public health bureaucracy? There are huge regional variations in the manner in which Ayurveda is incorporated into healthcare by different states in India. In South India, the neighbouring states of Kerala and Tamil Nadu adopted different strategies of integrative care, which as Sujatha and Payyappallimana (2022) have shown is in itself an interesting theme of study. Tamil Nadu not only endorsed Siddha medicine during Covid-19 but actively distributed the Siddha formulation *Kapa cura kutinīr* in its health centres, and it became a big hit among the masses (Sujatha 2024: 242).

Experience, knowledge and expertise under medical pluralism

It is clear from the above that the experiences of patients and Siddha physicians are not informed wholly by traditional or biomedical perspectives. Two factors facilitate our understanding of the dynamic of experience and knowledge in a mixed health culture like this (Sujatha 2021b). First, there is a need to factor in the social background and subjectivity of the Siddha doctors. My fieldwork (Sujatha 2019a) among the college-educated doctors of Siddha shows that there are several first-generation learners in the Siddha stream. They are the first in their family to enter college education and predominantly come from Tamil-medium schools in villages and small towns such that we can expect a greater number of them to belong to rural households and to have familiarity with local health traditions. There is a small group of Siddha doctors from the English-medium stream who come from educated families from small towns and thereby have greater social capital. This small group of the elite Siddha practitioners is also active in civil society in the promotion of traditional medicine.

The Tamil language of traditional texts provides freshers coming from Tamil-medium education with better access to Siddha medical knowledge. Siddha doctors are socialised in the health culture of the region and are trained in modern sciences at school and college. They review and analyse the traditional health practices that they witnessed in during their formative years. Diagnosis by clinical record-taking of symptoms continues to be the primary mode of diagnosis and even as the Siddha doctors analyse biomedical diagnostic test results, they also try to correlate the biomarkers and parameters with Siddha aetiology. After the Covid-19 pandemic was announced, Siddha doctors were not permitted to directly treat Covid patients in government health facilities. As a result, their access to the disease in the clinical encounter was limited to a small number of patients treated in the private sector in small towns. Government-affiliated Siddha expert followed the guidance of scientific publications that analysed symptoms and signs as their primary source of information. Symptom matching and sign correlation, which I mentioned earlier, are cognitive processes by which the Siddha doctors established a connection between Siddha medicine's descriptive pathology and accurate biomarkers and numerical parameters. This process of matching and correlation with visual and numerical indices is understood to explicate the underlying functional processes in Siddha pathology explained in the textual verses. Thus, there is also exchange and syncretism at the level of expertise. We require nuanced and in-depth studies to characterise this kind of inter-epistemic cognition. General terms like 'biomedicalisation' may not give us the analytical leverage to grasp the intricate flow of knowledge and expertise in the larger context of a pluralist health culture.

Second, it is crucial to note that the government of Tamil Nadu's decision to distribute *Nilavembu kutinīr*[27] for dengue and *Kapa cura kutinīr*[28] for Covid-19 on a mass scale is historically important. It represented a situation in which the state reinstated a disappeared folk health practice, involving consuming medicated waters containing herbs and spices during the spring season that is conducive to treating infectious fevers. *Nilavembu* (*Andrographis Paniculata*), the key ingredient in *Nilavembu kutinīr* that consists of seven items, is a herb widely used in Asia as

[27] Herbal and spice compound containing seven ingredients mentioned in the siddha texts and siddha formulary of India which is administered in the form of a watery decoction.

[28] Herbal and spice compound containing 15 ingredients mentioned in the siddha texts and siddha formulary of India which is administered in the form of a watery decoction.

an anti-inflammatory and antipyretic and is described in thousands of scientific publications (Chao and Lin 2010). The bureaucratic process by which this initiative was approved by the Chief Minister of the state was grounded in refereed publications on the ingredients. The state government's pharmaceutical unit played a key role in mobilising the herbal ingredients on a large scale. At the grassroots level, a notable innovation was the large-scale provision of medicated hot water in coffee vending machines, enabling it to be distributed in containment zones and schools as a preventive measure. The above measures have been discussed in detail (Sujatha and Payyappallimana 2022). The widespread popularity of the *kutinīr* among the Tamil public, the fact that private religious trusts and political parties distributed the *kutinīr*s and the public demand for *kutinīr*s in government health centres after the pandemic indicate how a household health practice embedded in everyday experience has undergone a full cycle of being validated by knowledge and expertise of various kinds to return as an icon of Siddha medicine in contemporary Tamil Nadu. This, however, does not imply a return to traditional health culture but rather that specific objects and products from traditional medicine, such as the *kutinīr*s, could emerge in the public healthcare system which is otherwise governed by a biomedical approach.

Conclusion

Epidemic outbreaks in the 21st century have been a turning point for Siddha medicine in terms of its role in public health as well as for the self-perception of Siddha physicians. The government-backed mass deployment of *Nilavembu kutinīr* for dengue in 2011 created a rupture in the trajectory of Siddha medicine that was consolidated during the Covid-19 pandemic. The institutional structures to scale up the distribution of medicated water (*kutinīr*) for a massive outbreak have been strengthened, and mechanisms for systematic documentation and research have been stepped up. The variety of evidence generated on *Nilavembu kutinīr* and *Kapa cura kutinīr* is quite wide-ranging, encompassing refereed publications from double-blind trials, observational, retrospective and open trials, case studies, unrefereed publications and hospital reports (Sujatha 2024; Thillaivanan *et al.* 2015; Natarajan *et al.* 2021; Rathinam Susheela *et al.* 2021; Ramaswamy *et al.* 2022; Christian *et al.* 2023). *Kutinīr* has thus emerged as a historical-epistemic object.

Drawing on Foucault, Ian Hacking proposes what he calls a 'historical ontology' in which one speaks 'about objects in general. Not just things, but whatever we individuate and allow us to talk about. That includes not only "material" objects, but also classes, kinds of people, and, indeed, ideas. Finally, if we are concerned with the coming into being of the very possibility of some objects, what is that if not historical?' (Hacking 2004: 3). This historical experience suggests that the trajectory of integrating Ayurveda and Siddha into government-run public health services may proceed through the adoption of specific objects and treatments from the medical tradition; the host-based approach cannot be holistic when it is integrated into the health bureaucracy. The dynamics of experience, knowledge and expertise in medicine in a situation of medical pluralism require careful consideration of epistemic and ontological aspects in three-dimensional space, where the dualism between the subject and object of medicine mutually influence each other.

References

Primary sources

Central Council for Research in Ayurveda and Siddha (CCRAS). (1979), *Teraiyar Compendium of Medicated Water (original and commentary) (Teraiyar Kutinīr)* (Tam.) (New Delhi: Central Council for Research in Ayurveda and Siddha (CCRAS)).

Kuppuswamy, M. (Tam.) (1936), *Siddha Medicine (General) (Siddha Marutuvam (Potu))* (Chennai: Department of Indigenous Medicine and Homeopathy).

Nāyanar, M. (ed.) (Tam.) (1898), *Yugimuni*, '*Vaitiyasintāmani*' (Printed in Chennai).

Varadarasan, M. (Tam.) (1972), *Tamizh Ilakiya Varalaru (History of Tamil Literature)* (New Delhi: Sahitya Academy).

Secondary sources

Abraham, L. (2013), 'Reproduction of Indigenous Knowledge in Plural Cultures: Ayurveda Education in Contemporary India' in G. B. Nambissan and S. Rao (eds) *Sociology of Education in India: Changing Contours and Emerging Concerns* (New Delhi: Oxford University Press), 245–72.

Asad, T. (2011), 'Thinking About the Secular Body, Pain, and Liberal Politics'. *Cultural Anthropology*, 26(4): 657–75. https://doi.org/10.1111/j.1548-1360.2011.01118.x

Canguilhem, G. (1989), *The Normal and the Pathological* (New York: Zone Books).

Chao, W.-W. and Lin, B. F. (2010), 'Isolation and Identification of Bioactive Compounds in Andrographis Paniculata (Chuanxinlian)'. *Chinese Medicine* 5(17): Article no. 17. https://doi.org/10.1186/1749-8546-5-17

Christian, G. J., Meenakumari, R., Shanthimalar, R., Sankar, G., Ravichandran, V. M., Elansekaran, S., *et al.* (2023), 'Safety and Efficacy of Siddha Management as Adjuvant Care for COVID-19 Patients Admitted in a Tertiary Care Hospital – An Open-label, Proof-of-concept Randomized Controlled Trial'. *Journal of Ayurveda Integrative Medicine*, 14(2): 100706. https://doi.org/10.1016/j.jaim.2023.100706

Foucault, M. (1975), *The Birth of the Clinic: An Archaeology of Medical Perception* (New York: Vintage Books).

Ganapathy, T. N., Arumugam, K. R. and Anand, G. (eds) (2006), *The Yoga of Siddha Tirumūlar: Essays on the Tirumandiram* (Quebec: Babaji's Kriya Yoga Trust).

Ganapathy, T. N. (2006), 'The Twilight Language of the Tirumantiram' in T. N. Ganapathy, K. R. Arumugam and G. Anand (eds) *The Yoga of Siddha Tirumūlar: Essays on the Tirumandiram Ganapathy* (Quebec: Babaji's Kriya Yoga Trust), 295–338.

Hacking, I. (2004), *Historical Ontology* (Cambridge, MA: Harvard University Press).

Jensen, T. R. and Moran, D. (2013), 'Introduction' in J. T. Rasmus and D. Moran (eds) *The Phenomenology of Embodied Subjectivity* (London: Springer), vii–xxxiii.

Kakar, S. (1990), *Shamans, Mystics and Doctors: A Psychological Inquiry into India and Its Healing Traditions* (Chicago, IL: The University of Chicago Press).

Kleinman, A. (1980), *Patients and Healers in the Context of Culture* (Berkeley, CA: University of California Press).

Leyder, D. (1992), 'A Tale of Two Bodies: The Cartesian Corpse and the Lived Body' in D. Leyder (ed.) *The Body in Medical Thought and Practice* (Dordrecht: Kluwer Academic Publishers), 17–36.

Morris, K. (2013), 'Chronic Pain in Phenomenological/Anthropological Analysis' in J. T. Rasmus and D. Moran (eds) *The Phenomenology of Embodied Subjectivity* (London: Springer), 167–84.

Mudaliar, K. (1936), *Siddha Medicine (General) (Siddha Marutuvam (Potu)* (Chennai: Department of Indigenous Medicine and Homeopathy).

Natarajan, S. P., Anbarasi, P, Sathiyarajeshwaran, P., Manickam, P., Geetha, S., Kathiravan, R., *et al.* (2021), 'Kabasura Kudineer (KSK), a Poly-herbal Siddha Medicine, Reduced SARS-CoV-2 Viral Load in Asymptomatic COVID-19 Individuals as Compared to Vitamin C and Zinc Supplementation: Findings from a Prospective, Exploratory, Open-labelled, Comparative, Randomized Controlled Trial, Tamil Nadu, India'. *Trials*, 22(1). https://trialsjournal.biomedcentral.com/articles/10.1186/s13063-021-05583-0

Obeyesekere, G. (1977), 'The Theory and Practice of Psychological Medicine in the Ayurvedic Tradition'. *Culture, Medicine and Psychiatry*, 1: 155–81.

Rammanohar, P., Suhila, K., Payyappallimana, U., Mangalath, P., Nampoothiri, V., Sharma, P., *et al.* (2022), 'Ayurvedic Clinical Profile of COVID-19 – A Preliminary Report'. *Journal of Ayurveda and Integrative Medicine*, 13(1). https://doi.org/10.1016/j.jaim.2020.05.011

Ramaswamy, M., Thangaraj, K., Sundaram, A., Sundaram, M. M., Shanmugapriya, P., Mariappan, A., *et al.* (2022), 'Clinical Outcomes Among COVID-19 Patients Managed with Modern and Traditional Siddha Medicine – A Retrospective Cohort Study'. *Journal of Ayurveda & Integrative Medicine*, 13(2): 100470. https://doi.org/10.1016/j.jaim.2021.06.010

Ram-Prasad, C. (2021), *Human Being, Bodily Being* (Oxford: Oxford University Press).

Rathinam, S., Muthiah, K., Parameswaran, P. S., Kavitha, T., Esaivani, S., Tamilarasan, K., *et al.* (2021), 'Analogy of *Kaba Suram* with COVID-19 Symptoms – A Siddha Literature Review'. *International Journal of Ayurvedic Medicine*, 11(4): 616–21. In *Compilation of COVID 19 Publication of CCRS* (Ministry of Ayush). Available at: http://Siddhacouncil.com/ccrs/wp-content/uploads/2022/01/CCRS_COVID-19_PUBLICATIONS_UPDATED_04012022.pdf. Accessed 25 June 2024.

Sathaye, B. (1986), *Padartha Vignana* (Goa: Gomantak Ayurveda College).

Singh, A. (2007), 'Action and Reason in the Theory of Ayurveda'. *AI & Society: Journal of Knowledge, Culture and Communication*, 21(1): 27–46. https://doi.org/10.1007/s00146-006-0041-x

Subhose, V., Srinivas, P. and Narayana, A. (2005), 'Biography of Madhavakara: His Scholarly Contribution'. *Bulletin of the Indian Institute for the History of Medicine*, 35(2): 113–30. https://pubmed.ncbi.nlm.nih.gov/17333668/

Sujatha, V. (2009), 'The Patient as a Knower: Principle and Practice in Siddha Medicine'. *Economic & Political Weekly*, 44(16): 76–83.

Sujatha, V. (2011), 'Innovation Within and Between Traditions: Dilemma of Traditional Medicine in Contemporary India'. *Science, Technology & Society*, 16(2): 191–213. https://doi.org/10.1177/097172181001600204

Sujatha, V. (2013), *Sociology of Health and Medicine: New Perspectives* (New Delhi: Oxford University Press).

Sujatha, V. (2019a), 'The Social Background and Subjectivity of Siddha Doctors'. Unpublished paper on 'Understanding Medical Syncretism: Subjectivity, Medical Knowledge and Institutions in Contemporary Siddha'. Paper presented at the international conference on *Medicine, Religion and Alchemy in South India* organised by Tübingen University, Germany, 25–27 July 2019. Available at: https://www.academia.edu/38505442/International_Conference_Medicine_Religion_and_Alchemy_in_South_India_Resources_and_Permutations_of_Siddha_Traditions_and_Siddha_Medicine_25_27_July_2019_Tübingen_University0.Accessed 25 June 2024.

Sujatha, V. (2019b), 'Beyond Medical Pluralism: Medicine, Power and Social Legitimacy in India' in Y. Arif and D. Mehta (eds) *Rethinking India: Essays in Celebration of 50 Years of Contributions to Indian Sociology* (London: Sage), 433–49.

Sujatha, V. (2021a), 'The Politics of Medicine in a Pandemic'. *Economic and Political Weekly*, LVI(30): 19–24. https://www.epw.in/system/files/pdf/2021_56/30/CM_LVI_29_240721_V_Sujatha.pdf

Sujatha, V. (2021b), 'COVID-19 Pandemic and the Politics of Risk: Perspectives on Science, State and Society in India'. *Contributions to Indian Sociology*, 55(2): 254–67.

Sujatha, V. (2022), 'Of Informal Practitioners of Biomedicine: The Interplay of Medicine, Economy and Society in India'. *Social Science and Medicine*, 317. https://doi.org/10.1016/j.socscimed.2022.115564

Sujatha, V. (2024), '"Not the Germ, It Is the Host": Siddha Medical Interventions in the Management of Infectious Fevers in Tamil Nadu'. *Asian Medicine*, 19(2): 239–72. https://doi.org/10.1163/15734218-12341562

Sujatha, V. and Payyappallimana, U. (2022), 'Public Health and the Politics of Knowledge: The Role of Traditional Medicine in the Management of COVID-19 in Two South Indian States'. *Journal of Health Management*, 25(2): 340–50.

Thillaivanan, S., Parthiban, P, Kanakavalli, K. and Sathiyarajeshwaran, P. (2015), 'A Review on "Kapa Sura Kudineer" – A Siddha Formulary Prediction for Swine Flu'. *International Journal of Pharmaceutical Sciences and Drug Research*, 7(5): 376–83. http://ijpsdr.com/index.php/ijpsdr/article/view/440/401

Uttamaroyan, K. S. (1983), *Siddha Maruthuvanga Surukkam* (Tamil, Summary of Components of Siddha Medicine) (Chennai: Department of Indigenous Medicine and Homeopathy, Government of Tamil Nadu).

Zimmermann, F. (1987), *The Jungle and the Aroma of Meats: An Ecological Theme in Hindu Medicine* (Berkeley, CA: University of California Press).

6

Iran's Clerical State and Modern Medicine in the Age of Covid-19

HORMOZ EBRAHIMNEJAD

Introduction

WHEN I STUDIED the cholera and plague epidemics in 19th-century Iran as case studies to understand how modern medicine developed amid the continued dominance of humoral medicine, I noticed some affinities between traditional and modern medicines in terms of aetiology and treatment. A similar affinity during the transition period at the end of the 19th century provided favourable ground for dialogue between traditional and modern medicines . In my previous work (Ebrahimnejad 2014), I argued that traditional humoral medicine, as the dominant discourse and paradigm, faded away by going through an internal transformation, which acted as a catalyst for the development of biomedicine. However, both at the height of the Covid-19 pandemic in 2020 and in the present day (2023–5) we have witnessed the use of herbal drugs and traditional treatment by the population in Iran alongside modern medicine, even as Covid-19 vaccines have effectively diminished the mortality caused by the virus.

The successes of microbiology in identifying the agents of plague and cholera at the end of the 19th century gave rise to the hope that modern science would put an end to all epidemic diseases; however, the outbreak of influenza between 1918 and 1920 put an end to this, causing between 40 and 50 million deaths (Byerly 2005: 5; Barro Ursúa and Weng 2020: 2). A century later, the Covid-19 pandemic was another blow to the confidence in microbiology's capacity to cure diseases. It is now time to look beyond the laboratory and evidence-based medicine (EBM), which has proved to have limitations when faced with ancient and novel pathogens in a new global and regional context. As Greenhalgh *et al.* point out, 'the pandemic is an epistemic opportunity for the EBM movement to come to better understand, debate, and embrace EBM+' (2022: 253). Social historians of medicine have for some time now agreed that the prevalence of modern medicine is not only due to

Proceedings of the British Academy, **278**, 112–137, © Authors 2025.

its actual efficacy but also to the expansion of modern medical institutions, which in turn involve politics and the economy. The role played by the modern medical profession and institutions (medical schools and hospitals) in forming modern medical discourse, including microbiology and EBM medicine, is not negligible (e.g. Nandy and Visvanathan 1990). Institutionalisation has also played an important role in the promotion of herbal and traditional medicine in modern times.[1]

In such a context, we have also witnessed the expansion of the herbal drugs market and of so-called alternative medicine. This is partly due to the pervasive development of the market economy and consumerism, which entails institutionalisation of traditional medicine such as through its incorporation into the healthcare system.[2] It is also a consequence of the fact that the line between the effectiveness of biomedical 'chemical medicine' and the ineffectiveness of herbal medicine is not always clear-cut (e.g. Negahban, Maleki and Abbassian 2019). With the increasing number of chronic diseases and the subsequent importance of preventive healthcare, herbal medicine has become increasingly popular and consumer friendly. Its availability has been enhanced through e-commerce delivery without people needing to go through the official healthcare system, obtain a prescription and be subject to higher costs. Furthermore, many herbal drugs for chronic diseases are advertised by specialist doctors and surgeons who warn against the harm caused by the chemical drugs' side effects, as opposed to the relative innocuity of herbal drugs. Such advertisements sometimes avoid mentioning that herbal medicines can also have side effects and, in combination with chemical drugs, can be harmful.[3] The growing audience for such adverts and the use of herbal medicine stems from a range of different factors, including an increasing tendency towards preventive medicine to avoid or postpone curative treatment; legal rulings in different countries; evidence of the harmful side effects of many modern medical treatments; and the bad reputation of pharmaceutical companies.[4] To this, we need to add clinical trials by some herbal drug companies, which could increase with the growing income of these companies. One example is the ephedra herb extract used to treat infectious diseases, specifically coronavirus, which has gone through several trial phases (Global Data 2024).[5]

According to a 2015 report by the WHO, about 80 per cent of the world population rely on traditional medicine for their primary healthcare needs

[1] One of the factors behind the rise of the herbal-based pharmaceutical industry especially in countries like India and South Korea is their institutionalisation (e.g. Hong 1989: 55–6).

[2] This is recommended by the WHO, but it is more frequent in the global south (e.g. Kofi-Tsekpo 2004).

[3] One such example is St John's wort in the form of a herbal preparation for relief of symptoms associated with mild to major depressive episodes. However, using it in combination with a number of other chemical medications including antidepressants and oral contraceptives can be deleterious (e.g. Nicolussi *et al.* 2020).

[4] On media reporting of profit-seeking pharmaceutical companies see, for example, Smedley (2015).

[5] Clinical trials of herbal drugs are, however, far from ubiquitous. The trials of herbal drugs vary from country to country but, in most cases, herbal drugs are not regulated by the state (Parveen *et al.* 2015).

(Parveen *et al.* 2015). In Iran, however, given the economic sanctions,[6] the herbal medicine market has not developed as it has in much of the rest of the world. The resurgence of herbal or traditional medicine in Iran was initially due to the clerical state's Islamist Cultural Revolution (*c.* 1980–3), aimed at fighting against Western influence. A late 20th-century resurgence has also taken place in Asian countries such as Japan, China and Korea for several other reasons (Hong 1989: 26–30). In the European Union, the Committee on Herbal Medicinal Products issues scientific opinions on herbal substances on behalf of the European Medicines Agency (EMA) (for details, see EMA 2024). Within the EU, individual countries also apply their national regulations.

This, however, is not the case in Iran. As we will see, the government and Public Health Ministry do not invest in 'Iranian and Complementary Medicine', a state-sponsored institution that was created at the beginning of the Islamic regime, because they prioritise modern medicine for political reasons, as I will explain below. In Iran, we find a paradox in the attitude of the state towards traditional medicine. On the one hand, the government initiated the revival of traditional medicine in the 1980s and, in response to WHO recommendations, later took further steps to integrate it into the healthcare system. On the other hand, it has often paid only lip service to these recommendations – and even to its own regulations – regarding the support and development of traditional medicine (see Negahban, Maleki and Abbassian 2019).

This paradox is the result of the complex political context arising from the 1979 Revolution, which later evolved into the so-called Islamic Revolution. Medical knowledge and practice are shaped in specific social, political, discursive and material contexts. There is a relationship between concepts, theories and models of knowledge on the one hand, and culture, politics and the economy on the other. It is from this perspective that we might be able to understand the commitment of the clerical regime to modern medicine despite its ideological inclination for tradition. In this chapter, I argue that the existential conditions of the clerical state played a key role in their paradoxical attitude towards traditional and modern medicines during the Covid-19 pandemic.

The persistence of miasma theory during the Covid-19 pandemic

Covid-19 took the global medical community by surprise, as it was not like the previous virus in the SARS family in terms of its diagnosis, the way it spread and its lethal effects. Dr Antony Fauci, who was the head of the National Institute of Allergy

[6] Iran has been under US sanctions since the US hostage crisis in November 1979. These sanctions expanded in the last two decades after the Islamic regime in Iran began to develop nuclear technology that Western countries claim to be aimed at producing atomic bombs.

and Infectious Diseases (NIAID) in the US from 1984 to 2022, acknowledged that the airborne pattern of transmission of the virus was not initially understood (quoted in Entekhab News 2020). Although there is now a general medical consensus that the virus is transmitted through droplets and not free-floating aerosols, scientists have suggested there could still be the possibility of airborne transmission (Bhagat and Linden 2020; Morawska and Milton 2020; Greenhalgh *et al.* 2021; Greenhalgh *et al.* 2022).

Uncertainty about the way Covid-19 was transmitted and lack of clarity about preventive measures against it prior to the production of a vaccine is reminiscent of the age-old vagueness of the concepts of 'contagion' and miasma that were deemed to have caused the cholera epidemics that shook the world in the 19th century. Even though a distinction was made between the theories of miasma and contagion with the introduction of anatomical pathology, traditional physicians in 19th-century Iran were often ambiguous on the question of whether plague was transmitted by contact or through foul air. In theory, they believed that *vabâ* (the generic term for all sorts of epidemics) was due to foul air (miasma), while the same physicians during epidemic outbreaks avoided any contact with the sick because they feared contagion. Hence, Shirâzi wrote his *Tâ'unia* (Treatise on Plague, 1831), criticising his contemporary colleagues for their fear of contagion. Even Shirâzi, who argued that plague was not contagious, when discussing the etymology of طاعون (*tâ'un*, plague) referred to the Arabic root طعن /*ta'n*, which he translated as 'piercing with a spear', a term that inherently carries connotations of 'contact and contagion'.[7] Another 19th-century source informs us that during the cholera epidemic of 1892 in Tehran, the only physician who was available to treat the infected people was a Jew, as all Muslim doctors stayed at home or left the city for fear of being contaminated when treating patients (Astarabadi in Ebrahimnejad 2004: 418–19).[8]

From the viewpoint of humoral aetiology, an epidemic-related fever is generated when corrupted air enters the heart and alters the body's temperature, which is called *harârat-e ghariba* (unnatural heat). This unnatural heat is transmitted through blood circulation to other body parts. When the organs are affected, the fever is light or *yawm* (day fever, lasting one day or so) but when the unnatural heat affects the *akhlât* (humours), it causes 'infectious fever' and epidemic fever is of this kind. We can see that fever and infection are related in humoral aetiology, just as in modern medicine.[9]

The theory of contagion did not gain currency among 19th-century traditional doctors in Iran because the concept of a 'seed', 'pathogen' or 'particle' as the agent

[7] The concept of 'piercing' used by Shirâzi is reminiscent of the bow and arrows used to represent the plague representation in the West in the 17th century (Delumeau 1989; Snowden 2019).

[8] Astarabadi's point is not that there were religious differences regarding beliefs about contagion per se; rather, he points out that the Jewish doctor took the opportunity to treat patients at a time when most other doctors avoided possible contamination.

[9] For a more general context on humoral understandings of infectious diseases, see Nutton (2021).

of disease transmission, first proposed by Fracastoro during the Renaissance,[10] was either unknown or seemed irrelevant to most of them. The problem with the theory of germs in contagion for those physicians who knew about the pathogen particle was that it could not explain why people who were not in contact with each other were affected by cholera or plague within a short period. However, from the critical essay of Shirâzi on plague, we learn that there were physicians who, although they could not explain how, believed in some kind of contagion because they avoided touching and treating bubonic plague patients. In other words, they were anti-contagionist in theory but contagionist in practice!

Although the theory of miasmas is no longer accepted in modern medical discourse, it continues to inform our understanding of the outbreak of Covid-19 and some of our public health measures globally.[11] This representation of infectious particles was still at work during the Covid-19 pandemic, during which public health recommendations such as 'social distancing' and avoidance of crowds in closed spaces were advised to prevent air corruption, since it was believed that coronavirus was airborne. Therefore, the windows of offices and classrooms were left open even in the winter to let the virus escape. Yet, it is unclear whether the wind is responsible for the movement of the virus. Some studies have shown that the virus travels in the air even when there is no wind. Early speculative reporting spread information that the virus is transmitted quicker when the humidity rate is 90 per cent. For example, it was reported in Iran that in July 2020, New Delhi saw the number of Covid-19 patients increase from 78,000 to 135,000 with the increasing temperature and humidity (Entekhab News 2020). In September 2020, reporting in Iran speculated that the coronavirus pattern of transmission showed that when the humidity increases (at any temperature), the virus spreads up to six metres even when there is no wind (ibid.). In traditional medicine, a sign of *vabâ* or epidemic is when, due to the weakness of the sun, putrid vapour does not ascend enough to transform into rain. We can see how analogous physical conditions have given rise to a similar epidemiological understanding in contemporary times. However, systematic scientific research has shown that low humidity (i.e. 10–20 per cent) is associated with higher risk of infection and that in conditions of high humidity (70–80 per cent) infection risk becomes 'moderate' (Ahlawat, Wiedensohler and Mishra 2020). However, a number of other environmental factors have also been identified as relevant to evaluating the risk of airborne transmission of Covid-19 (Feng *et al.* 2020; Zhao *et al.* 2022).

[10] Girolamo Fracastoro/Fracastorius (1484–1553) was the first person who, by introducing the concept of seed or germ, presented the scientific theory of contagious disease. This was later confirmed through the discoveries of bacteriology, notably by Pasteur and Koch (Ackerknecht 1982).

[11] According to Anne Marie Moulin, the idea of a virus in the air is almost the same as the concept of miasma, and one could see similar perspectives in France during Covid-19 in 2020 and the Marseilles plague of 1720–2 (Moulin 2023: 53–4).

Cultural and political dimensions

It can be observed that social, cultural and political factors are as influential as experimentally derived medical concepts in addressing the pandemic, as social groups and broader sociopolitical and economic contexts shape the perceived validity – and thus the impact – of medical discourses (Good 1993). Michel Foucault argued that a disease entity is not naturally 'given' but is made and defined through medical discourse (Conrad and Barker 2010: 69). The strict adherence to scientific criteria might result from excessive institutionalisation or bureaucratisation of medicine, which was lambasted by Ivan Illich (1975, 1976), who maintained, albeit to an extreme degree, that 'illness' is made up by doctors. Illich coined the term iatrogenesis (or doctor-caused) to describe some diseases. The medical establishment, according to Illich, has created institutions, laboratories and testing procedures that in many cases benefit doctors and other medical professionals more than patients and sometimes kill more patients than they save.

As has long been observed, the concept of illness is affected by a person's specific culture (Kim 1973). It is important to consider how disease and illness are perceived by society and different societal groups because illness and disease are not only natural incidences but also social, cultural and professional constructs. Despite the significance of the cultural, social and political dimensions in medicine, there are still publications that condemn what they call faked medical information to fight Covid-19 and that aim to discredit any medical treatment and advice that is not in line with evidence-based medicine, as defined by the WHO (e.g. Vraga and Bode 2017; Moreno-Castro *et al.* 2020; Tasnim, Hussain and Mazumder 2020; Vraga, Bode and Tully 2020). This approach still follows the above-mentioned classical dichotomy between 'correct' and 'false', 'legitimate' and 'illegitimate', and 'scientific' and 'folk' medicines, a dualism that should be called into question, considering the blurred line between modern and complementary medicines in terms of aetiology, epidemiology, diagnosis and treatment. Such a 'scientific' perspective is overly restrictive, failing to account for factors such as culture, belief and social standing, which – when examined through historical and social lenses – challenge clear-cut distinctions between traditional and modern medicine.

Significantly, traditional medicine in 19th-century Iran was more inclusive, unlike modern medicine which tends to be exclusive given that it has established well-defined boundaries in line with modern science. Traditional medicine in 19th-century Iran, on the other hand, while principally based on humoral physiology, did not exclude magic and folk medicine. In the same vein, traditional physicians did not always shy away from modern medical theory and practice (e.g. Ebrahimnejad 2014: 17, 37 *et passim*). This was because the dominant medical discourse variously ascribed epidemic diseases to environmental conditions, contagion, divine will or a mixture of all three. Furthermore, during the development of modern medicine in the 19th century, when traditional and humoral discourse was still dominant, there was still dialogue between biomedicine, Galenic and Hippocratic medicine.

This dialogue helped the conceptual evolution of traditional medicine, which in turn facilitated the integration of modern medical theories. However, political, and ideological factors – especially in the context of the Constitutional Revolution of 1907–11, which was captivated by modern science, and the subsequent modernisation under Reza Shah – gave rise to a belief in a dichotomy between tradition and the modern. Such a situation led to the predominance of modern medical discourse. Traditional medicine was marginalised, since the only legal medical practice belonged to those who had completed their studies at medical faculties grounded in modern Western medicine.

Practitioners of modern biomedicine were initially arrogant about its scientific findings and overestimated its efficacy. However, the emerging epidemics and etiological uncertainty have revealed its limits. This can explain, at least partly, why pluralism reappeared in a different form during Covid-19, giving rise to traditional and modern approaches adopted in parallel or in combination by Iranian society. Such a context potentially gives rise to eclecticism in medical theory and practice. The popular medical discourse which spread across social media developed its own anatomical narrative, according to which coronavirus enters the body through respiration and before reaching the lungs stays four days in the throat and produces a cough and sore throat. It was rumoured that as soon as one has a cough or sore throat, they should drink lots of water, inhale the steam of boiled thyme and gargle salty water with vinegar. This would stop the virus from reaching the lungs and would save lives. No matter whether these treatments, which circulated during the Covid-19 pandemic through Telegram or WhatsApp, are effective or not, the important point is that they determine the way that disease is addressed among the Iranian population at large.

Attitudes of social groups towards Covid-19

Unlike the official biomedical view that considers disease as a natural fact that is to be diagnosed and described unambiguously and objectively by scientists and physicians, disease and illness can also be seen as subjective phenomena following different norms. From a social constructivist standpoint, our perception of disease and illness is almost as important as scientific findings and shapes the way society and individuals respond to illness. The impact of social and political forces on the treatment of Covid-19 is therefore crucial. In Iran, we can identify three major societal categories involved in the shaping of public health and preventive or curative measures against Covid-19: the core of the clerical state, which officially applies modern medicine; the general population, whose default medical repertoire is to rely on alternative medicine whenever there is limited access to modern medicine, a lack of belief in it or diminished trust in biomedical practices; and the orthodox clergy (or the clerical estate in general), who refer to the Medicine of the

Prophet and the Imams, which also draws on folk medicine.[12] Each societal group's medical choices are shaped by distinct incentives: the clerical regime is motivated by the exercise of power; the population's preference for alternative medicine stems from a combination of cultural, religious, financial and political motivation (lack of confidence in the government); and the clerical estate's interest in traditional medicine resides in the theoretical foundation of their profession.

Medicine advocated by the clerical state

Although from the outset of its creation in 1979, the clerical state sponsored the revival of Islamic and alternative medicine and added it to the university curriculum,[13] it is highly significant that in the context of Covid-19, it did not adopt Islamic medicine or traditional humoral medicine to define and implement its public health policy. According to the semi-official *Iran* newspaper, the *Specialised Committee of the National Covid-19 Task Force* (announced in August 2020) was the only official body to enunciate the state's policy on Covid-19 (Magiran 2020). Even the supreme leader and other *marâje'* (plural of *marja'*), Shiite sources of emulation, commissioned the *Specialised Committee* to determine the hygienic measures to be observed in mosques, shrines and religious festivals. The government stated that the decisions made by this committee were entirely based on modern science, specifying that its policy was approved by the WHO (Magiran 2020). The government of Iranian President Ruhani (2013–21) was known for its relatively moderate policy in domestic and foreign affairs and was more relaxed in the application of religious codes, a posture that put it in some opposition to the hardliners. However, except for some discord between the two political factions within the government (the hardliners and the moderates) regarding the distribution of funds from state reserves for Covid-19, both had the same adherence to modern medicine. This contrasted with the perspective of the clerical estate (the traditional Shiite hierocracy that had developed since the 16th century in Iran), which should not be confused with the clerical state (the current regime of the Ayatollahs).[14]

The mouthpiece of the Islamic Revolutionary Guard Corps (IRGC), *Fars News*, regularly reports state-of-the-art scientific, technological and medical news,

[12] In one case (March 2020), Sheikh Motrezâ Kohansâl, a cleric from Langarud (north Iran), claimed that a liquid that he represented as 'the perfume of the Prophet' healed Covid-19 patients. He went to the bedside of Covid-19 patients without wearing a mask or gloves, and with his finger and a dropper rubbed the perfume on the back of the lips and around the mouth of patients (Deutsche Welle 2020).

[13] The clerical state refers to the state (Islamic government). The clerical estate is the traditional clerical establishment. Many clerics from this establishment are coopted by the state and others remains independent (a few of them dissident), although in a minority.

[14] On the development of the Shiite hierocracy, see Arjomand (1981).

but it does not refer to Islamic or traditional medicine (Fars News 2020a). On 20 September 2020, the *Fars News* reported:

> Researchers at the Royan Institute studied the mutations of the genome of Sars Covid-19, which is essential to finding treatment and controlling the disease.[15] They discovered that the genome of this virus mutates very fast. The researchers compared the genome of this virus in 20 Iranian and non-Iranian patients with a history of travel to Iran or contact with an individual. The results of this research published in Cell Journal show 44 differences in the level of the nucleotides and 26 differences in the protein that were caused by mutations. Comparison of these mutations with the global figures indicates that some of these mutations are seen only in the Iranian population.
> (Fars News 2020b)

The clerical regime, in order to showcase its power, endeavours to develop modern science and technology. At the height of the coronavirus pandemic, the spokesperson of the IRGC announced that this military organisation had invented an instrument that could detect coronavirus (as well as any other virus) from a distance of 100 metres.[16] There is of course no evidence for the accuracy of such an instrument, and, indeed, this claim has frequently been ridiculed on social media. In another example, in June 2023, the Iranian government claimed that they had produced 'the first quantum processing algorithm' (Iran International Newsroom 2023). Regardless of whether social media users found this to have been faked, the news indicates how enthusiastic the clerical regime is to display its command of modern science and technology. The regime's adherence to modern medicine is also for practical purposes, as modern science and technology enable it to exercise its power more effectively. For example, to realise its project of demographic growth, the supreme leader has allowed cloning of the organs, despite the fact that it could be interpreted by Sharia as an intervention in God's creation. Both religion and science are at the service of power under the clerical regime. Ayatollah Khomeini, the founder of the Islamic Republic, said in a speech on 16 November 1981:

> Today we are facing all the powers outside and inside who try to break this revolution and defeat and destroy this Islamic movement and the Islamic Republic … [T]he preservation of the Islamic Republic is more important than the preservation of one person, even if it is the Imam of the Age (Mahdi). Because the Imam of the Age sacrifices himself for Islam. All the prophets who came from the beginning of the world until now fought for the word of truth and the religion of God and sacrificed themselves. The Holy Prophet [Mohammad] and his Ahl al-Bayt (household) suffered all those hardships. They made sacrifices to preserve Islam and to establish the Islamic government [that has now been materialised in Iran] and maintaining this is an objective obligation for everyone [including the Hidden Imam].
> (Khomeini 1981)

[15] Fars News, 'Royan Research Investigates Specific Differences in Coronavirus Gene Mutations in Iranian Society'.

[16] The video in which the head of the IRGC demonstrates the device can be found at https://www.aparat.com/v/v41x66s (accessed August 2023).

More recently, on 6 November 2022, the cleric Hossein Jalâli, the deputy of Rafsanjan and a member of the Cultural Committee of the Majlis (Islamic parliament), opposed Shamkhani's (the secretary of the National Security Council) favourable talk about the moderate ex-president Khatami, by reminding him of the words of Ayatollah Khomeini in the following terms:

> Colleagues, Iran is the country of the Imam of the Age (Hidden Imam), the victory of the Islamic system is a divine promise. Global arrogance wants to present Islam as weak and the religious government as ineffective; they are all wet! Today Iran is powerful and strong after passing through crises and making amazing progress in the creation of knowledge-based enterprises, air and space, nuclear, Nanos, stem cells, nuclear medicine, and thousands of valuable achievements that some of our neighbors dream of having one of them, Iran has been able to become a dominant power in West Asia and soon you will see that it will show its strength as an undisputed power in front of America's hypocritical hymen … Mr. Shamkhani, maintaining the [Islamic] government is one of the obligatory duties, even more than preserving the life of Imam of the Age. You should not prioritize friendship with Khatami over the principle of the Islamic government.
>
> (Entekhab News 2022)

Through the development of biomedical engineering and science and seeking to implement state-of-the-art medicine, the regime has no other aim than asserting and strengthening its control of the population through demographic manipulation or increasing it for political reasons. Gone are the views of the 19th century, when the clerical estate opposed the dissection of the dead body – whether for the newly introduced anatomical pathology, post-mortem autopsies or criminology – because the body, even when dead, was considered sacred. For decades, this prohibition prevented the modern school of medicine from carrying out dissection for education; the anatomical knowledge of students was instead based on descriptive materials and illustrations. At that time, the clerical estate did not hold power.[17]

We should also consider the fact that Ayatollah Khomeini, the founder of the regime, advocating traditional medicine was in line with his opposition to whatever the Pahlavi regime had established, including modern universities and modern medical education and practice. It was thus politically motivated. When he came to be treated at the time of illness, however, Khomeini's attitude towards traditional medicine was radically the opposite. When he suffered a heart attack in March 1986, a private hospital for cardiology was established in the vicinity of his residence in Jamârân (north of Tehran), given that his health conditions made it risky for him to be transferred, in the case of any illness, to the existing hospitals

[17] We can see parallel developments elsewhere in the Islamic world. The Islamic bioethical code was approved by the International Academy of Islamic Jurisprudence in 1983 in Jeddah (Saudi Arabia), based on the principle of 'public interest or well-being' (*al-maslaha*) and 'the necessities outweigh prohibitions' (*al-darurat tubihu al mahzurât*). Blood transfusion and organ transplantation are among practices that normally should be prohibited in Islam but modern Islamic jurisprudence allows them (Houot 2013).

that were too distant from his residence. This hospital was equipped with the most modern instruments, including a PET scan that at that time existed only in three hospitals in Iran. When, about a year later, his medical team discovered that he had metastatic cancer of the stomach, his medical team operated on his stomach and then prescribed chemotherapy that might have been fatal. During his cardiac treatment, Ayatollah Khomeini not only did not refuse to take the medication prescribed by his medical team but also adhered strictly to their prescription and always asked which medication was good to treat for his various problems (Gooya News 2023). There are, however, no reports that he asked either those around him or his medical teams to use traditional medicine, which he had initially championed.

Civil society and Covid-19

The second social group comprises a large section of the population that due to the combination of several factors – including cultural background, lack of clear knowledge about coronavirus and financial affordability – have recourse to alternative or herbal medicine in their fight against Covid-19. To this, we should also add the factor of confidence in the political power that controls the medical system (hospitals, medical insurance, production and distribution of vaccines). Iranian society, in general, has been divided by the authorities into 'them' and 'us', which has badly affected trust in the government. The authoritarian approach to dealing with civil rights was much more pronounced during the pandemic when, for political and financial reasons, the supreme leader, despite the medical experts' opinion and the rising mortality, opposed the introduction of the newly produced Pfizer and AstraZeneca vaccines. This further dented the population's confidence in the government and its 'modern medicine'. The tendency to favour herbal drugs during the coronavirus pandemic can also be understood within this context.[18]

The clerical estate's response to Covid-19

The third social category consists of the orthodox clerics and their followers, who lambasted the government for restricting access to mosques or enforcing the closure of shrines and forbidding pilgrims to cross the border with Iraq to go to the shrines in Najaf and Karbala. The practice of social distancing obstructed religious ceremonies and pilgrimages and transformed some of the supporters of the regime into their opponents, as their belief in the healing 'properties' of the shrines came into conflict with the clerical government's closure of the shrines. The religious city of Qom, which hosts the Mausoleum of Ma'soumeh (sister of Imam Reza,

[18] Sanitary dictatorship as opposed to sanitary democracy in the case of France and Europe is examined by Moulin (2023: 125–35).

765–818, the eighth Imam of the Shiites), was the epicentre from which Covid-19 spread elsewhere in Iran. According to the Health Minister, the virus was introduced to Qom by Chinese travellers, and one of the first victims of Covid-19 in Qom was an Iranian merchant who made frequent business trips to China. The Ministry of Health advised the closure of the mausoleum but Ayatollah Sa'eedi, the curator of the shrine and the Friday Imam of Qom, strongly objected to this decision in the following terms: 'We consider this holy shrine as Dar al-Shafâ (abode of healing); Dar al-Shafâ means people come and get healed for mental and physical diseases. Therefore, it should be open here, and people should continue their pilgrimage even more than before. Of course, we also take necessary cautions and observe health matters.' The website of Ma'soumeh Shrine published a note protesting the decision of the Qom Province Supply Council to disinfect the shrine, claiming that 'there is no need to disinfect or close the shrine, as its faith-based architecture and silver structures are the best weapons against bacteria. The Supreme Leader's representative in Qom had previously said that the shrine is a place of healing and must remain open.'[19]

The opposition of a section of the clergy to the clerical state's public health Covid-19 policy originates in the foundation of the clerical estate. The popular belief in shrines as places of healing and intercession is the result of the work of the Shiite clerical establishment shaped under the Safavids (1501–1726) and consolidated under the Qajars (1797–1925). This cultural work, epitomised in the 110 volumes of *Behâr al-Anvâr* (Oceans of Lights) by Mohammad Bâqer Majlesi (1617–99), along with the creation of hundreds of mausoleums dedicated to the Shiite Imams' descendants, laid the foundations for the Shiite hierocracy and the power of the clerics today (Arjomand 1985; Ashtiani 1989). However, once at the helm of the state, the same clerics opposed the belief that the saint shrines could protect the faithful from Covid-19. We find a clear difference in attitudes towards Covid-19 between the Islamic clerical government and the clerical estate, even though both sides share the same ideology. However, those within the power structure sometimes attempt to reconcile traditional and modern medicine by drawing on their repertoire of hadiths and employing *ijtihad* – the capacity to derive rulings from the sources of Sacred Law – to justify the benefits of modern medicine. Allam al Hoda (the curator of Imam Reza mausoleum and the Friday Imam of Mashhad) stated that 'the Imams themselves were subject to natural law even though they can miraculously heal or protect … the fact that the saints heal, does not dispense us from observing hygienic measures' (Aftab News 2020). Allam al Hoda here endorsed the government's instructions that the faithful should not visit the shrines. And those who resisted, such as the individual who licked the shrine to prove that the virus can never infect saint locations, were arrested and jailed.[20]

[19] https://p.dw.com/p/3YTnh (accessed 20 June 2025).

[20] Usually, pilgrims kiss the shrine, but in order to show that this would not infect him he went even further.

In Shiism, *feqh*, or jurisprudence that determines the legal rights of individuals on every matter, is based on the expert opinion of the jurisconsult (*faqih*). However, in the Islamic regime, where the supreme leader is the ruling *faqih*, there are two kinds of *feqh*: the state and civil. According to the state *feqh* (*feqh-e hokumati*), people must comply with the state's prophylactic measures and failure to do so would be punishable by law. This is based on the principle of the mandate of the jurist (*velâyat-e faqih*), whose decree during Covid-19 must be obeyed (Khatami 2020).[21] According to section K of article 8 of the management of public services, improving public health and preventive measures against infectious and epidemic diseases is an example of the implementation of the decree of the supreme leader (*velâyat-e faqih*) (Sadat 2022). The adherence of the clerical regime in Iran to 'modern' medicine and international regulations set by the WHO is in line with its strategy of adopting modern science and technology, such as nanotechnology, cloning of organs and missile and nuclear technologies. Islamists in the modern age see no contrast between modern science and religion not least because they can use modern science and technology to boost their power while they oppose modern human social sciences, such as sociology and critical history.

The state media, while broadcasting the policy of the state on Covid-19, also aired the voices of orthodox Shiites, who are attached to traditional medicine and the Medicine of the Prophet and the Imams. The medical editor of *Tasnim*, the semi-official newspaper linked to the Islamic Revolutionary Guard Corps, lamented that 'eight months into the outbreak of corona in the country, no use was made of traditional medicine in dealing with the pandemic'. Dr Akbari, a pathologist and researcher in traditional medicine, was quoted as saying that he proposed that hospitals establish a department for practitioners of traditional medicine under the responsibility of one of the faculties of traditional and complementary medicine (Tasnim News 2020b).

In January 2021, another *Tasnim* article reported that the government was facing criticism for neglecting the promotion of traditional medicine, as it was allocated a budget of almost zero. Out of 155 trillion toman (£2,066,666,666) earmarked for public health in the 2021 budget, only 7.5 billion T (£100,000) was given to traditional medicine.[22] The article concluded that 'the government did not believe in traditional medicine, despite the high popularity of simple and herbal remedies, the public's predisposition toward traditional treatments for Covid-19, and the reportedly near-zero mortality rate among patients who used such methods'. The article further notes:

[21] This was a 'external lesson' 9 (*dars-e khârej*). External lectures are given at a higher level of seminary schools (*howza*) and can be defined as: 'argumentative presentation of the lesson without relying on a specific text'. In this lesson, the professor presents different opinions about the topic under discussion, recounts and criticises its evidence and finally presents his opinion.

[22] This conversion is made on the basis of the rate in March 2024 (1£= 75,000 toman).

> The government neglects the rich capacity of traditional medicine in the country, while, according to the Ministry of Health, the combined use of traditional and modern medicine in countries like China has helped greatly in treating patients with Corona and reducing the complications caused by the disease. Also, Iran is a vast country with historical roots and ancient medicine with more than 8000 plant species; for this reason, it is considered one of the most important countries in the field of 'ethnopharmacology' and has many study opportunities for research in this field.
>
> (Tasnim News 2021a)

The core argument of this group of doctors is that treatment based on traditional medicine would improve the immune system and reduce the mortality rate. Even the Deputy Minister of National Health acknowledged that what saves lives during Covid-19 is prevention and care and not cure through the prescription of drugs. Nevertheless, hospitals did not accept this suggestion and exclusively relied on modern medicine in tackling Covid-19.

The most immediate source of information on Covid-19 for the population in Iran was social media (WhatsApp, Telegram, immo, Instagram), where we find a mixture of modern and traditional prescriptions to prevent or cure Covid, with a preference for herbal and traditional medicine. To fight the corrupt or foul air due to coronavirus, one should fumigate the area by burning *espand* (rue or mustard seed). Infusions of herbs and spices such as *âvishan* (thyme), ginger, cinnamon, camomile (*bâbuneh*) and pennyroyal were advised to prevent coronavirus as well as simple colds.

With the growing disillusionment with the clerical regime, social media has been increasingly used, substituting the state-run information channels. Social media has also played a role in breaking the monopoly of the pharmaceutical industry that is controlled by the state in general and by the IRGC in particular. One of these social media posts (circulated throughout the Covid-19 pandemic: 2020–2) states that: 'pharmaceutical companies prefer to make a profit out of "our pains" by selling their chemical drugs, including those used in chemotherapy, rather than to inform us about alternative (herbal and natural) drugs and we know about this thanks to social media.' Another explains: 'The effects of lemon in killing cancerous cells [for example] are far greater than chemotherapy.' The same post on WhatsApp claims that 'the reason why we are left ignoring the benefits of lemon in treating cancer is that pharmaceutical companies have copied the properties of lemon in the form of chemical drugs and made a huge profit from it. So long as this secret is not made public, many die so that the huge profits of the said companies are secured.'[23] This message is grounded in widely accepted knowledge about the benefits of lemon peel (e.g. Lang 2019; Katiboina 2021), which is used to criticise pharmaceutical companies.

Sometimes, perhaps to lend greater credibility, these prescriptions are attributed to modern, formally trained physicians – reflecting the significant influence that

[23] Forwarded message on WhatsApp (author unknown), 'Read on the Benefits of Lemon Peel'. Posted in March 2023.

modern medical institutions exert on the population. For instance, the experience of Dr Jalal Yunes, who worked in a Cairo hospital treating Covid-19 patients, was widely circulated through WhatsApp. As a preventive measure against Covid-19, Dr Yunes advised that 'if everyone eats two onions per day with a meal, coronavirus will never affect them, even though they are in direct contact with Covid patients'. Dr Yunes also advised: 'Those experiencing respiratory difficulties due to Covid-19 should mince an onion, place it in a perforated plastic bag, and inhale its vapours for ten minutes. This, instead, would disinfect all lung infections.' He further asserted that 'if everyone repeats this for three weeks, Covid-19 would be completely eradicated.'[24] At the end of the WhatsApp post, it is stressed that this should be communicated to as many people and as fast as possible. According to another post widely forwarded through WhatsApp, a soup made of carrot, celery and other vegetables and herbs has been trialled at the University Hospital Masih Daneshvari (Educational, Research and Treatment Centre for Tuberculosis and Pulmonary Diseases), north Tehran, where many Covid-19 patients were hospitalised. The effectiveness of this soup was considered to be nearly certain. Such a phenomenon demonstrates the extent to which cultural and belief systems inform medical knowledge and practice.

Official 'scientific' discourse

In the official discourse, on the other hand, modern medicine dominates. At the peak of Covid-19 the Iranian Ministry of Health warned against self-treatment with alternative medicine advertised on social media but allowed physicians to use chemical antiviral drugs such as hydroxychloroquine, favipiravir and remdesivir, even though they had not yet received approval from the WHO and were still being clinically trialled (Fars News 2020c),[25] and despite some studies that were published in Iran showing that hydrochloroquine (for the treatment of malaria) and hydroxychloroquine (for rheumatism and arthritis rheumatoid) were ineffective in the treatment of Covid-19 (e.g. Singh *et al.* 2021).[26] It is worth noting that while in the West, the efficacy of drugs like remdesivir remained uncertain during the pandemic, in Iran, physicians were allowed to prescribe them for those Covid-19 patients who were wealthy enough to pay for them. Dr Akbari (previously quoted in *Tasnim News* above) stated: 'At the start of the pandemic, hydroxychloroquine was prescribed

[24] This information was widely circulated on WhatsApp during the pandemic in Iran. The only reference I have found is on a Facebook account belonging to the Afghan Academy posted on 16 November 2020. This post cites a letter by Dr Jalal Yunes sent to the Egyptian president advising that onion can cure and prevent coronavirus. It is interesting to note that Egypt is a major producer of onion!

[25] The US Food & Drug Administration (FDA) approved remdesivir on 22 October 2020 (FDA 2020).

[26] A similar opinion about these drugs was published on the website *Doctor-e to* (Your doctor) on 2 December 2020, although the post was revised in October 2024: https://doctoreto.com/blog/what-is-hydroxychloroquine-sulfate/ (accessed 17 November 2024).

for coronavirus but then it proved to be ineffective. Nonetheless, our authorities allow this medicine to be imported and prescribed but they refuse to systematically prescribe thyme and honey that have been widely used and proved to be effective in the treatment of corona.'[27] One can also conjecture that the pharmaceutical companies who imported hydroxychloroquine and remdesivir were more motivated by profit than by the duty of supplying the market with effective drugs.

The underlying factor, however, for the prevalence of modern medicine in the public health response to Covid-19 in Iran is the historiographical, political and medical discourse of modernity and modernisation, characterised by a dichotomy between the modern and the traditional. This discourse has survived the clerical regime's policy of incorporating traditional medicine within the university medical curriculum as part of its 'Cultural Revolution'. In this discourse, there is a sharp break between traditional and modern medicine, and one should adhere to one or the other. In such a context, social actors choose their medicine according to their ideological, economic, professional and political stance. However, in a situation where modern medical discourse dominates, religious conservatives within the power structure sometimes adopt a reconciliatory attitude and accept that their medicine could be practised in parallel to modern medicine, as was the case with Ayatollah Allam al Hoda mentioned above. A similar stance can be observed among practitioners of traditional medicine. This is not the case for most practitioners of modern medicine, who categorically reject the use of herbal drugs for treatment. Dr Malekzadeh, the Deputy Minister of Health, responding to a request to launch specialised complementary courses in traditional medicine, voiced concerns that traditional medical knowledge 'created more chaos in the Ministry of Health'. He said this despite the formal commitment of the Ministry at that time (2020) to fully support traditional medicine. *Tasnim News*'s article explicitly criticised the 'artificial dichotomisation' in medicine (2020b). Prior to this, in June 2015, Dr Malekzadeh had opposed the creation of a 'traditional medicine' department in the Health Ministry because he believed that there is only one type of medicine, which is what is recognised by the WHO standard.[28] In his long response (4 Azar 1399/ 24/11/2020) to the (*bassij*/mobilisation) students close to the Islamic Revolutionary Guard Corps (IRGC), who criticised him for not having allocated the 5 per cent fund earmarked for traditional medicine, Malekzadeh answered that first of all this was approved by the 735th meeting, dated 15 April 2013, of the Supreme Council of Cultural Revolution and the Headquarter for the Development of Science and Technology of Medicinal Plants and Traditional Medicine 'that is the decision-making authority … So, this question should be asked to the relevant institution.'

[27] The FDA first approved hydroxychloroquine for the treatment of Covid-19 on 28 March 2020 but later, on 15 June, cancelled the approval after clinical studies showed that it was ineffective for such treatment with some serious side effects, such as irregular heartbeat, in the patients who used it (Drugs.com 2024).

[28] Dr Malekzadeh said 'I don't believe there should be such a thing as traditional medicine because medicine is one' (MedVoice 2023).

He then insisted on the necessity of the 'independence of medical universities [from the Supreme Council of Cultural Revolution] … Secondly, research on herbal drugs was not exclusive to traditional medicine but the faculties of pharmacy and other disciplines could also research this' (Iran Science Watch 2020). In general, Malekzadeh refuted all use of herbal drugs before they are tested through research and clinical trials. In particular, he refuted the approach of complementary medicine faculties or establishments who referred to old medical textbooks and applied their prescriptions to their patients, as he believed that they could be harmful.

The use of alternative or complementary medicine when modern medicine has not always been successful in treating lethal cancers, chronic conditions and severe syndromes is not exclusive to non-Western countries and is also at work in the West. Likewise, the promotion of traditional medicine by the clerical regime is not the revival of what was at work before the creation of the modern faculty of medicine under Reza Shah in 1933. The School of Persian Medicine has been added to other schools of the University of Medical Science, including the School of Medicine, School of Dentistry, School of Pharmacy and School of Allied Medical Sciences. To become specialised in Persian (traditional and complementary) medicine, the candidate should have graduated from the Faculty of Medicine after seven years of studies and training in modern medicine. All the teaching staff and deanery of the School of Persian Medicine are graduates of the Faculty of Medicine. This means that a specialist in traditional medicine has already acquired modern medical knowledge and skills and would practise traditional medicine within the framework of modern medicine. In other words, modern medical discourse prevails even for traditional medicine. Dr Malekzadeh's stance aligns with the general policy of the clerical state, which withholds substantial and meaningful support from traditional medicine practitioners. Although the government has not banned traditional medicine, it deprives it of all chance of development insofar as it does not subsidise herbal products or locally produced herbal raw materials– while it does subsidise 'the pharmaceutical industry's importation of raw materials' (WHO 2001). This situation is evident in the official website of the School of Persian (traditional) Medicine, which is poorly populated with several of its links inactive. One of its links that is quite well updated belongs to the Basij (Mobilisation) medical students at this School, which broadcasts political news in line with hardliners' viewpoints.[29]

The rise of neo-traditionalism in medicine

The rise of what we might call neo-traditionalism in medicine in Iran is grounded in three interrelated factors. The first is ideology as an instrument of national identity and anti-imperialism, which was prominent in the 1979 Revolution

[29] An English summary page can be found here: http://en.tums.ac.ir/en/content/238/school-of-persian-medicine (accessed 12 July 2023).

and shared by both Islamist and secular opponents of the Shah. As explained above, this ideology was adopted by the clerical state as a hallmark of fighting against Western culture, while in fact the regime applies modern medicine in practice. The second factor is the availability and affordability of herbal drugs in comparison to the high cost or lack of effective chemical medicine during the Covid-19 pandemic. And the third factor is the professionalisation and institutionalisation of traditional medicine by its practitioners, who endeavour to attain official recognition that would allow them to expand their activities and market presence. In such a context, the practitioners of traditional medicine, for ideological and professional reasons, stay within the boundaries set by classical sources of Galenico-Hippocratic medicine by applying the content of this literature. They then try to prove the effectiveness of this medicine from the viewpoint of modern medical knowledge and terminologies as a way to legitimise their work. For example, according to a specialist in traditional medicine, *hejamat* (scarification by cupping) would increase the oxygen level in the blood of Covid-19-affected patients. It can also cure diabetes by improving insulin sensitivity; it can increase anti-depression hormones in the brain, which is why those who are subject to phlebotomy feel lighter and happier! (Tasnim News 2021b).[30] In general, traditional medicine claimed that the immune system would be boosted by bloodletting (of different forms) during Covid-19; it was also claimed that the use of garlic and onion, raw or cooked, as well as nigella or fennel seeds enhanced immunity against Covid-19 (Tasnim News 2021c).

Practitioners of traditional medicine also have recourse to the principle of research and trials, which is fundamental in modern medicine, to legitimise the use of herbal medicine. For example, on herbal drugs for Covid-19, they claim that:

> according to laboratory research, the following drugs are effective for the treatment of coronavirus: saffron, lavender, chamomile, black seed, jujube, liquorice root, medicine of Imam Kazem (peace be upon him), baking soda incense, mint inhalation extract, and in addition to the medicine, proper nutrition and sufficient rest are necessary. The order to use each of the above medicines is different according to the gender, age, and condition of each person and should not be used arbitrarily.
>
> (ISNA 2021)

As previously noted, only 56 herbal medicines have undergone clinial trials in Iran, even though more than 8,000 medicinal plants have been identified. In any case, there cannot be a systemic clinical trial of herbal medicine, simply because the government does not allocate any budget for it.

[30] The 'traditional doctor' in this source explains the physiological function of hejamat (scarification), including change of humour and increase in the level of oxygen in the blood to 96 per cent. It is noteworthy that hejamat prescribed in the medicine of the prophet is based on Galenic medicine. The practice of hejamat in folk/prophetic medicine in North Africa (Algeria, Egypt) is associated with magic and ritualistic preparations (Cherak 2013).

The modern pharmaceutical industry and political rents

The question of why the Health Ministry opposes the official and state-sponsored application of traditional medicine to treat Covid-19 requires further research. One of the critics of the government's reliance on modern medicine in the treatment of coronavirus claimed that the reason for the exclusion of traditional medicine in treating Covid-19 patients is the drug mafia: namely, that those involved in the Health Ministry in importing or producing chemical drugs try to preserve their monopoly on the pharmaceutical industry. As we saw earlier, this allowed them to benefit from drugs such as hydroxychloroquine and remdesivir that had not yet undergone clinical trials (see above). The charge of corruption is certainly an established issue, and as mentioned above, the budget allocated for traditional medicine was far from honouring the 'ideological' commitment of the clerical regime to traditional medicine. This, however, is only a by-product of the regime's policy to employ modern science and technology to strengthen its power and reinforce its control over society. The Tasnim News Agency criticised Dr Malekzadeh, for having created a pharmaceutical company and taken up the position of chairman of its board of directors while being in the position of Deputy Health Minister. To sharpen their criticism, they also added that this company had produced some ineffective drugs for the treatment of coronavirus and called for his resignation. Malekzadeh's response to this was the following:

> As a distinguished [emeritus] professor and faculty member of the Tehran University of Medical Sciences in the field of gastrointestinal disease, on 29/02/2015 I created, together with some other colleagues, the (private and knowledge-based) company of Fanâvarân Royan Mohaghegh Darou and was elected as the chairman of its board of directors. For the following reasons, my membership in this company is not subject to the law approved in 1994 that banned the accumulation of more than one job. …
>
> The final clause of Article 141 of the Constitution of the Islamic Republic of Iran exempts teaching positions and faculty members from the law that prohibits the accumulation of public jobs alongside managing private companies. … In addition, according to Note 4 under Article 17 of the Fifth Development Plan Law and Note 7 under Article 1 of the Law on Permanent Budget Decree, faculty members can also form 100% private knowledge-based institutes and companies with the approval of the board of trustees of the same university or participate in these institutions and companies.
>
> (Iran Science Watch 2020)

This amounts to what Kevan Harris calls 'capitalism from above as wide and disperse patrimonial networks have come to dominate the technocratic agencies' (Harris 2013: 66). The cumulation of positions and exclusive rights to create commercial companies by the elites of the Islamic regime has become a well-established trend. Dr Velayati, a paediatrist who became the Foreign Minister at the start of the Islamic Republic, has occupied 63 positions, including the one he created during the pandemic, which had the 'exclusive right to import Favipiravir from Japan to treat corona before a vaccine was produced and the first users of this drug were the men of the regime' or those wealthy enough to pay for it.[31] In 2023, the managing director of the Society of Thalassemia Patients raised concerns that the pharmaceutical companies inside Iran take advantage of the sanctions on importing drugs. They do so by changing the formula of foreign drugs to produce cheaper alternatives, yet market these less effective drugs as the imported drugs to the patients (Khabarban 2023). Whether such accumulation of activities reserved for those who benefit from political rents leads to corruption or the development of capitalism (from above), what is significant in the case under study here is that they have been devoted more to modern medicine than traditional and complementary medicine.

There is contradictory information about the commitments of the clerical state in integrating traditional medicine into the healthcare system. The two main healthcare systems according to the WHO are the 'integrative system', which recognises traditional and complementary medicine and employs them in all areas (research, education, regulation, insurance, etc.), and the 'inclusive system', which recognises traditional medicine but does not incorporate it in the healthcare system. Referring to this categorisation, Negahban, Maleki and Abbassian (2019) demonstrate that Iran has an inclusive system. In the WHO global report in 2019, it is said that the Islamic Republic of Iran has integrated national policy on T&CM issued in 1996 and revised in 2010 (WHO 2019: 104–5). However, when it comes to the insurance of herbal drugs, out of tens of thousands of registered herbal medicines, only 56 are national drugs (included in the National Essential Medicines List) and are covered by public health insurance (WHO 2019: 105). A comparison with India provides insight into the attitude of the clerical state towards traditional medicine. The Ministry of AYUSH in India, formed in 1995, focuses on developing education and research on naturopathy, Ayurveda, yoga, Unani medicine, Siddha and homeopathy (AYUSH) (Singh and Shuka 2021: 31). There are several bodies or legislation, including the Central Council of Indian Medicine Act, research councils, Department of AYUSH, and the Drug & Cosmetic Act 1940, that regulate herbal medicine in India. In a striking contrast to the modernisation of Ayurveda in India and traditional medicines in Japan, China and Korea – which not only represent the assertion of their national identities against Western colonial and imperialist rule but also respond to their economic ambitions by developing a global pharmaceutical industry – in Iran, despite the Islamic government's promotion of traditional medicine, no concrete and substantial steps have been taken to integrate traditional medicine and herbal drugs into education, research and medical insurance.[32] The institutional modernisation of traditional medicine in Asia can potentially break the

[31] https://fa.opensocietyalliance.org/s1202024021520/ (accessed 17 June 2024).

[32] On the modernisation of Ayurvedic medicine, see Gaudillière and Pordié (2014); on the modernisation of herbal medicine in China and Korea, see Kloos (2017); on the inclusion of traditional Korean medicine in the National Medical Insurance, see Son (1999).

tradition/modern dichotomy, fostering a dialogue between the two. However, as Anne Marie Moulin (2016) notes in the case of Ayurvedic medicine in India, this process entails an inherent contradiction – namely, how to incorporate innovations into a therapeutic tradition that is revered precisely for its strict adherence to ancient texts deemed inviolable. In Iran, by contrast, the emphasis on epistemological gaps and theoretical differences – articulated by Dr Malekzadeh for modern medicine and Dr Akbari for traditional medicine – reinforces a long-standing dichotomy between the two. This divide appears to serve the interests of the clerical state in consolidating state authority more than it advances the institutional and professional standing of traditional medicine.

Conclusion

Unlike the fundamental changes and discontinuities in medical knowledge that have occurred since the nineteenth century when the foundations of modern public health were laid, the Covid-19 experience brings to the fore striking continuities in the way Iranian society confronts epidemics as well as other diseases.

Following the 1979 Revolution, which brought the clerics to power, the clerical state worked towards the restoration of traditional and humoral medicine as part of its ideological agenda. Dr Velayati, a paediatrician educated in the US and the Minister of Foreign Affairs, was one of those who took the lead in this process. Thus, the revival of traditional medicine had political and ideological (rather than theoretical) foundations and incentives.

With the outbreak of Covid-19, in the absence of a vaccine, hazy (or lack of) knowledge about the virus and ineffective chemical drugs, traditional and herbal medicine were used and advertised as an alternative solution to respond to the pandemic. It is, however, significant that neither the ideological motivations nor the extensive use of herbal medicine during the pandemic led to its official recognition by the clerical regime, which instead remained attached to modern medicine in dealing with the pandemic; therefore, traditional medicine could not regain its former status. The opposition of the clerical regime to the use of vaccines made in the West at the start of the pandemic was due to its geopolitical agenda and anti-Western foreign policy, as well as to financial reasons. This enabled the government's medical institutions to receive a budget for the development of different vaccines, such as Noor and Barekat (produced by companies under the Headquarters of Imam) or Fakhra (under the Defense Ministry), as well as funding for some private companies, which are often directly or indirectly linked to the IRGC.

The use of modern medicine alongside other modern technologies, such as nanotechnologies, nuclear and missile technologies, as instruments of power by a regime that identifies itself with pre-modern knowledge and the supernatural power of the saints speaks volumes about the power component of a regime of knowledge. It is highly significant that the clerical establishment founded its power on religion but ended up upholding its power by relying on modern science and technology. Historically, this reflects the enduring cohabitation of religion, magic and science, reminiscent of patterns observed in previous centuries in the West. It also illustrates how the exercise of power often aligns religion and science as instruments of authority, rather than ends in themselves. Epistemologically, this phenomenon might align with what Habermas describes as 'reason-interested' (Habermas 1972 in Rillo and Carrillo 2023: 5). If we assume, as Habermas does, that 'the direction of the efforts in the acquisition of knowledge' emanates from (or is informed by) the intention behind the pursuit of knowledge, we could then arguably conclude that the reliance of the clerical regime on modern medical knowledge is merely utilitarian or practical rather than an act 'geared toward the preservation of a certain value entailed in the acquisition of a particular form of knowledge' (Dube 1977: 44). In other words, I believe that the original value of 'inquiry' or freethinking that Habermas refers to as the origin of knowledge does not necessarily apply to the application of modern science and technology in the so-called post-modern world.

References

Aftab News. (2020), 'Alam al-Huda: Gold and Silver of the Shrine Do Not Heal Anyone: Imam Reza Provides the Means to Prevent Corona', 14 Esfand 1398 / 4 March 2020. Available at: https://aftabnews.ir/fa/news/639970. Accessed October 2024.

Ahlawat, A., Wiedensohler, A. and Mishra, S. K. (2020), 'An Overview on the Role of Relative Humidity in Airborne Transmission of SARS-CoV-2 in Indoor Environments'. *Aerosol Air Quality Research*, 20(9): 1856–61. https://doi.org/10.4209/aaqr.2020.06.0302

Arjomand, S. A. (1981), 'The Shiʿite Hierocracy and the State in Pre-modern Iran: 1785–1890'. *European Journal of Sociology*, 22(1): 40–78. http://doi.org/10.1017/S000397560000360X

Arjomand, S. A. (1985), 'The Clerical Estate and the Emergence of a Shiʿite Hierocracy in Safavid Iran: A Study in Historical Sociology'. *Journal of the Economic and Social History of the Orient*, 28(2): 169–219. https://doi.org/10.2307/3631858

Ashtiani, A. (1989), 'Cultural Formation on a Theocratic State: The Institutionalisation of Shiism in Safavid Iran'. *Social Compass*, 36(4): 481–92. https://doi.org/10.1177/003776889036004005

Barro, R. J, Ursúa, J. F. and Weng, J. (2020), 'The Coronavirus and the Great Influenza Pandemic: Lessons from the "Spanish Flu" for the Coronavirus's Potential Effects on Mortality and Economic Activity'. *National Bureau of Economic Research*, Working Paper 26866. https://doi.org/10.3386/w26866

Bhagat, R. K. and Linden, P. F. (2020), 'Displacement Ventilation: A Viable Ventilation Strategy for Makeshift Hospitals and Public Buildings to Contain COVID-19 and Other Airborne Diseases'. *Royal Society Open Science*, 7(9): 200680. https://doi.org/10.1098/rsos.200680

Byerly, C. R. (2005), *Fever of War: The Influenza Epidemic in the U.S. Army During World War I* (London: New York University Press).

Cherak, F. Z. (2013), 'La thérapeutique de la rouqiya entre Algérie, Egypte et France' in A. M. Moulin (ed.) *Islam et révolutions médicales* (Paris: Karthala), 297–328.

Conrad, P. and Barker, K. (2010), 'The Social Construction of Illness: Key Insights and Policy Implications'. *Journal of Health and Social Behavior*, 51(1S): 67–79. https://doi.org/10.1177/0022146510383495

Delumeau, J. (1989), *Fear in the Western World: 1300–1800* (Cambridge, MA: Harvard University Press).

Deutsche Welle. (2020), 'Coronavirus: Islamic Medicine and the Controversy of Sheikh Morteza Kohansal', *Deutsche Welle Iran*, 22 March.

Drugs.com. (2024), 'An Update: Is Hydroxychloroquine Effective for COVID-19?', 26 August. Available at: https://www.drugs.com/medical-answers/hydroxychloroquine-effective-covid-19-3536024/. Accessed October 2024.

Dube, J. E. R. (1977), *Habermas' Proposal: The Unity of Knowledge, Interest and Action.* Master's thesis, University of Winsor, Canada. Electronic Theses and Dissertations. 2260. https://scholar.uwindsor.ca/etd/2260

Ebrahimnejad, H. (2004), 'Religion and Medicine in Qajar Iran' in R. Gleave (ed.) *Religion and Society in Qajar Iran* (London: Routledge), 401–28.

Ebrahimnejad, H. (2014), *Medicine in Iran: Profession, Practice and Politics, 1800–1925* (New York: Palgrave Macmillan).

Entekhab News. (2020), 'Surprising Facts About Coronavirus Airborne Movement / Virus Movement Through Moisture', 05 Mehr 1399/26 September. Available at: https://www.entekhab.ir/fa/news/576663/. Accessed October 2024.

Entekhab News. (2022), 'MP: Preserving the System Is Even More Important Than Saving the Life of the Imam of the Time', 15 Aban 1401/6 November. Available at: https://www.entekhab.ir/fa/news/701952. Accessed October 2024.

European Medicines Agency (EMA). (2024), 'Herbal Medicinal Products', European Medical Association website, European Union. Available at: https://www.ema.europa.eu/en/human-regulatory-overview/herbal-medicinal-products.

Fars News. (2020a), 'The Most Up-to-Date Results of Cell Therapy of the Corona Patient: Coronavirus Can Deceive the Immune System', 16 September. Available at: https://farsnews.ir/FarsNews/1600238157000853122. Accessed August 2023.

Fars News. (2020b), 'Royan Research Investigates Specific Differences in Coronavirus Gene Mutations in Iranian Society', 20 September. Available at: https://farsnews.ir/ScientificAcademic/1600588374000207045. Accessed August 2024.

Fars News. (2020c), Available at: https://farsnews.ir/social/1596007493000409949 Accessed October 2024.

FDA. (2020), 'FDA Approves First Treatment for COVID-19', *Federal Food and Drug Administration*, 22 October. Available at: https://www.fda.gov/news-events/press-announcements/fda-approves-first-treatment-covid-19. Accessed October 2024.

Feng, Y., Marchal, T., Sperry, T. and Yi, H. (2020), 'Influence of Wind and Relative Humidity on the Social Distancing Effectiveness to Prevent COVID-19 Airborne Transmission: A Numerical Study'. *Journal of Aerosol Science*, 147: 105585. https://doi.org/10.1016/j.jaerosci.2020.105585

Global Data. (2024), 'Tsumura & Co – Company Profile'. Available at: https://www.globaldata.com/company-profile/tsumura-co/premium-data/clinical-trials. Accessed 12 October 2024.

Good, B. J. (1993), *Medicine, Rationality, and Experience* (Cambridge: Cambridge University Press).

Gooya News. (2023), 18 June. https://news.gooya.com/2023/06/post-76946.php. Accessed 22 June 2023.

Greenhalgh, T., Fisman, D., Cane, D. J., Oliver, M. and Macintyre, C. R. (2022), 'Adapt or Die: How the Pandemic Made the Shift from EBM to EBM+ More Urgent'. *BMJ Journals*, 27(5): 253–60. https://doi.org/10.1136/bmjebm-2022-111952

Greenhalgh, T., Jimenez, J. L., Prather, K. A., Tufekcim, Z., Fisman, D. and Schooley, R. (2021), 'Ten Scientific Reasons in Support of Airborne Transmission of SARS-CoV-2'. *Lancet*, 397(10285): 1603–5. https:/doi.org/10.1016/S0140-6736(21)00869-2

Harris, K. (2013), 'The Rise of the Subcontractor State: Politics of Pseudo-Privatization in the Islamic Republic of Iran'. *International Journal of Middle Eastern Studies*, 45(1): 45–70. https://www.jstor.org/stable/43302954

Hong, S.-P. (1989), 'Traditional Korean Medicine in the Modernisation Process: Institutional and Attitudinal Changes'. Ph.D. thesis, Iowa State University. https://doi.org/10.31274/rtd-180813-8980

Houot, S. (2013), 'La *fatwâ*, un cadre pour la bioéthique contemporaine' in A. M. Moulin (ed.) *Islam et Révolutions Médicales* (Paris: Karthala), 123–43.

Illich, I. (1975), *Medical Nemesis* (London: Calder & Boyars).

Illich, I. (1976), *Limits to Medicine. Medical Nemesis: The Expropriation of Health* (London: Penguin Books).

Iran International Newsroom. (2023), 'Iran's Claim of Quantum Processor Draws Ridicule', 8 June, updated 25 October 2024. Available at: https://www.iranintl.com/en/202306086480. Accessed October 2024.

Iran Science Watch. (2020), 'Full Response of Dr. Malekzadeh, Resigned Deputy Minister of Research at the Ministry of Health to the Statement of the Student Basij of 11 Iranian Universities of Medical Sciences', 24 November. Available at: https://www.isw.ir/47166. Accessed October 2024.

ISNA. (2021), 'The Role of Traditional Medicine in the Prevention and Treatment of Coronavirus', *Iranian Students News Agency*, 9 March. Available at: https://www.isna.ir/news/1400120906855. Accessed October 2024.

Katiboina, V. (2021), '11 Benefits and Uses of Lemon Peel', *Medicine Net*. Available at: https://www.medicinenet.com/benefits_and_uses_of_lemon_peel/article.htm. Accessed October 2024.

Khabarban. (2023), 'The Monthly Cost of Treatment of Thalassemia Patients Has Increased by 5 to 7 Million / Monopoly in Domestic Pharmaceutical Companies', 21 June. Available at: https://38038781.khabarban.com/. Accessed October 2024.

Khatami, Ayatollah S. E. (2020), '*Dars-e khârej* (External Lesson) on Coronavirus 03-02-1399', Eshia.ir. Available at: https://eshia.ir/feqh/archive/text/khatami/feqh3/98/990203/. Accessed October 2024.

Khomeini, Ayatollah (1981), 'Speech on 16 November'. Available at: https://www.aparat.com/v/f01v218. Accessed October 2024.

Kim, K.-I. (1973), 'Traditional Concept of Disease in Korea'. *Korea Journal*, 13(1): 12–18.

Kloos, S. (2017), 'The Pharmaceutical Assemblage: Rethinking Sowa Rigpa and the Herbal Pharmaceutical Industry in Asia', *Current Anthropology*, 58(6): 693–717. https://www.journals.uchicago.edu/doi/pdfplus/10.1086/693896

Kofi-Tsekpo, M. (2004), 'Institutionalization of African Traditional Medicine in Health Care Systems in Africa'. *African Journal of Health Sciences*, 11(1–2): i–ii.

Lang, A. (2019), '9 Benefits and Uses of Lemon Peel', *Healthline.com*. Available at: https://www.healthline.com/nutrition/lemon-peel. Accessed October 2024.

Magiran. (2020), 'The President at the Meeting of the Specialized Committees of the National Headquarters for Combating Coronavirus', *Magiran*. Newspaper, No. 7419 (25/05/1399). Available at: https://www.magiran.com/article/4077443

MedVoice (2023), Available at: http://medvoice.ir/1807. Accessed on 14 April 2023.

Morawska, L. and Milton, D. K. (2020), 'It Is Time to Address Airborne Transmission of Coronavirus Disease 2019 (Covid-19)'. *Clinical Infectious Diseases*, 71(9): 2311–13. https://doi.org/10.1093/cid/ciaa939

Moreno-Castro, C. Vengut-Climent, E., Cano-Orón, L. and Mendoza-Poudereux, I. (2020), 'Exploratory Study of the Hoaxes Spread via WhatsApp in Spain to Prevent and/or Cure Covid-19'. *Gaceta Sanitaria*, 35(6): 534–41. https://doi.org/10.1016/j.gaceta.2020.07.008

Moulin, A. M. (2016), 'Book Review: *The Herbal Pharmaceutical Industry in India: Drug Reformulation and the Market*. Sous la direction de Jean-Paul Gaudillière et Laurent Pordié'. *Medical Science*, 32(10): 895–7. https://doi.org/10.1051/medsci/20163210024

Moulin, A. M. (2023), *La vie avec les virus* (Paris: Presses Universitaire de France).

Nandy, A. and Visvanathan, S. (1990), 'Modern Medicine and Its Non-Modern Critics: A Study in Discourse' in F. A. Marglin and S. A. Marglin (eds) *Dominating Knowledge: Development, Culture, and Resistance* (Oxford: Oxford University Press), 145–84.

Negahban, A., Maleki, M. and Abbassian, A. (2019), 'Policies and Laws Related to the Integration of Traditional and Complementary Medicine into the Iranian Health System Based on the WHO Definition: A Document Analysis'. *Journal of Education and Health Promotion*, 29(8): 221. https://doi.org/10.4103/jehp.jehp_321_19

Nicolussi, S., Drewe, J., Butterweck, V. and Meyer Zu Schwabedissen, H. E. (2020), 'Clinical Relevance of St. John's Wort Drug Interactions Revisited'. *British Journal of Pharmacology*, 177(6): 1212–26. https://doi.org/10.1111/bph.14936

Nutton, V. (2021), 'Epidemic Disease in a Humoral Environment: From Airs, Waters and Places to the Renaissance' in C. Thumiger (ed.) *Holism in Ancient Medicine and Its Reception* (Leiden: Brill), 357–76.

Parveen, A., Parveen, B., Parveen, R. and Ahmad, S. (2015), 'Challenges and Guidelines for Clinical Trial of Herbal Drugs'. *Journal of Pharmacy & Bioallied Sciences*, 7(4): 329–33. https://doi.org/10.4103/0975-7406.168035

Rillo, A. G. and Carrillo, B. E. M. (2023), 'Elements to Understand the Epistemology of Medicine'. *International Journal of Humanities and Social Science Invention*, 12(2): 3–14. https://www.ijhssi.org/papers/vol12(2)/B12020314.pdf

Sadat, S. M. M. (2022), *Mas'uliyatha-ye feqhi-ye dowlat va masuliyatha-ye madani-ye madrom dar dowran-e korona* (Legal responsibilities of the state and civil duties of people during corona), 05 Bahman 1400/25 January 2022: 8.

Shirâzi, M. M.-T. (1831), *Tâ'uniya (On Plague)*, in Arabic, lithograph, Majles Library, Tehran. 1264.

Singh, B., Ryan, H., Kredo, T., Chaplin, M. and Fletcher, T. (2021), 'Review of Hydroxychloroquine'. Available at: https://www.cochrane.org/fa/CD013587/. Accessed October 2024.

Singh, S. and Shuka, V. K. (2021), 'Current Regulations for Herbal Medicine in India'. *International Journal of Drug Regulatory Affairs*, 9(2): 30–4. https://doi.org/10.22270/ijdra.v9i2.466

Smedley, T. (2015), 'Big Pharma Attempts to Cast Off Bad Reputation by Targeting the Poor', *Guardian*, 25 June. Available at: https://www.theguardian.com/sustainable-business/2015/jun/25/big-pharma-attempts-to-cast-off-bad-reputation-by-targeting-the-poor. Accessed 17 December 2023.

Snowden, F. (2019), *Epidemics and Society: From the Black Death to the Present* (London: Yale University Press).

Tasnim News. (2020a), 'What Is the Reason for the Public Opposition to Traditional Medicine by Some Officials of the Ministry of Health?!' 3 October. Available at: https://www.tasnimnews.com/fa/news/1399/07/12/2361548. Accessed October 2024.

Tasnim News. (2020b), 'Report// The Mortality Rate of "Corona Patients" in the Field of "Traditional Medicine" Has Been Close to Zero!' 14 October. Available at: https://www.tasnimnews.com/fa/news/1399/07/23/2369250. Accessed October 2024.

Tasnim News. (2021a), 'Mr. Secretary! How Is It Possible to Promote and Develop Traditional Medicine Demanded by Leadership with a "Near-Zero Budget"!?!' 25 January. Available at: https://www.tasnimnews.com/fa/news/1399/11/06/2439588. Accessed October 2024.

Tasnim News. (2021b), 'Video// Prevention and Treatment of More Than 200 Diseases Through "Cupping"', 4 Khordad 1400 / June 2021. Available at: https://www.tasnimnews.com/fa/news/1400/03/04/2509314. Accessed October 2024.

Tasnim News. (2021c), 'Strengthening the Immune System During the Corona Period Using "Cupping and Cupping" + Nutritional Instructions', 30 January. https://www.tasnimnews.com/fa/news/1399/11/10/2440149. Accessed October 2024.

Tasnim, S., Hussain, M. M. and Mazumder, H. (2020), 'Impact of Rumors and Misinformation on COVID-19 in Social Media'. *Journal of Preventive Medicine and Public Health*, 53(3): 171–4. https://doi.org/10.3961/jpmph.20.094

Vraga, E. K. and Bode, L. (2017), 'Using Expert Sources to Correct Health Misinformation in Social Media'. *Science Communication*, 39(5): 621–45. https://doi.org/10.1177/1075547017731776

Vraga, E. K., Bode, L. and Tully, M. (2020), 'Creating News Literacy Messages to Enhance Expert Corrections of Misinformation on Twitter'. *Communication Research*, 49(2): 245–67. https://doi.org/10.1177/0093650219898094

World Health Organization (WHO). (2001), *Legal Status of Traditional Medicine and Complementary/Alternative Medicine: A Worldwide Review*, WHO/EDM/TRM/2001.2 (Geneva: World Health Organization). https://www.who.int/publications/i/item/WHO-EDM-TRM-2001.2. Accessed October 2024.

World Health Organization (WHO). (2019), *WHO Global Report on Traditional and Complementary Medicine, 2019* (Geneva: World Health Organization). Available at: https://iris.who.int/bitstream/handle/10665/312342/9789241515436. Accessed October 2024.

Zhao, X. Liu, S., Yin, Y., Zhang, T. and Chen, Q. (2022), 'Airborne Transmission of COVID-19 Virus in Enclosed Spaces: An Overview of Research Methods'. *Indoor Air*, 32(6). https://doi.org/10.1111/ina.13056

Part IV

Pragmatic Complementarity: Healing and Marginalised Epistemologies

MANY OF THE chapters in this volume contain studies of communities that integrate traditional and biomedical healing. Such pragmatism is often underpinned by rational choices that are seamlessly blended through the lived knowledge of multiple epistemes.

These three chapters provide compelling accounts of the multiple beliefs, experiences and forms of healing that can unfold for particular communities. Whether it is combining prayer with professional nursing practice (Ugba, Chapter 7), experiencing material-medical and other-dimensional healing in overlapping space–time dimensions within the context of hospital treatment (Bahia, Chapter 9) or the Korean state's support of *musok* practitioners to clear ancestor spirits to improve public order (Sarfati, Chapter 9), these case studies all demonstrate the capacity for religious subjects to effect pragmatic epistemic approaches to healthcare in which religio-culture and biomedical beliefs are seen as mutually supportive to the healing process.

7

Pentecostal Africans and Remaking of Divine Healing in 'Secular' Britain

ABEL UGBA

Introduction

MIGRATION, ESPECIALLY ACROSS international borders, exposes individuals to different cultures, languages and social norms, which can lead to an epistemological turn or significant shifts in their epistemological frameworks. This transformation extends beyond acquiring new information in a new migration context to a profound and challenging re-evaluation of one's beliefs, values and epistemic frames (Oliveira, Nada and Magalhães 2023). This transformative process provides migrants with new insights that challenge their pre existing values and notions of knowledge and practice. Moreover, the migration experience can also highlight issues of epistemic injustice (Fricker 2007), where the knowledge and experiences of migrants are often marginalised or devalued in their new contexts. This can trigger a critical reflection on power dynamics and the politics of knowledge, further contributing to an epistemological turn or awakening. This chapter focuses on Pentecostal Africans and critically assesses the nuanced ways and extent to which their migration context in Britain has transformed their divine healing epistemic frames and practices.

Migration and religion

Migration and religion are intertwined in countless, complex and consequential ways. For example, religious persecution and missionary activism have long been identified as major 'push' factors in international migration (Carling 2002; Gozdziak and Shandy 2002; Fiddian-Qasmiyeh *et al.* 2014). Religious ideologies have not only informed migration decisions and directions, but they have also impacted the acculturation of immigrants and shaped their aspirations in the migration destination (Mella 1994; Haar 1998; Ugba 2009; Adogame 2013; Vásquez and Dewind 2014).

Proceedings of the British Academy, **278**, 141–159, © Authors 2025.

The migration stories of believers often affirm their faith-inspired understanding of social realities, and they are reflected in their everyday religious activities. Their desires and challenges are threaded into their prayers, while their songs express the joys and triumphs of their journey. Although research on the interfaces between religion and migration has gained traction in recent decades, less attention has been paid to the challenges of remaking healing beliefs and rituals in an immigration context, and against the backdrop of a global pandemic. This analysis of the divine healing practices of Pentecostal Africans adds to the growing body of research (e.g. Hagan and Ebaugh 2003; Hagan 2008; Córdova and Dias 2021) that seeks to fill this lacuna.

In this chapter, I argue that divine healing as practised by Pentecostal Africans is rooted in a scripturally informed epistemology of illness and health that links effects and outcomes to spiritual causations and interprets healing more expansively and holistically to include spiritual salvation. By focusing on the substance of Pentecostalism and everyday immigrant religious practices, this chapter elevates an under-researched dimension of the study of African transnational Pentecostalism and highlights the pertinent interfaces between two distinct illness and health epistemologies. Relying on the self-construction and interpretations of the research participants, I discuss the dynamics and implications of mixing two distinct healthcare epistemes, as well as the innovative delineation of 'safe' spaces in secular and unconducive terrains to perform divine healing. My conclusions complexify narratives about illness and healing and invite the readers to look critically and beyond the dominant Western biomedical healing episteme.

Empirical data collection

The empirical data that informs the analysis in this chapter was obtained through in-depth semi-structured interviews with 12 members and officials of two Pentecostal churches in London, as well as direct observation of worship meetings and healing sessions.[1] All the interviews were conducted in English (with a mixture of pidgin in one case) in the church premises and home of one of the pastors. All interviews were conducted and transcribed by this author and a research assistant, a Ph.D. student who also served as the link between the author and the churches. Founded by immigrants from Ghana, the two churches each hosted about 120 worshippers on Sundays before the Covid-19 pandemic. They also held two mid-week meetings, which were mostly dedicated to teaching doctrines and, in one church, performing healing. Post-Covid, in-person meeting attendance decreased while the number and

[1] The visits to the churches and most of the interviews took place in the summer and autumn of 2019 as part of a larger project sponsored by the US-based John Templeton Foundation and Calvin College. Follow-up interviews were conducted with the leaders of the two churches in the summer of 2024 to discuss their Covid-19 and post-pandemic experience and those of their church members.

types of online mid-week meetings increased dramatically – five days a week in one church. The churches are led and mostly populated by educated and professional people, many of whom migrated from Ghana or have ancestral links to the country. In this chapter, the narratives of a few interviewees are prioritised as key stories (Chase 2005) because they capture the major themes that emerged from all the interviews. However, views from the other participants are interjected where they enrich, interrogate or problematise the key stories.

The next section begins with a concise explanation of divine healing as a scripturally informed health and wellbeing episteme that fits within the wide spectrum of non-medical complementary healthcare practices. This is followed by an abridged history of African-led Pentecostalism in Britain and a concise analysis of selected sociopolitical and legal developments that have impacted the Bible-informed episteme and healing practice of Pentecostal Africans in Britain. The section before the conclusion analyses some of the innovative healing practices that have enabled African Pentecostals to actualise divine healing in ways that acknowledge but also subvert the norms of secularism. It references Covid-19 as a public health emergency that has challenged as well as reinforced the divine healing beliefs of Pentecostal Africans. The conclusion reaffirms the sociological significance of the arguments in this chapter and their contribution to extant analyses of the everyday religiosity of African transnational migrants.

Divine healing

Pentecostalism's Bible-based healing epistemic frame expresses a dialectical relationship between the physical world and a spiritual one, where what happens in one triggers a reaction in the other. It affirms the willingness and capability of a supermundane being to rid believers of ailments (or supply the fortitude to bear them) and meet their psychological, material and spiritual needs. Several participants in the research for this chapter cite verses and instances from the Bible, including the healing miracles of Jesus and the apostles, to buttress their claims that illness is not merely a physiological phenomenon but also a spiritual one that is linked to sin, bad spirits, faithlessness and so on. Although healing is transmitted invisibly to the recipient, it is sought through prayer, laying on of hands, fasting and periodic abstinence from indulgences. In this epistemology of health and healing, healing is procured and confirmed not solely through empirical observation or scientific inquiry but also from religious experience and scriptural interpretation and the self-confession of the healing recipient. For many Pentecostals, this epistemic stance translates, in practice, into a dual approach to healthcare, where medical options are accepted but always assessed through the lens of faith and spiritual discernment, as this view by a female pastor demonstrates:

> If they go to the doctor and get medication, take it and get well, I believe it is still God that brought them healing by giving them the wisdom to know what medication to use

> for that ailment. The guy who produces the antibiotics, I don't know if he believes in Christ or not, but I think he got the knowledge from somewhere, from God. I believe that God caused the healing even if the person who is taking the medicine and the maker of the antibiotic do not believe it.

Divine healing is a core doctrine that unifies and identifies most Pentecostals although variations of it have been embraced by Catholics, especially those in the charismatic movement, and some mainstream protestant denominations (McGuire 1982; Csordas 1997). Given the centrality of healing to Pentecostalism, Cox (2011: xviii) asserts that 'healing practices are not only integral, but they often serve as the threshold through which new recruits pass into other dimensions of the movement', while Brown (2011: 8) argues that 'the primary appeal of Pentecostalism worldwide is as a religion of healing'. However, the mainstream Christianity that was diffused from the West to Africa and other parts of the world affirms its distinction from other permutations of Christianity, including African-led Pentecostalism, by prioritising Western values and epistemes, including the biomedical illness and healing framework. For some Pentecostals, the biomedical framework is limiting, not least because it does not lead to holistic healing and spiritual restoration. Spiritual salvation and physical healing, they claim, are among the entitlements restored to believers through the sacrificial death of Jesus Christ that erased the consequences of the Adamic sin, as this response by a female church leader confirms:

> I also believe that there are other areas of life that also need attention. The salvation of the soul is key. In the Bible, when the lepers were healed, only one of them came back to give thanks, and Jesus added to him that aspect of salvation. That's what I mean. Yes, there is that physical healing, but there is another element without which the healing process is incomplete.

Pentecostals are quick to cite direct personal or group experiences of healing, witnessing the healing of others or performing healing as proof that divine healing is a present-day reality and not simply confined to the pages of the Bible. As the pastor of one of the churches covered by this study puts it: 'I believe God can cure every sickness. In Malachi 3:6 it says I am the Lord I do not lie, in Hebrews 13:8 it says God is the same yesterday, today and forever.' Although this chapter focuses on Pentecostal Africans, divine healing has also been a key component of the beliefs and practices of indigenous British Pentecostal groups (Hollenweger 1997; Anderson 2004; Warrington 2005). Their healing practices, also inspired by biblical texts and precedents (Hunt 1998; Cartledge 2006; Kay 2007), share several similar characteristics with those of Pentecostal Africans. For example, participants in my research and subscribers to divine healing among the indigenous British Pentecostal groups consider divine healing superior to other healing options because it transcends physical and emotional healing to include spiritual salvation and wholeness. In the words of a female research participant:

> … the medicine that they give them can supress the issues, but it may not deal with them completely. And at times, when they give those medicines, they have side

> effects. So, to be honest, these medications are not faultless. You will need divine healing to be healed completely.

For a long time, secular analysts and writers derided divine healing as trickery and the indulgence of poor or uneducated zealots with little knowledge of, and poor access to, orthodox medical care. But Brown (2011: 8) critiques that interpretation, stating that the advancement of divine healing has been unabated 'even where biomedical science is most sophisticated, convenient, and affordable'. Divine healing practice by Pentecostals in sub-Saharan African countries such as Nigeria and Ghana has incorporated ideologies from African indigenous religions that ascribe illness and lack of general wellbeing to the machinations of witches, demons and aggrieved ancestors (Asamoah-Gyadu 2015b). By embedding the notion of witchcraft into its epistemology of illness, Pentecostalism has resonated more convincingly for Africans as a belief system that holds the solution to their quest for protection against material and spiritual adversities and adversaries. According to Kalu (2008), deliverance ministry involving exorcism and spiritual warfare against demonic forces is a significant feature of African Pentecostalism that indicates a contextualised response to traditional African beliefs about spiritual causation of material or bodily problems. Kalu's views cohere with Anderson's (2001) proposition that African Pentecostalism incorporates elements of indigenous African religious practices, including belief in spirits, witchcraft and symbolic rituals.

However, commitment to and approaches to healing vary among Pentecostals in sub-Saharan Africa and the African diaspora. For example, mainstream Pentecostal groups with strong connections to the version of Pentecostalism that spread from the US since the Azusa Street Revival (Bartleman 1980; Synan 1997) have often repudiated any links to African spiritistic practices, which they describe as the work of darkness. But some Pentecostal-like groups in West Africa, such as the Aladura movement and Christ Apostolic Church, which have their roots and nurturing in Africa, have tended to showcase a stronger commitment to African spirituality and ways of worship. However, despite these diverse approaches to divine healing, the African Pentecostal movement is unified by dynamic and expressive worship styles (Asamoah-Gyadu 2013), a strong commitment to community development and social transformation (Adogame 2016) and emphasis on the prosperity gospel (Gifford 2004).

Although Pentecostal Africans in Britain often conceptualise divine healing as superior to, and distinct from, other approaches, including the biomedical framework of the National Health Service (NHS), their healing beliefs and practices share many characteristics with, and can be categorised among the repertoires of, unorthodox and non-medical approaches that come under the broad category of 'alternative' or 'complementary' healing. The rich and diverse alternative healing landscape in Britain has included New Age philosophies and movements (Heelas 2008). The minority and 'complementary' status of divine healing and New Age movements, coupled with their epistemological estrangement from each other and from the mainstream biomedical framework, marks another layer of similarity between these alternative illness and healing frameworks. For example, some features of New Age spirituality that Heelas (2008) describes are discernible in the ideologies and practices of Pentecostal Africans in Britain. His suggestion that New Age teachings and practices locate spirituality within the depths of life (2008: 25) could be appropriated as an analytical frame to understand the attachment to Pentecostal ideologies by African immigrants in Britain. Moreover, the New Age movement's emphasis on the subjective experience of spiritual renewal echoes the claim by Pentecostals that spiritual rebirth, a major marker of the entry into Pentecostalism, is a subjective and internal experience. The two healing frameworks are examples of alternative health and wellbeing approaches that co-exist, contrast and compete with the dominant biomedical NHS framework in 21st-century Britain.

African-led Pentecostalism in Britain

African-led Pentecostal groups in Britain are generally categorised among the Black Majority Christianity (BMC) groups (Kalilombe 1997). BMC describes the dynamic presence of African and Caribbean Christian communities in the British religious landscape. This phenomenon gained prominence during the post-World War II period, and it was accelerated by the arrival of the Windrush generation and waves of migrations from the Commonwealth (Hunt and Lightly 2001). Vibrant worship styles, charismatic theology and strong community orientation are some of the characteristics of BMC. Their rise and entrenchment in Britain have diversified Christianity in the UK, leading Beckford (2000) to conclude that BMC churches challenge traditional British religious institutions and contribute to the reconfiguring of religious and cultural identities. Similarly, Rogers (2020) emphasises the significant role of these churches in urban regeneration and community development.

BMC churches range from large and affluent congregations that meet in ultra-modern auditoriums and are led by upwardly mobile leaders to much smaller groups that meet in front stalls, residential places and rented school halls (Burgess 2009; Olofinjana 2010; Adedibu 2012). They are a mix of mainstream Protestants who stick closer to traditional doctrines and practices that emanated from the Reformation (Noll 1994; Marsden 2006), classical Pentecostals and a plethora of African Indigenous Churches that have purposefully prioritised elements of African culture as their way of reinterpreting and resisting the heavily Westernised Christianity that the missionaries introduced to Africa centuries ago. Although these churches are differentiated by size, worship methods, doctrines and transnational links, they are unified by 'their self-proclaimed or ascribed Christian minority status and their common struggle to establish a place and a voice in the British society' (Ugba 2014: 65).

In the past 50 years, the numbers and characteristics of these churches have changed, reflecting the dynamics of migration to Britain. A 2015 report by the

Cambridge-based Woolf Institute identified 'a shift away from mainstream denominations and a growth in evangelical and Pentecostal churches' as a major trait of the changes in Britain's Christianity landscape in recent decades (Woolf Institute 2015). London, the location of the two churches that were investigated for this chapter, is characterised by what Vertovec (2007: 1024) has described as 'super-diversity', a city where 'increased numbers of new, small and scattered, multiple-origin, transnationally connected, socio-economically differentiated and legally stratified immigrants' cohabit. Pentecostals are among the largest and fastest-growing BMC churches, and they are more concentrated in London than in any other part of Britain. More churches and groups have, in recent years, been established by church leaders with a self-proclaimed mission to reverse the decline of Christianity in the West while simultaneously staking a claim in the global spiritual marketplace (Adogame 2013). Although the concept of 'reverse mission' has been subjected to much scrutiny and contestation (Kalu 2005; Kim and Kim 2008; Adogame 2013), most interpretations agree it describes the initiatives and quests by missionaries from former mission regions, such as Africa, Asia and South America, to revitalise and spread Christianity in the West.

The bulk of extant research (e.g. Hunt 2002; Gerloff 2004; Burgess 2009; Adogame 2013; Adedibu 2016) has focused on megachurches, for example, the Redeemed Christian Church of God (RCCG). Notable exceptions to this focus on the megachurches are Krause's work (Krause 2014) on Ghanaian Pentecostals and Fesenmyer's research (Fesenmyer 2020, 2019) on Kenyan Pentecostals. My research has focused on smaller groups to broaden, enrich and complexify existing theorisations of African-led Pentecostalism in Britain. Although divine healing in the megachurches and smaller ones is grounded in the same scripturally based epistemology of health and wellbeing, the actualisation of healing is differentiated and conditioned by local circumstances and the makeup of individual churches. The next section analyses the dynamics, challenges and innovations of actualising divine healing in secular and unreceptive spaces.

Divine healing in a secular context: conformity mixed with subversion

African Pentecostals' epistemology and practice of divine healing are rooted in specific Bible passages, as is shown in this response by a male pastor to a question about the authenticity of healing:

> I believe in divine healing. Oh yes, absolutely. I derived the belief from what the word of God says in Exodus 15:26 that 'I am the lord that healeth thee'. And one thing that I know about the word of God is that God doesn't lie; if he says I am the lord that healeth thee, I know he will.

While the long-term impact of Covid-19 on their attachment to divine healing will take longer to ascertain, the global pandemic has, without doubt, provoked critical reflections about new approaches to healing. The two pastors admitted that several church members, members of their family and they themselves had been infected with the virus. Some became seriously ill, and a few were hospitalised, but there were no casualties. Close relatives of some church members in the UK and outside of it died from Covid-19 complications. One pastor left all behavioural and treatment decisions about Covid-19 to individual church members, while the other actively encouraged members to avail of the vaccinations but also to rely on God for healing. As the latter explained: 'God will do his part, but we must do our part. In as much as we are praying, we must also look after ourselves. We prayed, which is important, but we also looked after ourselves.'

For him, 'looking after ourselves' included healthier diets and organised group light physical exercise in parks for church members. The group walks and exercise in the parks have continued even after Covid-19: 'Even today, we went to the park to exercise. In the past, we went to the beach for picnic but today we went to the park. It's only a small thing, but it helps.'

Both churches have been rebuilding organisationally and spiritually since the heights of Covid-19. In-person attendance has dwindled and the faith of members whose relatives died from the virus has suffered. Still, one of the pastors saw the pandemic as a sign of the end times that has tested and refined believers: 'COVID-19 has tested the commitment of worshippers. It has refined and purified believers. The non-rooted have deviated, but the faith of the rooted have been purified and made stronger.' The divergent approach to healing during Covid-19 mirrors the diverse explanations of divine healing generally. Both are unified by the emphasis they all put on divine healing's efficacy and desirability, even in a context where good medical care is widely accessible through the NHS. As a female church leader put it:

> … I don't think there is any sickness that only the NHS will be good enough for. You could have some cures without the NHS, but I don't think it is possible the other way around … If they give you a drug, pray over it. They can't do it, but God can.

The male pastor of one of the two churches, while affirming the necessity for, and superiority of, divine healing in the British context, cautioned against repudiating biomedicine – a view that is not uncommon in the long-running discourse about Pentecostals' relationship with modern medicine (Poloma 2003; Brown 2011; Lindhardt 2011). He advocated a middle-of-the-road position akin to the views of most participants:

> I don't allow my beliefs to override my belief in the use of medicine. In their use of medicines, God can also heal them … medicine will heal but there will be side effects. With divine healing, they will never find any traces that you've suffered from the sickness in the past. That is how I think divine healing should be seen – as overriding medical healing.

The unreceptive environment in general, but especially in the workplace, has motivated Pentecostal Africans to actualise divine healing in ways that simultaneously conform with and subvert the norms of secularism, as this narration by a female research participant and a nurse in an NHS hospital, reveals:

> In the hospital, not that I pray aloud. We've got a chapel and other things. I don't wait to get to the chapel. When I go to change my dress, I sit down in my changing room and say a word of prayer that God himself should heal. We are there to help. He's given us the wisdom to give medication or to care for the patients, but only God heals. We care but God heals. When I am in charge of the ward, I ask him (God) to take over. I ask the Holy Spirit to take control, for I don't have that power.

By carving out a 'safe place' on the premises of an NHS hospital to engage in divine healing, the respondent confronts and subverts secularist norms and biomedical standards that assume that such religious actions are undesirable, especially in an NHS hospital environment. Also, her action exemplifies the adaptation of a religious ritual in an immigration context. At the hospital in Ghana where she had worked, hospital staff routinely gathered for prayer at the start of their shift in an open show of religious devotion, as she explained:

> I was a nurse in Ghana before coming here. And every morning before we start, we pray together, and that is in the open. We thank God and commit the operations into God's hand, for him to come and take over because he is the healer ... here you can't do that. I remember in the news at one hospital one nurse went to pray for a patient, and she was sacked. She prayed for the patient before the surgery, and she was sacked! In this country you can't pray for individual patients, otherwise, you'll be in trouble ... I pray for them in my head before I do something, that God himself should touch them. Though they don't believe, he (God) says he loves them.

The prayers in the hospital in Ghana were longer, communal and more interactive, and they sometimes included exhortations from the scriptures. Although the adaptation of the divine healing ritual at the hospital in London is streamlined and devoid of embellishments, it nonetheless appears to meet the needs of the adherent. However, it raises questions about the authenticity of healing rituals in a diaspora context. For example, how authentic is a divine healing experience that circumvents some of the normative rituals when it is adapted to a new and unwelcoming environment such as a hospital ward?

Another incident narrated by the same participant confirms that her faith-inspired actions go beyond praying for the patients in her head. The following is her account:

> I have been in that hospital for about 11 years, but it was only one patient who asked me to pray for her. We drew the curtains and prayed. Because in this country, their law is so different, if you are doing something that will affect the next person, they can charge you. She had her Bible, and she called me, and said, 'sister, are you a Christian, can you pray for me before I go into the surgery?' So, I prayed for her and told her that the Lord will take her in and bring her back. Yeah, He did. She was discharged.

In this instance, the act of drawing the curtains symbolised the delineation of a 'safe' space where the African Pentecostal believer could 'perform' healing in a way that accords with her religious conviction. But this 'space' simultaneously symbolises the contest and 'confrontation' between two epistemes of healing in 21st-century Britain. Given that the participant had earlier referenced a media report about a nurse who was sacked for performing a similar religious act, her action could be interpreted as a religiously inspired but wilful and risk-laden defiance of the hegemonic and normative secular biomedical episteme of healthcare provision. Beyond demonstrating the deep-rooted nature of a religious ideology, the healing act confirms the resilience of African Pentecostal practices in less faith-friendly contexts in the West. It also showcases the flexibility and adaptability of Pentecostal healing rituals that have enabled it to co-exist with modern medicine, a point further emphasised in the following narratives about fasting, a key component of Pentecostal healing.

Acutely aware of well-publicised cases where church leaders have been accused of decreeing fasting for members that resulted in starvation and deaths, the pastor of one church, in the account below, articulated how he adapted the fasting rituals:

> I don't believe that fasting should be the prescription for every sickness even though it could be necessary for some instances. We do fast once a week, every Wednesday from 6 to 6, but to those who cannot do 6 to 6, I encourage them to start after 12. I encourage them to drink hot water while they're fasting and the idea is that it flushes and cleanses the system … part of divine healing is to exercise, go to the gym, don't eat too late.

By canvassing a semi or mini-fast and proffering alternative routes to good health, the pastor demonstrated the adaptability of healing rituals in an immigration context, and he strived to conform divine healing practices to societal norms while simultaneously subverting those norms. It is a path that is trodden by others as the following narration by another church leader confirms:

> We looked at the importance of health, why we should keep fit … And we looked at the various ways to get fit, the various sources of help, which of course now includes divine healing in addition to orthodox healing. You don't have to wait till you get sick to start living a healthy life … We looked at the need to exercise, to sleep well, to eat well. In fact, I suggested that they have vitamin supplements (A, D, C, and now we have E), because as ministers, sometimes we don't really have the time to eat well.

In the next section, I discuss the sociocultural and political contexts in Britain that have framed and arguably constrained the Bible-informed episteme of healing by African Pentecostals, focusing specifically on the climate of religious (un)freedom of worship and the passive hostility towards religiosity and public piety.

The religious 'other' in Britain

The empirical data and narratives of the research participants presented above demonstrate that although religious freedom is protected in Britain, religious minorities – especially the religiously devout – often find themselves in an environment that is less than conducive to public expressions of faith. While the right to freedom of religion and belief is enshrined in the Human Rights Act of 1998, which is based on the European Convention on Human Rights (2010), and anti-discrimination laws such as the Equality Act 2010 aim to prevent overt religious discrimination, these protections are increasingly challenged by the general anti-faith environment. The right to profess a religion may be absolute in contemporary Britain, but the right to manifest religious beliefs, for instance through religious clothing or public religious acts, is conditional and can be restricted if it is seen to interfere with the rights of others. This, according to my research participants, has led to a complex environment where African Pentecostals have encountered hostility for practising their faith publicly.

Several factors contribute to this situation, including contested exemptions within anti-discrimination laws that create a sense of 'unfreedom' for religious practitioners. Moreover, the media's portrayal of certain religious groups, particularly minority Christian groups and non-Christian religions, often fosters an anti-religious atmosphere (see Ugba 2014). Pro-secularist campaigns and nationalist sentiments also play a significant role in creating resistance to religious ideologies that deviate from the country's dominant Christian traditions.

Britain's religious landscape has undergone significant changes in recent decades. Scholars and commentators have highlighted two main trends: a steady rise in secularism, resulting in a decline in religiosity, and the increased presence of imported religions, including African-led Pentecostalism. A British Social Attitudes (BSA) report authored by Curtice *et al.* (2019: 5) confirmed that minority faiths such as African-led Pentecostalism have been growing, largely due to migration from regions such as South Asia, the Caribbean and West Africa, where religious ideologies and cultures are still deeply rooted. This shift has been paralleled by a sharp decline in the proportion of Anglicans, from 40 per cent in 1983 to around 17 per cent in 2014, and a similar drop in Roman Catholic numbers. Secularism tends to be more pronounced in urban areas. The BSA report reinforces the idea that Britain is moving away from religious identity, belief and observance. In 1983, two-thirds of the population identified as Christian, but by 2019 this figure had dropped to 38 per cent, with more than half of Britons (52 per cent) claiming no religious affiliation (Curtice *et al.* 2019: 5). This trend is generational, with each successive cohort being less likely to identify as religious. Non-religious parents, for example, are almost guaranteed to pass on their secular worldview to their children, whereas religious parents have only a 50 per cent chance of doing so (Curtice *et al.* 2019: 4). The Covid-19 pandemic, rather than driving people back to faith, had little impact on religious sentiment in the UK. A 2020 YouGov survey, though conducted at the height of the pandemic, found that over half of Britons remained non-religious during the pandemic, the highest proportion among the 14 countries surveyed (YouGov 2020).

Religion has not vanished from Britain, but the evidence seems to confirm its accelerated marginalisation in the public sphere. This development compels a critical reflection on secularisation theories that have long predicted religion's retreat in the modern world (Casanova 2011). I argue that the present developments in the religious landscape in Britain do not necessarily confirm the secularisation theory because despite the ascent of secularism, debates about faith and the role of religion in society persist. This, in my view, confirms the continued relevance and even influence of religion and religious actors and their healing epistemes. A more nuanced conceptualisation of secularisation is needed to enhance its usefulness as a concept for explaining the complexities of religious belonging and un-belonging in the 21st century. In this regard, Casanova (2011: 73) rightly called for 'a much more open analysis of non-Western civilizational dynamics' that is 'more critical of our Western Christian secular categories, in order to expand our understandings of the secular and secularisms'. The persistence of religious minorities like African Pentecostals in secular contexts such as Britain and other places in the West highlights the significance of a more critical re-evaluation of the concept of secularism, particularly its contextual or localised attributes. Although the number of Pentecostal groups in Britain is relatively small, their growth, fuelled primarily by immigration and descendants of immigrants, presents a challenge to the secularisation thesis. However, Bruce has argued that the periodic resurgences of Christianity in the last century, including the rapid growth of the worldwide Pentecostal movement, have not altered the progress of secularisation because these developments have 'failed to make even a small dent in the growing numbers of people free from any organized religious interest' (Bruce 2010: 138).

The contentions about secularisation aside, the presence of African Pentecostals in Britain, without a doubt, demonstrates how religious minorities navigate an environment that is hostile to public expressions of faith. Despite the legal framework that purports to protect religious freedom, Pentecostal groups often encounter both direct and indirect discrimination (Brener 2010). For example, workplace anti-discrimination laws are supposed to ensure equal treatment for people of all faiths, but in practice, religious accommodations are often overlooked. The European Court of Human Rights has been reluctant to recognise religious accommodation as a fundamental right, dismissing claims of indirect discrimination against faith practitioners (Henrard 2016).

High-profile court cases involving Christians who refused to perform actions that contradict their beliefs have further exposed the tensions between secular values and religious freedoms in contemporary Britain. Cases such as that of Lilian Ladele, a registrar who refused to conduct same-sex civil partnerships, and the guesthouse owners who refused to accommodate a gay couple have polarised public opinion (Guardian 2008; BBC 2013). These incidents, coupled with a rise in secularist activism, underline the difficulties faced by religious minorities like African Pentecostals. They are often compelled to navigate a public sphere where secularism is increasingly the default mode, and public displays of faith are met with scepticism or outright opposition.

African Pentecostals face unique challenges in this secularising context. As a relatively small religious community, they are often subject to indirect discrimination and bias, which are difficult to address through existing anti-discrimination laws. Despite these challenges, they continue to practise their faith and maintain their religious obligations. Their persistence represents a test case for theories of de-secularisation (Casanova 2011), as their presence in Britain adds complexity to the debate about religion's role in modern secular societies generally. African-led Pentecostalism in contemporary Britain exemplifies the struggle of religious minorities to maintain their beliefs and practices in the face of growing secularism and societal resistance.

Conclusion

This critical analysis confirms that divine healing ideologies and actions among Pentecostal Africans in Britain are vivacious and entrenched, and they are constantly and continuously being remade in ways that emphasise their resilience and adaptability. Based on an analysis of secondary quantitative data, Massey and Higgins (2011: 1) conclude that 'immigration is a disruptive event that alienates immigrants from religious practice rather than "theologizing" them'. Similarly, Beckford (2019) acknowledges that immigration can offer an escape from religion for some migrants. These views neither capture nor explain the experiences of Pentecostal African immigrants in Britain. From relatively small communities in the 1960s and 1970s, they have transformed into dynamic and larger entities that are increasingly socially and culturally relevant in Britain. Their phenomenal growth and expansive and multidimensional practices remain one of the most significant changes in the religious landscape in Britain in recent decades. Their ranks have been repeatedly renewed and enriched by successive waves of migration and the enlistment of children of first, second and third immigrant generations.

African Pentecostalism is being impacted in the migration contexts in Britain just as the religion itself, to some degree and in ways that are sometimes not obvious, is impacting British society. The healing practices of Pentecostal Africans highlight the creative and innovative adaptation of religious rituals to meet the physical, spiritual and emotional needs of believers – maintaining essential elements of this healing episteme – in an immigration context. Significantly, the creative adaptation of healing rituals is accomplished in ways that conform with, and simultaneously subvert, the norms of a secular society. This finding illuminates the challenges and complexities of transforming, transmitting and disseminating African Pentecostal ideologies and scripturally inspired illness and healing epistemology in a global world. The approach of Pentecostal Africans to illness and healing complements and challenges the biomedical framework of the NHS, raising the potential for conflicts but also enriching and diversifying public health ideologies and practice in Britain. The *Fair for All – Religion and Belief Matter* resources published by NHS Scotland in 2018 amount to official recognition of the challenges and possibilities in public health policies and delivery.[2] The analysis of the everyday practices of Pentecostal Africans confirms a dual approach to healing that sometimes brings together two seemingly parallel epistemes of healthcare.

Whereas mainstream and 'national' religions in the West appear to have made their peace with secularism and the resultant decimation of religiosity in the public sphere (Calhoun 2016), minority and 'fundamentalist' religions – characterised by a strict adherence to traditional doctrinal interpretations and resistance to modernist and liberal theological changes (Marty 1991; Almond, Appleby and Sivan 2003) – appear to be the last bastions against the dominance of secularism. Scholarly and media focus has so far prioritised the dramatic and sometimes violent actions of minority religions that have wittingly or unwittingly highlighted the conflict and collision between faith and secularism. The arguments in this chapter about the creative repudiation of secularist ideas about healing by African Pentecostals confirm that the conflict between faith and secularism in the West is hydra-headed and its manifestations are not limited to religiously inspired violent actions or the highly publicised campaigns about reasonable accommodation for religious minorities. It is a conflict, as the empirical data and claims in this chapter demonstrate, that is manifesting far less dramatically, but efficaciously, in street corners and hospital wards.

According to Beckford (2019: 3), 'critical and hostile responses to the global reach of even relatively modest religious activities have also intensified, especially in places where claims to religious freedom clash with doctrines of secularism and various forms of opposition to particular – or all – religions'. He further notes that 'globalisation has boosted processes of religious outreach and, in doing so, has also aggravated controversies and conflicts which can be particularly acute in relation to migrants' (2019: 3). The conflict that Beckford references here have no doubt fed into the wider debates about multiculturalism and cultural diversity in many Western countries, including Britain. Scholars and public commentators on the dimensions and implications of this conflict have mostly focused on the more populous and influential minority (in the West) religions, such as Islam (Farrar 2012; Tottoli 2015). This chapter has attempted to expand the discourse and chart a new path of scholarly inquiry by establishing the connectedness of African Pentecostalism to the conflict. Ultimately, the arguments in this chapter highlight important sociological questions about the implications of secularisation for all the residents of a secular society and the co-existence and conflicts between two distinct epistemes of illness and healing.

Beckford (2011: 55) reiterates the importance and topicality of this issue when he states that 'arguments about religion and migration have become at least

[2] A copy of this report is accessible via the website of NHS Scotland: https://interfaithscotland.org/wp-content/uploads/2018/07/Religion-and-Belief-Matter-a-resource-guide-for-healthcare-staff.pdf (accessed 13 September 2024).

as contentious as those about "race", class, language, nationality and ethnicity in discussions of social cohesion, integration or assimilation'. Similarly, Levitt (1998: 75) describes religious globalisation as 'the spread and thickening of transnational religious structures and movements that challenge the nation-state'. The arguments in this chapter demonstrate that Levitt's claim can be utilised as an explanatory frame for the conflicts and confrontation that result from actualising a Pentecostalism-informed episteme of healing in secular Western democracies. Therefore, this chapter expands and complexifies extant discourses about the transnational religious practices of immigrants in the West. It also enriches analyses of the impact of transnational migration on African Pentecostalism specifically, as well as the epistemologies of Pentecostalism in general. The remaking and truncating of healing rituals in diaspora contexts has amounted to an unintended but important critique of Pentecostal orthodoxies and some degree of repudiation of divine healing norms. For example, when divine healing rituals are performed and adapted in a hospital ward, longstanding constitutive elements are missed out to accommodate the norms of a secular workplace.

The research participants, referencing specific healing instances in the Bible, confidently asserted that the adapted practices are devoid neither of authenticity nor efficacy, although many admitted that they would perform the same healing rituals differently – and more elaborately – in a non-secular and non-restrictive environment. The justifications offered by the participants aside, the remaking of practice and rituals has historically not harmed or hindered Pentecostalism. On the contrary, adaptability and flexibility have long been identified as key features of Pentecostalism and are major reasons why this brand of Christianity has spread phenomenally in several parts of the world and penetrated various cultures with relative ease (Anderson 1999; Poloma 2001; Kalu 2003). Still, the remaking of practice in the diaspora context raises important epistemological questions about Africa-led Pentecostalism as it perches on the wings of mass migration to reach far-flung corners of the West in the era of globalisation.

Vertovec (2000: 280) surmises that 'the study of diasporas and their modes of adaptation can give us insights into general patterns of religious transformation'. Several participants in this research actively engage in sustained transnational activities with Africa, which include the frequent and dialectical exchange of religious ideologies and personnel between the two places. The adaptation of healing practices provides clear evidence of epistemic shifts and turns, some of which impact and are impacted by the flows between migration contexts and 'home'. The dramatic transformations in African Pentecostalism in the 21st century could not be fully explained and theorised without a systematic and evidence-based explanation of the contribution of its diaspora entities to the transformations. This research, which focuses on major aspects of the healing practices of African Pentecostal diaspora in Britain, has therefore significantly enriched extant academic explanations (Kalu 2008; Asamoah-Gyadu 2013, 2015a; Adogame 2013; Counted 2019) of current developments in, and transformation of, African Pentecostalism in general. Specifically, it showcases the conflicts, negotiations, adaptations and epistemic shifts and turns that have characterised the actualisation of divine healing by African Pentecostals in a secularising Britain.

References

Adedibu, B. (2012), 'Coercive Mimicry and Reflections on African Pentecostalism: The Case of the Redeemed Christian Church of God in Britain'. *Pentecostudies*, 11(1): 58–74.

Adedibu, B. (2016), 'Missional History and the Growth of the Redeemed Christian Church of God in the United Kingdom (1988–2015)'. *The Journal of the European Pentecostal Theological Association*, 36(1): 80–93.

Adogame, A. (2013), *The African Christian Diaspora: New Currents and Emerging Trends in World Christianity* (London: Bloomsbury).

Adogame, A. (2016), *The Public Face of African New Religious Movements in Diaspora: Imagining the Religious 'Other'* (London: Routledge).

Almond, G., Appleby, S. and Sivan, E. (2003), *Strong Religion: The Rise of Fundamentalisms Around the World* (Chicago, IL: University of Chicago Press).

Anderson, A. (1999), 'Introduction: World Pentecostalism at a Crossroads' in A. H. Anderson and W. J. Hollenweger (eds) *Pentecostals After a Century: Global Perspectives on a Movement in Transition* (Sheffield: Sheffield Academic Press), 19–31.

Anderson, A. (2001), *African Reformation: African Initiated Christianity in the 20th Century* (Trenton, NJ: Africa World Press).

Anderson, A. (2004), *An Introduction to Pentecostalism: Global Charismatic Christianity* (Cambridge: Cambridge University Press).

Asamoah-Gyadu, J. K. (2013), *Contemporary Pentecostal Christianity: Interpretations from an African Context* (Oxford: Regnum Books International).

Asamoah-Gyadu, J. K. (2015a), *Sighs and Signs of the Spirit: Ghanaian Perspectives on Pentecostalism and Renewal in Africa* (Oxford: Regnum).

Asamoah-Gyadu, J. K. (2015b), 'Witchcraft Accusations and Christianity in Africa'. *International Bulletin of Mission Research*, 39(1): 23–7. https://doi.org/10.1177/239693931503900107

Bartleman, F. (1980). *Azusa Street: The Roots of Modern-day Pentecost* (Plainfield, FL: Bridge-Logos Publishers).

BBC. (2013), 'Gay Snub Cornish B&B Owners Lose Supreme Court Appeal'. Available at: https://www.bbc.co.uk/news/uk-england-25119158. Accessed February 2021.

Beckford, J. A. (2011), 'Religious Diversity and Social Problems: The Case of Britain' in T. Hjelm (ed.) *Religion and Social Problems* (London: Routledge), 53–66.

Beckford, J. A. (2019), 'Religions and Migrations – Old and New'. *Quaderni Di Sociologia*, 80: 15–32. https://doi.org/10.4000/qds.2599

Beckford, R. (2000), *Jesus Is Dread: Black Theology and Black Culture in Britain* (London: Darton, Longman & Todd).

Brener, M. (2010), 'Religious Accommodation in the Workplace: Legal Rights and Responsibilities'. *Employee Relations Law Journal*, 36(4): 35–58.

Brown, C. G. (2011), *Global Pentecostal and Charismatic Healing* (Oxford: Oxford University Press).

Bruce, S. (2010), 'From Secularization to Resacralization' in B. Turner (ed.) *The New Blackwell Companion to the Sociology of Religion* (London: Wiley-Blackwell), 125–40.

Burgess, R. (2009), 'African Pentecostal Growth: The Redeemed Christian Church of God in Britain' in G. J. Hanciles (ed.) *Global Diasporas and Mission* (Farnham: Ashgate Publishing), 269–88.

Calhoun, C. (2016), 'How Does Religion Matter in Britain's Secular Public Sphere?' Available at: https://blogs.lse.ac.uk/politicsandpolicy/how-does-religion-matter-in-britains-secular-public-sphere/. Accessed 21 December 2020.

Carling, J. (2002), 'Migration in the Age of Involuntary Immobility: Theoretical Reflections and Cape Verdean Experiences'. *Journal of Ethnic and Migration Studies*, 28(1): 5–42.

Cartledge, M. (2006), *Testimony in the Spirit: Rescripting Ordinary Pentecostal Theology*. Farnham: Ashgate Publishing.

Casanova, J. (2011), 'The Secular, Secularizations, Secularisms' in C. Calhoun (ed.) *Rethinking Secularism* (Oxford: Oxford University Press), 54–74.

Chase, S. E. (2005), 'Narrative Inquiry: Multiple Lenses, Approaches, Voices' in N. K. Denzin and Y. S. Lincoln (eds) *The Sage Handbook of Qualitative Research*. 3rd ed. (London: Sage Publications), 651–79.

Córdova Quero, H. and Dias, N. (2021), 'Riding the Wave: Daily Life and Religion Among Brazilian Immigrants to Japan in the Age of Covid-19 Pandemic'. *Religions*, 12(11): 943. https://doi.org/10.3390/rel12110943

Counted, V. (2019), 'African Christian Diaspora Religion and/or Spirituality: A Concept Analysis and Reinterpretation'. *Critical Research on Religion*, 7(1): 58–79. https://doi.org/10.1177/2050303218823258

Cox, H. (2011), 'Foreword' in G. Brown (ed.) *Global Pentecostal and Charismatic Healing* (Oxford: Oxford University Press), xvii–xxii.

Csordas, T. (1997), *Language, Charisma, and Creativity: The Ritual Life of a Religious Movement* (Berkeley, CA: University of California Press).

Curtice, J., Clery, E., Perry, J., Phillips, M. and Rahim, N. (eds) (2019), *British Social Attitudes: The 36th Report* (London: The National Centre for Social Research).

European Convention on Human Rights. (2010), *The European Court of Human Rights* (Strasbourg: Council of Europe).

Farrar, M. (2012), *Islam in the West: Key Issues in Multiculturalism* (London: Palgrave Macmillan).

Fesenmyer, L. (2019), 'Bringing the Kingdom to the City: Mission as Placemaking Practice Amongst Kenyan Pentecostals in London'. *City & Society*, 31(1): 34–54.

Fesenmyer, L. (2020), '"Living as Londoners Do": Born-again Christians in Convivial East London'. *Social Anthropology*, 28(2): 402–17.

Fiddian-Qasmiyeh, E., Loescher, G., Long, K. and Sigona, N. (eds) (2014), *The Oxford Handbook of Refugee and Forced Migration Studies* (Oxford: Oxford University Press).

Fricker, M. (2007), *Epistemic Injustice: Power and the Ethics of Knowing* (Oxford: Oxford University Press).

Gerloff, R. (2004), 'The African Diaspora in the Caribbean and Europe from Pre-Emancipation to the Present Day' in O. U. Kalu (ed.) *African Christianity: An African Story* (Pretoria: University of Pretoria Press), 353–70.

Gifford, P. (2004), *Ghana's New Christianity: Pentecostalism in a Globalizing African Economy* (Bloomington, IN: Indiana University Press).

Gozdziak, E. M. and Shandy, D. J. (2002), 'Editorial Introduction: Religion and Spirituality in Forced Migration'. *Journal of Refugee Studies*, 15(2): 129–35. https://doi.org/10.1093/jrs/15.2.129

Guardian. (2008), 'Landmark Rulings Strengthen Gay Rights in Workplace'. Available at: https://www.theguardian.com/world/2008/dec/20/gayrights-law. Accessed February 2021.

Haar, G. (1998), *Halfway to Paradise: African Christians in Europe* (Cardiff: Cardiff Academic Press).
Hagan, J. (2008), *Migration Miracle: Faith, Hope, and Meaning on the Undocumented Journey* (Cambridge, MA: Harvard University Press).
Hagan, J. and Ebaugh, H. R. (2003), 'Calling Upon the Sacred: Migrants' Use of Religion in the Migration Process'. *International Migration Review*, 37: 1145–53.
Heelas, P. (2008), *Spiritualities of Life: New Age Romanticism and Consumptive Capitalism* (Malden, MA: Blackwell Publishing).
Henrard, K. (2016), 'Duties of Reasonable Accommodation on Grounds of Religion in the Jurisprudence of the European Court of Human Rights: A Tale of (Baby) Steps Forward and Missed Opportunities'. *International Journal of Constitutional Law*, 14(4): 961–83. https://doi.org/10.1093/icon/mow061
Hollenweger, W. J. (1997), *Pentecostalism: Origins and Developments Worldwide* (Peabody, MA: Hendrickson Publishers).
Hunt, S. (1998), *The "New" Black Pentecostal Churches: The Growth and Theology of the Redeemed Christian Church of God.* CESNUR Conference Proceedings.
Hunt, S. (2002), '"Neither Here nor There": The Construction of Identities and Boundary Maintenance of West African Pentecostals'. *Sociology*, 36(1): 147–69.
Hunt, S. and Lightly, N. (2001), 'The British Black Pentecostal "Revival": Identity and Belief in the New Nigerian Churches'. *Ethnic and Racial Studies*, 24(l): 104–24.
Kalilombe, P. (1997), 'Black Christianity in Britain'. *Ethnic and Racial Studies*, 20(2): 308–15.
Kalu, O. (2003), 'Globalisation and Religion: The Pentecostal Model in Contemporary Africa' in G. ter Haar and J. Cox (eds) *Uniquely African? African Christian Identity from Cultural and Historical Perspectives* (Trenton, NJ: Africa World Press), 215–40.
Kalu, O. (2005), *African Christianity: An African Story* (Pretoria: University of Pretoria Press).
Kalu, O. (2008), *African Pentecostalism: An Introduction* (Oxford: Oxford University Press).
Kay, W. (2007), *Healing, Prosperity and Faith: A History and Sociology of the Faith Movement* (Paternoster Press).
Kim, S. and Kim, K. (2008), *Christianity as a World Religion* (London: Bloomsbury).
Krause, K. (2014), 'Space in Pentecostal Healing Practices Among Ghanaian Migrants in London'. *Medical Anthropology*, 33(1): 37–51.
Levitt, P. (1998), 'Local-Level Global Religion: The Case of U.S.-Dominican Migration'. *Journal for the Scientific Study of Religion*, 37(1): 74–89.
Lindhardt, M. (2011), *Practicing the Faith: The Ritual Life of Pentecostal-Charismatic Christians* (New York and Oxford: Berghahn Books).
Marsden, G. (2006), *Fundamentalism and American Culture* (Oxford: Oxford University Press).
Marty, M. E. (1991), *Modern American Religion, Volume 1: The Irony of It All, 1893–1919* (Chicago, IL: University of Chicago Press).
Massey, D. S. and Higgins, M. E. (2011), 'The Effect of Immigration on Religious Belief and Practice: A Theologizing or Alienating Experience?'. *Social Science Research*, 40(5): 1371–89. https://doi.org/10.1016/j.ssresearch.2010.04.012
McGuire, M. (1982), *Pentecostal Catholics: Power, Charisma, and Order in a Religious Movement* (Philadelphia, PA: Temple University Press).
Mella, O. (1994), *Religion in the Life of Refugees and Immigrants* (Stockholm: Centre for Research in International Migration and Ethnicity (CEIFO)).

Noll, M. (1994), *The Scandal of the Evangelical Mind* (Grand Rapids, MI: Wm. B. Eerdmans Publishing Co.)

Oliveira, T., Nada, C. and Magalhães, A. (2023), 'Academic Migration and Epistemological Value: Exploring the Experience of Migrant Academics in Portugal'. *Education Sciences*, 13(7): 720. https://doi.org/10.3390/educsci13070720

Olofinjana, I. O. (2010), *Reverse in Ministry and Missions: Africans in the Dark Continent of Europe* (Bloomington, IN: AuthorHouse).

Poloma, M. (2001), 'The Millenarianism of the Pentecostal Movement' in S. Hunt (ed.) *Christian Millenarianism: From the Early Church to Waco* (London: Hurst), 166–84.

Poloma, M. (2003), *Main Street Mystics: The Toronto Blessing and Reviving Pentecostalism* (Walnut Creek, CA: Altamira Press).

Rogers, A. (2020), *Congregational Geography: Churches, Place, and Space in Post-War England* (Leiden: Brill).

Synan, V. (1997), *The Holiness-Pentecostal Tradition: Charismatic Movements in the Twentieth Century* (Grand Rapids, MI: Wm. B. Eerdmans Publishing Co).

Tottoli, R. (2015), *Routledge Handbook of Islam in the West* (London: Routledge). https://doi.org/10.4324/9781315794273

Ugba, A. (2009), *Shades of Belonging: African Pentecostals in Twenty-First Century Ireland* (Trenton, NJ: Africa World Press).

Ugba, A. (2014), 'Self-representation by Black Majority Christianity in Britain' in A. Adogame (ed.) *The Public Face of African New Religious Movements in Diaspora: Imagining the Religious 'Other'* (Farnham: Ashgate Publishing), 65–84.

Vásquez, M. and Dewind, J. (2014), 'Introduction to the Religious Lives of Migrant Minorities: A Transnational and Multi-sited Perspective'. *Global Networks*, 14(3): 251–72. https://doi.org/10.1111/glob.12058

Vertovec, S. (2000), 'Religion and Diaspora' in P. Antes, A. W. Geertz and R. R. Warne (eds) *New Approaches to the Study of Religion* (Berlin: Verlag de Gruyter), 275–304.

Vertovec, S. (2007), 'Super-diversity and Its Implications'. *Ethnic and Racial Studies*, 30(6): 1024–54. https://doi.org/10.1080/01419870701599465

Warrington, K. (2005), *Healing and Suffering: Biblical and Pastoral Reflections* (Carlisle: Paternoster Publishing).

Woolf Institute. (2015), *Living with Difference: Community, Diversity and the Common Good. Commission on Religion and Belief in British Public Life* (Cambridge: Woolf Institute).

YouGov. (2020), 'International Study: How Has Coronavirus Affected People's Personal Lives?' Available at: https://yougov.co.uk/topics/international/articles-reports/2020/12/10/impact-coronavirus-personal-lives. Accessed January 2021.

8

Covid-19 and the Understanding of Illnesses in Urban Korean *Musok*

LIORA SARFATI

Introduction

IN JULY 2020, at the peak of the Covid-19 pandemic anxiety, Yi Hae-gyŏng performed on the well-respected stage of Korea's national theatre. Yi is a *manshin*, a Korean spiritual mediator practising spirit possession, and the performance was an innovative version of *kut*, a ritual performed by *manshin* to seek blessing and healing through supernatural interventions.[1] The performance seamlessly blended traditional dance and song, accompanied by three large screens projecting images captured during the ritual. On these screens, the practitioner appeared in complete ritual attire, engaging in a song and dance sequence while beseeching the gods for the healing of individuals as the nation grappled with the Covid-19 outbreak.

The performance emerged as an artistic collaboration between a renowned photographer and a religious healer celebrated for her proficiency in executing intricate traditional rituals. Yi identifies herself as a traditional spiritual mediator and healer, indicating that she has undergone initiation and apprenticeship under a formidable mentor, or *shinŏmŏni* (spirit mother). Since the 1990s, much of her time has been dedicated to divining the future and asking gods for good health, prosperity, blessings of business ventures, new homes and marriages. Possessing the knowledge to prepare and perform various types of rituals, she is also capable of identifying and initiating novices into the Korean practice of *musok*.[2] Despite

[1] All translations and transliterations from Korean to English are mine. I use the McCune-Reischauer transliteration system, adding a comma between syllables of first names, and using shi instead of si to facilitate proper pronunciation.

[2] The term *musok* reflects a variety of spiritual practices, some including possession, while others do not. Although it has often been translated as *shamanism*, I avoid this term here as it is too inclusive and generalised. It is also worth noting that the term *musok* originated during the colonial period and thus even this common term is laden with value judgement (for more on this debate see Sarfati (2021),

Proceedings of the British Academy, **278**, 160–178, © Authors 2025.

her traditional roots, Yi sees no conflict in embracing the intersection of cameras and innovative ritual forms. She perceives her active participation in this fusion of performance art, video art and ritual as both efficacious and crucial during the times of the pandemic. Moreover, she used one of the photos documenting the event as her Facebook profile image.

While public performances for the common good have been documented in Korea's pre-modern monarchy and increasingly since the 1980s (Robinson 1993; Kendall 2009), the global Covid-19 pandemic incorporated more extensively the usage of digital media in covering these performances and inviting screen-mediated audiences. During 2020–2, restrictions on gatherings in enclosed spaces prevented many individuals from conducting private rituals. Yi, too, refrained from the crowded settings typical of the ceremonies she used to lead before the pandemic. This event presented an opportunity to showcase her skills on stage with a minimal number of participants while still reaching a vast audience through mediated means.

The event was streamed live on YouTube for a duration of 70 minutes under the title 'A New Kut Stage Performance' (*kut sŭt'eji*). One of the primary objectives of this performance was to seek blessings from the spirit of the War General (Changgun) during the global pandemic. Throughout the ritual, various spirits and gods manifested through the performer, including Sanshin (the mountain god), renowned for his merciful and benevolent nature with healing capabilities. Additionally, spirits of deceased ancestors and ghosts, believed to require constant appeasement and veneration to ward off illnesses and disasters, were also invoked. This would be a common assemblage of venerated entities in any healing *kut* ritual, but this time it was aimed at healing the whole nation and, as an extension, the whole global population suffering from the Covid-19 outbreak. The traditional role of *musok* as a means to control pandemics such as smallpox, which was frequent in pre-modern Korea, was re-enacted as will be discussed below.

This chapter addresses two key questions. The first explores the micro level concerning the ritual participants: Why did contemporary urbanites in South Korea seek such a spiritual blessing? The second delves into the macro-level organisational aspects that facilitated this innovative ritual during times of health-related national distress: Why did a government establishment, such as the national theatre, take the initiative to sponsor this event?

These questions, alongside related inquiries, form the foundation of my ethnographic exploration.[3] To unravel how *musok* intersected with hypermodernity, modern biomedicine and the state during the pandemic, I explore three facets of

introduction). Each region in the Korean peninsula boasts a distinct ritual style meticulously studied and documented by devoted folklorists over the years (for example, Ch'oe 1978, 1981, 1991).

[3] I began my ethnographic observations and interviews in Korea in 2005 and have since visited there regularly and lived in Seoul for periods between weeks and years. During these fieldwork sessions I participated in many *kut* rituals, interviewed *manshin* and clients, spent time with them in their daily activities, ritual preparations and pilgrimages, and frequented several *musok* goods stores (see Sarfati 2021, 2023, 2024).

these intricate relationships. Initially, I delve into the *musok* perspective on illness and its interpretation of the surge in Covid-19 cases. Subsequently, I examine preventive methods offered by *musok*, and finally, I explore *musok*'s perception of the healing potential inherent in spiritual mediation.

These three aspects illustrate, in various ways, that in Korea the *musok* understanding of illness places it within diverse manifestations of disharmony between people and supernatural entities. In this respect it can be discussed as a vernacular religion in which healing is an important aspect or as a healing system, which has spiritual and religious bases. In conclusion, I posit that even during the Covid-19 pandemic, *musok* has been generally perceived in Korea as a distinct realm of practice, seemingly unrelated to modern medicine. However, *manshin* do not insist on exclusivity from their patients. On the contrary, they actively encourage collaborative treatment approaches, in which rituals address the spiritual causes of illness, while biomedical doctors attend to its physical manifestations. Therefore, they were advocates of vaccination and medical attention to the virus, alongside veneration activities to enhance better healing through blessings from gods and spirits. Yi, mentioned above, posted on her Facebook page direct encouragements to take the vaccines throughout the pandemic.

Thus, while in pre-modern Korea the main epistemic framework explaining illness and healing was based on spiritual inflictions, the advent of biomedicine in the 19th century created a sphere of competing explanations and treatments that managed to co-exist because they served different purposes. As will be explained below, the *musok* perspective detects the spiritual vulnerability of a particular person or family which allows the illness to affect them, while the biomedical explanation details the physical aspects of the patient's condition. Biomedicine has also competed with traditional herbal and mineral medicines prescribed by vernacular healers and Buddhist priests, which are still popular in contemporary Korea. These different healing practices are not viewed as mutually exclusive but rather as complementary. Both physical and spiritual aspects of the illness should be treated to reach full recovery, and ancient local healing methods can be combined with scientific ones.

Korean *musok* intersections with hypermodernity and modern biomedicine

First, it is crucial to acknowledge the active and vibrant presence of *musok* in contemporary urban South Korea. *Musok*'s mystical worldview, with an ancient cosmology and a complex belief system and associated practices, did not experience a revival solely to offer hope amid the Covid-19 health anxiety. Rather, it has sustained a broad base of followers into the 21st century (Kendall 2009; Sarfati 2021), extensively documented since the early 20th century (Akamatsu and Akiba 1938; Ch'oe 1978; Kendall 1988). *Musok*, viewed as a women's practice given that around 80 per cent of the *manshin* are female, has survived persecution by the (mostly male) neo-Confucian monarchy in the 14th–19th centuries and disapproval by the monotheistic Christian churches that became prevalent in Korea, with around 30 per cent of the population adhering to it today. This success through decades of marginalisation has been assisted by the vernacular nature of this belief system and practice, which has allowed it to incorporate new terminologies and adjust ritual procedures to align with the hypermodern lifestyle of individuals residing in 21st-century Seoul.

Hypermodern lives have been characterised by fast communication, innovative technologies, excessive consumption and increased manifestations of spectacle in social life (Gottschalk 2018). These characteristics fit the *musok* culture as it increasingly involves digital communication; it has become a part of consumer culture through online advertising and purchase options; and has always been based on sumptuous altars, lively performances and materially laden ritual spectacles (Sarfati 2021, introduction).

The thriving of *musok* in Korea was emphasised on 28 March 2023, in the opening statement of an article published in the mainstream newspaper, *The Korea Herald*:

> In [the opening scene of] episode 15 of [the] Netflix's drama series 'The Glory,' the shaman [*manshin*], who is involved in the antagonist Park Yeon-jin's shady family business, suddenly drops dead in the middle of performing a ritual, leaving viewers bewildered by the sudden plot twist involving a supernatural scene. Shamanism [spiritual mediation] may appear out of place in a modern-day revenge thriller, but superstitions and shamanistic practices are not far removed from the daily lives of many Koreans, even in their tech-savvy and fast-paced world.
>
> (Jung 2023)

Indeed, many contemporary urbanite Koreans do not perceive a conflict between this ancient belief system and contemporaneous perspectives, and the incorporation of such scenes in Korean television programmes, dramas and in films has become commonplace. Moreover, these rituals offer a spectacle that can be captured beautifully through cinematic strategies and therefore have become a common feature in many Korean films and television programmes, fostering broad awareness of the availability of this healing method (Sarfati 2021).

Musok, literally meaning the customs of spiritual mediation, is the Korean term for a broad spectrum of spiritual practices. In these practices, communication occurs between people and supernatural entities through a specialised spiritual mediator. In cases involving spirit possession by *manshin*, the communication is bidirectional, as the mediator embodies spirits and gods, conveying their words. A hereditary version of *musok* (*sesŭpmu*), which does not involve possession by supernatural entities, has been declining in recent decades (Mills 2007). *Musok* is employed to address a wide array of issues, with healing diseases being just one aspect. Other misfortunes such as bankruptcy, family strife and accidents are also addressed through these practices.

To undergo initiation, every *manshin* must successfully engage in direct communication with gods, spirits and ancestors in a practice known as 'opening the gate of words' (Bruno 2002). This direct communication takes place through spirit possession, during which the *manshin* invites specific spirits into her body. While embodying the supernatural, the *manshin*'s apprentices and assistants question her about the clients and the supernatural origins of their afflictions.

Shinbyŏng is a unique illness associated with *musok*. It is caused by spirits or gods demanding that an individual becomes their venerator by becoming a *manshin*. All the *manshin* I am acquainted with have undergone *shinbyŏng*. Many of them had limited knowledge about *musok* before being identified as destined to be *manshin*. Such destiny is revealed through dreams, visions and various kinds of ailments, which are perceived as sent by supernatural entities who try to signal this destiny to the *shinbyŏng* patient. The symptoms vary, but their cause is an attempt to draw the person's attention to the required choice of a *manshin* vocation. Typically, these patients sought out a *manshin*'s assistance after years of unsuccessful biomedical treatments for various forms of suffering like joint pains, nightmares, psychiatric disorders, depression, severe headaches and cancer. Through experienced *manshin*, they learned that their ailments were ways in which the spirits sought to communicate their demand for daily veneration and possession during rituals. These supernatural entities particularly enjoy *kut* rituals, where they can be embodied in the *manshin*, partaking in activities like eating, drinking, dancing and enjoying celebrations in ways not possible without such embodiment. Healing *shinbyŏng* is believed to occur only if patients undergo an apprenticeship process.

Severe illness and near-death experiences consistently emerge as commonly cited signs of a shamanic calling across various cultures. In 1951, Mircea Eliade elucidated the significance of such experiences in the shamanic cultures he compared in his seminal work, *Shamanism: Archaic Techniques of Ecstasy*. He conveyed that the illness is typically severe, 'but the future shaman is cured in the end, with the help of the same spirits that will later become his tutelaries and helpers' (Eliade 2004: 28). While debates surround many aspects of his book, and some argue that its generalisations are overly broad, Korean scholars of *musok* have often cited it (for example, Ch'oe 1999). The notion of initiatory illness, and the idea that 'the initiation of the candidate is equivalent to a cure' (ibid.: 27), persists in contemporary ethnographies about shamans. Examples include Buryat culture (see Quijada 2011), Taiwan (see Liu 2021) and even Neo-shamanism in the UK (see Ivanescu and Berentzen 2020).

In Korea, a unique set of healing rituals is necessary when the patient has *shinbyŏng*. Healing this spirit-inflicted illness can only be achieved if the patient agrees to become a *manshin*. Several *kut* performed for this specific type of illness mark the gradual progress of the apprentice from being ill to becoming a healer. The peak of these rituals is the initiation ritual (*shin naerim kut*), after which the apprentice is declared a full-fledged *manshin*. *Shinbyŏng* occurs without the person's desire to become a *manshin* (Sarfati 2020).

The ritual style practised in the screen-mediated ritual described above originated in the northern part of the Korean peninsula, specifically in the Hwanghae-do region, which is now located within the borders of the North Korean state (for more on this regional style, see Hong 2006). During the Korean War in 1951–3, many practitioners of this spirit mediation practice fled to the South due to concerns that the Northern communist regime might suppress their faith and venerational practices. In the South, they have flourished to the extent that they were showcased at the national theatre in 2020 during a period of national uncertainty.

The screen-mediated ritual by Yi Hae-gyŏng in 2020 shows how *musok* practitioners can opt to create an innovative form of ritual while keeping certain aspects of their traditional practices. In the Hwanghae-do *kut* that Yi performs, various spirits and gods are invited to enter the practitioner's body. A tangible manner to invite them and to symbolise their embodiment in the *manshin* is the *shinbok*, a unique outfit prepared for each deity. In the screen-staged ritual, Yi changed more than five *shinbok*, symbolising each time the current venerated deity. The outfits were very elaborate, colourful and uniquely Korean, serving also as a marker of heritage and national culture. Another aspect that the filmed ritual maintained was the unique *kut* music, which required several musicians to be on stage. On the innovative side, the photographer Kang Yŏng-ho was an active performer. Seated on a wheeled chair, he moved around Yi, photographing her from various angles and dancing with her. This video was portrayed on the huge screens behind, and the stage was filmed and broadcast live on YouTube, as well as being documented in the photographer's blog (Kang 2020). Yi insists that these innovations did not diminish the focus on the stated ritual intention to alleviate the pandemic's spread in Korea and neither did its efficacy decrease. This insistence stems from the *musok* perspective on illness and healing.

What constitutes illness in the *musok* perspective?

Musok practitioners in 21st-century Seoul embrace the foundational paradigms of modern medicine. They do not dispute the existence of germs and viruses, nor do they overlook the significance of biological genes and behavioural influences on health and sickness. All of these factors are collectively considered as reasons for the apparent symptoms of illness and disease, and they can be addressed through modern biomedical interventions.

However, a distinction arises in understanding why a specific individual succumbs to a particular disease, while another, with similar preconditions, remains unaffected. This distinction is attributed to the spiritual realm. In other words, the harmony or disharmony in the human–spirit relationship plays a crucial role. What a biomedical doctor might categorise as misfortune or mere coincidence finds a supernatural explanation in *musok*.

This episteme has remained pertinent in Korea and is accepted by the *manshin*'s patients. It has survived the urbanisation and modernisation processes by bridging the gaps in the biomedical explanation of illness. In the case of the Covid-19 pandemic, *musok* explained cases where contemporary biomedicine could not account for why a certain patient became severely ill while others exposed to the same conditions did not. It was offered as a causal explanation where biomedicine had little assurance, and many accepted it. It is difficult to estimate the extent of belief in this tradition, but we know that more than 300,000 registered practitioners are listed in the largest professional association of *musok* in South Korea. Similarly, a *manshin* can attribute a car accident to the manipulation of a grudging spirit while acknowledging the driver's mistake. The *manshin*'s insight answers questions like why the driver made that specific mistake and why the accident resulted in severe injury or not. These are aspects perceived as outcomes influenced by the agency of spirits. Since such explanations do not delve into the actual symptoms but rather focus on the reasons for the spiritual weakness that allowed symptoms into the patient's body, these explanations do not compete with the biomedical account of the mechanism causing the physical damage to the body.

An example can help elucidate this relationship and its impact on a person's health. In a ritual I observed in July 2015 for a 65-year-old woman grappling with chronic muscle weakness, she sought the *manshin*'s assistance after multiple doctors informed her that there was no treatment available except for painkillers. During the ritual, the *manshin* became possessed by the spirit of a middle-aged woman who proclaimed herself as the biological mother of the patient. Despite the patient's protest, stating that her actual mother was still alive, albeit old and suffering from dementia, the woman possessing the *manshin*'s body insisted on being recognised as the mother.

According to the narrative unfolded by the spirit, she was the secret lover of the patient's father, both of them being married to other individuals. When she became pregnant, the patient's father insisted that the baby be raised in his official family with his wife registered as the mother. The biological mother agreed to this arrangement out of fear that the baby might appear markedly different from her actual husband, with whom she had been unable to conceive for several years. She informed her husband that the baby had died shortly after birth, received a lump sum of money, and agreed to sever ties with the lover and his family. During the ritual, the spirit expressed that her heart was shattered after leaving her newborn from the love affair. She passed away a few years later without having any other children. Now, she had returned as a ghost to visit her only child after feeling neglected and unacknowledged for many years.

The possessed *manshin* negotiated with the patient through the mediation of the younger apprentices present, and an agreement was reached. The patient committed to creating a small altar for the spirit of her purported biological mother and acquiring a special princess costume for the *manshin*'s collection. The costume would bear the embroidered name of the deceased ancestor. Whenever the *manshin* danced in this costume, it would serve as an acknowledgement and appeasement for the spirit of the biological mother. The ritual concluded with the ceremonial departure of the ancestral spirit, separating her from her living daughter. The patient pledged to light incense for her every year at a mountain altar during the lunar harvest moon holiday (*Chusŏk*).

Did the patient truly believe that the woman she thought was her mother was, in fact, only her father's wife? Several friends who observed the ritual, seated on floor cushions beside me, speculated that she had always sensed resentment from her mother, potentially explaining their tense relationship since a young age. Given the mother's dementia and the deceased status of the father and his sisters, uncovering facts leading to the complete truth would prove challenging. Moreover, further investigation into the scandal might create strife in the family and eventually harm the woman who was so far considered a full-fledged daughter. Had the mother been alive or born other children, it might have some benefits to find the biological family, but given Korea's conservative society, more harm than benefit could be expected. After the ritual concluded, and the patient rejoined her friends, they embraced her, expressing hope that she felt better. While the patient expressed a similar sentiment, she did not sound entirely convinced. In subsequent meetings with the *manshin*, I learned that the patient had become a regular client, seeking divination and consultation every few months. According to the *manshin*, the woman experienced less pain since the ritual.

We could interpret this case through psychological explanations that focus on the problematic relationship between the client and her mother. However, for the suffering woman, the spiritual explanation played a role, and she was not obligated to fully embrace it in her thinking and feelings. For the *manshin*, proof of the ritual's success was reaching an agreement with the spirit rather than the daughter's acceptance of the story. The *manshin* express their devotion to the supernatural as central to their work more than satisfying their human clients. Thus, a typical *musok* diagnosis in a consultation with a *manshin* might attribute an illness to an angered ancestral spirit lingering around the person, seeking attention even in cases where the clients are reluctant to accept it. When ignored, the spirit might resort to extreme measures, such as causing illness or disasters like car crashes or fires, in an effort to gain recognition. Other potentially harmful spirits include those of the house or gods of natural elements attempting to convey a message. The *manshin* asserts that appeasing such spirits does not necessitate clients believing in their existence; performing veneration acts is deemed sufficient. Similarly, the *manshin* in Seoul offered their clients various veneration practices that could presumably prevent a severe Covid-19 infection, mostly performed without a face-to-face meeting. Some even created special online promotion campaigns for this purpose.

Acceptance of a modern biomedical perspective on illness does not contradict the *musok* viewpoint and therefore both beliefs can co-exist in one person's understanding of illness. It is more difficult for Christian Koreans to accept *musok* healers than for non-Christians to be clients of *manshin* and biomedical doctors at the same time because the basic worldview of *musok* contradicts monotheism. Healing in *musok* is entwined in a religious belief system. The *manshin* often inquire whether their patients are undergoing modern medical treatment and, if not, encourage them to consult with a doctor. For example, an acquaintance who is a doctor asked me to connect a *manshin* with a cancer patient in the advanced stages of the illness seeking spiritual guidance, which the doctor did not deem potentially harmful.[4] When I approached a *manshin* I knew and asked if she was willing to meet the cancer patient, she responded that he must first see a doctor. Only after she ensured serious medical treatment was in progress did she agree to provide spiritual consultation. She explained that when the body is severely afflicted, appeasing angry spirits may not suffice to reverse the damage already done, and biomedical treatment becomes necessary. Moreover, as explained above, it is believed that even with the most elaborate biomedical treatments the initiatory illness cannot be cured if one does not become a *manshin.*

In cases where illness is not considered initiatory, the ancient *musok* episteme perceives it as an uninvited guest (*sonnim*). The 'visit' can be concluded through rituals in which the spirit of the disease is invited to partake in a feast, ultimately persuading it to leave the patient's body. This perspective was also notable in the context of Covid-19, where the severity of illness among those infected was linked to their level of harmony with the world of spirits and gods. There is no reason to avoid biomedicine because if the angry spirits are appeased, they should support the healing of the body with any measure possible, including modern ones. The *manshin* believe that restoring harmony with the supernatural and also the blessing of biomedical procedures can both help mitigate the dangers of the illness. Consequently, traditional healing rituals (*pyŏng kut*) were extensively performed during the Covid-19 pandemic.

On 7 December 2022, when she endured a severe Covid-19 infection for two weeks, one of my *manshin* acquaintances shared photos of her positive Covid-19 test on Facebook and wrote, 'I was sick for six days, even though I took the booster shot. Omicron symptoms all began … I was always proud of being with the gods, but maybe I did not pray enough.' She explained that she contracted the virus from one of her apprentices, but the question of supernatural protection was tied to the intensity of the symptoms she experienced. She believed these symptoms were the result of her insufficient veneration activity. Furthermore, several *manshin* told me in the summer of 2022 that the global pandemic is a distress signal expressed by the gods of nature due to immoral norms associated with neoliberalism, extreme capitalism and excessive consumption that disregard ecosystems. I have not heard *manshin* criticise biomedicine as part of the problem, but in several cases they expressed hopes for collaboration with doctors in the initial stages of the illnesses,

[4] I was asked to keep this in full discretion since the patient was a well-known figure in the business world and someone perceived as rational science-oriented person. Thus, no further details can be supplied.

in a manner that might prevent the physical damage that usually happens during the extended periods that pass until clients come to see them. For most Koreans the *musok* treatment is viewed as the last resort, after biomedicine options have been explored. In the summers of 2023 and 2024, several *manshin* that I interviewed asserted that we have not achieved global harmony with the supernatural, and the ongoing wars in Ukraine and the Middle East were discussed as proof that much spiritual work is still needed. The engagements of *manshin* with current global concerns over human morality and responsibility have become widespread. Such discourses serve to demonstrate how *manshin* have adapted to hypermodern conditions, in contrast with those in Korea who view them as irrelevant remnants of ancient cultural trends.

How can illness be prevented in the *musok* perspective?

If illness arises from problematic relations with spirits of ancestors or gods of nature that created disharmony with the supernatural, then prevention can be achieved by appeasing these entities, hoping that they will not feel the need to make an uninvited 'visit' to the ritual sponsors. This does not imply that *manshin* avoid advising their patients to maintain a healthy lifestyle, make informed food choices and engage in regular exercise. All the *manshin* I have encountered view preventive modern biomedicine as a way to keep the body strong. They were not among the groups strongly opposing Covid-19 gathering restrictions, in contrast to several Christian denominations and new religious groups in Korea (Kin and Noh 2022).

In the *musok* worldview, when the body is weak, an angry spirit might easily inflict illness. Angry spirits can cause harm in various ways, not just through illness, and people need to be cautious in their daily interactions, even when making efforts to appease such harm-causing supernatural entities. For *manshin*, preventing illness is akin to averting other calamities. One must strive to maintain a safe environment both within the body and in the surrounding world. Additionally, ensuring that the spiritual aspects are secure can be achieved by consulting a *manshin*.

During a typical preventive consultation, the client usually meets the *manshin* either in her home shrine or downtown office. If the spirits are regularly appeased, there might not be a need for an elaborate full *kut* ritual, making the difference between a brief consultation costing a few hundred euros and a full-scale event costing thousands. In brief consultations, the central feature of the office is a large altar adorned with various depictions of gods and spirits in paintings and statues, alongside offerings ranging from durable jade candlesticks and paper flowers to biodegradable fruits, candies and hard liquor. For the *manshin*, these offerings constitute a daily preventive practice that safeguards both them and their clients.

Each morning, the *manshin* places fresh water on the altar, lights incense and offers prayers. If there are angry entities present, they might communicate their grievances through her, providing an opportunity for discussion on how to appease them. The Covid-19 pandemic was a time of special caution for many of the *manshin* I know. They conducted their daily reverence with prayers for national and global health improvement and went on pilgrimages to the mountain to plead with Sanshin, the mountain god known for healing. The common perspective is that 'the ancestors never kill a person outright, though they might send an illness that can result in death if not properly treated' (Janelli and Janelli 1982: 161). Therefore, where calamities, such as a severe Covid-19 infection, occur, the *manshin* see their role as crucial in preventing the death of their clients.

Certain patients are deemed to be at special risk. These individuals are often those whose families have endured the loss of a child or a young unmarried person, particularly if the death resulted from violence. The spirits of those who passed away prematurely, without having the opportunity to leave offspring, are perceived as hungry and neglected (Janelli and Janelli 1982: 154). Unlike spirits whose descendants perform the traditional Confucian ancestor rites during major holidays, those without offspring are excluded from these customary rituals, as in Korea such veneration is typically the responsibility of the deceased's sons. Consequently, spirits without children may feel hungry and linger around their siblings or parents, sensing exclusion from the festive observances.

If the *manshin* discovers that there has been a premature death in her client's family, she may propose regular veneration of the spirit at her home shrine to mitigate any potential harm to the family. The client might contribute children's clothes and toys to place on the *manshin*'s altar, attaching the name of the deceased to demonstrate to the spirit that it has not been forgotten. Some *manshin* engage in venerating the spirits of children during extended *kut* rituals, adopting childish voices and inviting audience members to participate in games. This form of veneration aims to pacify potential illnesses caused by spiritual unrest. Additionally, certain regional styles incorporate spirit weddings into their practices. In these ceremonies, they symbolically marry a deceased boy and girl to alleviate their loneliness, thus reducing the likelihood of frequent 'visits' to their living relatives.

During the Covid-19 pandemic, my *manshin* acquaintances reported that their workload did not decrease as might have been expected with people's tendency to reduce their number of outings and their strong trust in the biomedical solutions to the pandemic; on the contrary, the general anxiety increased their workload, attesting to the prevailing perception that *musok* is efficacious in ontological aspects, that is, that *manshin* can really heal. To adapt to the circumstances, most *manshin* expanded their online divination methods, utilising platforms such as the KakaoTalk chat app and YouTube live video streaming. When Covid-19 restrictions were enforced, they conducted rituals without a live audience, broadcasting them to the sponsoring clients. Many sought assistance to cleanse their homes of restless spirits, fearing these spirits might be linked to severe Covid-19 cases. Others requested rituals to appease ancestors who might be upset due to the absence of customary gravesite visits and holiday festivities.

The new *kut* stage performance in the national theatre, discussed in the opening of the chapter, served as a preventive ritual for general blessing and protection. It was the responsibility of *musok* practitioners to maintain the spirits' contentment, preventing them from causing illnesses and other calamities. All the religious activities of the *manshin* are perceived as efforts to prevent illnesses of different kinds, some bodily, some mental and some social. *Manshin* describe their daily commitment to appeasing spirits as a constant endeavour. They engage in short prayers and offerings multiple times each day and remain vigilant for any irregularities in their surroundings, which may indicate spirits' dissatisfaction. Additionally, most *manshin* undertake pilgrimages to holy sites like mountains and seashores, where they regularly venerate their guardian spirits.

How is healing believed to be attained according to *musok*?

If illness is rooted in disharmony with the supernatural, and the gods of nature and spirits of ancestors are perceived as causal factors of illness, then when it strikes severely, this supernatural disharmony must be rectified. The supernatural entities are depicted anthropomorphically in sacred painting (*mushindo*) in the shrines and are also portrayed in statues. Communication and prayers are held daily in front of these depictions and the *manshin* attest that they also see them in dreams and visions. This visualisation helps when the healer needs to diagnose which entities have been aggravated, by whom and why. Subsequently, negotiations with the entities commence until an agreement is reached, and they promise to cease causing harm. All of this is accomplished through direct communication and embodiment of the entities.

The process begins with short consultation meetings where the cause of the problem is revealed. These consultations differ from preventive consultations as they are conducted with a clear problem at hand. The illness or disaster has already occurred, and the patient's condition requires repair. Patients would usually not visit a *manshin* unless they experienced severe afflictions, but during the Covid-19 pandemic, many sought the *manshin*'s help right when they were diagnosed, in line with the general feeling of despair and fear.

If there is a straightforward solution, such as resuming ancestral veneration rites neglected for several years, the *manshin*'s involvement in the process might conclude, and the treatment of physical symptoms can be left to biomedicine. However, if the *manshin* cannot identify the source of the problem in a brief meeting, she might prescribe an extensive *kut* ritual. *Kut* events used to extend over several days and nights until the 1980s, but due to Korea's rapid urbanisation, they are now typically condensed to a single day (Kendall 2009: 108, 113, 125). The sequence of each ritual is meticulously planned based on the specific issue at hand. In the aforementioned *pyŏng kut* for healing, the *manshin* calls upon gods known for their benevolence and mercifulness, such as Sanshin (the mountain god) and Ch'ilsŏng (the spirit of the constellation Ursa Major). Conversely, a ritual for economic prosperity venerates more extensively spirits of historical generals and government officials recognised for their courage and manipulativeness.

Rituals aimed at peacefully guiding the deceased to the afterworld specifically invoke the spirits they intend to aid, along with the spirits of deceased *manshin*, historical kings and government officials, and warrior generals. All these spirits play a role in persuading the departed to sever their connections with their living relatives. The ritual for sending the dead varies in name across regions; for instance, *tari kut* is the term used in P'yŏngan pukdo, an area now situated in the North Korean state. The distinctions in the ritual's purpose are evident in its structure, texts and offerings. When the reason for the illness is diagnosed as an ancestor who has not passed peacefully to the afterworld, the healing *kut* is combined with sending off the dead.

Each *kut* is divided into several parts (*kori*), each associated with a different kind of possession sequence. Every *kut* commences with cleansing the space of any harmful influences and arranging small altars around the ritual area for hungry spirits who might arrive uninvited upon hearing the music and song. On these altars, the *manshin* places small amounts of rice cakes, fruit, water, meat, rice wine (*makkŏlli*) and other delicacies. This spirit-nourishing aspect plays a crucial role in the efficacy of the ritual and is conducted with utmost seriousness, typically before the arrival of patients, clients, musicians and other participants. Within the primary shrine, there stands a large altar adorned with additional delicacies, along with paper-cut decorations and flowers. These serve as offerings for the gods and spirits who will be summoned to partake in the festivities together with humans, and are a reflection of their anthropomorphous nature.

Most *kori* in the possession-centred *kut* rituals involve the recitation of myths, the invitation of spirits to possess the *manshin*, and a possession trance where divination, negotiation and blessings are exchanged between supernatural entities and the *manshin*. Some scholars have debated whether these performances include a real embodiment of supernatural entities and trance (Kendall 2009: 207 n.3). I use *possession trance* here as the emic meaning conveyed by my *manshin* interlocutors. They are always cautious when angry spirits are reluctant to leave and offer further promises and entertainment. Therefore, the final stage of the rituals is crucial because when the spirits bid farewell, it means having accomplished the intended goal. This does not necessarily imply that the patient is fully healed; rather, it indicates that the spiritual reasons for the affliction and the severity of the disease have been addressed. Physical symptoms might take a while to heal.

According to modern biomedicine, symptoms are linked to the body, and healing can only be achieved when the body undergoes specific manipulations, either through physical interventions or the introduction of chemical substances. In contemporary *musok*, the healing process can sometimes be conducted without the physical presence of the client because it does not exclusively target the body. While many patients personally meet the *manshin*, communication can also occur through phone calls, online platforms or even through personal artefacts like undergarments. The *manshin* utilises these methods to inform the spirits and gods about the identity of the patient she is treating. The supernatural entities can provide information about the issue that led to the ailment even without the person being physically present in the ritual space.

The increasingly prevalent use of screen-mediated rituals in Seoul is facilitated by the understanding in *musok* cosmology that there is no specific permanent location where a spirit or god resides, enabling their influence to extend everywhere. The *manshin* attest that pilgrimages to places of special supernatural connection, such as mountain tops and gravesites, are not necessary in every case, since the entities communicate with the *manshin* everywhere, even when the practitioners travel abroad. The ritual's purpose and the patient's condition determine the proper spiritual handling of the situation. This characteristic of *musok* belief has enabled the continuity of *kut* performances even during the most stringent stages of Covid-19 restrictions, with small-scale *kut* in sacred outdoor sites or a video conference meeting. Patients were not obligated to leave their homes, and large gatherings were not a prerequisite for conducting the healing spiritual mediation.

Sometimes the conclusion of a ritual was that the client had to perform acts of veneration in person, but these could be carried out in various open-air places, such as mountains, ancestral gravesites or beaches. The essential ritual guests, without whom no healing can be achieved, are supernatural entities, and they were not regulated by the Covid-19 restrictions of the Korean Ministry of Health.

During the ritual, several procedures are performed to check the efficacy of the veneration acts and to verify that certain spirits have been appeased. The most common one seen in Seoul involves throwing a pair of knives near the shrine's door. When both knives point outwards, it means that the spirits have been pleased. Otherwise, more rites are performed, and then the knives are thrown again. This process can be repeated as long as needed until the *manshin* is sure that the offerings have been accepted. These acts were common in rituals before the pandemic and continued to be practised as a means to verify supernatural satisfaction and promise of healing. The main difference was the absence of the clients in the actual ritual space.

Another common method of assessing the success of the ritual involves sacrificial animals, such as pigs and cows. These animals are often balanced on a large trident stuck in a small bag of uncooked rice. Balancing the entire pig's carcass can take several attempts, accompanied by song, chanting and prayers. If the process takes too long, the *manshin* encourages the clients to make promises to the spirits, which may involve buying more food or ritual goods. To fulfil these promises, clients place money bills on the pig's skin or in its mouth, rub their hands in supplication and bow. Balancing the pig should be achieved within 15 minutes or half an hour. The *manshin* leaves the pig on the trident without touching it for a few minutes to ensure it works and then hits it with a stick until it falls.

Post-Covid-19 *musok*

The explanations provided by the *manshin* for the Covid-19 pandemic are reminiscent of pre-modern interpretations of smallpox, known as *hogu pyŏlsŏng* (spirit of illness) for male spirits and *hogu aegisshi* (girl spirit of illness) for female spirits. The disease was colloquially referred to as *sonnim* (the guest) and was traditionally expelled through exorcism and celebratory rituals. These spirits were often associated with young individuals who had succumbed to illness (Kim 1993). Similarly, with the onset of the Covid-19 pandemic, many *manshin* engaged in preventive purification rituals and sought to pacify potentially irate spirits that posed increased risks to individuals exposed to the virus.

State-sponsored rituals intertwined traditional arts and religious practices, with museums and theatres accentuating the artistic value of Korean heritage, while *manshin* placed precedence on their spiritual beliefs. Since the 1990s, being sponsored by the government or local council through the intangible human asset system has become a sought-after nomination by successful *manshin* since it boosts their potential client base and increases their public legitimacy (Howard 1998). The sponsoring organisations relied on the recognised definition of *musok* as a national heritage. This classification has been prevalent since the 1960s for several traditional arts, and from the 1980s the government started designating *manshin* as Intangible National Heritage Holders (*ingan munhwajae*). This title mandated them to train younger performers in *musok* song and dance. However, inclusion in the sponsored folk arts repertoire of Korea does not necessarily imply official acceptance of the religious episteme related to illness. Innovative technology has allowed many *manshin* who are not designated officially as 'human assets' to achieve fame and success. Online live broadcasts allowed audiences to participate for various reasons, and for laypeople, there was no obligation to subscribe to beliefs in the appeased spirits.

Tensions between the national health system and privately sought spiritual healing in Korea have antecedents in pre-modern conflicts between the ruling male neo-Confucian scholars and the mostly female *manshin*. While Confucianism emphasises order and hierarchy, *musok* veneration is vernacular, and therefore less regulated. Each *manshin* has a different pantheon that derives from her initiatory process, her family history and place of residence and worship. The series of gods and spirits that she venerates do not adhere to a fixed hierarchy; rather, for each case, the relative importance of certain entities is determined according to healing needs. In the early 20th century, this characteristic of *musok* was called *parallelism* by the famous folklorist Yim Sŏk-jae, and this terminology has recently returned to research elaborations on this belief system (Kwŏn 2023). *Manshin* have been viewed by the male elites as subversive both in their epistemology and their practices because of their flexible interpretations of serious life-related issues. For Christian Koreans, the polytheistic nature of *musok* is unacceptable.

Similar disdain has been expressed by biomedical doctors who prefer a clear definition of illness, one that does not change according to each client's spiritual condition. This stigma against *manshin* began during early encounters of Koreans with Western medicine in the early 20th century when politicians and newspapers claimed that *manshin* did not understand science. 'Indigenous female health practices were de-legitimized through a modernizing discourse to advocate newly institutionalized practices and products' (Hwang 2012: 49–50). Thus, the conflicts then and now do not stem from a clear-cut distinction between the efficacy of different healing methods but more from the subversive nature of *musok*. The practitioners are mostly independent in their decision-making process, and their acts cannot be verified in a generalisable scientific manner. Moreover, their education to be healers does not have an official script or fixed stages; rather, it is achieved through another inspired healer, the spirit mother, who is also independent of regulations and institutions. For some scientific-oriented Koreans, such individualised healing treatments seemed especially dangerous amid the general anxiety of the pandemic. Others embraced it as a reassuring tradition.

For the *manshin*, the pandemic became a defining moment in their profession, despite scepticism in parts of the medical community. Additionally, it facilitated more integration of screen technology as a substitute for face-to-face meetings. This shift proved convenient for clients who preferred to keep their consultations with the *manshin* confidential, such as professed Christians, and for those residing far from their preferred healer. Some *manshin* with young children mentioned that it was particularly advantageous, as maintaining an orderly home shrine for clients to visit was challenging. A brief Zoom session could be more manageable in a crowded home. While screen-mediated consultations and rituals had been utilised for several years prior to the pandemic, they were not favoured by all practitioners and were less commonly used for elderly clients. However, with the perception of the Covid-19 virus as particularly dangerous for the elderly, these clients began to accept screen-mediated *musok* healing and divination out of fear of encountering many people outside their homes.

The Covid-19 restrictions served as a catalyst for obtaining ritual artefacts through telephone orders from *musok* goods stores. Even before the pandemic restrictions, the dense traffic in Seoul had compelled *manshin* to rely on telephone orders for costumes, *pujŏk* amulets, decorations, brass bells and paintings of gods. However, each *manshin* has a preferred store where she has established a trusted relationship with the owner and can stay informed about the latest gossip in the field. These store owners are aware, for instance, when a spirit mother quarrels with apprentices to the extent that they leave her group, or when a *manshin* receives a special honour such as a government title as an Intangible Culture Holder. I have spent many days in such stores, learning a great deal about the politics of various performance teams. Nevertheless, when face-to-face meetings with the store owner were not possible, the *manshin* were confident that by explaining what they needed, the ritual props would safely arrive at their shrine through a delivery service.

The pandemic did not significantly integrate marginalised knowledge and the *musok* epistemology of illness into national health strategies, and biomedicine is still the most practised healing method in contemporary Korea. Instead, *musok* was utilised to comfort people by performing a celebrated uniting heritage, and perhaps, for the genuine believers, by appeasing angry spirits and gods to achieve harmony with the supernatural. The *manshin* who perform on stages and broadcast their rituals on television or YouTube channels assert that gods and spirits are pleased with these innovations because they appreciate human attention in various forms. The most noteworthy innovation that the post-Covid-19 *musok* world is experiencing is a greater reliance on screen-mediated divination, rituals and performances without an on-site audience.

Conclusion

In contrast to the biomedical understanding of illness, which centres on exploring the patient's body during diagnosis, the *musok* perspective focuses on the spirits and gods outside the patient's body that cause suffering. According to *musok* beliefs, illness shares similar causes with accidents and other problems, and healing occurs when the spirits and gods are appeased, restoring harmony. Bodily aches are considered symptoms of spiritual weakness.

This paradigmatic contrast leads university-trained doctors to criticise *manshin*, often dismissing their beliefs as superstitions. However, some patients assert that *manshin* treatments saved their lives, a sentiment shared by most *manshin* who found relief from spirit-inflicted illnesses that biomedical experts could not cure. *Manshin* apprenticeship and initiation were the only effective cures, according to their life narratives.

Thus, the two questions posed at the beginning of this chapter have been addressed. At the micro level, I demonstrated that contemporary urbanites in South Korea seek spiritual blessing and healing when biomedicine fails to help, and during times of anxiety, resorting to traditional beliefs becomes even more reassuring than in normal times. The *manshin* facilitate the maintenance of spiritual practices by adapting them to current concerns, such as avoiding large crowds during an infectious pandemic. At the macro level, the data has shown that organisations such as museums and theatres have embraced innovative screen-mediated ritual performances to assert national unity through artistic heritage displayed by the *manshin* while sidestepping the religious and spiritual implications of the ritual's healing capacities. Such acceptance by mainstream institutions decreased the public's fear of *manshin*, which has stemmed from their daily interactions with spirits of the dead. In several interviews I held in summer 2024 I learned that young people view *musok* as a fun practice, compared to its perception as scary by people over 50. This shift has also been visible in the recent media depictions of *manshin* as cute professionals who wish to help people in contrast with the scary mean characters portrayed in the 1970s films (for a discussion of these image shifts see Sarfati 2021, chapter 3).

The success and expansion of *musok* healing practices in Korea should not be dismissed as superstition born of ignorance. In many cases, prioritising biomedical science may not be automatic; instead, biomedical doctors could consider collaborations, as seen in other cases discussed in the book, particularly in Brazil. In Seoul, where the biomedical system has been long established and is mostly government sponsored, it might be more problematic to combine traditional and scientific treatment, but other cases have shown this to be possible, for example, in the Navajo reserves in the US (Kunitz and Levy 1997: 119–20). Settling spiritual and familial unresolved grudges of the deceased can be crucial for patients' wellbeing, even if not provable through scientific tools. Diversifying healing options to include a broader range of choices could prove beneficial. For example, the healthcare system could enhance patients' ability to make personal healing choices by allocating funding to non-scientific treatments of their preference. Complementary epistemes of healing can exist side by side as seen in the Korean case. It should be beneficial to embrace such diversity when assessing the relative contribution of treatments to the wellbeing of patients and societies in times of health-related anxieties.

References

Akamatsu, C. and Akiba, T. (1938), *Chōsen Fuzuko no Kenkyū* (Study of Korean Shamanism). (Tokyo: Osakayago Shōten).

Bruno, A. L. (2002), *The Gate of Words. Language in the Rituals of Korean Shamans* (Leiden: University of Leiden Press).

Ch'oe, K. (1978), *Han'guk Musok ŭi Yŏn'gu* (Research of Korean Shamanism) (Seoul: Asia Munhwasa).

Ch'oe, K. (1981), *Han'guk Musongon* (About Korean Shamanism) (Sŏul: Hyŏngsŏl Ch'ulp'ansa).

Ch'oe, K. (1991), *Han'guk Muga 2: Kyŏngbok, Kangwon, Cheju, Sŏul, Hwanghae-do* (Shamanic Text of Korea 2: Kyŏngbok, Kangwon, Cheju, Seoul, and Hwanghae-do) (Sŏul: Asea Munhwasa).

Ch'oe, K. (1999), 'Shyamanijŭm ŭi Pigyo (Comparison in Shamanism)' in I. Ch'oe (ed.) *Pigyo Minsokhak kwa Pigyomunhwa* (Comparative Folklore and Culture) (Sŏul: Minsogwŏn), 357–72.

Eliade, M. (2004), *Shamanism: Archaic Techniques of Ecstasy* (Princeton, NJ: Princeton University Press).

Gottschalk, S. (2018), *The Terminal Self: Everyday Life in Hypermodern Times* (New York: Routledge).

Hong, T. (2006), *Hwanghae-do ŭi Muga* (Shamanic Texts of Hwanghae-do Province) (Seoul: Minsogwŏn).

Howard, K. (1998), 'Preserving the Spirits? Ritual, State Sponsorship, and Performance' in K. Howard (ed.) *Korean Shamanism Revivals, Survivals, and Change* (Seoul: Seoul Press), 87–217.

Hwang, M. (2012), 'Shamans and Superstitious Mothers: Modern Healthcare Discourse in 1920s-30s Korea'. *Asian Journal of Women's Studies*, 18(1): 30–61.

Ivanescu, C. and Berentzen, S. (2020), 'Becoming a Shaman: Narratives of Apprenticeship and Initiation in Contemporary Shamanism'. *Religions*, 11(7): 362.

Janelli Roger, L. and Janelli, D. Y. (1982), *Ancestor Worship and Korean Society* (Stanford, CA: Stanford University Press)

Jung, M. (2023), 'Shamans, Curses and Superstitions in Contemporary South Korea', *The Herald Times*, 28 March. Available at: https://www.koreaherald.com/view.php?ud=20230328000549. Accessed 1 October 2024.

Kang, Y. (2020), 'Contacting with God and Inhaling Spirit – Shaman and Photographer'. Blog post, *Yongho Kang Photography*. Available at: http://www.younghokang.com/shaman-and-photographer. Accessed 1 October 2024.

Kendall, L. (1988), *The Life and Hard Times of a Korean Shaman: of Tales and the Telling of Tales* (Honolulu, HI: University of Hawai'i Press).

Kendall, L. (2009), *Shamans, Nostalgias, and the IMF: South Korean Popular Religion in Motion* (Honolulu, HI: University of Hawai'i Press).

Kim, Ok-ju (1993), 'Chosŏn Malgi Tuch'ang ŭi Yuhaeng kwa Mingan ŭi Taeŭng' (Smallpox Epidemics and Popular Responses in the Late Chosŏn Period). *Ŭisahak* (Korean Journal of Medical History), 2(1): 38–58.

Kin, C. and Noh, M. (2022), 'COVID-19, Shincheonji, and the Limits of South Korean Secularism: The Devil in Patient 31'. *Religion, State and Society*, 50(3): 316–37.

Kunitz, S. J. and Levy, J. E. (1997), 'Dances with Doctors: Navajo Encounters with the Indian Health Service' in A. Cunningham and B. Andrews (eds) *Western Medicine as Contested Knowledge* (Manchester: Manchester University Press), 93–123.

Kwŏn, H. (2023), 'Pyŏlip Singwan ŭi Ilonjŏk Uisang' (Parallelism: Yim Suk-Jay's Theory of Korean Shamanism). *Hanguk Minsokhak (Korean Folklore)*, 77: 7–27.

Liu, P. (2021), 'Shamanism and Gender Construction Among the Kavalan of Taiwan: Men and Women's Illness Caused by Different Spirits' in D. Torri and S. Roche (eds) *The Shamaness in Asia* (London and New York: Routledge), 208–24.

Quijada, J. B. (2011), 'Symptoms as Signs in Buriat Shamanic Callings' in D. G. Anderson (ed.) *The Healing Landscapes of Central and Southeastern Siberia* (Alberta: The University of Alberta Press), 13–27.

Mills, S. (2007), *Healing Rhythms: The World of South Korea's East Coast Hereditary Shamans* (Aldershot: Ashgate).

Robinson, M. E. (1993), 'Enduring Anxieties: Cultural Nationalism and Modern East Asian' in H. Befu (ed.) *Cultural Nationalism in East Asia: Representation and Identity* (Berkeley: Institute of East Asian Studies), 167–86.

Sarfati, L. (2020), 'Healing Through Gender Inversion in Korean Possession Trance Rituals'. *The Drama Review*, 64(3): 16–32.

Sarfati, L. (2021), *Contemporary Korean Shamanism: From Ritual to Digital* (Bloomington, IN: Indiana University Press).

Sarfati, L. (2023), 'The Cosmopolitan Vernacular: Korean Shamans (Mudang) in the Global Spirituality Market'. *Religions*, 14(189): 1–21.

Sarfati, L. (2024), 'From Rural Outcasts to Urban Cosmopolitans: Spiritual Healers in Seoul'. *Urbanities*, 14(1): 84–100.

9

Spiritual Technologies: Afro-Brazilian Religious Epistemologies and Healing During Covid-19

JOANA BAHIA

Introduction

In the present chapter, I deal with the mediation between health, care and bodies through technologies and spiritual agency (Latour 2021), transiting between different types of epistemes produced by practitioners, clients, leaders of Afro-Brazilian religiosities and the non-human agents in this worldview. Inspired by Latour's ideas (2021), I define spiritual technologies as materialities manufactured under the agency of spirits, humans (adepts, religious leaders), plants and animals. All substances made as offerings connect humans and non-humans because the action of both is present in their production. The combination of objects (flowers, pots), herbs and sacrificed animals, added to the knowledge of prayers and magical utterances and actions of the religious adepts' bodies, produces new objects and actions that make it possible to instrumentalise healing. The substances involved in the offerings in Afro-Brazilian religions comprise multiple realities and beings, and their production also involves the presence of the spirits attracted by the prayers, animals, plants and the context in which the offering is produced. The offering is a form of knowledge itself, and it is produced by the combination of all things (human and non-human) with spiritual action; all is connected.

Epistemology as a way of seeing, perceiving and producing knowledge in the Afro-religious field is produced by contact with ancestry, in other words, with the spirit world. The spirit world brings knowledge about herbs, minerals and vegetables – in short, knowledge about various other human and non-human beings. All this knowledge is produced by humans and non-humans in interaction with the spiritual world, and these are elements that are in dialogue with the visions and tools of science, especially bioscience (medicine). One of the ways to get in touch with

Proceedings of the British Academy, **278**, 179–195, © Authors 2025.

this divine aspect is through the divinatory game played by the cowrie shells. This technological knowledge is produced over the years by the experience acquired by the body/mind in ritual practice, oral tradition and contact through trance and mediumistic learning.

The whole ensemble involved in making the religious offering shows the interweaving of episteme produced through spiritual connection. In the ethnography I carried out between 2020 and 2023, I interviewed Afro-Brazilian religious practitioners and leaders, and I perceived the importance of spiritual agency; the modes of production of sacred technologies in hospitals, Afro-Brazilian temples and other territories; and the interpretations these religions made regarding Covid-19, based upon mediumistic experiences. The analysis presented below is based on the fieldwork I did during and after Covid-19 with various Afro-religious groups, but in the current chapter, I focus in depth on one case study containing reports of near-death and post-mortem experiences. The leaders and some of the clients I interviewed are initiated into and have knowledge about different types of Afro-Brazilian religiosities, ranging across Umbanda, Quimbanda (Leistner 2014), Batuque, Candomblé and Ifá.

After introducing Afro-Brazilian religions, there will be three examples which highlight the ancestral *ebós* technologies which enable the experience of multiple ontologies coexisting and evidenced through experiential and visionary epistemes. In this context the efficacy of biomedical technologies is determined by non-physical actors, a spiritual entity, namely *exu*, and other spirits such as *erês*. These different ontologies would be seen by the standard Euro-Christian-scientific model as being mutually exclusive or competing worldviews. Yet in the experience of those subjects described below, these competing ontologies are not mutually exclusive in any way; in fact, healing is only possible in many cases through accessing and communicating at the crossroads of standard empirical and visionary/spiritual epistemologies.

Afro-Brazilian religions

Afro-Brazilian religions are a variety of religious expressions of African origin, which were codified in Brazil during the Afro-Atlantic slave trade between the 16th and 19th centuries. Parés (2018) argues that within Afro-Brazilian religiosity, there are distinct religiosities originating among the peoples of West Africa (the Gbe and Yoruba) and those marked by the traditions of Central Africa (the Bantu). In the first group, we have the Tambor de Mina, Xangô and Candomblé. In the second we have Candomblé de Caboclo, Macumba, Quimbanda and, finally, Umbanda. Of the West African traditions, Candomblé is a religion that was constituted in the 19th century in the Brazilian state of Bahia, drawing upon the Yoruba tradition. Ifá is first an *orisha* (deity) in Yoruba traditional religion and also a complete system of divination. As an oracle, Ifá plays a practical and significant role in Yoruba traditional religion by offering answers and solutions to existential problems in the form of ritual offerings and sacrifices to the appropriate deities. From the Central African (Bantu) grouping, Umbanda is perhaps the most prominent and based upon possession by spirits. Its origins lie in the beginning of the 20th century in Rio de Janeiro, and Umbanda blends African religions with Catholicism, Spiritism and considerable indigenous lore. In Umbanda, one worships and incorporates spirits (not African gods as in Candomblé) (Parés 2018).

Afro-Brazilian religions recreate African principles (Rabelo 2014; Parés 2016) in which there is no separation between the subject, spirit, body, community and nature (animals and plants), and which include the ancestors, the living, the dead, the unborn and a whole range of African gods. Healing and religion are connected, and in the Afro-Brazilian logic there is no separation between body and spiritual vitality, seen and unseen, as there is in the West (Asante and Mazama 2009; Onongha 2022: 197). The body is seen as a great repository of knowledge (Bahia 2021), and all the elements that involve it in the religious experience (Rabelo, Alvez and Souza 1999) – community, nature, spaces, times and objects – constitute its experience. The technologies (Latour 2021) and objects that involve these sacred bodies are paradoxically visible and invisible. They also produce sacredness (Beliso-de Jesús 2015; Capponi 2017), being part of the production of the healing process.

According to Afro-Brazilian cosmology, each medium can be surrounded by a group of entities around them. A medium's body builds its mediumship by dreaming and thinking, responding to ideas and gestures coming from an array of sensory experiences brought about in rituals and in contact with their entities. Sharing these experiences with the family of a saint or others allows the medium to perceive changes in body posture and to observe the gradual construction of their mediumship (Bahia 2021: 10).[1] This whole experience is part of the pre-initiation process in which the spiritual agency is decisive, and which will lead to the initiation rites in the religious community. After initiation, the strength of the spiritual and corporeal connection between a person and their *exu* becomes inseparable. To reflect this, the name of their most active *exu* is added to their name as a second identity. For example, the surname Rafael becomes Rafael do Tranca Rua das Almas. In almost all Afro-Brazilian religions, people connect their names to those of their spirits, which are incorporated into their surnames.

These religions have been historically persecuted in Brazil since the times of the Portuguese Empire, when the country was under the control of the Catholic Church and run by the Emperor. Brazil was proclaimed a republic in 1889 when the state sought to separate the Catholic Church and the state, but this plan was never consolidated (Bahia 2023). Between 1930 and 1940, the Church built strong alliances with the state and – through the employment of racial rhetoric – composed new forms of control in the public sphere. Afro-Brazilian religions were accused

[1] Saints are the highest ranks of Candomblé priests, those who care for the *orishas*.

of charlatanism and illegal medicine. Beginning in 1941, the police invaded Afro-Brazilian temples, initially prohibiting their activities and then demanding their registration until 1970 (Bahia 2023).

Since the 1940s, the presence of Evangelical Christianity has increased in Brazilian print, television and radio media. It has been increasingly active in digital spaces since the 1980s and entered national politics from the 1990s onwards as part of a power project extending across several Latin American countries (Guadalupe 2019). This project is linked to the ultra-right Catholic camp, and a growing conservative advance is intensifying religious intolerance against Afro-Brazilian religions. Since the 1990s, the 'invasion' of *terreiros* (Afro-Brazilian temples), the assassination of Afro-religious leaders by conservative evangelical followers, and a greater public regulation of the Afro-religious presence in the political and social sphere have all become increasingly common.

On 20 July 2023, the Brazilian National Health Council, through Resolution 715, recognised the importance of religions of African origin as complementary to the Unified Health System (Sistema Único de Saúde; SUS) and as a first access for individuals seeking healing for emotional and psychological issues. Although the healthcare system recognises Afro-religious knowledge, the majority of hospitals do not allow it in. Brazilian society is guided by an identity as a Christian nation, permeating various institutions such as the legal field, healthcare system and others.

Afro-Brazilian responses to Covid-19

There are no academic works on how Brazilian Afro-religious communities responded to the pandemic. When the issue is raised, religious leaders generally address it in terms of how religious cosmology favours protection and the idea of seclusion as part of a holistic spiritual/bodily treatment. Such analyses explain isolation as part of the learning processes of Afro-religious culture in creating sacred bodies and healing processes; religious values are used to encourage preventive health habits.

Although Afro-Brazilian religions are not authorised by the state (which favours Catholics and Evangelicals) to enter hospital spaces, this does not mean that their practitioners do not transgress these determinations to protest against the excessive Christian presence in public spaces. The strong sympathy for popular practices on the part of the intellectualised and more politicised segments of the population has intersected with growing denunciations from Afro-religious social movements, with the support of non-conservative Christians; the result has been increased pressure for its presence within the Brazilian state to be regulated (Bahia 2023).

We take as our basis of analysis an understanding that the borders between people's lived experiences in Afro-Brazilian religion and those in the digital worlds of devices and machines are porous (Oosterbahn, Van de Kamp and Bahia 2020; Panagiotopoulos and Roussou 2022: 3–4). During the pandemic Afro-Brazilian religious technologies entered hospital gardens and were transmitted to the sick via prayers and thoughts, in Yoruba or in other languages. They crossed the thresholds of hospital doors and windows. Afro-Brazilian spiritual agency entered all these restricted spaces of medical care. Connected by video cameras and mobile phones, the production of objects for healing rituals circulated through the semi-occult spaces of Messenger, WhatsApp and Instagram. The spiritual agency operates in diverse spaces and can use technological elements to transform the sacred into something present, blurring the line between online and offline.

During the pandemic, I observed that some *terreiros* maintained religious rituals in online spaces, recreating them in the face of physical absence and the need to provide comfort to many of their members and clients.[2] Many fathers and mothers of saints attended online, but some only gradually returned to the calendar of public activities in the physical temples after the first round of Covid-19 vaccinations. Despite the pandemic, temple maintenance activities, as observed in my fieldwork, and the feeding of the gods continued,[3] but these duties involved few members and a rotation of people performed them. The epistemological flexibility of Afro-Brazilian religions leads to adaptations to extreme situations in which healing can be produced in different realities.

Although analysis of Afro-Brazilian traditions usually emphasises how the body is a spiritual vehicle, during the pandemic consultations and religious services were carried out through media in biomedical spaces, for example, using online services and a variety of objects and technological devices that are central to Afro-Brazilian healing practices. In understanding this apparent contradiction, we follow Meyer (2016), who emphasised how aesthetics evokes sensations (Serres 2001; Stoller 2022). Even when mediated through Messenger, WhatsApp and Instagram, those embedded in the Afro-Brazilian epistemologies continued to have bodily experiences of the active mediation of spirits and *orishas* in their healing processes.[4]

The currency of exchange became images of spells sent by mobile phone cameras. Instructions for the continuity of religious services were passed through WhatsApp groups. The commerce through which objects and animals were purchased for ritual was also part of a spell's modus operandi. The local animal breeders who largely supplied the *babalawos* (Afro-religious leaders) began to get more work than the more central large markets. Despite restricted physical

[2] *Terreiros* are communities of initiates and Afro-Brazilian temples, also called *roça* and *ilê*.

[3] Food is related to the logic of Asé and gift, connecting initiates, priests and gods. Asé is transmissible. It is passed on by material and symbolic means and it can accumulate. It is a force that can be acquired by means of introjection or contact. It may be transmitted both to objects and human beings (Santos 1986). Asé always seems to need a material vehicle to be transmitted and food, in the form of offerings, is generally the main means of transmission. Minerals and ingredients from the vegetable kingdom, as well as animal sacrifices, can be used individually or in combination as food offerings. These offerings are made to the *orishas*, *eguns* and sometimes to the person's double (Souza 2015).

[4] *Orishas* are African gods venerated in Candomblé as mediators between Olorun and humankind.

circulation, mobility was possible, managed by sorcerers and their clients and families, as well as by the places and machines through which the sick circulated.

Online services made religious continuity possible for old clients while forming networks of new clients (and) sons of saints in Brazil and in other countries. Interviews with several Quimbanda masters show that when cases of Covid-19 began to decrease due (likely) to increases in vaccination, many apprentices began to be initiated in the houses of their masters in Brazil. While there are Quimbanda initiations that do not require the physical presence of the apprentice, physical presence is necessary in other cases (of other types of Quimbanda).

Many lectures and readings on social media by *terreiro* leaders presented Obaluaié – the *orisha* of illness and health and the owner of the land[5] – as someone who understood the pandemic as a reflection of the evils caused by humanity against nature and as resulting from the imbalances caused by not considering the Earth as one of the social actors of our times and society. Many images shared on social media depict this *orisha* healing the planet from the pandemic, cleaning bodies and places with popcorn (Obaluaié´s food used in many rituals). This interpretation was very common among the followers of Afro-religions, who understand the Afro-religious technological apparatus as an important and complex system of healing knowledge production.

For example, *ebós* are understood as ancestral technologies, since they bring together multiple forms of knowledge about the world, connecting human and non-human beings to the *orisha*s. *Ebós* are sacrificial offering to an *orisha* which can rebalance a person's life. *Ebós* are understood as a physical and energetic instrument for the circulation of the *Asé* between biological bodies, a powerful healing technology.[6] An example of how this works in practice is provided in the following case study.

Case study: tubes, machines and multiple agencies in the healing process

This case study shows multiple agencies, with different social actors being part of the healing experience: not just the healer and the patient but all their attendant social entourages. Families of blood and saints, sorcerers, doctors and different spaces of life and death appear here, along with the full technological apparatus that connects them (Stolow 2013).

On St George's Day, 23 April 2021, Mr Francisco returned from a 40-day intubation in hospital caused by Covid-19. He had gone to cardiac arrest for 10 minutes and had seen his inert body being resuscitated for 6 minutes, after which he

[5] See https://www.cartacapital.com.br/blogs/dialogos-da-fe/e-a-doenca-que-nos-ensina-que-saude-e-um-bem-precioso/ (accessed 23 August 2024).

[6] See note 3.

was left alone for 4 minutes. In that final spacetime, he slowly returned to life. His *exus* are very present both in his reports and in the visions that he had in the hospital, but several other entities appear in his spiritual experiences as well. Francisco had a sensitive experience in a place that was a mixture of a spiritual hospital and a home, which he called 'hell': a good and positive place containing many entities from various currents of Afro-Brazilian religions.

His relatives claim that *exus* were close to Mr Francisco's daughter, as it was she who spoke with great authority and conviction and took him and his wife to the hospital. The hospital doors were opened and closed by *exus* for the daughter to pass through at various times during her stay in the institution. Since she is a nurse by profession, she was the one who had the best access to the doctors and to her parents.

In Mr Francisco's narrative, he says that his *exu*, Exu Tranca Ruas de Embaré,[7] took his hand right at the beginning of his hospitalisation, and Francisco followed him on a long journey. During the second day of his hospitalisation, Francisco asked his *exu* to put an end to his suffering. According to Francisco's doctor, Francisco could not breathe, 90 per cent of his lungs were infected and he was in constant agony. In Francisco's vision, Exu Tranca Rua was a Black man, two metres tall, who took Francisco by the chest, extracted his essence and left his body there.

Francisco was no longer in his body. He looked down and saw himself being intubated by nurses. At that moment, his *exu* took him to a new place, with a waterfall that plummeted from a rock. Two women in silver robes gave him a white liquid that tasted like coconut water. They cleaned him up, since Francisco's body was covered in slime and scabs. He was taken care of morning and afternoon as he laid there, imbibing the liquid. He saw his body in the spiritual hospital. After he managed to walk better, Embaré and Exu Marabó appeared to guide him, to show him where he was. It was a place that looked like a very extensive medieval stone castle. There were many people there with orange robes hanging down to their feet, wearing hats with a white sign. They were spiritual doctors.

On the right side, there were women with red and white shirts who also cared for the sick. These were the helpers of the spiritual doctors. Their faces were visible, but the spiritual doctors' faces were not, nor were their hands and feet. Everyone was as busy as the doctors and did not have time to go home.

Francisco reported that in this place there was a 13-year-old boy who was responsible for his treatment. The boy was called Xere,[8] which is the name of an *erê*,[9] Francisco's son's entity in Candomblé. Breath gives life to things, enchanting and consecrating (Serres 2001). This process is controlled by divine children like the *erês*. Despite the differences between these entities, children are associated

[7] Another type of *exu* in Quimbanda, related to St Anthony of Embaré.

[8] The name of the spirit evokes the idea of a ritual rattle in the cult of the orisha Xangô.

[9] A childlike manifestation of an *orisha*. It manifests during a shallower trance, in which the person possessed speaks and behaves like a child.

with *erês* and *ibejis*, who are understood as child spirits with great healing power (Capone 2020: 304). They have been associated in popular Brazilian Catholic culture since the 16th century with Saints Cosimo and Damian, who are the patron saints of doctors and surgeons.

Francisco experienced Xere giving him information, transmitting and producing knowledge, and passing medicines to his doctor in the biomedical hospital. Francisco's body was dying 'downstairs' in the medical hospital, and the doctor was hitting the table, saying 'I can't lose Mr. Francisco!' Francisco saw Xere come from the place where all of the spiritual doctors were working, and he went into Francisco's doctor's ear in the hospital and said something. The doctor said: 'I already know what I'm going to give him.' There was a huge fistula in Francisco's intestine that would not close, but with Xere's medicine, the doctor was able to control it.

Francisco experienced this *erê*, Xere, as working day and night while acting with a certain playfulness. Xere laughed, joked and did not take anyone very seriously. However, his absence was a sign of desperation because there was a device, according to Mr Francisco, that 'breathed in the medical hospital down here'. Everyone imagined that this device (a bipap) was controlled by nurses in the material hospital, but Francisco experienced that the biomedical machine was controlled by Xere, who regulated the machine that made Francisco's breathing possible.

While his body was in hospital, Francisco's *exus* took him to many places. There, in that spiritual place, he felt at home, happy, with no desire to return to Earth. He saw many people arriving and tried to help find a way out for all the souls that were arriving. Deaths of all kinds were occurring, beyond the people dying from Covid-19.[10] In that place, there was a leader, and Francisco was invited to go into that leader's home. This spiritual city was a hospital for souls.

During these journeys with Xere, Francisco described coming into Lucifer's presence. In *Quimbanda* symbology, Lucifer is an *exu*. It is in his presence that persons are received into the spiritual plane. Francisco described Lucifer as very big and muscled. Francisco greeted him and asked if Lucifer wanted anything, given that he was restoring Francisco's life. Lucifer replied: 'My son, you are a good son. You don't owe me anything. Continue being the person you are.' Francisco insisted: 'If I give you a black goat, will you be happy with me?' Lucifer replied: 'I'm happy, but I don't want anything from you. You don't have to give me anything.'

[10] In July 2020, there were more than 80,000 deaths and a further 2.1 million people infected, with a rate of 38 deaths per 100,000 inhabitants in Brazil. This made the country the second in absolute number of cases in the world, behind the US alone, which had a death rate of 43 deaths/100,000 inhabitants. In Latin America, only Chile and Peru have higher mortality rates than Brazil: Chile, with 330,930 infected and 8,503 dead, had a death rate of 45 deaths/100,000 inhabitants, and Peru, with 353,590 infected and 13,187 dead, had a death rate of 41 deaths/100,000 inhabitants. In Brazil, the pandemic created tensions in the health sector that fueled, among other factors, the political and information crisis that plagued the country, in which religion appeared as one of the protagonists. See: https://covid.saude.gov.br/, https://www.nytimes.com/interactive/2020/world/coronavirus-maps.html (accessed 20 July 2020).

Francisco praised his Lucifer with a song. Lucifer left, and Francisco was left between Exu Tranca Rua and Marabó. Up came a very thin gentleman with a pita rope tied around his waist. In Francisco's vision, this was Obatalá, the creator, who said that it was time to return his son to the material world. At that moment, Francisco saw his dogs, his water fountain and his home.

In that spiritual place, Francisco's body was muscular and healthy, unlike his physical form. The place had sloping stone beds on which the sick lay. The white liquid distributed to them twice a day was a spiritual technology, developed by the family of women in the silver robes. An extract from the tree of life, only this spiritual family could manufacture the liquid, not just anyone knew how to produce it. Some things only exist in the spiritual world.

In the morning, Francisco counted down the hours until dawn to take a bath with scented herbal extracts in a river of warm waters. The spiritual beings took him to a feast for Oxossi (African god, a hunter who possesses the knowledge of all the beings that exist in the forest), where they were roasting a whole deer. Francisco could not eat it, however, as it was only for those who already lived in that realm. Oxossi came to talk to him. Ogun (African god of technology and new paths) from Cappadocia also came to see him and said that he was taking Francisco out of that place. Ogun said that Francisco was Ori Meji, an expression in Yoruba that means 'double head', that is, an individual who has an *Orí* (head) governed by two *orishas* at the same time and was accompanied by Ogun on his spiritual path. Francisco felt the presence of his *exu*, Tranca Rua, who came to him, smiling, when Francisco returned to life after 10 minutes of cardiac arrest. Francisco was resuscitated with more faith in his beliefs. His religous episteme strengthened as a result of his near-death experience. Francisco thinks people should know that 'religion is solid and fights for its children. Your religion is listening; your gods listen to you. Your African gods are Black, respectful and listen to their children.'

Francisco believed that the hospital's doctor was put into his life by the *exus*. The doctor was a 34-year-old man who had gained a certain visibility and recognition in the region where he works. The doctor joked that he saved Francisco, but in fact, it was Francisco's illness that saved him first, since he was in crisis. The doctor had lost all of his intubated patients to Covid-19. He saved only Francisco and another patient. Francisco narrated that this was possible because the *exu* cleansed that hospital of *eguns*,[11] spirits of the deceased which can be hazardous to the living but also important actors in rituals when controlled by the *exus*, and several other intubated patients began to return to life.

During his journey, Francisco had learned that his family was spiritual and that it had an important mission. On a spiritual level, Francisco learned about

[11] A spirit of the dead. Contact with them can be very dangerous in Candomblé. In Quimbanda, they are hazardous but also important in the rituals, and they serve the *exus* and the *pombasgiras*, performing most of the spiritual services.

the importance of his family when he visited Pentagram (the ruler of the spiritual city).[12] He participated in meetings, outlining the future of the place in relation to the disease, and had the right to express his opinion. Everyone at the meeting in the spiritual hospital knew that Covid-19 was a spiritual phenomenon and that this disease was allowed to happen to a limited number of people, so that they could learn from their imperfections – from what they cannot master.

Dead and alive, animate and inanimate, human and non-human beings (Blanes and Espírito Santo 2014) can all be found in Francisco's hell. New forms of communication between different beings are marked by sensations and images. Blowing, inhaling, expelling, the laying on of hands, observing, smelling, eating, bending, and various uses of the body and its sensory suite (Serres 2001) are all present in spiritual agency (Hayes 2011; Johnson 2014; Lambek 2014) and in the mediations of this with other beings.

When Francisco was hospitalised, his son asked the *exus* of his house for help and asked everyone to 'drop their irons' (their settlements) to take care of his parents in the hospital.[13] The hospital garden was filled with Afro-Brazilian offerings by Francisco's son. On the day of his father's hospitalisation, Francisco's son called his *babalawo* of Ifá, who saw Iku (death) in the game and said that his mother would return, but that his father would not return if he didn't make an *ebó*, an offering used for spiritual cleansing and healing.

The *ebós* and all the magical works were accompanied by Ya Nádia (Afro-Brazilian female leader), who died shortly after her parents returned from the hospital. Many things were done for the Iaymins,[14] since they are the owners of blood, the organs and the body in general, and they are one of the great pillars of Candomblé. When Olodumare created the world,[15] he soon created the Iaymins, who had greater strength because not even an *exu* could face them. The *orishas* could bring blessings, but they could also bring discord. Xapanã, Obatalá, Oxossi,

[12] An alchemical symbol, present in European witchcraft but also in Quimbanda, it can have multiple meanings depending on how it is used. It can be a concentration, an expansion, an energetic prison or a symbol of decay. Everything depends on the situation in which it is worked. The most important symbol is the magical incantation scratched out in drawings on the floor, which represents the signature of the Spirits, and the spirits invoked.

[13] This is the material representation of the sacred force of the divinity. It is made of clay, ceramic or wooden containers holding a stone (otan) symbolising the initiate's head.

[14] A name representing all mythical female progenitors. For example: Odudua, Nanã, Yemanja, Oxum. They are attached to the gourd which contains a bird: the procreated element. This bird represents the African Iyamin; its power is primordial, absolute, dangerous and sovereignly feminine.. They are simultaneously Destroyer and Generator. In Yoruba thought, iaymis can be situated among sorceresses as well as creation gods. Their action mediates excesses of power. They contribute to the distribution of power and social position (Verger 1992: 37). The anger of the iaymis explains the diseases and their remedies. The restlessness and anguish they represent are part of Yoruba culture.

[15] Olodumare or Olorun is the traditional name in Yoruba cosmology for the Supreme Being. He is present in every spark of life.

Ogun, Exu and other *orishas* only exist in Nigeria.[16] Francisco's son did not have time to do most of the spiritual works because of visiting his father in hospital and everyday life, so they called the *babalawo*, and he consulted the oracle and made the *ebós*.[17]

One of the first spells was directed at Francisco's head to calm him down. On the day of his father's intubation, Francisco's son got very nervous, and he heard his Xangô Airá,[18] who asked him to calm down and understand the need for intubation. Every day the son made an *abará* for Xangô,[19] opened it, prayed and left it in the flowerbed next to the hospital. It was his *orisha*. He heard his voice inside the hospital almost all the time. It was the father's time to talk to the son – in this case, Xangô talking to him. At the end of Francisco's treatment, there were more than 60 *abarás* scattered throughout the garden.

From there, Francisco's son went to perform the first spell, among several, going to the bush to offer a pig's heart and two roosters to Exu das Matas,[20] one of the healing *exus* in Quimbanda. He put the offerings on the ground and began to call the *exu*, and the weeds began to creak under his feet. He made the offering in the first place that his father had taken him to take care of this *exu*. The wind started blowing leaves around it, the trees started shaking and noises of jaguar grunts and various animals approaching could be heard. That day the father's heartbeat improved. Conditions or illnesses that would normally take three or four days to improve were expedited with the use of spells. Francisco's son offered his blood to Tranca Ruas de Embaré and Marabó.[21] He asked Beelzebub and the *exu* for a black cape. He asked for aid from the Preto Velho and the Caboclo Sete Setas, his father's entities. All the animals they raised went to the *ebós*, and they still had to buy more animals for the *babalawo*'s offerings. Francisco's son did not have time to play the Quimbanda oracle,[22] so most of the offerings were a mix of what he knew, along with his intuition, guiding him in what to do. In the meantime, he activated his

[16] Xapanã is he who cleans the body, thus taking the *egun* to another plane. His main symbol is the xaxará, made with straw extracted from the palm leaf, decorated with whelks and beads. With this 'weapon' he sweeps away diseases, spells, misery and incurable evils. Oxossi owns the forests, being the hunter orixá. Egungun is an ancestral spirit venerated on Caparica Island in Bahia, Brazil. The traditions of the *egúngún* cult teach about life. Those initiated into the secret – the *õjê* – do not disappear. They return to *ìtun lá* (house, a place of rebirth), a conception that represents the structure, in a way that is understood not as a mystery but as something that is very close to life. It is the certainty of renewal expressed in the exchange between life and death.

[17] A sacrificial offering to an *orisha*, or a positive magical work.

[18] *Orisha* of justice, fire and storms.

[19] *Abará* is ritual food offered to Xango. It consists of ground fried bean dumpling with dried shrimp and onions, seasoned with dende oil and pepper and steamed, wrapped in a banana leaf.

[20] *Exu* from the kingdom of the forests, considered to be the place of knowledge.

[21] You can offer your own blood if you have nothing else to offer. Only in a situation of extreme urgency would one offer up some of one's own life force in exchange for more life force.

[22] A type of divinatory practice in Quimbanda, generally performed with 7 cowrie shells but which can also be performed with 4, 16 or 21 cowrie shells.

entire Quimbanda, Umbanda, Candomblé and Ifá networks. During the drumming, Obatalá warned that he would return.

This knowledge is transmitted through religious learning brought in the first instance by mediumship (dreams, visions, malaise, fainting, pain and various bodily reactions to the presence of spirits) and then completed with subsequent initiation into the Afro-religion. Each Afro-religious segment has a different length of time for learning. A person who has already been initiated learns something else about their emotions and their experience with their entities. The Afro-episteme constantly incorporates new input from the other-than-human members of this ontology to ensure that the healing technologies continue to be effective.

At various times, Obatalá appears in these narratives, in the offerings and in the positive responses to Francisco's return to life. In *itans* (mythological accounts) recounted in Candomblé, Olodumare asked Obatalá to mould the physical bodies of human beings in clay. When this was done, Olodumare breathed on the lifeless bodies, and they became living people. After that, the created beings went to the *ori* (inner head), from where they chose their destinations because the head gives direction to the body, the path a person should follow in life. In this cosmology the head is the most important part of the body.

The *babalawo* had to go back to Nigeria for treatment after taking care of Francisco. At Ifá, the *babalawo* helped someone else, but he didn't charge for this service. He asked for lunch with his parents, but this is not considered a charge for the spirit world. If the person does not charge, they become part of the problem in the sense of not creating any kind of distinction between the patient and the *babalawo*. In such a case, the *babalawo* would share the negativity of the person they were trying to help, as well as their bad luck, and could attract spiritual attacks onto themselves. As Iku, Death, wanted to take Mr Francisco, if the *babalawo* took that target away from him, then that target's fate was now the *babalawo*'s problem. Iku pursues the *babalawo* to take his life because he has attracted negative energy to himself. The economy in the spirit world is different from ours. The epistemologies of healing, whether spiritual or hospital based, are not opposed but go hand in hand.

Ethnographing the cure

The importance of the body is evident in the construction of the experiences related above (Merleau-Ponty 1994), as well as how such bodies can be affected differently. I accept such bodily interpretations and value their sensations throughout the entire long process of illness and healing. As mediums, the patients, doctors and their spirits transit between *terreiros*, hospitals, cemeteries and other spaces engaged in multiple and various healing rituals. The healing processes in Afro-religions are part of their cosmological worldview, in which they do not separate their knowledge from others; even if they are different epistemes, they can engage in dialogue and intermingle with each other.

The understanding here is that disease is not just a biological or cultural determination (Csordas 2002: 287). It is not a mechanical association between signs and symptoms (Rabelo, Alves and Souza 1994). Subjects' bodies are central in these narratives and are intertwined with spirits, which – in turn – produce substances, blow breaths through the air, and handle devices and machines. This is not a question of thinking about a relationship in which religious discourses invade scientific ones or vice versa. Here, technological forms of 'enchantments' are being managed by social actors, things, spirits and means. Humans and their spirits drive the apparatus/machines, whether in the hospital ward or the immaterial ones in the spirit world. Afro cosmology does not separate these worlds. The biomedical technology of life-support machines is activated by the 'technology' of mediation and communication with the *exus*, who can effect healing with as much agency as biomedical interventions. There is no inherent objection to 'mechanical technology', but its effectiveness is mediated by the *exus*. In this sense, the body is not an object or a text (Merleau-Ponty 1994) but a locus of subjectivity; a contingent configuration, never static or permanent but capable of composing hybrids (Taylor 2005: 750).

Eres and *exus* have spiritual agency (Hayes 2011). They are part of the daily lives of the people I interviewed who went through different ways of dealing with suffering by activating their multiple religious networks. This highlights not only the importance of religious life as a valuable public asset but also shows that emotions and spiritual agency create ways of thinking about Covid-19 and the urgency of the pandemic. The *ebós*, the offerings, the spiritual agency, the mediumship that produces dreams and visions are all ways of being, present in the production of Afro-religious sacredness, which consequently produce knowledge about the experiences of illness and healing. This is the constantly adapting episteme of the Afro-Brazilian healing traditions.

All stages of the pandemic were complex in Brazil, as there were restrictions on access to various places. There was also a lot of creativity at play, however. Many Pais de Santo and Mestres (religious leader of Quimbanda) relied on the help of their religious family's networks to seek solutions, share doubts about their own mediumship, discover new substances and ways of performing spells in unimaginable spaces, or even as an extension of the hospital. Producing healing is also possible in this great dialogue about doubts and discoveries, in the sharing of this multiple knowledge. The power of the *exus* takes over the bodies of their mediums and shows how affliction and healing are experienced. This situation brings new challenges for mediums who experience doubt, a broken body and the power of agency that the spirits bring them. The *babalawo* of Ifá had to recover from their experiences, as they had violently been in direct contact with death. These principles and practices derive from religious worldviews that do not exclude other forms of knowledge. Divinatory systems used by *babalawo* bring knowledge not only about illness but about where in the body one is not paying attention, how to relate parts of the body to the emotional, how illness is related to the worlds of the dead and how to take care of them. What role do entities play in understanding, producing or even treating illness? Illness is amplified by this knowledge, which goes beyond just treating it.

Spiritually living in what Francisco calls 'hell' (his beliefs in Quimbanda) also made him think of the world of the dead that temporarily became his home. It is worth remembering that in some of the African traditions inherited by Afro-Brazilian religiosities, the dead continue their existence in the spiritual world. Consequently, the family and community ties enjoyed in the physical world do not end when someone dies: people continue to maintain these ties in the spirit realm. In the spirit realm, however, they are called 'ancestors' (Asante and Mazama 2009: 36). In this state of existence, they remain closely related to those who are still alive in the physical world, although these spirits are no longer considered to be human. Even though mortality might overtake Francisco, he will continue to be part of his family in unseen ways. Death is not the end. The idea of life and death is cyclical and is a central part of Afro-religious cosmology, to which Francisco belongs.

Exus, enchanted ones, *orishas*, saints, demons, the living and the dead, and objects such as images, amulets, candles, food, herbs, medicines and *ebós* are present in the daily lives of the faithful and in the different contexts through which all these agents and objects flow. These agencies are not limited to the extraordinary dimension or circumscribed to the domains of the religious. We saw that the lawns of the hospitals gained a new life through the *abarás* deposited upon them. This is because it is necessary to feed that space to enter the world of the dead, since in the *itans* of Xangô this becomes possible. All of this permeates everyday choices and attitudes and materialises, in different ways, in the things experienced during the urgency of the pandemic.

In the case study explored in this chapter around Afro-Brazilian religious encounters with Covid-19, we have decentred humans and come to know other possible existences. The agency and mediation of other beings (Latour 2012), the flows of life that animate materials and that provide a flowing character to stable entities (Ingold 2012) or interspecies connections (Tsing 2015), demonstrate the fluidity between the different spheres of existence (Oosterbahn, Van de Kamp and Bahia 2020: 10–12). It is in this context that we find strong Black men like *exus*, 13-year-old child doctors and beings of many races in Mr Francisco's hell, all governed by the Pentagram. Even though these spheres are ontologically related to other spheres, Sloterdijk (2016) maintains that social life is produced by (or in) bubbles and that humans reproduce bounded spheres in which social life is made possible.

Sound creates a sense of communication in which the material and immaterial, visible and invisible worlds are not separated. The word *is* a meaning even before it *has* meaning (Stoller 2022: 183–4). The word of the healer (master or *babalawo*) is thus worth a lot because it is an energy. Its power of enchantment brings life to many things, substances, objects, food, people and animals. The verbal dimension is important in words and prayers, as it attributes power to actions and creates movement. One cannot experience the sacred by reducing it to this single dimension, however (Favret-Saada 1980).

We understand that many studies have been interested in how people mobilise spiritual and material agencies linked to 'supernatural' realities in situations of struggle, disputes and identity construction (Lambek 2014; Blanes and Espírito Santo 2014; Johnson 2014). Entities (such as enchanted people, spirits, saints and ghosts) and 'animated' objects (such as images, amulets, candles, plants, medicines and offerings) are all present in the daily lives of the people we have interviewed. These agencies are not limited to ethereal planes or the domains of the explicitly religious, as if the sacred were a separate world. Spirits and objects are part of everyday attitudes, and their effects materialise in different ways in daily experience. Even if the biomedical episteme cannot incorporate the healing of the Afro-Brazilian epistemology, the working episteme of the Afro-Brazilian healers can and does adapt to coexisting with biomedical epistemes and technologies.

Ebós technologies entered hospital gardens, prayers and thoughts, whether in Yoruba or in other languages. They crossed the thresholds of doors and windows, and spiritual agency entered all these restricted spaces of medical care. Connected by video cameras and mobile phones, the production of objects and things for healing rituals circulated through the semi-occult spaces of Messenger, WhatsApp and Instagram. Clothes of the sick and their objects circulated from hospitals to *terreiros*, among the deities and their multiple spaces. Messages, incorporations, objects and mentalisations moved from axé houses to libraries, doctors' offices and cemeteries. This coming and going of things, animals and people constitutes the lexicon of magic (Kapferer 2015).

Interaction between bodies, materials and nature is a spiritual technology that circulates Asé and enables the possibility of transforming these elements into others. Techniques, the actions of time and the perennial nature of substances are all transformed and recycled into others (Latour 2021). Baking, processing, frying, cooking and other forms of food production, along with offerings and baths that decompose, ferment and alter their compositions, materially translate the power of temporal processes and how the idea of the perennial underpins the very idea of thinking about life.

As well as *ebós* being technologies that connect worlds (Capponi 2017; Latour 2021), acting on humans and non-humans in places like gardens, cemeteries and hospitals, we emphasise the actions of spirits. These articulate their sacred knowledge to issue reports, intubate people, mobilise doctors, open and close doors, and prescribe spells through transmissions and communications via mobile phones (Hayes 2011). The spirit world is in the bodies of the mediums and on the screens performing healing (Beliso-de Jesús 2015).

The notion of technology for thinking about *ebós* is based on epistemes produced by non-Western cosmologies and ontologies. Epistemologies in Afro-religions constitute a form of knowledge shared by the religious community from mediumistic development and initiation into the religion, and do not exclude other forms of production about the body, such as medicine or related areas; this knowledge is reworked in the spiritual field. These epistemes produce Asé through *ebós*, baths, prayers and various sacred materialities, restoring health from the intersection of knowledge and substances between human, non-human and machine agents (Stolow 2013).

References

Asante, M. (ed.) (2009), *An Encyclopedia of African Religion* (Los Angeles, CA: Sage Publications).

Bahia, J. (2021), 'Multiple Space-Times of the Transnational Mediumship: Case Studies in Afro-Brazilian Religions'. *Shaman*, 29(1–2): 5–20.

Bahia, J. (2023), *O Rio de Iemanjá* (Rio de Janeiro: Editora Telha).

Beliso-de Jesús, A. M. (2015), *Electric Santería: Racial and Sexual Assemblages of Transnational Religion* (Columbia, OH: Columbia University Press).

Blanes, R. and Espírito Santo, D. (eds) (2014), *The Social Life of Spirits* (Chicago, IL: The University of Chicago Press).

Capone, S. (2020), 'As crianças divinas: ibejis, erês e egbé orún nas reigiões afro-atlânticas' in R. Menezes, M. Freita and L. Bártolo (eds) *Doces Santos: devoções a Cosme e Damião* (Rio de Janeiro: Museu Nacional, Universidade Federal do Rio de Janeiro), 289–325.

Capponi, G. (2017), 'Deuses ou ciborgues? Uma análise multiespécie do conceito de assentamento no candomblé'. *Anais da VI Reunião de Antropologia da Ciência e Tecnologia*, no. 3: 3–18.

Csordas T. (2002), *Body/Mind/Healing* (New York: Palgrave).

Favret-Saada, J. (1980), *Deadly Words: Witchcraft in the Bocage* (Cambridge: Cambridge University Press).

Guadalupe, J. L. P. (2019), *Evangélicos y poder en América Latina*. 2nd ed. (Lima: Konrad Adenauer Stiftung (KAS); Instituto de Estudios Social Cristianos (IESC)).

Hayes, K. (2011), *Femininity, Sexuality and Black Magic in Brazil* (Berkeley, CA: University of California Press).

Ingold, T. (2012), 'Trazendo as coisas de volta à vida: emaranhados criativos num mundo de materiais'. *Horizontes Antropológicos*, 18(37): 25–44.

Johnson, P. C. (ed.) (2014), *Spirited Things: The Work of Possession in Afro-Atlantic Religions* (Chicago, IL: The University of Chicago Press).

Kapferer, B. (2015), 'Feitiçaria, modernidade e o imaginário constitutivo: continuidades hibridizantes'. *Religião e Sociedade*, 35(2): 18–44.

Lambek, M. (2014), 'Afterword: Recognizing and Misrecognizing Spirit Possession' in P. Johnson (ed.) *Spirited Things: The Work of Possession in Afro-Atlantic Religions* (London: University of Chicago Press), 257–6.

Latour, B. (2012), *Reagregando o Social: Uma Introdução à Teoria do Ator-Rede* (Salvador: Edufba).

Latour, B. (2021), *Sobre o culto moderno dos deuses fetiches: seguido de Iconoclash* (São Paulo: Editora Unesp).

Leistner, R. M. (2014), *Os outsiders do além: um estudo sobre a Quimbanda e outras 'feitiçarias' afro-gaúchas*. Ph.D. thesis, Universidade do Vale do Rio dos Sinos.

Merleau-Ponty, M. (1994), *Fenomenologia da percepção* (São Paulo: Martins fontes).

Meyer, B. (2016), 'How to Capture the "Wow": R.R. Marett's Notion of Awe and the Study of Religion'. *Journal of the Royal Anthropological Institute*, 22(1): 7–26.

Onongha, K. (2022), 'Illnesses and Cures' in I. S. Aderibigbe and T. Falola (eds) *The Palgrave Handbook of African Traditional Religion* (Cham: Palgrave Macmillan), 197–206.

Oosterbahn, M., Van de Kamp, L. and Bahia, J. (2020), 'Lusospheres: The Globalization of Brazilian Religion' in M. Oosterbahn, L. Van de Kamp and J. Bahia (eds) *Global Trajectories of Brazilian Religion: Lusospheres* (London and New York: Bloomsbury Academic), 1–20.

Panagiotopoulos, A. and Roussou, E. (2022), 'We Have Always Been Transreligious: An Introduction to Transreligiosity'. *Social Compass*, 69(4): 614–30.

Parés, L. N. (2016), 'Desdobramento atlânticos, diálogos e reconfigurações' in *O rei, o pai e a morte* (São Paulo: Companhia das Letras), 347–59.

Parés, L. N. (2018), 'Religiosidades' in L. M. Schwarcz and F. dos Santos Gomes (eds) *Dicionário da escravidão e liberdade: 50 textos críticos*. 1st ed. (São Paulo: Companhia das Letras), 395–402.

Rabelo, M. (2014), 'O terreiro como lugar de multiplicidade' in *Enredos, Feituras e Modos de cuidado. Dimensões da vida e da convivência no candomblé* (Salvador: Edufba, Salvador), 279–85.

Rabelo, M., Alves, P. C. and Souza, I. (1999), *Experiência de doença e narrativa* [online] (Rio de Janeiro: Editora Fiobcruz).

Santos, J. (1986), *Os nagô e a morte. Pàde, Àsèsè e o culto Égun na Bahia* (Petrópolis: Vozes)

Serres, M. (2001), *Os cinco sentidos* (Rio de Janeiro: Bertrand Brasil).

Sloterdijk, P. (2016), *Esferas 1 (Bolhas)* (São Paulo: Estação Liberdade).

Souza, P. (2015), 'Food in African Brazilian Candomblé'. *Religion and Food, Scripta Instituti Donneriani Aboensis*, 26: 269.

Stoller, P. (2022), *O gosto das coisas etnográficas: Os sentidos na antropologia* (Rio de Janeiro: Papéis selvagens).

Stolow, J. (2013), *Deus in machina: Religion, Technology, and the Things in Between* (New York: Fordham University Press).

Taylor, J. (2005), 'Surfacing the Body Interior'. *Annual Review of Anthropology*, 34: 741–56.

Tsing, A. (2015), *The Mushroom at the End of the World: On the Possibility of Life in Capitalist Ruins* (Princeton NJ: Princeton University Press).

Verger, P. (1992), 'Esplendor e decadência do culto de Iaymi Osoronga entre os yorubas "minha mãe feiticeira"'. *Artigos. Tomo* 1 (São Paulo: Corrupio).

Part V

Bridging Strategies: Experience and Biomedical Research

THESE THREE CHAPTERS consider possible futures for biomedical research in which there is better integration with religio-cultural paradigms such as *qi* (Cheung, Chapter 10), Daoist visualisation (Steavu, Chapter 11) or yoga (Newcombe, Chapter 12). In such future frameworks, biomedical research would open up to taking the healing benefits of such practices seriously enough to warrant planning and executing clinical trials at sufficient scale, such that any test results, positive or negative, could lead to meaningful conclusions within the context of clinical practice.

Such moves would need to consider both the episteme of the religio-cultural practices, as well as developing encultured and embodied means of identifying and analysing both harms and benefits from within a non-biomedical episteme. This would take the research on minority epistemic practices beyond sample studies, pilot projects and inconclusive results towards substantial knowledge-building in the clinical domain about these healthcare systems. It entails rethinking some of the epistemological assumptions in the clinical frame about benchmarks, baselines and valid bases of truth. It equally requires being more critical about (often political) insider claims in relation to religious 'authenticity' or appeals to 'ancient wisdom' and 'timeless tradition'. Within such future clinical research, experience and reports of healing experiences would need to be taken more seriously or accepted as legitimate or valid ways of arriving at truth. Such epistemic conversations have the potential to enrich standard biomedical epistemes as well as promote a more critical integration of embodied systems of alternative health on their own terms.

10

Placebo Effects, *Qi* and Intention: How Biomedical Hegemony Polices Competing Paradigms

KIN CHEUNG

Introduction

JOSEPHINE BRIGGS SERVED as the second Director of the National Center for Complementary and Integrative Health (NCCIH, formerly National Center for Complementary and Alternative Medicine or NCCAM) at the National Institutes of Health (NIH) from 2008 to 2017 in the US. After she delivered the keynote address on 3 June 2015, at the *Mindfulness and Compassion: The Art and Science of Contemplative Practice* conference held at San Francisco State University, I asked her a few questions. Her answers were frank and have implications for the problems with how medical research is conducted in the US. When asked to provide a working definition of health, Briggs said NCCIH has none and admits this is surprising and something that caught her off guard. This glaring lack of attention to the philosophy and intellectual history of medicine and health may not be surprising to those familiar with the day-to-day operations of medical research centres and the pressure to secure funding and deliver results.[1] When asked about research on acupuncture and *qi*, she flatly told me she would not fund experiments that have no theoretical basis she can understand.[2] Her dismissal of everything included in a paradigm – in this case, one of *qi* – because it is incommensurable with the currently hegemonic one, the biomedical – should not surprise anyone aware of Thomas Kuhn's point on scientific paradigms (Gillies 2005). However, Briggs is not just any medical researcher. She was the decade-long director for a leading

[1] See Cheung (2016) on how underlying philosophical assumptions of health affect wellness research. See Cheung (2020) on what is at stake in defining health and what it may take to change paradigms.

[2] She mentioned explicitly her disdain for experiments measuring whether or not external emission of *qi* could heal cancer cells in a petri dish.

Proceedings of the British Academy, **278**, 199–222, © Authors 2025.

research centre on complementary/alternative and integrative health. Perhaps Briggs's attitude is directly in response to the centre facing 'repeated criticism for funding studies of what many consider to be dubious treatments with very little supporting scientific evidence' (Allen 2015: n.p.).[3] Exactly what *should* or *could* be considered as scientific evidence is precisely what needs to be questioned.

In this chapter, I will focus on the uses of science to defend or debunk acupuncture and healing through/with *qi*. Debunkers relegate and then dismiss acupuncture as a placebo. To be sure, not everyone who claims that the efficacy of acupuncture comes from placebo effects dismisses the practice since there are medical professionals and organisations, in the UK among others, that accept the placebo explanation for acupuncture and still recommend its use. This includes the NCCIH, which has changed its stance on acupuncture (but not *qi*).[4] However, I argue, placebos are precisely what challenges biomedicine. The hegemonic paradigm of biomedicine defines itself as scientifically verified and delineates itself against pseudoscience or practices unverifiable by scientific standards. I argue that healing through *qi* may very well be *unverifiable*, not because it is spurious, but because the standards used to measure, include and legitimate medical practices preemptively rule out healing practices through *qi* due to their underlying paradigm's incommensurability with biomedical worldviews of healing and mind–body. The biomedical call for 'evidence-based' practices ignores the bias of what *counts* as evidence in the first place and the theoretically informed ways evidence is understood and *interpreted*. Double-blind randomised controlled trials are the gold standard for biomedicine, but this type of study (artificially) *severs the precise mechanism* for healing *qi*: the therapeutic relationship and exchange of *qi*.

Qi (氣; *chi*) has been translated as soul, '[p]*neuma*, *ki*, *prana*, air, breath, vital energy, energy, magnetism' (Stanley-Baker 2022: 23), psychophysical energy phenomenon, bioenergy, physical force, ether and more (Yuasa 1993). Translating *qi* has always been political (Zhang 1999). It is a key term in understanding Chinese philosophical-religious traditions, physical and moral self-cultivation practices (e.g. martial arts, meditation), mind–body, health, medicine and more. *Qi* has been examined not only in the disciplines of philosophy (ontology and metaphysics, epistemology, ethics) and the field of religious studies (ritual studies) but also through the disciplinary lenses of political science, linguistics (*qi* as grammar), fine arts and literature (Yuasa 1993; Stanley-Baker 2022). In other words, *qi* is not one thing.

[3] The original name of the center in 1991 was The Office of Alternative Medicine. 'The NIH is notoriously risk averse. The agency is not forgiving of failure, and grant applications are rarely renewed when results are not encouraging. The agency also requires applicants to provide clearly defined deliverables for their projects, and they often have to provide preliminary evidence prior to receiving funding for a project' (Schryvers 2020: 90).

[4] I thank anonymous reviewers for pointing this out ('Acupuncture' 2022) and providing other helpful feedback. I am grateful for the suggestions from the participants at the *Beliefs, Religious Worldviews and Public Health after Covid: Plural/Competing Epistemologies* conference, especially the convenors (editors of this volume) and my respondent. In the UK, the National Institute for Health and Care Excellence (NICE) recommends acupuncture without mentioning placebo, though they distinguish between 'a neurobiological paradigm' (i.e. biomedical) and one based on *qi* (NICE 2021: 6).

Healing through/with *qi* can be done with *qigong*, meditation or visualisation exercises, acupuncture or *fengshui* object placement.[5] Though there exist studies conducted on *qigong*, the majority of research on healing through manipulating *qi* is done on acupuncture. Advocates cite large bodies of scientific studies to defend the legitimacy of acupuncture. Critics are unconvinced. They cite other scientific studies to debunk the practice, commonly dismissing acupuncture as a mere or 'theatrical' placebo (Colquhoun and Novella 2013). It is important to note that researchers of placebo effects recognise the theatre of biomedicine as well, with surgery as the example par excellence of ritual performance.[6]

The label of placebo serves to contain unexplained – only from the biomedical perspective – healing. While acknowledging empirical evidence for efficacy, the placebo moniker dismisses practices thus marked because these outliers threaten the hegemonic paradigm. This type of boundary work allows biomedicine to go unchallenged. I argue that placebo effects point to precisely the cracks and fault lines of biomedicine. I broaden the calls from researchers of placebos to investigate placebos alongside ritual studies, by incorporating multidisciplinary perspectives from the humanities and social sciences in order to provide a much-needed corrective for the status quo of insular and provincial medical research. In this chapter, I wish to explore placebos as a theoretical tool.[7] This is to ask: How do placebos solve intellectual problems? (The impetus for this chapter is a contribution to a 2023 British Academy/Wellcome Conference,[8] in which placebos featured prominently in discussions of belief and competing epistemologies – and religion as well, since *qigong* is typically presented as religious healing.) This question is especially important after the Covid-19 global pandemic brought to the fore other incommensurable paradigms of health and healing. Elsewhere, I have written on the difficulty faced by state-backed public health programmes that assume a biomedical understanding of SARS-CoV-2 when they conflict with religious minority paradigms of health and illness.[9] 'What is at stake here is how

[5] The discourse on healing with *qi* usually revolves around acupuncture or *qigong* and does not address in tandem manipulation of *qi* via *fengshui*. This is especially the case for biomedical studies. A 5 July 2024 search for acupuncture and *qigong* on PubMed yielded 45,262 and 1,213 results, respectively (with approximately 2,000 results each for acupuncture-adjacent practices of acupressure and shiatsu), while a search for *fengshui* yielded 14 results (and the majority of these are not studies on *fengshui* as a medical intervention). See Cheung (forthcoming) for a case study on a contemporary Chinese American healer who employs *fengshui*, *qigong*, Buddhist chants and other Chinese medical arts with his immigrant community in the New York City-area and how the healer code-switches among medical paradigms.

[6] See Wartolowska *et al.* (2014).

[7] I thank Jolyon Thomas for this suggestion and the audience at the 2022 American Academy of Religion Annual National Meeting in Denver for their feedback on my argument for understanding acupuncture as medicine *and* placebo.

[8] *Public Health After COVID: Beliefs, Religion and Competing Epistemologies* funded by the British Academy and Wellcome Trust. The conference was co-hosted by The Open University and King's College London and was held at King's College London, 26–27 May 2023.

[9] See Cheung and Noh (2022) for analysis of the Shincheonji Church in South Korea and how their members were portrayed in Korean and Anglophone media.

state power to immunise and quarantine rationalises and legitimates itself by claiming to protect the majority, at the expense of (religious) minorities' (Cheung and Noh 2022: 316). This is not only an issue for minority populations. In China and certain pockets of the world, even though the state –like all modern states – officially espouses biomedicine, Chinese medical arts that rest on the foundation of *qi* are accepted and practised by the majority (though such a majority may be marginalised or minoritised in terms of power). The larger question is how to deal with incommensurability.

I note here that incompatibility is only a problem from within the biomedical paradigm because of its need to assert dominance, though anthropologists point out that biomedicine itself has glaring internal inconsistences among different groups following the same biomedical paradigm.[10] Clearly, biomedicine is not a monolith. Though chiropractic counts as *acceptable* 'evidence-based' medicine in the UK, it is not given the same level of acceptance in the US.[11] The historian of medicine Helen Tilley explains that medical paradigms outside of the biomedical 'spark[s] the most controversy when its advocates insist on the idea that people can occupy different "conceptual realities" and bodily "modes of existence" at one and the same time. Ironically, this is exactly what so many people – including scientific experts – do all the time' (Tilley 2020: n.p.). She notes that despite the hegemony of biomedicine, 'polyglot therapeutics' continue to persist. Rather than being uncomfortable with plural or competing paradigms, many people oscillate among multiple incommensurable worldviews. Though I write mainly about paradigms, there is considerable overlap between Kuhn's use of paradigms and Foucault's use of epistemes. They both 'provide the conditions of possibility of knowledge and are both part of an approach to the history of science that emphasizes discontinuity over continuity', yet they differ in scope and methodology (Pirozelli 2021: 300). The epistemes I address are found in the communities who heal using *qi*. The anthropologist Elisabeth Hsu contrasts the standardised and verbal reasoning employed by biomedicine with non-verbal knowing in her ethnography of a *qigong* healer in Kunming, China. In the context of her participant experience learning from teachers of *qigong* and Chinese medical arts, Hsu distinguishes among the following forms of knowing: secret, personal, standardised and non-verbal (Hsu 1999: 225–31). In other words, the experiential and familial are paths to trusted knowledge. Though Foucault highlights the ruptures between successive epistemes, Kuhn proposes possibilities for translation and interpretation between paradigms (Pirozelli 2021: 288). After explaining code-switching among medical-religious languages below, I will elaborate on the need to attend to power differences in the process of translation between such languages.

[10] See Mol (2002) on how atherosclerosis (plaque buildup in the arteries) is radically different for patients, doctors, hospital administrators, etc.

[11] NICE recommends chiropractic for lower back pain as part of a treatment package with exercise (NICE 2020: 1.2.7).

In the sections below, I: (1) provide evidence of exactly how comprehensively hegemonic biomedicine is established around the world; (2) explain the intractability of working with incommensurable paradigms; (3) argue for problems with 'evidence-based' medicine and its reliance on randomised controlled trials; (4) consider in depth how and why acupuncture is dismissed as a placebo; (5) argue for why placebos challenge biomedicine; (6) propose a theory of healing with *qi* focusing on intention as an alternative to the biomedical paradigm; and (7) conclude with suggestions for incorporating a multidisciplinary approach for communities of practice using ritual studies, humanistic and social scientific perspectives to continue investigating placebos.

The hegemony of biomedicine and incommensurability

The global hegemony of biomedicine is not simply a result of the paradigm being the most effective or true or real. It also depends on government power to establish biomedicine above all other competing paradigms through state laws and what Tilley calls soft laws, or ideology.

> This matrix of legislation and jurisprudence, rules and regulations, did its own boundary work by setting standards and guidelines – those elusive soft laws – for how to *classify disease* (nosology and etiology), *think about human bodies* (physiology, neurology, psychiatry, immunology, biochemistry, endocrinology, racial and reproductive sciences), *interpret environments* (epidemiology, ecology, climatology, toxicology), and *marshal evidence* (forensics, genetics, biometrics) that effectively occluded other ways of representing the world.
>
> (Tilley 2021: 13–14, emphasis in the original)

Yet, despite these enormous efforts, other forms of therapeutics continue to exist.

The scholar of religion Robert C. Fuller notes that such boundary-making by the state puts up a veneer of rational judgement to hide its 'artificial and even hypocritical' delineations between legitimate (bio)medicine and every/anything else (Fuller 2021: 399). He states: 'Governments have long recognized the need to regulate the quality, safety, and efficacy of medical treatments. They do so, however, in largely idiosyncratic ways, making it next to impossible to identify normative patterns in the regulation of complementary and alternative medicine' (Fuller 2021: 401). Specifically addressing healing with *qi* and Chinese medical arts, and more generally any non-biomedical system, Fuller explains:

> NCCAM distinguishes such systems, which also include homeopathy and naturopathy, from biologically-based therapies such as supplements and diets, manipulative therapies such as chiropractic and osteopathic manipulation, mind-body therapies such as meditation and breathing exercises, and energy healing therapies such as Reiki and Therapeutic Touch. The fact that Chinese medicine includes therapies from the other four categories (e.g. herbs, massage, and internal and external *qigong*) demonstrates the arbitrariness of this delineation.
>
> (Fuller 2021: 399)

In other words, Chinese medical practices based on the *qi* paradigm are sliced apart and jammed into artificial containers that fit biomedical shapes, leaving the remains to be discarded as other, as lesser. This process is hidden and presented as self-evident to the wider public. Hegemony requires maintenance. These 'border skirmishes' continue to play out in court (Fuller 2021: 396). Since resources are required to police borders, there must be much to gain or possibly lose.

Defenders of biomedicine do not necessarily do so with an underlying agenda. Rather, biomedicine's hegemony is reinforced by deep incommensurability that separates it from other worldviews. Thomas Kuhn's influential idea of incommensurability can be explained from a commonly taught example in the history of biomedicine: that of Ignaz Semmelweis and the germ theory of disease. As a physician in 19th-century Vienna, Semmelweis operated under the then dominant paradigms of miasma and contagion theories of disease. Though he conducted empirical experiments and found that washing hands with strong antiseptics led to saving lives, the medical profession dismissed his advice even though it was backed with data and 'evidence' because there was no germ theory of disease at that time to account for how such practice could be effective (Gillies 2005). The abstract ideal of medical science advancing through research ignores the concrete reality of medical scientists routinely rejecting 'evidence' that does not already fit within their theoretical frameworks. Unfortunately, the undergraduates majoring in nursing and health sciences, whom I teach, learn about Semmelweis as an example of how science progresses and improves, moving ever closer towards a more accurate account of medical knowledge. The lesson they should be learning instead is how within the miasma and contagion paradigms, Semmelweis's colleagues dismissed his 'evidence' because there was no conceivable mechanism for disease to spread from a doctor's hands coming into contact with cadavers immediately before delivering babies – thus causing childbed fever. The evaluation of what Semmelweis observed and recorded is done from a theoretically informed perspective, such that the exact same 'evidence' would be judged differently by physicians operating within incommensurable paradigms of disease.

The philosopher Alasdair McIntyre notes the temporal nature of incommensurability, that is, that rival paradigms have irreconcilable standards to judge evidence and consider what qualifies as evidence in the first place over *specific periods* of time (McIntyre 1991).[12] Though he acknowledges the seeming intractability of adjudicating incommensurable paradigms, McIntyre argues for hope moving forward by stating the only three possibilities: (1) describing paradigm B(iomedicine) within the standards of C(hinese medical arts); (2) describing paradigm C within the standards of B; or (3) describing the paradigms of B and C within the standards of A(nother paradigm). Option 3 is conceivably as numerous as there are various A's that can describe both B and C. In other words, to envision future possibilities of learning from rival paradigms, he argues one must use at least

[12] I thank Amod Lele for informing me of this argument by McIntyre via personal communication.

two of the three possible steps. McIntyre acknowledges the difficulty for any one person to fully offer an adequate description outside their own paradigm, and hence there is a need for collaboration and discussion among multiple perspectives. He states the two conditions for such dialogue are the 'admission of fallibilism' (that one may be wrong regarding the paradigm they have settled on) and that 'we have no neutral, independent standpoint' (McIntyre 1991: 120). To make this explicit about biomedicine and admit these conditions is already a challenge against its hegemony that is not normally made. If Tilley's point on people oscillating among paradigms is considered, then such work might be more feasible than McIntyre predicts, although Tilley has in mind medical paradigms, while McIntyre is writing about ethical ones. Tilley's oscillation can be applied to paradigms outside the medical since empirical evidence from experimental philosophy shows that inconsistent ethical intuitions are held by the general public. Decades after his work, Tilley has advanced in the direction that McIntyre treaded and the contemporary relevance can be seen when approaching other competing narratives around the globe.

Returning to medicine, even with intentions to reconcile incommensurability, problems arise for state governments in managing public health when there is little time to pursue the options McIntyre listed. In the case of Covid-19, biomedical recommendations – though relatively swift in comparison to past efforts and contested in the early stages of this novel virus – were sought and then implemented with varying degrees of success and failure. Tilley's point about the persistence of 'traditional' medicines is reinforced by their use to address Covid-19. The second of McIntyre's three options by can be found in the various studies done within the biomedical paradigm to evaluate the outcomes of alternatives including Chinese medical arts and Ayurveda.[13] However, to merely take one option without considering the others only strengthens the hegemony of biomedicine. This dominance is reinforced rhetorically when champions of biomedicine stress that their paradigm relies on 'evidence-based' medicine, implying that other paradigms have little, weak or no 'evidence'.

Problems with 'evidence-based' and randomised controlled trials: 'evidence-*biased*' and 'randomised controlled *crime*'

The term 'evidence-based medicine' (EBM) began to circulate during the 1990s in an effort to improve healthcare (Solomon 2015: 105). Though its origins stem from the desire for direct clinical evidence over nebulous expert judgement by physicians in order to make medical decisions, the term has since been used to reinforce the hegemony of biomedicine against alternative paradigms that are assumed to

[13] Within the Anglophone context, a search on 5 July 2024 using the term 'Chinese medicine COVID' yielded 9,636 results on PubMed.gov and 'Ayurved* (to include Ayurveda and Ayurvedic) COVID' yielded 383 results.

lack supporting evidence. 'Evidence-based' is evoked to dismiss, among others, homeopathy as lacking *acceptable* evidence. Although writing on EBM attends to potential biases, such as publication bias, these criticisms are still from the standpoint of biomedicine. Philosophers of science and medical statisticians argue that EBM is often unsupported by the evidence within its own paradigm due to methodological problems such as 'misalignment between research hypotheses and statistical hypotheses' (Lawler and Zimmermann 2021: 307). Furthermore, EBM relies heavily on a problematic way of obtaining 'evidence'. 'Evidence-based medicine places the highest weight in randomized controlled trials' (RCT) because this type of study is considered 'the highest quality evidence available' (Tenny and Varacallo 2022). What this internal (to biomedicine) criticism ignores is how RCTs as the gold standard already are themselves a biased form of collecting, measuring and interpreting evidence. The philosopher of medicine Miriam Solomon sums up the problem when she states: 'It seems obvious that medicine is based on the evidence, yet perplexing that evidence-based medicine seems to dismiss a good deal of strong evidence' (Solomon 2015: 226). I will return to this epistemological issue later, but first, this section will address why RCTs are incommensurate with obtaining 'evidence' for *qi*. The historian of medicine Tamara Venit Shelton points out the 'problem of biomedicalization is the fundamental incompatibility between randomized controlled trials and traditional Chinese medicine. Such trials privilege therapeutics and outcomes that researchers can reduce, isolate, and replicate; traditional Chinese therapies are inherently eclectic, holistic, and particular' (Shelton 2019: 259). This is to say, again, that collecting 'evidence' is not paradigm neutral.

The medical anthropologist Vincanne Adams reveals how the reliance of evidence-b(i)ased medicine on RCTs functions more to police professional borders around biomedicine than to evaluate empirical data when she writes on 'randomized controlled crime'. Adams explains how RCTs assume and reinforce biomedical hegemony by predefining disease, presenting a value-free interpretation of data and setting themselves 'in opposition to the "spiritual" or "religious"' (Adams 2002: 680). These 'randomized controlled crimes' are used in legal battles within Tibet and the US against practices by Tibetan healers and to outlaw certain Tibetan medicine that competes with biomedicine (Adams 2002: 663–4).

Nevertheless, RCTs are considered *the* gold standard, supplying the highest-quality 'evidence'. To be sure, there are internal criticisms of time, cost, feasibility and ethics against RCTs, but they are still considered the best way to minimise bias. This is despite methodological problems. For instance, philosophers and statisticians point out that 'one cannot gain proper evidence regarding the hypothesis that, say, some medication is *better* than a placebo by examining whether there is any difference whatsoever between the parameters of interest' (Lawler and Zimmermann 2021: 313, emphasis in the original) because of the misalignment due to indirect testing via 'pairing a directional research hypothesis with a non-directional statistical hypothesis' (Lawler and Zimmermann 2021: 308). I quote the above on placebos because the origin of the double-blind RCT stemmed from biomedicine's need to evaluate the effectiveness of an intervention against a placebo (Shapiro and Shapiro 1997: 20).

The randomisation in RCTs eliminates the precise mechanism of healing through *qi*.[14] For instance, a 2009 study that is cited 285 times is representative of this methodological issue of forcing biomedical assumptions onto the paradigm of Chinese healing through *qi*. Researchers used an RCT to compare 'individualized acupuncture, standardized acupuncture, simulated acupuncture, or usual care' for back pain and found that the different types of acupuncture were more effective than the typical treatment (Cherkin *et al.* 2009: 858). However, because the effects of simulated acupuncture were not significantly different from individualised acupuncture or standardised acupuncture, researchers questioned the purported mechanism of acupuncture and considered the therapeutic effects were caused by a placebo. I will return to this charge of a placebo effect below and show how this claim sustains the hegemony of biomedicine. Other researchers point out the 'methodological challenges in design and conduct of randomised controlled trials in acupuncture' by laying out serious problems, including – most relevant to the 2009 study previously mentioned – neglecting the 'importance of patient-practitioner interaction' (Fei *et al.* 2022: e064345). In raising these issues, Fei *et al.* are still staying within the framework of biomedicine, describing the importance of the interaction between healer and patient through concepts of care, communication and trust. However, what they fail to consider is the mechanism of healing within the paradigm of *qi* – namely, the exchange of *qi* between healer and patient.

This is also a problem with *single*-blinded RCTs on *qigong*. In conducting their RCT, Larkey *et al.* note that: 'Beyond the successful blinding of participants to the preferred intervention, and blinding of study staff, it was impossible to blind the instructors' (Larkey *et al.* 2015: 10). Blinding can only be used to eliminate conscious knowledge or intention but not un/sub-conscious intention to heal. The former is biomedicine's attempt to 'explain' placebo effects, while the latter is integral to alternative medical paradigms. The instructors of 'sham' *qigong* knew their patients *needed* healing.[15] This knowledge, as the researchers note, 'could have *unintentionally* biased the results' (Larkey *et al.* 2015: 10, emphasis added). They found the puzzling – only from the biomedical perspective – result that 'sham' *qigong* and *qigong* showed improvement for depression and sleep dysfunction, while only *qigong* but not 'sham' *qigong* showed improvement for fatigue. What is ignored is the emic logic within the paradigm of healing *qi* that considers exchange of *qi* and intention and which will be discussed in detail below. My point is that the gold standard of EBM is inadequate to assess alternative healing paradigms because it is already assuming a biomedical standard. A different study using RCTs

[14] See Cheung (2022: 145–8) for more on how double-blind RCTs are problematic for healing in alternative medical paradigms, including Buddhist medicine and the mechanism of karma.

[15] I thank Karen O'Brien-Kop for pointing out how the term 'sham' is morally laden yet commonly used in biomedical research that have control arms of 'sham *qigong*' or 'sham acupuncture'.

to examine *qigong* simply states: 'Blinding the participants to the allocation was not possible due to the nature of intervention' (Ho *et al.* 2012: 162) and thus, these researchers used those on a waitlist as a control group to compare against those practising *qigong*.

Both EBM and RCTs hinge on evaluating the 'evidence' of a therapeutic intervention against a placebo. However, placebos are precisely the quarantined section of biomedicine that is its greatest threat.

Placebo effects

In popular discourse regarding healing with *qi*, scientific studies are used by defenders and debunkers as 'evidence' for accepting or dismissing Chinese medical arts, especially acupuncture. A 2023 article on the NBC website quotes a clinical oncologist interviewed on the use of 'Eastern remedies', which include Chinese, Middle Eastern and Indian medicine, to treat long Covid. She states: 'Is there a good, robust evidence base for acupuncture? The answer is probably no, because of the difficulties and methodological challenges of doing acupuncture studies' (Brendix 2023: n.p.). Since she does not make explicit what exactly she means by 'good, robust evidence base', I assume she means RCTs. A few paragraphs later in the article, a cardiologist expresses worry about 'predatory providers' and explains why some respond to therapies such as acupuncture as follows: 'They may be getting benefit because of a placebo effect' (Brendix 2023: n.p.). This is a representative example of how non-biomedical therapies are dismissed as placebos. A 2013 issue of *Anesthesia & Analgesia* published articles debunking and defending the 'evidence' for acupuncture. 'Acupuncture is Theatrical Placebo' (Colquhoun and Novella 2013) has been cited 176 times compared to its debate counterpart, which has been cited 44 times (Wang *et al.* 2013). The two arguments speak past each other and the discourse continues to be at an impasse. Part of this is not related to any evidence regarding acupuncture per se but rather the reliance on comparing any therapeutic intervention against placebos. That acupuncture can heal animals is evidence against dismissing it as 'theatrical placebo',[16] but my point here is that 'evidence' is not enough to convince anyone to switch paradigms due to the nature of incommensurability.

Defining placebos in the first place, in order to study them, is not straightforward. The medical doctor and philosopher of medicine Howard Brody explains the confusion that arises from stipulating that placebos are inert yet have effects, 'operating by means *other than* the recognized pharmacological or physiological pathways to which biomedical sciences currently attributes drug responses' (Brody

[16] Oh and Kim (2021) provide a literature review that includes the effects of acupuncture on digestion and inflammation that cannot be dismissed as a therapeutic consequence of mice participating in a 'theatrical' performance.

1997: 79, emphasis in the original). He states: 'It is hard to define "placebo effect" without engaging in a small-scale project to reform modern medical thinking, making the definition useless for the unconverted. This central feature of the concept of "placebo" makes it a problem for writers of definitions but an opportunity for investigators and clinicians' (Brody 1997: 79). By 'unconverted', he means his interlocutors who are uninterested in questioning biomedicine, which is a powerful majority. Even with the minority who question it, popular discourse reflects hegemonic assumptions. I will offer suggestions towards challenging biomedicine in the conclusion of this chapter.

Research on placebos from within the biomedical paradigm proposes that effects result from expectation, reward and conditioning responses that release chemicals in the brain and body. Yet, perspectives from the social sciences (especially medical anthropology) and the humanities (especially the history and philosophy of medicine) note the inadequacy of biomedical blinders zooming in on dopamine. 'Neither clinical trials nor neurobiology, for example, has managed to explain how and why red placebos stimulate whereas blue ones calm, four placebos work better than two, or sham interventions can perform on par with successful drugs and operations' (Jong and Harris 2016: 4). I have written elsewhere on how a ritual studies approach is the middle ground between a neurological reductionist and an irreducibly social approach in studying placebos, including the limits of double-blind RCTs in studying placebos.[17] I will return to this middle ground below.

Claude Lévi-Strauss analysed a case study that can shift the perspective on what it means to call a therapeutic intervention a placebo. He applied his theory of structuralism to the psychology of shamans and their community through an examination of 'a fragment of the autobiography of a Kwakiuti Indian from the Vancouver region of Canada, obtained by Franz Boas' (Lévi-Strauss [1958] 1998: 133). The autobiographer Quesalid began as a sceptic of the shamans in his community. 'Driven by curiosity about their tricks and by the desire to expose them', Quesalid became apprenticed to a prominent shaman who revealed the secret to performing his ritual healing (Lévi-Strauss [1958] 1998: 133). The shaman's 'trick' was to conceal a piece of feather in his mouth. During the climax of the ritual, the healer bit his tongue to draw blood in order to mix that blood with the feather, which is then spit out and shown 'to his patient and the onlookers as the pathological foreign body extracted as a result of his sucking and manipulations' (Lévi-Strauss [1958] 1998: 133). The story, however, does not end with a myth-busting campaign by Quesalid. Before he gets a chance to do so, he 'was summoned by the family of a sick person who had dreamed of Quesalid as his healer' to perform the ritual – his very first – which 'was an outstanding success' (Lévi-Strauss [1958] 1998: 133). Lévi-Strauss writes that Quesalid 'interpreted his success in psychological terms: it was successful 'because he [the sick person] believed strongly in his dream about me' (Lévi-Strauss [1958] 1998: 133). The story continues with Quesalid

[17] See Cheung (2022: 148).

performing more rituals and growing his reputation in his and neighbouring tribes. Later, when he is confronted with and compares his rite with that from a different tribe, Quesalid is subjected to an analysis by Lévi-Strauss that is directly relevant to the problem of placebos and competing epistemologies. Lévi-Strauss states:

> Thus our hero grapples with a problem which perhaps has its parallel in the development of modern science. Two systems which we know to be inadequate present (with respect to each other) a differential validity, from both a logical and an empirical perspective. From which frame of reference shall we judge them? On the level of fact, where they merge, or on their own level, where they take on different values, both theoretically and empirically?
>
> (Lévi-Strauss [1958] 1998: 133)

In other words, Lévi-Strauss articulates the aforementioned intractability of adjudicating incommensurable paradigms described by McIntyre. The story ends with Quesalid having a long career as a shaman. He went on to expose others whom he deemed 'false' shamans – that is, ones who were ineffective in healing, and continued to heal with the feather technique that he learned.

The lesson here is not that shamans are deceptive, but, rather, this case study should compel a re-examination of the dominant biomedical paradigm from the perspective of the community members who were healed by Quesalid. Imagine if such populations came across the biomedical *ritual* of wearing white lab coats (ritual attire), using stethoscopes (ritual implements) and pronouncing a diagnosis with a Latin name for the medical condition (ritual labelling), and then prescribing various pills (climax of ritual healing). This is not to say that all of biomedicine is a placebo. To be sure, placebos are measured to be effective for a subset of ailments. Further research should be done on which ailments are more or less affected by placebos, and *why* that is the case.

In writing about placebos, the anthropologist Daniel Moerman (2002) points out that placebos are often erroneously understood as only belief by the patient. In fact, it is a web of belief within a community. Research on placebos shows how the belief of the *healer* (and *not* the patient) impacts the effects. Moerman asks: If placebos are merely in the mind, then why are people unable to 'trick' themselves into using a piece of candy to heal whatever ails them? His answer is that there is no community who takes seriously candy having the power to heal.[18] At the end of his monograph on placebos, Moerman explains that after everything he has written about the power of ritual in healing and the 'meaning response', which he suggests as a better term than placebo, he would still use pills deemed effective by biomedicine. Before he takes them, he would remind himself of what he and his social circle *accepts* – the tenets of biomedical research that relies on EBM and RCT testing of drugs in pill form, which is considered to have therapeutic efficacy. Moerman's points draw attention towards placebos or the 'meaning response' as

[18] The professor of psychology Ellen Langer makes a distinction between a 'traditional placebo' that 'fools the mind' and an 'active placebo' as one that 'enlists the mind', using the example of hypnosis employed to cure warts (Langer 2014: 174).

questioning all the factors involved in healing, rather than simply using placebo as a label to dismiss and contain.

The placebo label is a convenient way for the unexplained to be contained in order for the hegemony of biomedicine to continue without question. It at once acknowledges empirical evidence for the healing efficacy of any treatment deemed to be a placebo, yet delineates such healing as an outlier, since it threatens the paradigm.[19] Placebos challenge the norm when taken seriously. Brody states:

> In this sense [regarding the American model of medicine], we need to talk about how, if you're going to make placebo a more central part of medicine, then somehow in the process you are going to have to reform medical thinking across the board. You can't really define placebo and not challenge the biomedical model and the dominant thought patterns.
>
> (Brody 1997: 241)

What is at stake here is what the scholar of American literature, secularism and history of criticism Emily Ogden explains as *asserting dominance* – when one group charges another of being misled by false beliefs of healing.[20]

Ogden's work on 19th-century US mesmerism shows how mesmerists explained their superiority over others who believed in a false 'idol' – in their case animal magnetism – alleged to have healing power. Defenders of biomedicine may be doing something analogous when they relegate acupuncture as a placebo and hence attempt to contain the threat that empirical data on acupuncture's healing efficacy – and therefore the alternative paradigm of *qi* – poses to biomedical hegemony, epistemologically and ontologically. Ogden writes:

> There is a surprising consequence involved in accusing other people of believing in things that do not exist. The aim is to deprive these idols, these nothings in the world, of their power. And yet the end result is to give some placeholder – 'belief' or 'idolatry' or 'imagination' – all the power that the idols once had. As humbug-buster David Reese would write in 1838, by which time mesmerism not only still existed but was the primary target of Reese's ire, 'an *idol* is nothing, and *error* is nothing, but these *nothings* are the most dangerous things in the world'.
>
> (Ogden 2018: 29; emphasis in the original)

The assertion of dominance is justified through the biomedical logic that believers of false medicine are not fully modern, and hence, the ones who have knowledge of true or real medicine (i.e. biomedicine) have permission to educate and disabuse others of their ignorance (Ogden 2018: 7–8). Ogden continues to explain what debunkers need to do:

> The debunker is obliged to supply an *idol-function*: a cause to account for the effects formerly attributed to the idol animal magnetism. The trouble is that whatever this idol-function may be, it necessarily must have many of the powers attributed to the

[19] It is important to ask what else act like placebos and are also used to contain and dismiss in order to allow biomedicine to continue unchallenged?

[20] I thank Jolyon Thomas for helping me make this connection between placebos and Ogden's work.

> idol itself. In the case of the 1784 commission, the idol-function was a combination of things, including credulity, imagination, and imitation. Imagination, the leading cause in this group, soon came to be almost as powerful and worrisome as animal magnetism. To disenchant, then, is to invent idol-functions that explain the behavior of other people. And it is often to become unnerved by these inventions of your own.
>
> (Ogden 2018: 30; emphasis in the original)

To complete the analogy, debunkers of acupuncture use placebo as the idol-function to explain the false healing that acupuncture is observed to provide. The 'theatrical' move by debunkers is to explain away healing inconsistent with biomedicine without offering any substantial explanation at all. This is a pattern found in power struggles between competing epistemes, which shows how history repeats itself.

Will placebo studies fracture and magnify fault lines in the current paradigm, or will it be one of the many tools of the master that will never dismantle the master's house? Though admittedly a flawed comparison, I invoke Audre Lorde on racism here advisedly. Race in this context is classification. I follow Geraldine Heng's conception of race to emphasise how it 'is a structural relationship for the articulation and management of human differences, rather than a substantive content' (Heng 2018: 27). Racial analysis of biomedical hegemony illuminates how biomedicine is positioned as modern, despite how '*new* or recently assembled medical cultures were labelled "traditions" and often placed in an explicit ethnonational lineage, eventually becoming something pervasively called "traditional" or "indigenous" medicine (e.g., traditional Chinese medicine or Maori medicine)' (Tilley 2021: 5, emphasis in the original). Tilley is referring to the newly created 'Traditional Chinese Medicine' in the 1950s. Furthermore, she continues:

> Consider why professional scientists and doctors, often of European descent, have insisted that other people's cognitive and perceptual expertise is unreal – pseudoscience, superstitious, and dangerous – while their own analyses of faith and health, mind and matter, language and effect, and even energy flows, produce judicious and dispassionate understandings of reality.
>
> (Tilley 2021: 16)

That race is imbricated in biomedical hegemony should not be surprising since power along one axis often supports dominance along others. It should be fruitful to subject the hegemony of biomedicine along analyses of gender, religious, disability and other intersections of privilege.

Returning to the aforementioned middle ground between the poles of a biomedical reductionist approach and an irreducibly social approach of understanding placebos, in the next section I wish to extend the insights from Ted Kaptchuk. 'Trained as an acupuncturist, Kaptchuk is a pioneer in placebo research. In his attempt to address the ethical problem of deception in placebo research, his studies found that *patients who were told they were taking placebos still reported higher rates of healing* (Kaptchuk et al. 2010)' (Cheung 2022: 148, emphasis in the original). His 2011 article titled 'Placebo Studies and Ritual Theory: A Comparative Analysis of Navajo, Acupuncture and Biomedical Healing' argues that employing ritual studies will help understanding of placebos. A key finding of this study is that '[d]ifferent healers can have different effects on patients even when they perform an identical prospectively defined precise scripted interaction' (Kaptchuk 2011: 1856). In this research, Kaptchuk is still working within the biomedical paradigm of EBM and RCTs. However, as mentioned earlier, RCTs remove the mechanism of healing from the perspective of alternative paradigms. The individual healer matters, not just the scripted ritual.[21] Whether that mechanism is a harmonious relation with spirits and the earth, karma or *qi*, alternative paradigms explain healing as intricately connected to the specific healer, including the role of intention.[22]

Qi and intention: an alternative to the biomedical paradigm

That *qi* is psychophysical dissolves the problem that placebos represent in biomedicine. Since placebos are inert nothings but have consistent healing effects arising only from mental belief, biomedicine's assumption of mind–body dualism needs neurochemical explanations to explain placebo effects. Within the paradigm of *qi* however, acupuncture being dismissed as a placebo, or merely in the mind, is a bizarre claim since conscious intention is used to clear blockage of *qi* or unbalanced *qi* that causes bodily disease. Furthermore, what Kaptchuk is puzzled by, that different healers have different effects, is explained by an obvious corollary in the paradigm of *qi*: healing involves an exchange of *qi* and each person has a different *qi* makeup. Ultimately, the way forward involves openness to paradigms of healing outside the biomedical. Now, I turn to the role of intention as an alternative paradigm.[23]

In the rest of this section, I offer a preliminary proposal towards a theory of healing with *qi* focusing on intention as an alternative to biomedical explanations, or lack thereof, regarding placebos. The aforementioned studies on acupuncture and *qigong* carried out under the biomedical paradigm, with the common uses of 'sham' acupuncture and 'sham' *qigong*, puzzle researchers precisely because they ignore intention. Researchers of *qigong* who do acknowledge intention state: 'The role of intention, or the human mind, in *qigong* therapy is probably the most controversial

[21] For a description of how biomedicine is strikingly similar to a pilgrimage ritual that includes confession and being reborn, see Cundiff-O'Sullivan *et al.* (2023, 46–7). Nevertheless, that book chapter and entire edited volume at once acknowledge the importance of ritual in healing but situate ritual efficacy as the idol-function to explain placebo effects without actually explaining its (neuro/psycho) biological mechanisms (such as expectancy and conditioning), which are still the 'real' explanations in the biomedical paradigm. Cundiff-O'Sullivan *et al.* accept biomedical use of rituals without the lesson learned from Lévi-Strauss, leaving, yet again, biomedical hegemony unchallenged.

[22] It is unclear from Kaptchuk's 2011 article what exactly is the mechanism for Navajo healing, which may be intentional due to the intended audience of that journal or unintentional as a result of the hegemony of biomedicine. One possibility for this mechanism is *hózhó* (balance and beauty) and another is the journey that the healer has undergone in terms of training.

[23] Intention is a philosophically rich topic, as is its connection to mind and consciousness. See Li (2022) for a comparative treatment of Husserl's phenomenology and Yogacara Buddhism on these matters.

and most significant issue for understanding bioenergy healing' (Shao *et al.* 2009: 568). Researchers commonly conflate intention with mind or consciousness and do not distinguish among those terms, using them interchangeably. Although *qi* can be directed by intention, the two are distinct. I believe a further distinction is important between *conscious* and un/sub-conscious intention, to be addressed shortly.

Multiple studies have examined the growth rate of various strains of bacteria, comparing the growth rate of bacterial cultures that are directed by the conscious intention of *qigong* healers to promote rapid growth with others that are directed to inhibit growth or induce death of the bacteria. The results show statistically different growth rates among the two experimental groups and the control group: compared to the control group, the bacteria grows the most when *qigong* masters direct external *qi* with the intention to promote growth of the culture, and the bacteria grows the least when the intention is for them to die. Despite issues with declining effects of such experiments when repeated, researchers note the 'potential role of intention … [to] posit a new research paradigm in life science' (Shao *et al.* 2009: 568). In presenting a qualitative review of research on external *qigong*, the medical researcher Paul Posadzki suggests a theory of external *qigong* that is 'grounded in Eastern and Western paradigms' by combining insights from *qigong* and health psychology (2012: 50). In other words, researchers understand intention and *qigong* as a new or alternative paradigm to the biomedical.

Researchers would benefit from being in conversation with physicists and electrical engineers who have replicated experiments on how intention changes measurable properties of matter, in order to situate intention within a broader context. A team of researchers led by the engineering physicist William Tiller and his associates – including electrical engineers, medical doctors and nurses – have published experiments on the measurable effects of intention on health and the pH of water. Results include arthritis pain that did not respond to mainstream medicine but did improve after use of an 'intention host device' that imprints human intention (Manek and Tiller 2013). The improvement was verified by both subject reports and MRI. The research team have conducted numerous experiments on intention host devices and have measured their impact on altering the acid/alkaline balance (pH) of water (Panjuen *et al.* 2009).

Relevant to my point on intention, they found the following: 'When human energy-based activities such as meditation, yoga, *t'ai chi*, and reiki took place in adjoining rooms, slight to moderate oscillations in the pH level were noted over a period ranging from several hours to several days after the activity' (Panjuen *et al.* 2009: 965). They argue that the *rate* of pH change over time cannot be explained with conventional understanding of chemical processes that affect pH. Specifically, their measurements of water increasing pH at an exponential rate for 48 hours (from 5.95 to 6.05), then staying the same for a few days, then increasing at a linear rate for another few days (from 6.05 to 6.15) is incommensurable with the current paradigm of how pH changes. The devices were imprinted with human intention to raise the PH of water.

A later study found that such intention host devices could be imprinted passively by being in proximity to *Maitreya* Buddhist relics. The researchers note that: 'Crucially, a verbal request from a deep meditative state by 4 humans appeared to be a necessary condition for this "imbedded loving kindness essence" to manifest itself in this way', raising the pH of water over an extended exposure of thousands of hours (Tiller *et al.* 2012: 381). In the first 2,200 hours, no intention instructions were given, and accordingly, there was no significant measurable change in the water pH. In the subsequent 2,500 hours, the Buddha relic-imprinted intention host device was requested 'that the excess thermodynamic free energy aspect of this loving kindness essence be made manifest in this space so that its thermodynamic magnitude could be experimentally measured via the pH-sensor reading' (Tiller *et al.* 2012: 379). The result was a significant change in pH from 5.8 to 9. In other words, these preliminary studies suggest that researchers should take seriously the measurable effects of intention.

Therapeutic intent is not unique to *qigong* or Chinese medical arts, as it can be found in numerous medical cultures.[24] Though intention is not *qi*, the intention to heal is related to the conscious intention to direct the movement of *qi*. Hand, arm, shoulder and bodily movements help train the mind-body to direct *qi* circulation – whether within oneself, emitted externally towards others or exchanged with the natural environment.

The relevant type of intention or *yongyi* (用意) requires knowledge of the need for healing and a desire for healing, either of oneself or another. The use of consciousness/awareness *yishi* (意識) to heal is expressed in acupuncture through the exchange of *qi* between the healer and patient. It is enacted in *qigong* through the will to circulate *qi* within oneself or among other sentient beings and the natural environment. Thus, I propose shifting research on placebos to account for the ontological and epistemological consequences of observable changes due to the intention to heal.

Some research questions to pursue include testing how much the cultural or communal assumptions of the efficacy of *qi* impact the rate of healing. If *qi* is psychophysical, how much do limiting or hindering beliefs of a patient block their own healing? In other words, is there evidence that patients who believe they are not worthy of good health – perhaps due to a guilty conscience or other reasons – impact their health? How much does the reputation of a healer impact the results of *qigong* intervention? Researchers of placebos acknowledge that patients' level of trust and their sense of the healer's empathy or care impacts the effects of placebos.

The Chinese term for placebo is *anweiji* (安慰劑) or literally 'comfort dose', which I would translate as medicine that consoles. In my field research with a contemporary religious healer in the New York City-area who employs *qigong*

[24] See Schwartz (1990) for an overview of therapeutic intent in various healing cultures and times. Note that in his presentation, Schwartz still privileges biomedicine.

and other Chinese medical arts, I was told by my interlocutor that belief impacts healing.[25] That *qigong* healer mentioned the example of people using incense ash from temples as medicine. He explained that the efficacy could be due to the ingredients commonly found in incense to be medicinal plants as well. In addition, he stated that what matters is the solemn respect towards the ritual use of incense, the reputation of the temple and the awareness that others in the community frequent the temple. Related to this is trust. He shared another anecdote that if young children are too scared of needles to receive acupuncture treatment, a parent or doctor may use a toothpick on the child's acupressure points and tell the child that this is just as effective as a needle but will not pierce their skin. His point is that the trust the child has towards an authoritative adult factors into healing. This reinforces Moerman's point that community is important in recognising the efficacy of whatever healing ritual is performed such that a healer cannot simply tell a patient that a small piece of candy – though quite similar in ingredients to placebo pills but is not accepted as medicine by the wider community – will cure them. It may be interesting to research whether candy would be more or less as effective as placebos on children of various ages.

Thus far, I have considered the conscious intention to heal. I want to draw attention to the un/sub-conscious wish for healing of others. This takes us back to the problems with studies that employ 'sham' *qigong* or 'sham' acupuncture. That healing does occur with the 'sham' treatments can be explained within the paradigm of *qi* through the un/sub-conscious therapeutic intention of the person performing the 'sham' intervention. This is because they have knowledge that the patients are in need of healing.[26] Instead of dismissing the healing effects of *qigong* and acupuncture as a mere placebo, using the paradigm of healing with *qi* to require intention provides a different lens through which to evaluate the results of the exact same experiments. In other words, theoretical paradigms influence interpretation of evidence. In this case, the question is how to make sense of placebo effects. How can the focus on intention reorient the study of placebo effects in a way that disrupts biomedical hegemony?

Conclusion

When placebos are taken seriously, do biomedical assumptions and axioms unravel, or do such questions elicit RCTs to 'test' and find 'evidence' in order to ultimately subsume a therapeutic intervention, such as acupuncture, under biomedicine?

[25] See Cheung (2022) and Cheung (forthcoming) for more context on this healer and his community. I do not claim this *qigong* healer is representative. Rather, I am proposing alternative theory and research avenues based on his understanding of *qi*, intention and healing.

[26] Elsewhere I have written on how the impact of the *knowledge* of mice needing healing from cancer explains their higher rate of recovery than expected. See Cheung (2022: 146).

Biomedical hegemony, ever evolving, is systemically reinforced by institutional and state power, and competing paradigms such as *qi* could be assimilated or exiled.

If Kaptchuk is correct in proposing ritual studies as the way forward in studying placebos, then religious studies,[27] and humanistic (history and philosophy) and social scientific (sociology and anthropology) perspectives on medicine and healing should inform this multidisciplinary pursuit. Tilley uses linguistic metaphors that are helpful. She states:

> Officials have likewise tended to eschew the very idea that medical experts could code-switch, or move linguistically, between therapeutic cultures, often leaving those labors to scholars in the humanities and social sciences (and to the small number of medical doctors who have also done PhDs in medical anthropology or history). Why? In part, because anyone able to move between different worlds of meaning might also question whether dominant approaches to health were legitimate, and they might even point to some of their fictional foundations. Polyglot therapeutics have been so threatening to states and institutions (and, on a more mundane level, so challenging logistically), because anyone with these diverse abilities has tended to find it difficult to trade in absolutes about reality or health.
>
> (Tilley 2021: 15)

It is important to note that her use of code-switch and polyglot is not the same as the use of 'medical bilingualism' because the latter assumes a straightforward one-to-one translation of terms between medical languages.[28] What happens when therapeutics are untranslatable? Rather than translation, Tilley proposes oscillation. Elsewhere, I have written on the use of code-switching to understand how a contemporary healer's change in code does not signal any one code is more real than another, just like multilingual speakers do not find one language to better capture reality (Cheung forthcoming). Rather, code-switching is done to combine codes to best communicate reality, one in which there is no hierarchy among languages. When applied to medical paradigms, biomedicine then is relocated from its hegemony (as medical bilingualism is typically used to express how someone is able to translate an alternative paradigm into the language of biomedicine).

The broader issues at play include medical epistemology and public health policy. The philosopher of science Helen Longino reminds us of the social dimensions of scientific – including medical – knowledge. She writes: '*Values* play a direct role when they provide direct motivation to accept or reject a theory;

[27] See Salguero (2023) on Mahayana Buddhism's theory of placebos: all bodies and practices are empty; Buddhist interventions, medical and otherwise, are skillful means but are used anyway to address suffering. My stance on a Buddhist theory of placebo takes after Yogacara's position that everything is mind-dependent and experience is co-created by a combination of the mental–physical.

[28] See Salguero (2014) on the difficulties and complexity of translating Buddhist medicine, including how it is done through multiple versions aimed at different audiences. He shows the assumptions of medical bilingualism fail because they ignore the body and bodily understanding. See also Gorvett (2020) on untranslatable illnesses.

they play an indirect role when they play a role in evaluating the consequences of accepting or rejecting a claim, thus *influencing what will count as sufficient evidence* to accept or reject' (Longino 2019: n.p., emphasis added). For public health policy, this means recognising the plurality of values and epistemic standards (including, aforementioned 'idiosyncratic' ones explained by Fuller) among individuals and medical communities and how those oscillate within individuals and communities. Solomon concludes her analysis of medical knowledge by pointing out 'a developing but untidy' nature of the 'methodological pluralism' employed by the contemporary biomedical community, noting the simultaneous utility and shortcomings of EBM alongside those of consensus conferences, translational medicine and narrative medicine (2015: 224). She compares medical methods to jazz solos: as they riff off each other, 'they build on earlier themes, sometimes fitting together, sometimes competing, and sometimes changing each other. None of the voices disappear, although they can fade into the background. No solo lasts forever. The music is always developing, never finished, and always a little rough around the edges' (Solomon 2015: 229). As raised earlier, in my application of Lorde on race and power to the construction of medical knowledge, I am still unsure if the biomedical band will ever leave the stage of global medicine, even if research on placebo effects moves in my proposed direction.

In this chapter, I have focused on placebos because there is a lot at stake. The historian of science Allan Brandt states: 'Defining the placebo effect is a question at the core of how medicine works, or what it means to say that medicine works in the first place' (Harrington 1997: 243). How do placebos help us understand or solve the problem of incommensurability? McIntyre points out the difficulty of the problem. Maybe it is not realistic to follow his suggested paths, even with Tilley's point on oscillation. My position is that of strong agnosticism. In contrast to weak agnosticism, which is withholding judgement – that is, not taking an ontological position on, for example, the existence of *qi* – strong agnosticism is an epistemic position – one that doubts it is ever possible to marshal any 'evidence' that can convince someone to accept a different medical paradigm. Furthermore, the institutional structures of biomedicine resist code-switching because hegemony is about maintaining power. This means translating all other codes or subsuming them under the biomedical paradigm. The historical lesson from the example of Semmelweis in the 1840s, when the medical profession rejected his 'evidence' about washing hands, is this: what does biomedicine reject today that the next paradigm shift will judge to be so obvious that to doubt it is incomprehensible? That people oscillate among paradigms supports my position of strong agnosticism because of the difficulty, if not impossibility, of fully integrating competing epistemes. This is not to say I believe there is no hope in moving forward, in exchange and mutual learning. Rather, it is an open question as to whether or not studying placebos could result in a Kuhnian revolution that overturns biomedicine. The possibility for this is enough reason to take this path.

References

'Acupuncture: What You Need to Know'. (2022), National Center for Complementary and Integrative Health (NCCIH), October. Available at: https://www.nccih.nih.gov/health/acupuncture-what-you-need-to-know. Accessed 10 July 2024.

Adams, V. (2002), 'Randomized Controlled Crime: Postcolonial Sciences in Alternative Medicine Research'. *Social Studies of Science*, 32(5–6): 659–90. https://doi.org/10.1177/030631270203200503

Allen, S. (2015), 'Will a Name Change Make NIH Research Center Less Controversial?' American Association for the Advancement of Science (AAAS), 19 February. Available at: https://www.aaas.org/will-name-change-make-nih-research-center-less-controversial. Accessed 10 July 2024.

Brendix, A. (2023), 'For Some Long Covid Patients, Acupuncture and Other Eastern Remedies Offer Relief', *NBC News*, 11 March. Available at: https://www.nbcnews.com/health/health-news/long-covid-acupuncture-eastern-remedies-rcna74358. Accessed 10 July 2024.

Brody, H. (1997), 'The Doctor as Therapeutic Agent: A Placebo Effect Research Agenda?' in A. Harrington (ed.) *The Placebo Effect: An Interdisciplinary Exploration* (Cambridge, MA: Harvard University Press), 77–92.

Cherkin, D. C., Sherman, K. J., Avins, A. L., Erro, J. H., Ichikawa, L., Barlow, W. E., *et al.* (2009), 'A Randomized Trial Comparing Acupuncture, Simulated Acupuncture, and Usual Care for Chronic Low Back Pain'. *Archives of Internal Medicine*, 169(9): 858–66. https://doi.org/10.1001/archinternmed.2009.65

Cheung, K. (2022), 'Miracle as Natural: A Contemporary Chinese American Religious Healer' in K. R. Zwier, D. L. Weddle and T. D. Knepper (eds) *Miracles: An Exercise in Comparative Philosophy of Religion*. Comparative Philosophy of Religion 3 (Cham: Springer International Publishing), 131–54. https://doi.org/10.1007/978-3-031-14865-1_8

Cheung, K. (forthcoming), 'Healing (With) *Qi* via *Qigong*, Acupuncture, and *Fengshui*: Code-Switching and the Case of a Chinese American Healer' in J. Strube, M. Thaler and D. Zoehrer (eds) *Subtle Energies in Therapy, Spirituality, Arts, and Politics. 1800–Present*. Numen Book Series: Studies in the History of Religions (Leiden: Brill).

Cheung, K. and Noh, M. (2022), 'COVID-19, Shincheonji, and the Limits of South Korean Secularism: The Devil in Patient 31'. *Religion, State and Society*, 50(3): 316–37.

Colquhoun, D. and Novella, S. P. (2013), 'Acupuncture Is Theatrical Placebo'. *Anesthesia & Analgesia*, 116(6): 1360–3. https://doi.org/10.1213/ANE.0b013e31828f2d5e

Cundiff-O'Sullivan, R. L., Oula, D., Shafir, R. and Colloca, L. (2023), 'Cultural Influences on Placebo and Nocebo Effects' in L. Colloca, J. Noel, P. D. Franklin and C. Seneviratne (eds) *Placebo Effects Through the Lens of Translational Research* (Oxford: Oxford University Press), 38–54.

Fei, Y-T., Cao, H-J., Xia, R-Y., Chai, Q-Y., Liang, C-H., Feng, Y-T., *et al.* (2022), 'Methodological Challenges in Design and Conduct of Randomised Controlled Trials in Acupuncture'. *British Medical Journal*, 376: e064345. https://doi.org/10.1136/bmj-2021-064345

Fuller, R. C. (2021), 'Policing the Boundaries of Medical Science: Causality, Evidence, and the Question of Religion' in D. Lüddeckens, P. Hetmanczyk, P. E. Klassen and J. B. Stein (eds) *The Routledge Handbook of Religion, Medicine, and Health* (New York: Routledge), 391–405.

Gillies, D. (2005), 'Hempelian and Kuhnian Approaches in the Philosophy of Medicine: The Semmelweis Case'. *Studies in History and Philosophy of Science Part C: Studies in

History and Philosophy of Biological and Biomedical Sciences, 36(1): 159–81. https://doi.org/10.1016/j.shpsc.2004.12.003

Gorvett, Z. (2020), 'What We Can Learn from "Untranslatable" Illnesses', *BBC*, 7 June. Available at: https://www.bbc.com/future/article/20200604-what-we-can-learn-from-untranslatable-illnesses. Accessed 10 July 2024.

Harrington, A. (ed.) (1997), *The Placebo Effect: An Interdisciplinary Exploration* (Cambridge, MA: Harvard University Press).

Heng, G. (2018), *The Invention of Race in the European Middle Ages* (Cambridge: Cambridge University Press).

Ho, R. T. H., Chan, J. S. M., Wang, C-W., Lau, B. W. M., So, K. F., Yuen, L. P., *et al.* (2012), 'A Randomized Controlled Trial of Qigong Exercise on Fatigue Symptoms, Functioning, and Telomerase Activity in Persons with Chronic Fatigue or Chronic Fatigue Syndrome'. *Annals of Behavioral Medicine: A Publication of the Society of Behavioral Medicine*, 44(2): 160–70. https://doi.org/10.1007/s12160-012-9381-6

Hsu, E. (1999), *The Transmission of Chinese Medicine*. Cambridge Studies in Medical Anthropology 7 (Cambridge: Cambridge University Press).

Jong, V. de and Harris, C. S. (2016), 'Introduction: Placebos in Modern Society' in A. Raz and C. S. Harris (eds) *Placebo Talks: Modern Perspectives on Placebos in Society* (Oxford: Oxford University Press), 3–14.

Kaptchuk, T. J. (2011), 'Placebo Studies and Ritual Theory: A Comparative Analysis of Navajo, Acupuncture and Biomedical Healing'. *Philosophical Transactions of the Royal Society B: Biological Sciences*, 366(1572): 1849–58. https://doi.org/10.1098/rstb.2010.0385

Kaptchuk, T. J., Friedlander, E., Kelley, J. M., Sanchez, M. N., Kokkotou, E., Singer, J. P., *et al.* (2010), 'Placebos without Deception: A Randomized Controlled Trial in Irritable Bowel Syndrome'. *PLoS ONE*, 5(12): e15591. https://doi.org/10.1371/journal.pone.0015591

Langer, E. J. (2014), *Mindfulness (25th Anniversary Edition)* (Boston, MA: Hachette Books).

Larkey, L. K., Roe, D. J., Weihs, K. L., Jahnke, R., Lopez, A. M., Rogers, C. E., *et al.* (2015), 'Randomized Controlled Trial of Qigong/Tai Chi Easy on Cancer-Related Fatigue in Breast Cancer Survivors'. *Annals of Behavioral Medicine: A Publication of the Society of Behavioral Medicine*, 49(2): 165–76. https://doi.org/10.1007/s12160-014-9645-4

Lawler, I. and Zimmermann, G. (2021), 'Misalignment Between Research Hypotheses and Statistical Hypotheses: A Threat to Evidence-Based Medicine?'. *Topoi*, 40(2): 307–18. https://doi.org/10.1007/s11245-019-09667-0

Lévi-Strauss, C. ([1958] 1998), 'The Sorcerer and His Magic' in P. J. Brown (ed.) *Understanding and Applying Medical Anthropology* (Mountain View, CA: Mayfield Publishing Company), 129–37.

Li, J. (2022), *Comparing Husserl's Phenomenology and Chinese Yogacara in a Multicultural World: A Journey Beyond Orientalism* (London and New York: Bloomsbury Academic).

Longino, H. (2019), 'The Social Dimensions of Scientific Knowledge' in E. N. Zalta (ed.) *The Stanford Encyclopedia of Philosophy*. Available at: https://plato.stanford.edu/archives/sum2019/entries/scientific-knowledge-social/. Accessed 10 July 2024.

Manek, N. and Tiller, W. (2013), 'P05.09. Feasibility of Information Medicine as Delivered by Intention Host Devices: A Case Report'. *Global Advances in Health and Medicine*, 2 (1_suppl.). https://doi.org/10.7453/gahmj.2013.097CP.P05.09

McIntyre, A. (1991), 'Incommensurability, Truth, and the Conversation Between Confucians and Aristotelians about the Virtues' in E. Deutsch (ed.) *Culture and Modernity: East-West Philosophic Perspectives* (Honolulu, HI: University of Hawai'i Press), 103–21.

Moerman, D. E. (2002), *Meaning, Medicine and the 'Placebo Effect'* (Cambridge: Cambridge University Press).

Mol, A. (2002), *The Body Multiple: Ontology in Medical Practice* (Durham, NC and London: Duke University Press).

National Institute for Health and Care Excellence (NICE). (2020), *Low Back Pain and Sciatica in Over 16s: Assessment and Management NG59* (London: NICE). Available at: https://www.nice.org.uk/guidance/ng59. Accessed 30 August 2024.

National Institute for Health and Care Excellence (NICE). (2021), *Chronic Pain (Primary and Secondary) in Over 16s: Assessment of All Chronic Pain and Management of Chronic Primary Pain [G] NG193* (London: NICE). Available at: https://www.nice.org.uk/guidance/ng193. Accessed 3 July 2024.

Ogden, E. (2018), *Credulity: A Cultural History of US Mesmerism*. Class 200: New Studies in Religion (Chicago, IL: University of Chicago Press).

Oh, J.-E. and Kim, S-N. (2021), 'Anti-Inflammatory Effects of Acupuncture at ST36 Point: A Literature Review in Animal Studies'. *Frontiers in Immunology*, 12: 813748. https://doi.org/10.3389/fimmu.2021.813748

Pirozelli, P. (2021), 'The Grounds of Knowledge: A Comparison Between Kuhn's Paradigms and Foucault's Epistemes'. *Revista Kriterion*, 62(148).

Posadzki, P. (2012), 'Therapeutic Intention of External Qigong Practitioners: A Qualitative Analysis and Implications for Practice'. *Integrative Medicine*, 11(1): 50–3.

Salguero, C. P. (2014), *Translating Buddhist Medicine in Medieval China*. Encounters with Asia (Philadelphia, PA: University of Pennsylvania Press).

Salguero, C. P. (2023), 'Are the Dharma's Healing Powers Just Placebo?' *Lion's Roar*. Available at: https://www.lionsroar.com/dharma-healing-powers-placebo/. Accessed 10 July 2024.

Schryvers, P. (2020), *Bad Data: Why We Measure the Wrong Things and Often Miss the Metrics That Matter* (Amherst, NY: Prometheus).

Schwartz, S. A. (1990), 'Therapeutic Intent and the Art of Observation'. *Subtle Energies & Energy Medicine Journal Archives*, 1(1). ii–viii.

Shao, L., Zhang, J., Chen, L., Zhang, X. and Chen, K. W. (2009), 'Effects of External Qi of Qigong with Opposing Intentions on Proliferation of Escherichia Coli'. *The Journal of Alternative and Complementary Medicine*, 15(5): 567–71. https://doi.org/10.1089/acm.2008.0408

Shapiro, A. K. and Shapiro, E. (1997), 'The Placebo: Is It Much Ado about Nothing?' in A. Harrington (ed.) *The Placebo Effect: An Interdisciplinary Exploration* (Cambridge, MA: Harvard University Press), 12–36.

Shelton, T. V. (2019), *Herbs and Roots: A History of Chinese Doctors in the American Medical Marketplace* (New Haven, CT: Yale University Press).

Solomon, M. (2015), *Making Medical Knowledge* (Oxford: Oxford University Press).

Stanley-Baker, M. (2022), '*Qi* 氣: A Means for Cohering Natural Knowledge' in V. Lo and M. Stanley-Baker, with D. Yang (eds) *Routledge Handbook of Chinese Medicine* (New York: Routledge), 23–50.

Tenny, S. and Varacallo, M. (2022), 'Evidence Based Medicine' in *StatPearls*. (Treasure Island, FL: StatPearls Publishing). Available at: http://www.ncbi.nlm.nih.gov/books/NBK470182/. Accessed 10 July 2024.

Tiller, W. A., Tiller, J. E., Dibble, W. E., Manek, R. and Manek, N. (2012), 'The Buddha Relics and Evidence of Physical Space Conditioning with Unimprinted Intention Host Devices'. *Journal of Alternative and Complementary Medicine*, 18(4): 379–81. https://doi.org/10.1089/acm.2011.0817

Tilley, H. (2020), 'How to Make Sense of "Traditional (Chinese) Medicine" in a Time of Covid-19: Cold War Origin Stories and the WHO's Role in Making Space for Polyglot Therapeutics', *Somatosphere*, 25 May. Available at: http://somatosphere.net/2020/tcm-covid-19.html/. Accessed 10 July 2024.

Tilley, H. (ed.) (2021), *Therapeutic Properties: Global Medical Cultures, Knowledge and Law*. Osiris. Vol. 36 (Chicago, IL: University of Chicago Press).

Wang, S.-M., Harris, R. E., Lin, Y-C. and Gan, T-J. (2013), 'Acupuncture in 21st Century Anesthesia: Is There a Needle in the Haystack?' *Anesthesia & Analgesia*, 116(6): 1356–9. https://doi.org/10.1213/ANE.0b013e31828f5efa

Wartolowska, K., Judge, A., Hopewell, S., Collins, G. S., Dean, B. J. F., Rombach, I., *et al.* (2014), 'Use of Placebo Controls in the Evaluation of Surgery: Systematic Review'. *BMJ (Clinical Research Ed.)* 348: g3253. https://doi.org/10.1136/bmj.g3253

Yuasa, Y. (1993), *The Body, Self-Cultivation, and Ki-Energy*. Translated by S. Nagatomo and M. S. Hull (New York: SUNY Press).

Zhang, Q. (1999), 'Demystifying Qi: The Politics of Cultural Translation and Interpretation in the Early Jesuit Mission to China' in L. H. Liu (ed.) *Tokens of Exchange: The Problem of Translation in Global Circulations* (Durham, NC and London: Duke University Press), 74–106.

11

Daoist Meditation as Guided Framework in Psychedelic Self-Care and Therapy

DOMINIC STEAVU

Introduction

THE SUCCESSIVE LOCKDOWNS of the Covid-19 pandemic produced the ideal conditions for the rediscovery of inner space. While some people turned to yoga and mindfulness meditation as self-care for anxiety, stress, sleeping disorders, addiction and depression during periods of confinement, others – surfing the recent wave of interest in all things fungal – ventured down the psychedelic path, with surprising results. Indeed, a slew of recent clinical studies have highlighted the tremendous promise of the therapeutic applications of psilocybin, the psychoactive compound found in psilocybe mushrooms. However, the explosion in its popularity and the destigmatisation of its consumption, both fuelled by the pandemic, have generated a 'psychedelic renaissance' and opened up even vaster horizons of potential in clinical research. Some of these vistas sketch out a therapeutic landscape in which 'spiritual' benefits of psychedelics overlap with the mental health benefits of psychedelics – a phenomenon already observed with certain contemplative practices.

Daoism, during its two-millennia-long history, has at various times in the past intertwined meditation and psychedelics. Some of its earlier, medieval-period practices stand out as a natural complement to psychedelic therapies for mental health issues and, more importantly, as a remedy to some of the problems that arise from their application. In clinical settings, there are few or no guidelines on how to navigate a psychedelic experience.[1] This lack of direction can mitigate positive outcomes, resulting in unremarkable therapeutic results. More directly, the absence of experiential protocols can also generate adverse outcomes by occasioning

[1] This is not the case outside of clinical settings, of course, where guidelines abound. Nevertheless, no single protocol has emerged as a standard one. For some examples of reliable recreational guidelines, see Fadiman (2011) and Strassman (2022). My thanks to the reviewers for pointing out these sources.

Proceedings of the British Academy, **278**, 223–245, © Authors 2025.

'bad trips' that cause new traumas and deter individuals from pursuing treatment. With its experience-focused and detailed ritual programme of guided psychedelic visualisations, Daoist meditations from the medieval period can buttress positive psycho-spiritual outcomes of therapy (i.e. providing personal meaning or depth to the experience of the treatment, reinforcing social bonds and enhancing the feeling of interconnection with others or nature) while also potentially diminishing 'bad trips'.

Having developed a familiarity with Daoist primary textual sources from the 3rd to 13th centuries, especially in the context of my work as a historian of medicine and historian of Chinese religions, the potential contribution of historical Daoism to contemporary approaches to health and wellness is a particularly exciting prospect. Far from proving incongruous with clinical settings, I argue that experience-based Daoist knowledge about psychedelic mushrooms and meditation is epistemologically compatible. Daoist-derived meditations deployed clinically in conjunction with psychedelic therapies have the potential to go beyond the subordinate and supportive role vis-à-vis 'Western' allopathic medicine typically reserved for Complementary Alternative Medicines (CAMs). They are poised to yield new insights into mental health and healing, propelling public health policy, practice and discourse in exciting, uncharted directions during the post-Covid era.

Covid-19 confinements and the rediscovery of inner ecology

For a time, the Covid-19 pandemic annihilated traditional modes of social interaction in America and other parts of the world. The previously shared and communal outside space was off limits for close to two years, or partially accessible only through a panoply of sanitary restrictions that severely limited direct contact with others. Exposure to people outside one's household was mediated through the distortive digital veil of the virtual, profoundly modifying the ways in which people interact, even today.

The cordoning off of the outer social space, however, also spurred many to rediscover and remap their inner space. To explore it, lockdown psychonauts turned en masse to methods of recreational introspection such as mindfulness meditation. According to Fitbit app data collected from US users for instance, the practice of meditation increased by 2,900 per cent during the pandemic (McGroarty 2024). The confined also turned to less traditional and less publicised paths to exploring their inner world; 'shifting' (alt. 'reality shifting' or RS) was a notably popular method on social media. Consisting of a blend of auto-hypnosis and guided absorptive meditation, it enables practitioners to inhabit 'desired realities' or fantasy worlds (often based on the Harry Potter novels) for extended periods of time (Somer *et al.* 2023). The 'trips', akin to self-induced ecstatic journeys or lucid dreaming, last a few hours, sometimes as many as eight, but to 'shifters' they can feel like weeks- or months-long excursions. Practitioners construct parallel worlds in which they interact with others, forge meaningful relations and have careers, all in their mind's eye. No external aids or substances are employed and the ends are chiefly recreational: shifting offers an escape from the loneliness, dreariness and anxiety of imposed isolation.

To date, the practice is viewed with suspicion by mental health professionals who consider it a possibly dysfunctional expression of maladaptive daydreaming or pathological fantasy-making that negatively impacts the development of real-life coping strategies for loneliness and anxiety.[2] Yet, reality shifting appears to have significant therapeutic benefits in those struggling with mental health issues occasioned or exacerbated by the pandemic. It uses the escapist coping strategy, usually considered 'negative', to artificially create an environment free from the factors that occasion anxiety and loneliness in the first place. Thus, the method is associated with stress reduction (Somer *et al.* 2023: 11423–4). It is also associated with positive outcomes when used to treat connected pathologies such as anxiety and depression – although, according to accounts on Reddit, it can also generate anxiety or be harder to successfully undertake for those with depression (Reddit 2021a, 2022a).

Other, more conventional forms of visualisation or meditation – often revolving around secularised mindfulness meditation – were also employed as self-care during the pandemic to cope with the explosion of mental health issues. Beyond serving as an entry point to an inner ecology, as a practice for improving spiritual acuteness or as a method for attaining a more general state of wellbeing, meditation has exponentially garnered interest as a type of therapy in clinical settings since the Covid-19 pandemic.[3] Numerous studies have looked at meditation more specifically as a viable form of self-care during the lockdown, with many concluding it has a measurable beneficial effect on mental health (Behan 2020; Nur Hasina *et al.* 2021; Deguma *et al.* 2022). Even popular meditation apps which experienced unprecedented growth and commercial success during the pandemic, such as Calm or Headspace, were shown to have some beneficial effects on users (Lahtinen 2023; O' Donnell, Dunbar and Speelman 2023). Be that as it may, what concerns us here is their role as indicators of widespread interest in new accessible forms of self-care for mental health.

The psychedelic renaissance

Another (relatively) accessible form of therapeutic self-care that experienced a surge in popularity during the pandemic was the use of psychedelic substances, in particular psilocybe fungi, 'magic mushrooms' or 'shrooms' as they are colloquially known. Even before the pandemic, psychedelics were undergoing a

[2] Maladaptive daydreaming can be defined as the propensity to engage in prolonged bouts of escapist daydreaming in order to cope, or avoid coping, with a problem. See Somer *et al.* (2023: 11424).

[3] There are a plethora of studies available, but for a recent overview of the applications and effectiveness of meditation across a variety of therapeutic contexts, see Kim *et al.* (2022).

renaissance. Starting in 2000, a number of regulatory roadblocks were lifted in the US, and research on psychedelics – which had been banned there since 1973 when psychotropic drugs were classified as Schedule I substances – could be resumed under certain conditions.[4] In 2006, a milestone study titled 'Psilocybin Can Occasion Mystical-Type Experiences Having Substantial and Sustained Personal Meaning and Spiritual Significance' was published in the journal *Psychopharmacology* (Griffiths *et al.* 2006). It underscored positive outcomes associated with psilocybin-rich mushrooms and their potential therapeutic applications, effectively sparking a renewal in psychedelic research. Soon thereafter, more restrictions on psychedelic research were lifted and the number of studies began to steadily increase. Recognising the uptick in academic/clinical and popular interest in psychedelics, Ben Sessa coined the term 'psychedelic renaissance' in 2012 (Sessa 2012). By 2019, Johns Hopkins Medical School founded the Center for Psychedelic and Consciousness Research, the first and currently still largest of its kind in the world.

Meanwhile, in the early to mid-2010s, and very likely as a result of the renewed clinical interest in psychedelics, Silicon Valley cadres were experimenting with microdosing protocols for LSD and psilocybes. They consumed the hallucinogens not for the purpose of getting high, however, but in order to increase creativity in high-stress environments where out-of-the-box thinking is rewarded (Kuchler 2017; Swisher 2018). The trend sparked a regional West Coast revival of interest in psychedelic drugs, dovetailing with the full legalisation of cannabis in Western states (Colorado and Washington in 2012; Oregon in 2014; California and Nevada in 2016). This psychedelic boom also coincided with (or produced?) a string of new, popular publications on fungi, most notably Michael Pollan's *How to Change Your Mind: What the New Science of Psychedelics Teaches Us About Consciousness, Dying, Addiction, Depression, and Transcendence* (2018) and Paul Stamets' *Fantastic Fungi: How Mushrooms Can Heal, Shift Consciousness and Save the Planet* (2019), both of which resulted in Netflix shows/series.

In parallel and not unconnected to the psychedelic renaissance, mushrooms in general garnered a renewed interest, both academic and popular, marking a mycological boom: Anna Tsing's *The Mushroom at the End of the World: On the Possibility of Life in Capitalist Ruins* (2015) and Merlin Sheldrake's *Entangled Life: How Fungi Make our Worlds, Change our Minds and Shape our Futures* (2020) reflect the renewed general engouement for all things fungal that defined the zeitgeist. At any rate, by the time the pandemic lockdowns were enacted, magic mushrooms were no longer perceived as mere recreational drugs procuring a temporary and euphoric reprieve from reality; they were regarded as introspective or creative aids as well as substances that could positively contribute to treating anxiety, addiction

[4] See the Beckley Foundation's informative 'Psychedelic Research Timeline' (Beckley Foundation 2016). Brad Stoddard provides a welcome and more granular overview of psychedelic research since the late 1800s, its legal challenges, as well as its relation to spirituality in a pair of articles (Stoddard 2023a, 2023b).

and depression by resetting some of the recurring neural patterns that enable those conditions. The stage was thus set during the Covid-19 pandemic for the popular rediscovery of psychoactive mushrooms.

The combination of new knowledge (via published research) about the potential benefits of psychedelics for mental health, in conjunction with changing social attitudes towards their consumption and shadow epidemics of anxiety, addiction and depression spurred by the pandemic, formed the ideal conditions for many to experiment with magic mushrooms for the first time. Various sources reported that consumption of psychotropic drugs reached an all-time high, reaching a peak of 4.7 per cent of young adults in 2021 (NIDA 2022). For many new users, consuming psychedelic mushrooms during the pandemic was not driven by the traditional recreational aims or aspirations of increased creativity/workplace performance. Rather, it was a concern for wellness and self-care that motivated them (Winstock *et al.* 2021). In some cases, local authorities even encouraged these forms of self-administered therapy: protocols for microdosing psilocybin notably appeared on the Oregon Health Authority's 'Prevention and Wellness' website in 2022 but were removed in 2023.[5]

These factors – new research, an increase in social acceptability and pandemic self-care – coalesced into a psychedelic renaissance. Current clinical and popular interest in psilocybin, specifically, overshadows even the enthusiasm of the 1960s psychedelic counterculture, with this second wave of mushroom fervour aligning with mainstream values and cultural trends.

The 'spiritual' or wellness argument for therapeutic applications

As an illustration of the recent openness surrounding psychedelic use, a student-run and university-approved UCSB Psychedelics Club was founded in late 2019/early 2020 at the University of California, Santa Barbara.[6] It is advertised in the university newspaper and meets weekly during the academic year to discuss topics ranging from 'proper dosing' to 'psychedelics and spirituality'; the club also runs crossover sessions with the UCSB mindfulness club on a regular basis. Its organisers routinely host speakers, specialists in their field, who lecture on subjects including 'psilocybin, depression, and neuroplasticity' or 'psychedelics and meditation' (Crommelin 2019; Smith 2020).[7] Spiritual concerns are mentioned in the same breath as mental wellness. At meetings, 'tripping' or 'getting high' are

[5] See Oregon Health Authority (2023) for the updated version. Some of the earlier materials were archived and remain accessible; see Stauffer (2022).

[6] Comparatively, a number of other universities, especially in the UK (the University of Kent, for instance), have benefited from active student-run psychedelic societies since the early 2010s. My thanks to the reviewer for pointing this out.

[7] The UCSB Psychedelics Club also maintains a public Instagram page (UCSB Psychedelic Club 2020).

rarely mentioned as motivational factors in taking mushrooms; the focus is more squarely on introspection and self-care, which considerably overlap in the minds of participants.

Psilocybin was decriminalised in Colorado in 2019 and was both decriminalised and legalised (for supervised non-medical use) in Oregon in 2020. Although, as of 2025, California as a whole has not yet decriminalised psilocybin for therapeutic use, some cities have, including Santa Cruz, San Francisco and Berkeley. Overall, state and local enforcement agencies do not consider the illicit consumption of mushrooms a high-priority issue. Exploiting this 'live and let live' attitude on the part of authorities as well as prosecutorial grey areas on the matter, some dispensaries have begun discreetly selling psilocybe mushrooms. Zide Door in Oakland has been doing so since 2019, when the city became the first to decriminalise psilocybin in California. The shop remained open during the pandemic and with the concomitant increase in demand, the shop ended up being a victim of its own success; it was raided by Oakland police in 2020.

Following the raid, Zide Door filed a lawsuit against the city and the police department, arguing that they were in fact a religious organisation – the Church of Ambrosia (sometimes referred to as the Church of Entheogenic Plants) – and that consuming entheogens such as psilocybe mushrooms was part of their ritual practices (Church of Ambrosia 2022). Thus, Zide Door maintains that it offers religious sacraments in exchange for donations. Services are held at 4:20 pm on Sundays, but sacraments are available to church members throughout the week during regular business hours. For context, at the federal level, the United States Supreme Court ruled in the 2006 *Gonzales v. O Centro Espírita Beneficente União do Vegetal* case that, under certain circumstances, the consumption of illicit psychoactive substances as religious sacraments was protected for Americans under the Religious Freedom Restoration Act of 1993 (which afforded Native Americans an exemption for consuming peyote, a Schedule I drug) (Stoddard 2023b: 4–5). Zide Door eventually dropped its lawsuit in the hope that it would facilitate the obtention of a conditional use permit, but the affair prompted significant attention in the local media, enough so that the clientele/membership grew larger and more diverse.

Even before the lawsuit, Zide Door did indeed have a spiritual dimension to its activities. From the outset, it drew inspiration from predecessors such as Baba Kilindi Iyi's (d. 2020) radical African American religio-spiritual psychedelic community in Detroit. Much in the image of Zide Door and, to some extent, the UCSB Psychedelics Club, many of the new grassroots second-wave organisations that have emerged in the context of the psychedelics revival have an avowed spiritual scope, if not an openly religious one. These, of course, did not emerge ex nihilo but stand on the shoulders of an earlier generation of pioneers, most recently the psychedelic churches of the 1960s and 1970s.[8] Before that, William

[8] On the psychedelic churches of the mid- to late 20th century, see Marinacci (2023).

James's theories of mysticism had paved the way for the modern Euro-American discourse about accessing religious experiences via intoxicants.[9] And even earlier, in the North American context still, First Nations and Indigenous traditions had, for hundreds of years, included certain psychedelics as sacraments in their entheogenic programmes. They have continued to do so throughout the 20th and 21st centuries, their actors defending the substances' capacity for healing mental, physical or spiritual ailments (often one and the same) and otherwise occasioning meaningful improvements in a person's quality of life (Stoddard 2023a: 3).

Similarly, actors in the latest spiritual/religious/mystical groups that integrate psychedelics in their practices are quick to stress the positive outcomes of consuming such substances when it comes to wellness – a general sense of plenitude that is described as physical, mental and spiritual, all at once. Recent studies that have documented self-reported descriptions of the effects of psilocybin read like a laundry list of spiritual awakening. One of these, aggregating results from previous studies, usefully groups them into broad untitled categories, enumerating the following effects among others (Lowe *et al.* 2023, Tables 3, 4 and 5):

1 mystical, divine, or transcendental experiences; connection or communication with God/gods/the divine.
2 open-mindedness/change in perspective of the world; noticing intricacies in one's environment.
3 egolessness, ego dissolution; sense of unity and connection to nature, people, other living things; feeling at one with universe.
4 euphoria, happiness, joy, contentment; an overwhelming feeling of love or gratitude; peacefulness, calmness or quietude.
5 clarity, awareness; insight or enlightenment.
6 improvement in physical and mental wellbeing; lighter, limber, more energetic; reduction in psychological distress.

These positive outcomes have been shown to be acute and persistent over time, as psychedelics can effectively redraw the neural architecture in order to avoid the recurring mental pathways that lead to depression, anxiety, PTSD, addiction and other conditions (Lowe *et al.* 2023).

However, users also consistently report negative outcomes, whether in clinical settings or self-administered contexts with statistically significantly higher rates of occurrence in unguided settings (Schlag *et al.* 2022; Evans *et al.* 2023). The potential for adverse effects is conspicuously absent from public discourse around the topic of psychedelics and only recently have a few key studies started to probe the matter (Carbonaro *et al.* 2016; Bienemann *et al.* 2020). Generally, the negative outcomes associated with psilocybin consumption are nausea, headache, vomiting,

[9] William James expounds his theory of mysticism in *The Varieties of Religious Experience*; see Stoddard (2023: 3–4) for a summary.

disorientation, loss of control over bodily functions, temporary paralysis, visual or aural hallucinations, increased anxiety and, in rare cases, psychotic episodes.[10]

Significantly, very similar negative outcomes are sometimes reported by novice meditators who jump into practice without the necessary preparation or with a disordinate focus on the self. Collectively known as 'meditation sickness' or 'meditation malady', these symptoms have been signalled for centuries by Buddhists, who have prescribed certain countermeasures to offset them.[11] Only recently have practitioners begun, via the work of scholars of religion who have recovered these ancient remedies from the forgotten annals of history, to turn to early sources on meditation sickness to find more balanced approaches to their practice.

With its history of complex introspective meditation practices and mushroom-related practices, Daoism, in some of its earlier iterations, constitutes an alternative source of entheogenic knowledge that has been hitherto overlooked. What is more, these iterations charted the landscape of ecstatic trips and can therefore provide roadmaps in navigating the sometimes-bumpy road of psychedelic journeys. They can contribute to the minimisation of negative outcomes and supply a safe ritual framework for maximising positive outcomes.

Daoism

Daoism is a 2,000-year-old religious tradition from China concerned with biospiritual self-cultivation. On account of its focus on maintaining health and extending lifespan, it significantly intersects with indigenous Chinese disciplines including medicine, proto-chemistry and pharmacology, as well as botany and mycology.

From around the turn of the first millennium, psychoactive and hallucinogenic plants were integrated into practices shared by mediumistic currents and proto-Daoist longevity/immortality cults. Fungi were part of the entheogenic curriculum as well. Early murals depict immortals and deities grasping or surrounded by *lingzhi* 靈芝, 'numinous mushrooms', considered life-extending panaceas that enabled direct communication with the divine (Steavu 2018, 2025).[12] In later, institutional Daoism – which started to take shape from the mid-2nd century – these sacred

[10] In addition to clinical studies, Reddit provides anectodal but highly informative insights; see Reddit (2020, 2021b, 2022b).

[11] For studies based on historical accounts, see Ahn (2008, 2017, 2021) and Greene (2017). Eskildsen (2008) has published an eye-opening article on the lesser-known cases of meditation sickness in Daoism; some of his findings are applicable to contemporary settings as well. Salguero (2023) looks at both the historical and present-day contexts. As a complement to her work on the neuropsychological mechanisms of meditation-related benefits, Willoughby Britton has also researched neuroscientific concerns about mindfulness meditation today; see Britton *et al.* (2021), for example.

[12] Issues of identification regarding the term *lingzhi* are discussed in Steavu (2018) and Steavu (2026).

fungi took on more dignified indexical roles as gauges of immortality and divinity or ritual offerings on altars (Steavu 2026). Eventually, numinous mushrooms were appreciated for their symbolic functions alone, their entheogenic function gradually disappearing from official sources since the 14th century. Today, Daoism does not employ psychoactive substances in their rituals or practices, and this has been the case for at least the last century or two.

For much of the medieval period, however, eschewing public scrutiny and tucked away from the limelight under the cover of esoteric rites, mushrooms retained some of their original entheogenic applications. A passage from a 4th-century Daoist scripture intended for initiated readers illustrates this with relative clarity. In it, a legendary immortal transmitting his prized teachings to a disciple bestows the ultimate lesson:[13]

> By means of the stone mushrooms, red stem [mushrooms], and several other numinous mushrooms that I have offered to you for ingestion, my teaching is complete. … Bow respectfully to receive this teaching and retire for fasting. Perform the ablution of the five aromatics, do not sleep for seven days and seven nights. Should you feel any apprehension, sit with hands joined and reflect on the supreme Dao. Then, at dawn [on the eighth day], burn incense, face north, bow respectfully, and ingest these divine mushrooms. Within five years, you will be able to see things beyond five thousand *li*, your body will be light, you will leap over ten spans [in one bound], and be capable of travelling 500 *li* in one day. You will be able to hide or manifest your form [at will], to sit in contemplation undisturbed until you forget yourself, and to tour the famous mountains to seek instruction among immortals.[14]

These lines leave little doubt as to what type of mushrooms are under discussion. We may readily identify some of the effects of psychedelic fungi in the second part of the citation – and even if the text mentions a five-year frame for the substances to take action, this likely refers to the length of time required to train oneself in order to experience the Daoist-specific outcomes listed. The preparatory fasting and sleep deprivation (for a full week) would in and of themselves be sufficient to elicit visions, but in combination with psychoactive mushrooms, the entheogenic effects would undoubtedly be powerful and immediate.

We may glean another example from a 7th- or 8th-century text, the 'Secret of Divine Immortals' (Shenxian bishi 神仙祕事), which provides detailed instructions on how to grow four types of numinous mushrooms. After locating an appropriate site on a propitious day, practitioners must dig a hole and fill it with a variety of substances, from plants and roots to minerals, animal products, oils and ale. After a few weeks, special mushrooms will grow. These must be ritually harvested, on particular days and times, after making previous offerings and using

[13] All translations from Classical Chinese into English are mine.

[14] *Ziyang zhenren neizhuan*, 7a. 今以《守三一之法》、《靈妙小有之書》二百事傳子，石菌、朱柯、若乾芝與子服之，吾道畢矣。[…] 君再拜受教，退齋，沐浴五香，七日七夜不寐，但危坐接手，存念至道。乃以平旦燒香，北向再拜，服此神芝。五年之間，視見千里之外。身輕，能超十丈，日步行五百里。能隱能彰，坐在立亡。能巡行名山，尋索仙人。

knives fashioned from specific and ritually meaningful materials. Then, the text stipulates one should:

> … return the mushroom to shade for one hundred days and process it into grounds. Ingest one spatula-full and take it thrice daily by means of fragrant well water. When the mushroom is entirely consumed, you will immediately be able to feel light and float about. Gods will arrive to welcome you. You will ascend to Heaven in broad daylight and be as limitless as Heaven and Earth.[15]

The passage unambiguously lists the sensation of flying or floating, communication with the divine, travelling to other realms and a feeling of unity with all of creation – all hallmarks of the psychedelic experience – as effects of consuming numinous mushrooms. Given the esoteric nature of entheogenic practices, such accounts are fairly uncommon in the Daoist canon, but those that survive generally align with (equally sparse) descriptions of other Daoist methods that rely on entheogenic substances. I will not go into detail about these here, but calamus (*chuangpu* 菖蒲), monkshood (*fuzi* 附子), ephedra (*mahuang* 麻黄), henbane (*langdan* 莨菪) and cannabis flowers (*mabo* 麻勃; *mahua* 麻花) are among the documented substances that were featured in Daoist rituals, self-cultivation techniques (including meditation/visualisation) or healing rites (Steavu 2026). Their effects were described in terms very similar to those employed for numinous mushrooms, lending weight to the argument that the fungi consumed by Daoists for some practices were indeed psychedelic.

Despite the fact that the use of entheogens was not widely advertised, there is no question that Daoists were keenly aware of the properties of psychedelic mushrooms since the 3rd or 4th century, if not earlier (Steavu 2026). The 5th- or 6th-century *Commentary on the Classic of Materia Medica* 本草經集注 by the Daoist patriarch and physician Tao Hongjing 陶弘景 (456–536) contains entries concerning mushrooms that overlap with the self-reported effects of psilocybin, listed above (I include numbered references to their categories in square brackets): thus, they are found to be 'detoxifying' (解毒) [6], to 'heighten vision and hearing' (耳目聰明) [5], 'pacify the spirit' (安神; alt. 安精魂) [4], to make one 'harmonious and joyful' (*he le* 和樂) [4], 'make the body light' (輕身) [6], 'increase vitality' (益精氣) [6], and 'extend one's years' (不老延年) [6].[16] Other entries on mushrooms from the same source are even more explicit, with mentions of 'communicating with spirits and interacting with the numinous' (通神明; alt. 通神而致靈) [1] and 'laughing uncontrollably' (令人笑不止) [4].[17]

Excluding medical sources such as the *Commentary on the Classic of Materia Medica*, many of the texts or passages that centre on numinous mushrooms associate them with visualisation practices; very often, they include ecstatic

[15] *Shangqing mingjian yaojing*, 10a–10b. 歸，陰乾百日，治為屑。服一刀圭，以井花水，日服三。芝盡，即能輕舉，當有神來迎之，白日昇天，與天地无窮矣。

[16] *Bencao jing jizhu*, 3.184–5, and 187.

[17] Ibid., 3.187–8 and 2.183.

journeys or components thereof. This is also true of materials that do not focus on fungi but merely mention them in passing. The following lines from a 4th-century compilation illustrate the point:

> Ponder the essence of the sun descending and entering through your nostrils. Swallow it twenty-seven times so that it fills your heart. In your heart, there are three people. On the left there is Great Unity, the father; on the right there is Dark Radiance, the mother; and in the center there is the Red Child, a small lad. He is seated on a golden recliner with jade cushions, holding a jade platter of celestial mushroom plants and jade cup filled with the divine liquor of jade essence. If you visualize him eating [the mushrooms] and drinking [the liquor], accordingly, you will not know hunger nor thirst and you will be long-lived.[18]

In these cases, it is possible that psychedelics were ingested immediately before the visualisations, as an esoteric divine sacrament. If they were not, at the very least, practitioners were intended to identify with the Red Child, who ingests the mushrooms (and is elsewhere described as the 'true self' [*zhenwu* 真吾]). Thus, even when no actual mushrooms were involved, Daoist meditations played on the experiential overlap and kinship between structured, scripted or guided contemplations and psychedelic journeys.

Indeed, a good deal of Daoist visualisations appear to be devised and designed in such a way as to simulate psychedelic visions: exploring the inner landscape, travelling to distant stars or other realms, conversing with immortals, interacting with gods, peering into the future, bending time and space, dissolving oneself in the lunar and solar essences of the cosmos, tapping into the primordial vital breath of creation, or uniting with all in the expanse of Heaven and Earth. None of these are static experiences. There is almost always movement in Daoist visualisations, in scale or in distance, in terms of the practitioners' gaze or their travelling spirit-body, regardless of whether the methods are psychedelically augmented or not. Visionary travel is part of the very genetic code of Daoism.[19]

As I have argued elsewhere on the basis of medieval sources, 'purification rites' (*zhai* 齋) – ritual preparations that adepts undertook prior to embarking on elaborate meditation practices – and the mystical states they occasioned were sufficiently potent to elicit psychedelic-like experiences without relying on external substances. After days on end of intense isolation, silent introspection, repetitive intoning, as well as sensory, food and sleep deprivation (the latter, up to a week), adepts could seamlessly initiate a scripted and rehearsed ecstatic journey through the mind's eye that would feel just like a psychedelic trip (Benn 1991; Steavu 2018). Mystical religious experiences and psychedelic substances have indeed been shown to share

[18] *Lingbao wufu xu*, 1.25b. 因思日精來下，入鼻孔口中，嚥之三九，滿心中。心中有三人，左即太一父也，右即玄光母也，中央即赤子小童也。坐金牀玉榻，執玉柈玉杯，杯中玉英神酒，并天芝草見在，食飲之，仍不饑渴而長生矣。

[19] For a survey of meditation technique that incorporate ecstatic flight and trance journeys in Daoism, see Robinet 1993: 171–225 and Kohn 1993: 249–76.

similar neural pathways (Goodman 2002). When psychedelics were additionally ingested, either as part of the purification rites or in the context of the meditative practice, the potency of the visions would undoubtedly be exponentially multiplied.

Significantly, all of the complex visualisations were learned and rehearsed well ahead of time; when they were actually undertaken with chemical aids, the experiential path, although unquestionably intensified, was well trodden. The specifics of the ecstatic journey, the particularities of its content remained open-ended but the parameters were set, providing familiarity and stability. This quasi-predictable dimension to the process provided a failsafe, a talismanic 'home base' to return to in case of a sudden loss of direction or heightened anxiety. To put it succinctly, it guarded against bad trips.[20] Instead of giving free rein to their mind and ending up in uncharted territory, practitioners could stick to an internalised ritual script that involved relying on pre-suggested visions and provided a structured, measurable progression towards realisation.

Past trends and future directions: Daoism as a ritual guardrail or outcome anchor in post-Covid psychedelic meaning-making therapies

Meditation has been shown to have positive outcomes for depression, anxiety and addiction (Hoge *et al.* 2023) while also occasioning a general sense of wellbeing, quietude and a heightened mood. Psychedelic mushrooms offer much of the same benefits (Argento *et al.* 2021) with perhaps more marked clinical results. Combining meditation with psychedelic therapies promises to compound positive outcomes or reinforce them at the least. Daoism is one of the only existing traditions with a documented track record in both meditation and psychedelics, especially in its medieval incarnations. To be clear, while contemplation techniques continued to enjoy widespread currency in later periods, into the present day, Daoist entheogenic practices that relied on psychoactive substances largely fell into disuse after the medieval period and have been since relegated to the dustbin of history. Contemporary Daoists, particularly clerics, would deny any connection between psychedelic mushrooms and their tradition.

[20] On bad trips in Daoism, see Eskildsen (2008), where the author, drawing on primary sources, identifies mental disorders ('mania', 'delusion', 'the threat of insanity') and physiological harm ('physical agonies', 'suspension of breathing and pulse', 'danger of death') that can potentially stem from visualisation practices. Eskildsen does not refer to entheogens in his discussion, but his findings can be applied to psychedelic-aided practices as well since both varieties are reliant on trance states (a hallmark of visionary travel/ecstatic journeys as explained above). Of note, unpleasant mental or physical effects sometimes reflect the successful outcome of a practice since they manifest the purging of pathogens, for example. The approaches listed for avoiding negative experiences emphasise staying focused, practising earnestly and following the prescribed regimen. The presence of attendants or guides are also highlighted as a preventive measure.

Daoist practitioners benefitted from this two-pronged therapeutic approach in the medieval period and although it was abandoned during the early modern and modern periods, it can thankfully be excavated and redeployed due to its preservation in the archive. Its tested episteme and its trusted ritual programme can provide experiential guardrails as well as an outcome anchored in clinical settings by supplying pre-scripted parameters and teleological narratives for the psychedelic experience.

In the US, some groundwork has already been completed in recognising Daoism's position at the crossroads of meditation and psychedelics as well as its potential contributions to therapy. On the heels of the Beat Generation and the subsequent mid-century countercultural infatuation with Zen Buddhism, Gia-Fu Feng 馮家福 (1919–85), a Chinese banker turned Daoist sage, founded the Stillpoint Taoist Meditation Center. It was first established in Los Gatos, California (1966), and was then briefly moved to Vermont (early 1971), before finally being relocated to Colorado (late 1971). Feng also published a number of books, some of them translations, on the topics of Daoist thought and Daoist practice.[21] Prior to founding Stillpoint, Feng spent a formative decade on the West Coast with figures such as Allan Watts (1915–73), who were at the intersection of the Beats and the psychedelic movement (Stoddard 2023a). Watts would eventually go on to author a respected introduction to Daoism, published posthumously in 1975 (Watts with Huang 1975). Feng notably shared a close friendship with Dick Price (1930–85), co-founder of the Esalen Institute in Big Sur, California. He was actually one of the first staff members at Esalen, where he handled accounting and taught Taiji quan 太極拳 (alt. tai chi). He did not openly advocate ingesting psychedelics, but he did provide Price with insights about Chinese traditions and Daoist meditation in particular.[22] Various forms of meditation, including Daoist-inspired ones, were and continue to be taught at Esalen. Price had a pronounced interest in research into altered states of consciousness, so it is not unreasonable to suppose that he might have asked Feng about how they were understood (or even generated) in Daoism. Speculation aside, the Esalen Institute was certainly known for holding psychedelics workshops and hosting pioneers in psychedelics advocacy since the 1960s – some of them, including Aldoux Huxley (1894–1963), overlapping with Feng's tenure there.

Timothy Leary (1920–96) was another guest speaker of repute at Esalen, one who investigated the intersection between Asian traditions and psychedelics more seriously. Although most remembered for his Harvard Psilocybin Project (1960–2), the ensuing debacle and his subsequent role as countercultural icon, Leary also authored or co-authored over two dozen books. The first book he co-wrote after experimenting with 'magic mushrooms' in 1960 (his second overall)

[21] See Feng (1970); Feng and English (1972, 1974). A fourth book, Feng (1986), was published posthumously.

[22] For an enlightening biography of Feng, see Wilson (2019).

was *The Psychedelic Experience*, where he compared the interior journey of psychedelics to the Tibetan Buddhist process of death and rebirth (Leary, Metzner and Alpert 1964). It remains his best-known work to date. Shortly thereafter, he published *Psychedelic Prayers After the Tao Te Ching*, refining his understanding of the compatibility between Asian traditions and chemically induced mystical states (Leary 1966). In it, he reframed the psychedelic experience in terms of Daoist principles and more specifically in terms of the tradition's foundational text, the *Scripture of the Way and Virtue* (*Daode jing* 道德經; alt. *Tao Te Ching*). The prayers – which can also be described as mystical poems or trance hymns – that make up the book were composed on Crank's Ridge, near the town of Almora, Uttarakhand, in the Himalayas under the influence of LSD and hashish. They are, as he puts it, a 'translation' of the Daoist scripture into 'psychedelese', through which he exhorts readers to tap into their deeper tiers of consciousness, at the cellular and molecular levels, in order to access a perennial state of becoming in its natural condition as energy in constant flux (Leary 1966: 4).

With such a rich and relatively recent history in popular culture/counterculture, it is somewhat surprising that clinical studies have not looked more closely at the potential value of Daoist meditation in conjunction with psychedelic therapies. That is not to say the subject has been completely ignored. Building on the success of secularised Buddhist practices such as mindfulness, clinical trials on the benefits of Daoist-derived meditations have already begun with the expectation of applicability in therapeutic contexts. One example, 'Chinese Taoist Cognitive Therapy' or CTCT, a modern, comprehensive and culturally sensitive psychotherapy derived from Daoist ideas that was developed in China in 1998, has already shown promise in the treatment of depression and anxiety across cultural and geographical boundaries (Ding *et al.* 2020; Cohen 2024). Psychedelic therapies enhanced by more traditional but adapted Daoist visualisation practices would likely have similar if not a higher potential for clinical applications. By virtue of their structured and predetermined ritual paths, they can provide epistemological road maps that gradually shepherd patients through the psychedelic experience. In other words, to borrow Leary's terms, Daoist meditations can supply the 'set' (the mindset and outcome expectations for psychedelic therapies) to complement the therapeutic 'setting', thereby stimulating positive outcomes along an anticipated teleological path and reducing negative outcomes such as 'bad trips'.

Perhaps just as importantly, if not more so, because of their inherently introspective and ecstatic content (and not necessarily religious in the Western or Abrahamic sense of the term), Daoist practices can supply a genuine spiritual dimension to therapies – an aspect that is inevitably lacking or underdeveloped in clinical settings. Adding this dimension to the treatment of anxiety, depression, eating disorders or addiction can buttress the positive outcomes by providing the patient with *meaning* to process the neurological/psychological changes that psilocybin enables. It is common for recreational psychonauts to report ingesting psychedelics for the purposes of 'self-discovery', 'self-care' and 'self-acceptance' or 'healing the self'; some are motivated by the benefits of 'focusing on the self and forgetting the world' (Reddit 2022c). For them, the emphasis is squarely on the self and the individual: how to improve one's sense of fulfilment and peace in a result-oriented, output-driven world; how to reconnect with a lost 'self' in today's fast-paced society, and so on. Like Transcendental Meditation, mindfulness meditation and global yoga, meditation-supported psychedelic treatments run the risk of being over-secularised, commodified and co-opted into self-help narratives typical of late-stage capitalism. These narratives break up society into infinitesimally smaller units of consumption and production, displacing widespread societal issues onto a constructed 'self' who is then solely responsible for all shortcomings, failings or imperfections (including those pertaining to mental health). That 'self' is left with the arduous task of healing and rebuilding itself back up into a productive (i.e. consumerist) integrated member of the social whole (Purser 2019).

Daoist meditation is equipped with mechanisms that can act as a counterweight to these narratives. Many of its visualisations emphasise an interconnectedness with all living beings (through a shared constitutive essence) and the understanding of humans as mere cogs in the great wheel of the Dao. This is in stark contrast to other East Asian traditions, including Confucianism and even Buddhism, that adopt a more anthropocentric view grounded in human exceptionalism. In Daoist contemplations, the self is dissolved in the infinity of living things, each of which is on a plane of ontological equality with any other. In parallel to constituting a rampart against the hyper-individualisation and commodification of alternative or emerging treatments and maintaining some of the countercultural cachet of the first psychedelic wave, Daoist meditation reinforces positive sensations of depersonalisation and connectedness that are often central to successful outcomes in psychedelic treatments. If such treatments are unguided, intense sensations of egolessness – which the artist Henri Michaux (1899–1984) referred to as 'experimental psychosis' – can sometimes result in existential nihilism, reinforcing anxiety or deep depression.

But Daoist meditation, with its established idiom of fusion between subject (self) and object (the world), can ensure the dissolution of ego is experienced positively. One of the hallmarks of Daoist meditation is precisely the erasure of this distinction between our perceived self and the outside world that we inhabit. For example, in many practices, Daoism promotes an alignment of the internal rhythms of the body and of the inner space with those of the external world – one's immediate environment, nature writ large and the cosmos as well. Meanwhile, for some patients, psychedelic therapy results in an increased sense of synergy and relatedness to nature (Kettner *et al.* 2019; Gandy 2020). Daoist meditation as a therapeutic complement would not only have the potential to heighten and prolong those effects; once unpacked and reframed, it could eventually contribute to the articulation of a genuine (psychedelic-initiated) environmental ethic that sees a genuine identity between individuals and all living things – the antithesis to anthropocentric diktats that subjugate and instrumentalise nature for exclusively human (and individual) profit. While elaborating such an environmental ethic from psychedelic therapies may seem overly ambitious at present, at the very least, Daoism – with its unique heritage of guided visualisation methods and entheogenic know-how – can certainly provide an alternative framework for psychedelic therapies. The 'set' that it provides can promote positive outcomes and decrease negative ones.

In addition to supplying the 'set', Daoist meditations can also contribute the 'setting', to return to Leary's concept. But here, it is not in the physical sense of the term, the immediate environment or clinical context as it were, but rather the social, communal or species-wide episteme. Daoist meditations invariably situate their practitioners in a vast collective tapestry of living beings. This sense of insertion and belonging is at the antipodes of the alienating individuality that prevails in contemporary society and is sometimes at the root of mental health issues. In this respect, a guided and jointly meditative-psychedelic protocol for patients would constitute a genuine meaning-making therapy.

Conclusion

Daoist entheogenic and non-entheogenic meditations have historically developed in close proximity, sometimes intertwining with Classical Chinese medicine. Outside of Asia and in Euro-American settings in particular, they are habitually classified under the aegis of CAMs (Complementary and Alternative Medicines). Despite operating under sometimes different epistemic regimes, these systems have gained increasing currency in conventional medical practice over the last decade or two (Stanley-Baker, Yoeli-Tlalim and Yang 2021). Not only are they recognised in their own right as legitimate traditions of healing, but they are sometimes interwoven with allopathic 'Western' biomedical therapies, as in Integrative Medicine. Nevertheless, there remains some suspicion about them on the part of health professionals, researchers and patients, precisely because of their reliance on different grammars of healing, according to which the patient's experience, for example, is privileged or at the least taken into account when devising the course of therapy.

For many, this difference in epistemes of healing is perceived to be one of culture. 'Western' biomedicine is assumed to be opposed and inherently superior to other healing traditions from the Global South. This reductive view of CAMs and associated practices has prevented their broader deployment. In my own experience, I have found it to be an important stumbling block in attempting to establish the effectiveness of Daoist-derived therapeutic complements. I previously designed a meditation protocol to be used in conjunction with psychedelic therapy; together with a pharmacologist colleague, we drafted a proposal for a clinical trial and reached out to several clinical scholars at institutions that engage in psychedelic research. The few who responded expressed uneasiness with the 'spiritual' and 'culturally specific' aspects of the proposed research.

Yet, the argument is precisely that Daoist-inspired programmed psychedelic sessions should not be reduced to their culturally and historically specific settings of origin. To date, the rare studies that have seriously engaged with the healing potential of therapies derived from Daoist meditation have defended their value in culturally circumscribed applications, ideal for mental health patients with East Asian cultural backgrounds (Chang *et al.* 2020; Ding *et al.* 2020). While they can surely be useful in this respect, my position is that they have a broader, transcultural applicability. What is more, in current psychedelic therapies, it is seldom recognised that the cultural context of particular patients, regardless of their specific background, will invariably impact clinical results; the focal point remains on the psychoanalytically constructed 'self' of late-stage industrial societies and on the discovery of one's all-important 'mental cabinet' in order to initiate healing (to say nothing of the impact of the clinician's individual framing of the patient's experience and their dictating the terms in which the patient will live and recount it). A psychedelic treatment protocol that integrates a guided meditation component inspired by Daoist visualisations would not only displace the emphasis from the hyper-centripetal notion of the individual to a socially integrated, interconnected understanding of being, migrating from a particularist view of illness and healing to one that is universalist (applicable to all living beings); it could also provide a common language of meaning-making for both patient and clinician.

For although meditation-based therapies traditionally privilege an experiential episteme for truth claims, their relevance as therapies can also be established through clinical proof – via randomised control trials for instance – their effects verifiable and reproduceable according to the standards of validity of biomedicine. The congruence between different healing systems, including CAMs and conventional medicine, is gaining wider acceptance. The emerging field of placebo studies (see Cheung, Chapter 10), for example, has opened exciting new lines of inquiry into the biological consequences of experience, social interaction and intentionality. David Moerman, in particular, has highlighted the crucial role of making meaning, 'a human universal', as a trigger for endogenous biological mechanisms of healing and recovery (what he refers to as the 'meaning response') (Moerman 2002). Certain more focused studies have shed light on how prayer, meditative absorption or *qi* 氣 ('vital energy') may function in healing from a biomedical perspective, foregrounding the relevance of classical Chinese medicine and Buddhist meditation beyond their initial context (Smigielski *et al.* 2019). Kin Cheung, a contributor to this volume, makes the same point while innovatively arguing for the limitations of evidence-based legitimation mechanisms typical of allopathic medicine (Cheung 2022). Daoist meditative and healing practices are no different. They operate according to a different epistemology than that of biomedicine, but one that is nevertheless compatible and even convergent, especially when it comes to psychedelic therapies.

This epistemological overlay should also address lingering concerns about the 'religious' or, more appropriately, the 'spiritual' dimensions of an integrated meditative-psychedelic therapy. To reiterate, these are more about providing meaning to the experience than they are about complying with ritual expectations or theological positions. In making Daoist-inspired meditations available to a wide and diverse demographic of patients, certain adjustments to the original practices must of course be made. Yet, to begin with, Daoism could be construed as a deistic or even atheistic tradition under a certain light: its visualisations usually invoke deities that are mere avatars of impersonal cosmic and nature principles, as may be gleaned from the brief sample of passages above. But the idea would not be to completely secularise the practices, since maintaining some 'spiritual' aspects, especially if they are couched in neutral terms related to the natural world, ensures the production of meaning – a requisite for healing and recovery if we are to take Moerman's findings seriously. In and of itself, secularising or 'desacralising' practices is highly problematic from a number of perspectives. Through the appropriation and unilateral reformulation of religious phenomena, secularisation imposes an epistemic violence that has concrete, far-reaching and long-lasting effects.

With respect to Asian traditions that deal with healing and/or wellness, there are usually two scenarios, each fraught with colonial undertones. In the sphere of popular culture, secularising results in commodification. A practice or aspect of a tradition is orientalised, essentialised and pigeon-holed as a self-help product of consumer culture; when co-opted into the sphere of health, it results in selective, reductionist reframing along with a subjugation to a (usually hegemonic) biomedical discourse of validity. Yoga provides a vivid precedent for how these mechanisms operate, with a modern (i.e. ahistorical), transnational (i.e. non-Asian), highly commodified version of yoga now dominating popular discourse. The medicalised health-optimised version of yoga is discussed in terms that likewise leave little or no room for historical or cultural contexts, let alone religion or spirituality; its virtues are described in the most clinical terms alone. There are exceptions of course, especially in countercultural and CAM or Integrative Medicine-related settings (Stephens 2017; Newcombe 2019).[23]

As far as Daoist meditations are concerned, instead of suppressing their spiritual component to make them more compatible with mainstream allopathic approaches, foregrounding their spiritual dimensions will highlight the necessity of meaning-making for all mental health therapies. The current industrialist biomedical 'one-size-fits-all' model is problematic for numerous reasons; chief among them for our purposes is the fact that it does not account for the value of the diversity in meaning-making mechanisms for healing. On account of their experiential episteme, Daoist-derived therapeutic meditations esteem the plurality

[23] Newcombe (2019) considers both mainstream secular and countercultural spiritual forms of yoga in 20th-century Britain. In the medical sphere, Stephens (2017) is a good example of a study that argues for the relevance of yoga as a healing or wellness therapy on the basis of 'objective' biomedical evidence-based standards of validity while at the same time acknowledging, albeit timidly, the practice's contribution to patients' 'spiritual well-being'.

of cultural, gendered, class-based experiences of meaning-making in healing while avoiding the pitfalls of indulgent navel-gazing individualism, ultimately transcending the particular through their promotion of interconnective, relational understandings of mental health. In conjunction with psychedelic therapies, at a more basic level perhaps, Daoist meditations can furnish a pre-scripted and guiding teleological programme to avoid negative outcomes and encourage positive ones, an Ariadne's thread to follow through the sometimes-daunting labyrinth of psychedelic healing.

References

Primary sources

Bencao jing jizhu 本草經集注 [Commentary on the Classic of Materia Medica]. Liang dynasty, ca. 500. Tao Hongjing 陶弘景 (456–536), critically annotated by S. Zhijun 尚志鈞 and S. Yuansheng 尚元勝 (eds) (1994), *Bencao jing jizhu jijiao ben* 本草經集注輯校本 (Beijing: Renmin weisheng chubanshe).

Lingbao wufu xu 靈寶五符序 [Array of the Five Talismans of the Numinous Treasure]. Eastern Jin (265–420) or earlier. Daozang DZ 388.

Shangqing mingjian yaojing 上清明鑑要經 [Scripture on the Essentials of the Bright Mirror (Method) of the Highest Clarity]. 7th or 8th century. Daozang DZ 1206.

Ziyang zhenren neizhuan 紫陽真人內傳 [Inner Biography of the Perfected of Purple Yang]. Late 4th century. Daozang DZ 303.

Secondary sources

Ahn, J. (2008), 'Zen and the Art of Nourishing Life: Labor, Exhaustion, and the Malady of Meditation'. *Japanese Journal of Religious Studies*, 35(2): 177–229.

Ahn, J. (2017), 'Getting Sick Over Nothing: Hyesim and Hakuin on the Maladies of Meditation' in C. Salguero (ed.) *Buddhism and Medicine: An Anthology of Premodern Sources* (New York: Columbia University Press), 390–7.

Ahn, J. (2021), 'Meditation Sickness' in M. Farias, M. Lalljee and D. Brazier (eds) *The Oxford Handbook of Meditation* (Oxford: Oxford University Press), 887–906.

Argento, E., Christie, D., Mackay, L., Callon, C. and Walsh, Z. (2021), 'Psychedelic-Assisted Psychotherapy After COVID-19: The Therapeutic Uses of Psilocybin and MDMA for Pandemic-Related Mental Health Problems'. *Frontiers in Psychiatry*, 12: 716593.

Beckley Foundation. (2016), *Psychedelic Research Timeline*. Available at: https://www.beckleyfoundation.org/psychedelic-research-timeline-2/. Accessed August 2024.

Behan, C. (2020), 'The Benefits of Meditation and Mindfulness Practices During Times of Crisis Such as COVID-19'. *Irish Journal of Psychological Medicine*, 37(4): 256–8.

Benn, C. (1991), *The Cavern-Mystery Transmission: A Taoist Ordination Rite of A.D. 711* (Honolulu, HI: University of Hawai'i Press).

Bienemann, B., Ruschel, N. S., Campos, M. L., Negreiros, M. A. and Mograbi, D. C. (2020), 'Self-Reported Negative Outcomes of Psilocybin Users: A Quantitative Textual Analysis'. *PLoS One*, 21(15): e0229067.

Britton, W., Lindhal, J. R., Cooper, D. J., Candy, N. K. and Palitsky, R. (2021), 'Defining and Measuring Meditation-Related Adverse Effects in Mindfulness-Based Programs'. *Clinical Psychological Science*, 9(6): 1185–1204.

Carbonaro, T., Bradstreet, M. P., Barrett, F. S., MacLean, K. A., Jesse, R., Johnson, M. W. and Griffiths, R. R. (2016), 'Survey Study of Challenging Experiences After Ingesting Psilocybin Mushrooms: Acute and Enduring Positive and Negative Consequences'. *Journal of Psychopharmacology*, 30(12): 1268–78.

Chang, D., Ng, N., Chen, T., Hung, T., Miao, I. Y., Cao, Y. and Zhang, Y. (2020), 'Let Nature Take Its Course: Cultural Adaptation and Pilot Test of Taoist Cognitive Therapy for Chinese American Immigrants with Generalized Anxiety Disorder'. *Frontiers of Psychology*, 11: 547852.

Cheung, K (2022), 'Miracle as Natural: A Contemporary Chinese American Religious Healer' in K. Zwier, D. Weddle and T. Knepper (eds) *Miracle: An Exercise in Comparative Philosophy of Religion* (New York: Springer), 131–54.

Church of Ambrosia. (2022), *Church of Ambrosia Homepage*. Available at: https://ambrosia.church/. Accessed August 2024.

Cohen, E. (2024), 'The Dao of Dialogue: Daoism, Psychology, and Psychotherapy'. *Journal of Daoist Studies*, 17: 99–117.

Crommelin, S. (2019), 'So Mushroom for Growth: New Psychedelic Club at UCSB Aims to Shift Conversation and Culture', *The Daily Nexus*, 31 October. Available at: https://dailynexus.com/2019-10-31/so-mushroom-for-growth-new-psychedelic-club-at-ucsb-aims-to-shift-conversation-and-culture/. Accessed August 2024.

Deguma, M., Lumayag, C. G., Villaganas, M. C., Delos Reyes, N. R. T. and Deguma J. J. (2022), 'From Anxious Loneliness to Meditation: A Mental Health Self-Care Strategy to Cope with the Covid-19 Pandemic'. *Journal of Public Health*, 44(3): 402–3.

Ding, Y., Wang, L., Chen, J., Zhao, J. and Guo, W. (2020), 'Chinese Taoist Cognitive Therapy for Symptoms of Depression and Anxiety in Adults in China: A Systemic Review and Meta-Analysis'. *Frontiers of Psychology*, 11: 1–12.

Eskildsen, S. (2008), 'Some Troubles and Perils of Taoist Meditation'. *Monumenta Serica*, 56: 259–91.

Evans, J., Robinson, O. C., Argyri, E. K., Suseelan, S., Murphy-Beiner, A., McAlpine, R., *et al.* (2023), 'Extended Difficulties Following the Use of Psychedelic Drugs: A Mixed Methods Study'. Public *Library of Science (PLoS) One*, 18(10): e0293349.

Fadiman, J. (2011), *The Psychedelic Explorer's Guide: Safe, Therapeutic and Sacred Journeys* (Rochester, VT: Park Street Press).

Feng, G. (1970), *Tai Chi, A Way of Centering & I Ching, a Book of Oracle Imagery*. (New York: Collier Books).

Feng, G. (1986), *Yi Jing: Book of Changes* (Mullumbimby, Australia: Feng Books).

Feng, G. and English, J. (1972), *Lao Tsu / Tao Te Ching* (New York: Vintage Books).

Feng, G. and English, J. (1974), *Chuang Tsu / Inner Chapters* (New York: Vintage Books).

Gandy, S. (2020), 'The Potential Synergistic Effects Between Psychedelic Administration and Nature Contact for the Improvement of Mental Health'. *Health Psychology Open*, 7(2): 2055102920978123.

Goodman, N. (2002), 'The Serotonergic System and Mysticism: Could LSD and the Nondrug-Induced Mystical Experience Share Common Neural Mechanisms?' *Journal of Psychoactive Drugs*, 34(3): 263–72.

Greene, E. (2017), 'Healing Sicknesses Caused by Meditation: "The Enveloping Butter Contemplation" from the Secret Essential Methods for Curing Meditation Sickness' in C. Salguero (ed.) *Buddhism and Medicine: An Anthology of Premodern Sources* (New York: Columbia University Press), 373–81.

Griffiths, R. R., Richards, W. A., McCann, U. and Jesse, R. (2006), 'Psilocybin Can Occasion Mystical-Type Experiences Having Substantial and Sustained Personal Meaning and Spiritual Significance'. *Psychopharmacology*, 187(3): 268–83.

Hoge, E., Bui, E., Mete, M., Dutton, M. A., Baker, A. W. and Simon, N. M. (2023), 'Mindfulness-Based Stress Reduction vs. Escitalopram for the Treatment of Adults with Anxiety Disorders: A Randomized Clinical Trial'. *Journal of the American Medical Association, Psychiatry*, 80(1): 13–21.

Kettner, H., Gandy S., Haijen, E. C. H. M. and Carhart-Harris, R. L. (2019), 'From Egoism to Ecoism: Psychedelics Increase Nature Relatedness in a State-Mediated and Context-Dependent Manner'. *International Journal of Environmental Research and Public Health*, 16(24): 5147.

Kim, D., Hong, S., Jang, S., Park, S., Noh, J., Seok, J., Jo, H., *et al.* (2022), 'Systematic Review for the Medical Applications of Meditation in Randomized Controlled Trials'. *International Journal of Environmental Research and Public Health*, 19(3): 1–22.

Kohn, L. (1993), *The Taoist Experience: An Anthology* (Albany, NY: State University of New York Press).

Kuchler, H. (2017), 'How Silicon Valley Rediscovered LSD', *Financial Times*, 10 August. Available at: https://www.ft.com/content/0a5a4404-7c8e-11e7-ab01-a13271d1ee9c. Accessed April 2024.

Lahtinen, O. (2023), 'The Effects of App-Based Mindfulness Practice on the Well-Being of University Students and Staff'. *Current Psychology*, 42: 4412–21.

Leary, T. (1966), *Psychedelic Prayers After the Tao Te Ching* (New Hyde Park, NY: University Books).

Leary, T., Metzner, R. and Alpert, R. (1964), *The Psychedelic Experience: A Manual Based on The Tibetan Book of the Dead* (New Hyde Park, NY: University Books).

Lowe, H., Toyang, N., Steele, B., Valentine, H., Grant, J., Ali A., *et al.* (2023), 'The Therapeutic Potential of Psilocybin'. *Molecules*, 26(10): 2948.

Marinacci, M. (2023), *Psychedelic Cults and Outlaw Churches: LSD, Cannabis and Spiritual Sacraments in Underground America* (Rochester, VT: Park Street Press).

McGroarty, B. (2024), 'Meditation Up 2,900% Globally during Pandemic, According to Fitbit Data', Global Wellness Institute. Available at: https://globalwellnessinstitute.org/global-wellness-institute-blog/2020/12/01/meditation-up-2900-globally-during-pandemic-according-to-fitbit-data/. Accessed August 2024.

Moerman, D. (2002), *Meaning, Medicine, and the "Placebo Effect"* (Cambridge: Cambridge University Press).

Newcombe, S. (2019), *Yoga in Britain: Stretching Spirituality and Educating Yogis* (Bristol, CT: Equinox Publishing).

NIDA (National Institute on Drug Abuse). (2022), *Marijuana and Hallucinogen Use Among Young Adults Reached All-Time-High in 2021.* Available at: https://nida.nih.gov/news-events/news-releases/2022/08/marijuana-and-hallucinogen-use-among-young-adults-reached-all-time-high-in-2021. Accessed August 2024.

Nur Hasina, S., Noventi, I., Livana, P. H., and Hartono, D. (2021), 'Mindfulness Meditation Based on Spiritual Care to Reduce Community Anxiety Due to the Impact of Pandemic Coronavirus Disease'. *Macedonian Journal of Medical Sciences*, 9: 41–6.

O' Donnell, K., Dunbar M. and Speelman, D. (2023), 'Effectiveness of Daily Mindfulness Meditation App Usage to Reduce Anxiety and Improve Well-Being During the Covid-19 Pandemic: A Randomized Controlled Trial'. *Cureus*, 15(7): e42432.

Oregon Health Authority. (2023), 'Oregon Psilocybin Services'. Available at: https://www.oregon.gov/oha/PH/PREVENTIONWELLNESS/Pages/Oregon-Psilocybin-Services.aspx. Accessed August 2024.

Pollan, M. (2018), *How to Change Your Mind: What the New Science of Psychedelics Teaches Us About Consciousness, Dying, Addiction, Depression, and Transcendence* (New York: Penguin Press).

Purser, R. (2019), *McMindfulness: How Mindfulness Became the New Capitalist Spirituality* (London: Repeater Books).

Reddit. (2020), 'Bad Shrooms Trip'. Available at: https://www.reddit.com/r/Drugs/comments/m4q3wv/bad_shrooms_trip_has_anyone_else_experience_this/. Accessed August 2024.

Reddit. (2021a), 'An Updated Thought for Depressed Shifters'. Available at: https://www.reddit.com/r/shiftingrealities/comments/r671xs/an_updated_thought_for_depressed_shifters/. Accessed August 2024.

Reddit. (2021b), 'First Bad Trip'. Available at: https://www.reddit.com/r/shrooms/comments/pdxn40/first_bad_trip_what_went_wrong/. Accessed August 2024.

Reddit. (2022a), 'Your Reasons for Shifting'. Available at: https://www.reddit.com/r/shiftingrealities/comments/te4qtj/general_your_reasons_for_shifting. Accessed August 2024.

Reddit. (2022b), 'I Took Mushrooms'. Available at: https://www.reddit.com/r/self/comments/tpw1yv/i_took_mushrooms_and_im_having_a_bad_trip/. Accessed August 2024.

Reddit. (2022c), 'LSD or Psilocybin for Self-knowledge'. Available at: https://www.reddit.com/r/Psychonaut/comments/y9mwty/lsd_or_psilocybin_for_selfknowledge/. Accessed August 2024.

Robinet, I. (1993), *Taoist Meditation: The Mao-Shan Tradition of Great Purity*. Translated by J. Pas and N. Girardot (Albany, NY: State University of New York Press).

Salguero, C. (2023), 'Meditation Sickness in Medieval Chinese Buddhism and in the Contemporary West'. *Journal of Buddhist Ethics*, 30: 169–211.

Schlag, A., Aday, J., Salam, I., Neill, J. C. and Nutt, D. J. (2022), 'Adverse Effects of Psychedelics: From Anecdotes and Misinformation to Systematic Science'. *Journal of Psychopharmacology*, 36(3): 258–72.

Sessa, B. (2012), *The Psychedelic Renaissance: Reassessing the Role of Psychedelic Drugs in 21st Century Psychiatry and Society* (London: Muswell Hill Press).

Sheldrake, M. (2020), *Entangled Life: How Fungi Make Our Worlds, Change Our Minds and Shape Our Futures* (New York: Penguin Random House).

Smigielski, L., Kometer, M., Scheidegger M., Krähenmann, R., Huber T. and Vollenweider, F. X. (2019), 'Characterization and Prediction of Acute and Sustained Response to Psychedelic Psilocybin in a Mindfulness Group Retreat'. *Scientific Reports*, 9: 14914.

Smith, R. (2020), 'UCSB Psychedelics Club Explores Psychedelic Usage and Research', *The Bottom Line UCSB*, 14 April. Available at: https://thebottomline.as.ucsb.edu/2020/04/ucsb-psychedelics-club-explores-psychedelic-usage-and-research. Accessed August 2024.

Somer, E., Cardeña, E., Catelan, R. F. and Soffer-Dudek, N. (2023), 'Reality Shifting: Psychological Features of an Emergent Online Daydreaming Culture'. *Current Psychology*, 42: 11415–27.

Stamets, P. (2019), *Fantastic Fungi: How Mushrooms Can Heal, Shift Consciousness and Save the Planet* (San Rafael, CA: Earth Aware Editions).

Stanley-Baker, M., Yoeli-Tlalim, R. and Yang, D. (eds) (2021), 'Special Issue: Asian Medicine and Covid-19', *Asian Medicine*, 16.

Stauffer, C. (2022), *Oregon Health Authority: Microdosing*. Available at: https://www.oregon.gov/oha/PH/PREVENTIONWELLNESS/Documents/Psilocybin%20Microdosing_wn2022.01.20.pdf. Accessed August 2024.

Steavu, D. (2018), 'The Marvelous Fungus and the "Secret of Divine Immortals"'. *Micrologus*, 26: 353–83.

Steavu, D. (forthcoming, 2026), 'Did Daoists Do Drugs? Psychedelic Mushrooms in Daoism' in D. Steavu (ed.) *The Sage and the Dao: Essays on Daoism in Honor of Fabrizio Pregadio* (Leiden: EJ Brill).

Stephens, I. (2017), 'Medical Yoga Therapy'. *Children*, 4(2): 12.

Stoddard, B. (2023a), 'Entheogens: Psychedelic Religion in the United States, Part One'. *Religion Compass*, 17(10): e12474.

Stoddard, B. (2023b), 'Entheogens: Psychedelic Religion in the United States, Part Two'. *Religion Compass*, 17(11): e12477.

Strassman, R. (2022), *The Psychedelic Handbook: A Practical Guide to Psilocybin, LSD, Ketamine, MDMA, and Ayahuasca* (New York: Ulysses Press).

Swisher, K. (2018), 'How and Why Silicon Valley Gets High', *New York Times*, 23 August. Available at: https://www.nytimes.com/2018/08/23/opinion/elon-musk-burning-man-drugs-lsd.html. Accessed August 2024.

Tsing, A. (2015), *The Mushroom at the End of the World: On the Possibility of Life in Capitalist Ruins* (Princeton, NJ: Princeton University Press).

UCSB Psychedelics Club. (2020), *UCSB Psychedelics Club Instagram Account.* Available at: https://www.instagram.com/ucsbpsychedelicclub/?hl=en. Accessed August 2024.

Watts, A. with Huang, A. C. (1975), *Tao: The Watercourse Way* (New York: Pantheon).

Wilson, C. (2019), *Still Point of the Turning World: The Life of Gia-fu Feng* (Portland, OR: Amber Lotus).

Winstock, A. R., Maier, L. J., Zhuparris, A., Davies, E., Puljević, C. and Kuypers, K. (2021), *Global Drug Survey 2021 Global Report*. Available at: https://www.globaldrugsurvey.com/wp-content/uploads/2021/12/Report2021_global.pdf. Accessed April 2024.

12

The Importance of Interrogating the Experiential Episteme: Yoga, Indian Medicine and Rhetorical Strategies of Epistemic Capital

SUZANNE NEWCOMBE

Introduction

AT THE HEIGHT of the Covid-19 pandemic, many were surprised to see highly educated, middle-class people in Europe and North America protesting against public health messaging and refusing vaccines and mask-wearing directives (Guerin 2021). In Europe and North America, there were notable numbers of wealthy, white and well-educated yoga practitioners who shared alternative theories of the origin of the Covid-19 virus, both online and offline, and participated in vocal questioning of public health directives. In Britain, *The Guardian* asked, 'How did self-care turn so nasty?' (Kale 2021), and in the US the Centre for Tackling Digital Hate identified several prominent yoga teachers and wellness influencers as among the 12 most influential online spreaders of Covid 'conspiracy theories' (CTDH 2021). First broadcast in May 2020, *Conspirituality* became a popular podcast,[1] foregrounding the popularity of beliefs and practices found within yoga and similar milieus (e.g. guru-led transnational organisations) which actively undermined public health messaging and were associated with other kinds of harmful behaviour such as sexual abuse and coercive control (Beres *et al.* 2024).

Certainly not all, or even a majority of, yoga practitioners were opposed to vaccinations or lockdown policies. Yet there was a significant minority of yoga practitioners who were very vocal about the central importance of bodily autonomy

[1] Since first airing in May 2020, this podcast has produced over 220 episodes (as of August 2024) and is estimated to be in the top 0.1 per cent of listened to podcasts by ListenNotes (2024).

Proceedings of the British Academy, **278**, 246–271, © Authors 2025.

(to what extent do I accept the state limiting my body's choices?), the safety of vaccines (have they been properly tested, and do they contain any harmful additives?) as well as bodily integrity (is a particular biomedical intervention necessary at all? Could boosting internal immune system defences be equivalent or superior to vaccines?). These ideas often combined with other evidence-based concerns, such as doubts about the ethical integrity and profit motive of pharmaceutical companies (e.g. the aggressive marketing of OxyContin by Purdue Pharma and its role in the 'opioid epidemic' in the United States (Alpert *et al.* 2022)).

During the uncertainty that characterised the period of public lockdowns, mainstream media often characterised the population's responses to medical advice and mandates into factions of 'us' versus 'them'. From the perspective of government and medical authorities, 'us' were people who obediently followed the advice of medical experts and government directives, while 'them' were those who were misled by conspiratorial thinking and 'misinformation' into taking actions which put their own and others' health in jeopardy. However, from the perspective of those protesting against lockdown mandates and vaccines against the virus, 'them' were conversely identified as those in power, restricting individual liberty and encouraging people to behave obediently (i.e. 'like sheep') rather than 'doing one's own research'. This situation was many things, but among other descriptions it could be understood as an epistemological crisis point. That is, not only was there disagreement over the substance of what was known, but the very basis for valid knowledge upon which decisions could be reached was sharply contested between these polarised positions.

I postulate that if we take the epistemic validity of experiential knowledge more seriously, we might improve the quality of public health policy and communication. If we could more intelligently analyse and nuance the varieties and significance of experiential knowledge, we would both be raising the cultural value of experiential knowledge as well as increasing our ability to discuss and cultivate sensory sensibility intelligently. In many ways this argument is a continuation of the focus on embodiment found in Thomas Csordas and Bryan Turner's work as well as the more recent attempts from various scholars to refocus anthropological and religious studies' attention on the sensorium. What is new and significant about this chapter's argument is the link with a growing awareness of an 'epistemological crisis' where the foundations of collective truth – that is, the description of reality upon which societies can debate appropriate courses of action – have experienced a moment of rupture.

This crisis of epistemic uncertainty was exemplified in both individual and collective reactions to the Covid-19 crisis of 2020–2 (Beer and Hariman 2020) and has also been evidenced in responses to the climate crisis in the United States (Crockford 2023). Here what we are concerned with is not so much a socially constructed embodiment, although that certainly plays a part in experiences of health and healing (e.g. Turner 1987; Kuriyama 1999; Csordas 2002, 2007). Rather, this chapter more directly follows Amanda Fricker's proposal for 'training sensibility' to counter epistemic injustice and to create a more moral and accurate description of reality (2007: 81–5).[2] The central argument of this chapter is a call for more prioritisation of the role of sensorial training for both practitioners and patients involved with health and wellbeing. Taking the epistemic mode of experience more seriously, articulating and analysing it with more nuance, could transform how health and healing are evaluated and discussed, leading to more effective public health strategies.

Admittedly, we cannot know the effect that more value and nuance in cultivating sensory sensibility might have upon future public health discussions. However, there is strong evidence that the experiential episteme was devalued in health and healing as part of the modernist scientific framing of medicine. There is also evidence that the epistemic mode of personal, experiential knowledge is central in promoting health and healing. This chapter will focus on developing these two points – with the assertion that we, as both members of the educated public as well as in capacities of specific professional expertise, can do better in evaluating and analysing knowledge derived from personal, sensory experience. It is not good enough simply to allow 'if it feels right (to me), it is true' to stand without contextualisation and evaluation. As patients, or people with bodies who need healing – as well as for those in a position to provide professional evaluations of the efficacy of health interventions – it is possible to nuance the experience of 'feels right' with more evaluative frameworks. Some important evaluative criteria are around external context (e.g. potential of harm, social context, confounding variables), but more attention to sensory information, which sensory information is most important and which sensory information might be being ignored (and why) can provide the basis for a more educated engagement with sensory experience and subsequently promote better health. Not all sensory information is equally useful for bringing about a positive resolution of a particular health or social problem.

In order to set up the conceptual framework for this argument, I will first introduce and modify an articulation of epistemic capital developed by Robertson (2016: 45–53, 2025: 67–9). Then I will concentrate on two exemplar case studies found within Indian medical traditions which, although separated in time by 100 years, both reveal the centrality of sensory sensitivity to the working episteme of practitioners that has been obscured by a need to justify and narrate healing techniques using mainstream scientific epistemic frameworks.

First, the chapter will detail how the 1923 Usman Report successfully framed the efficacy of Indian medical traditions around 'scientific' rhetoric. This formulation

[2] In this work Fricker is primarily identifying two forms of epistemic injustice, testimonial injustice and hermeneutical injustice: 'Testimonial injustice occurs when prejudice causes a hearer to give a deflated level of credibility to a speaker's word; hermeneutical injustice occurs at a prior stage, when a gap in collective interpretive resources puts someone at an unfair disadvantage when it comes to making sense of their social experiences' (Fricker 2007: 1). This chapter's call for developing better sensory sensibility in regard to health and healing has overlaps with both forms of epistemic injustice identified here by Fricker and draws upon her discussion of 'training sensibility' to prevent these forms of injustice.

successfully allowed for limited resources to be used to support the traditional forms of healing that most of the Indian population accessed in the context of the British colonial administration. I will argue that the emphasis on 'science' obfuscated the centrality of sensory knowledge in the Indian medical tradition for both practitioners and patients. The second extended example will illustrate how a cultivation of sensory sensitivity (for both practitioners and patients) was essential to the improved health experienced by those participating in a long Covid pilot yoga intervention in the autumn of 2021.

These two examples are connected in the centrality of transmitting expertise based on *experiential* knowledge, which continues to be underexplored in contemporary justifications of yoga therapy. One hundred years after the Usman Report, in a postcolonial context, justifications of yoga-as-therapy continue to be based on a formulation of non-sensory scientific epistemes to achieve legitimacy. In conclusion, I will suggest that developing the linguistic and cultural capacity to acknowledge and give more nuance to the experiential episteme could be a partial way of addressing the epistemological crisis. A greater facility in critical analysis of the experiential episteme on the part of both patients and practitioners will lend more evidence-based legitimacy to evaluating this valid way of knowing, with the possibility of better bridging the apparent factions between those who follow the scientific epistemic consensus and those who rely (apparently) uncritically on their felt sense of 'truth' (e.g. Mbembe 2021: 27).

Modelling epistemic capital

In seeking to understand how authority was established and what epistemic modes were drawn upon in online spaces characterised by a mixture of religious and conspiratorial ideas (such as UFOs or QAnon conspiracy theories),[3] Robertson articulated a useful model of epistemic capital.[4] This concept borrows from Michel Foucault's articulation of sociohistorically contingent epistemes, that is to say different strategies for establishing 'truth' that are closely linked with particular forms of power in specific historical periods. It has now been widely accepted that scientific knowledge has been 'the most prominent form of epistemic capital in European culture and its colonies' since the 18th century (i.e. Foucault's modern post-Enlightenment episteme), even if the 'boundaries of scientific knowledge are less clear-cut than is generally acknowledged' (Robertson 2021: 29). By formulating a theory of epistemic capital, Robertson also highlights the relative

[3] Argentino and Amarasingam use this definition of QAnon: a 'decentralized ideology rooted in an unfounded conspiracy theory that a globally active "Deep State" cabal of satanic pedophile elites is responsible for all the evil in the world' (Argentino and Amarasingam 2021: 19).

[4] This model is based upon Robertson's previous work on epistemic strategies (Robertson 2016: 45–53) and the role of epistemic capital in establishing charismatic authority (Robertson 2018: 250–2) and is further articulated in Robertson (2025: 67–9).

efficacy of epistemic strategies to gain power by building upon Pierre Bourdieu's theories of symbolic/cultural capital. Five primary categories (i.e. modes) of epistemic capital are articulated in this model: (1) science, (2) tradition (which can be further subdivided into tradition as determined by either institutions or social groups), (3) experience, (4) channelling and (5) synthetic knowledge. This is visualised in Figure 12.1.

From European modernity onwards, scientific knowledge claims have been privileged in the hierarchy of epistemic capital. Consequently, scientific claims, as well as claims for traditional authority via institutional or organisation structures, are the dominant ways of asserting epistemic authority. In the realm of health and wellbeing, it should come as no surprise that scientific and traditional epistemic modes are the ones frequently appealed to as authoritative. However, the relative status or 'value' of a particular form of knowledge will be dependent upon the specific context, so while there is a hierarchical aspect to this format, it should not be read as either rigid or universally normative.

Robertson also notes that in some contexts, knowledge claims might be further bolstered by reference to individual, internal knowledge (e.g. eyewitness accounts

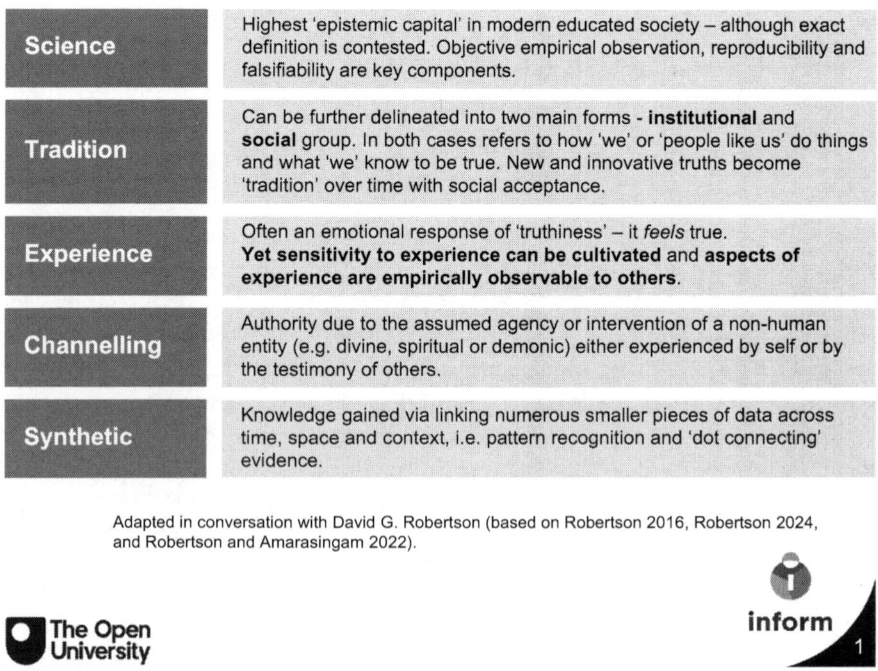

Figure 12.1 Five primary categories (modes) of epistemic capital. Adapted in conversation with David G. Robertson (based on Robertson 2016, Robertson 2024, and Robertson and Amarasingam 2022).

or personal experience) and/or through external or collective authority (e.g. a canonical text or legal precedent). Therefore, this framework should be read as an ideal-typical framework to assist with observation and analysis of both the mode being used to justify a truth and the relative value placed on each mode in any given context. Different epistemic modes may need to be added, explained differently or the relative value reimagined when applying this tool to more accurately understand other specific contexts or case studies.

Because contemporary global culture ascribes relatively low value to the experiential mode, there has been a cultural blindness in articulating, identifying and analysing the mechanisms through which experiential knowledge can be refined and transformed. Arguably, this is a kind of epistemic injustice as a kind of 'wrong done to someone especially in their capacity as knower' (Fricker 2007: 1). Culturally, the experiential mode is both reified as unassailable 'truth' as well as relegated to one of the lowest rungs of value in epistemic capital. On the one hand, that which is personally experienced and 'feels true' is not generally seen as available for challenge from different epistemic modes. Although relatively unassailable, this kind of personal, experiential knowledge is also not considered generalisable. While it is often accepted as a valid reason for personal decision-making, it is not widely considered a valid basis on which to make policy decisions affecting groups of people. The exception to this is when experiential knowledge is verified through quantitative survey models, that is, verified by a scientific epistemic mode. Through this process, some experiences are assumed to be a characteristic experience of a more generalisable group such as 'women', an ethnic minority or those with a specific disability or health condition. Here I am proposing that we consider something different in our evaluation of the experiential mode. Following Fricker's lead I propose that, as a culture, we need to gain capacity in sensory sensibility in order to better articulate and evaluate the experiential mode central to many health and healing traditions.

The next section will demonstrate why and how scientific rhetoric came to dominate more nuanced expressions of experiential knowledge in Indian indigenous medical traditions which date back to at least the first millennium BCE. Indigenous Indian medical traditions, which encompass yoga and meditation techniques, draw on multiple epistemic modes to know what they know. The 1923 Usman Report represents a clash of practices and epistemes, demonstrating the potency of appealing to the scientific epistemic mode (and its associated cultural capital) alongside emphasising traditional (written) sources of authority to justify efficacy to the colonial administration. But the testimony recorded in the Usman Report also betrays the centrality of the experiential mode to the knowledge basis of the Indian indigenous medical traditions and this mode's transformative potential for healing. The rhetorical conflation of epistemic modes in justifying a medical intervention can mystify and obfuscate both the mechanisms that promote health and healing and even potentially exacerbate errors in judgement and harm.

Justifying yoga for health

The Indian subcontinent has a deep and rich history of traditions of health and healing. However, the historiographical exploration of this rich and dynamic history is relatively recent in origin. Projit Mukharji confidently dates the initiation of modern historical investigation of these medical traditions to Charles Leslie's *Asian Medical Systems* (1976), although he argues that historical study only began to expand in earnest from the 1990s onwards (Mukharji 2011: 887). Therefore, there are many gaps in the academic understanding of the development of Indian medical practices.

It is difficult to gauge what Indian healers and physicians (*vaidya*s in the Ayurvedic tradition) were doing in their daily practices before the 20th century. Social and historical evidence for historical Indian medical practices examined to date has largely been drawn from the observations in travelogues of foreign visitors to the Indian subcontinent.[5] While significant sources for the historian, these etic descriptions come laced with the cultural assumptions of the observer, and often emphasise differences from their home culture rather than emic details which might be relevant to understand the nature of treatment and the experience of the physician and patient.[6] However, from extant historical evidence we can surmise that medical practitioners, including at times ascetics and 'yogis', were found in the courts of local rulers who also undertook some financial responsibly for providing medical care for the populations under their jurisdiction (Sujatha 2014: 149–52).

British colonisation of the Indian subcontinent disrupted established systems of financial patronage for supporting the provision of medicine for local populations and the training of *vaidya*s.[7] European-style hospitals were established in Madras (1664), Bombay (1676) and Calcutta (1707–8), initially to serve the British army and colonial administration. Local Indians were trained and employed at these institutions, which initially also incorporated local traditional healing arts into their practices (Sujatha 2014: 154–60). However, these European institutions

[5] For early travel accounts of medical practice see Zysk (2000: 27–8); for yogis see Singleton (2010: 36–44). Important historical primary sources of travelogues already noted by medical historians include al-Bīrūnī's Arabic monograph on India (*c.* 1030), known as the *Kitāb al-Hind* (see Maas and Verdon 2018). Honigberger (1852: 92–5, 116) records observing a 'faqueer' acting as one of several medical advisors to those in power in Lahore during the early 1800s. The terms 'yogi' and 'fakir' were often used interchangeably for ascetics in the accounts of Europeans at this time without necessarily any recorded attention to sectarian affiliation, although the term 'fakir' is a Persian word more closely associated with ascetic, nomadic Sufis than affiliates of the other sectarian groups also found seeking alms in pre-modern South Asia. This is an area in which there are probably plentiful sources for further historical research and analysis, particularly in the under-researched area of vernacular Indian historical sources.

[6] Important works in understanding 19th-century encounters and reformulations of indigenous Indian medicine include Sivaramakrishnan (2006).

[7] However, the local rulers of Baroda, Cochin, Gondal, Gwalior, Hyderabad, Indore, Jaipur, Mysore, Rewa and Travancore managed to continue to provide significant financial support for indigenous medical practitioners and traditional medical training systems (Wujastyk 2008: 49).

were generally operated for and by the colonial elite; historians generally agree that the influence of the European 'biomedical' episteme (with its prioritisation of the scientific epistemic mode) on healthcare provision for the indigenous Indian population was limited until the end of the 19th century (Arnold 1993: 240–90; Sujatha 2014: 160). Into much of the 20th century the majority of Indian's rural population did not have easy access to 'European' medical care.[8] Certainly, the influences of 'European' biomedical science into the concepts and practices of more traditionally trained *vaidya*s and *hakim*s (Unani medical practitioners) was marked by creative innovation and assimilation rather than wholesale conversion (Berger 2013; Mukharji 2016).[9] However, the impact of colonial framings and the political dominance of the European scientific episteme had a profound impact on the development of indigenous medical interventions.

The first detailed primary source we have of *vaidya*s describing medical practice in their own words is the *Report of the Committee on Indigenous Systems of Medicine, Madras* (1923). This report was commissioned by the colonial government of Madras in 1921 and was overseen by Sir Muhammad Usman, KCSI (1884–1960); it became known as the 'Usman Report'. This remarkable document solicited testimonies from medical practitioners spanning India which were submitted in Sanskrit, Urdu, Tamil, Telugu, Malayalam, Kannaḍa and Oriya as well as in English.[10] This report was initiated as part of a growing movement to improve the reputation and financial investment in indigenous medical practitioners that served the majority of the population of Madras state (roughly present-day Tamil Nadu).

Social movements in defence of indigenous medical practices had been gaining momentum for some decades as part of the growing unrest about colonial rule. The Usman Report can be understood as a direct response to a previous report on indigenous drugs published in 1920 on behalf of the Madras Presidency, which claimed 'there is very little if anything to be learnt from the methods of treatment followed by practitioners of the indigenous systems' (quoted in Gayathri 2012: 185–9). Vociferous criticism, calling out the Presidency government's prejudice against indigenous medicine was published in many vernacular papers, as well as in the English-language newspaper *The Hindu*. Opposition to the Koman report inspired a joint public statement in protest by the local Ayurvedic practitioner professional

[8] For example, the Usman Report (1923) estimated that the Madras Presidency held a population of about 42.3 million people, served by around 4,000 European-trained medical professionals and no less than 21,000 (self-described) indigenous practitioners (Vol. 1, 16). 'European medicine' or 'allopathy' were the terms used in the Usman Report, referring to what was later called 'Western' or biomedical traditions of medicine.

[9] Unani (*tibb yūnānī*) is the medical tradition of the Indian subcontinent that is closely associated with Islamic practitioners and populations, with close links to Persian and Arabic medical texts as well as to ancient Greek humoral systems of understanding the human body. Unani was impacted by colonialism and biomedicine; see Attewell (2007) and Alavi (2007), the latter for Unani medicine during the Mungal period.

[10] Translations into English of the vernacular submissions can be found in Wujastyk and Barois (2022).

bodies (Barois, Newcombe and Wujastyk 2022: xiii–xv). Pressure mounted to the extent that Usman was commissioned to gather evidence around the efficacy and scientific basis of indigenous medical traditions to bolster both financial support and social prestige.

The Usman commission was specifically attempting to present the indigenous medical traditions of India with the same evidence-based criteria that the Western-trained biomedical professionals used to justify their practices. The stakes were high. The British administration actively withheld both economic support and social prestige from the indigenous medical practitioners and the general population of India for whom allopathic medical care was inaccessible and unaffordable. In its call to evidence, the Usman committee was explicit in wanting evidence to support indigenious medical traditions 'based on by proofs or testimony acceptable to modern science', specifically:

1) 'evidence of directly demonstrable or observable facts, or of facts indirectly inferable, by logical methods of the nature of induction and deduction, known to modern science,' or
2) 'by showing that a proposition has the hypothetical certainty of a coherent system of assumptions or the practical or pragmatic certainty of a hypothesis that works best.'

(Usman Report 1923, Vol. 1, Appendix II: 97)

This was clearly defining what was considered in scope for the scientific mode at the time. Moreover, those submitting evidence to the commission were 'requested to note that the authority of revelations or venerated texts or uncriticisable tradition, however high its evidential value may be in other matters, are not accepted by modern science as valid' (ibid.). Therefore, appeals to traditional, channelled or experiential bases for medical knowledge (using the Robertson 2025 framework outlined above) were requested to be sidelined in preference for the scientific criteria of evidence for efficacy-based indicative or deductive logic and rigorous hypothesis testing.

In response to a questionnaire sent all over India, the committee claimed to have received 183 written submissions and published a selection of these in the second volume of the report (Barois, Newcombe and Wujastyk 2022: xvii–xviii). The first two questions around defining the system of medicine and formulating its theories of disease led to the longest, most articulate and most revealing responses. These responses refer again and again to a short, compressed description of how the physician should undertake diagnosis found in the canonical Ayurvedic text the *Suśrutasaṃhitā*. There are six ways or agencies through which diseases can be definitely known – by the five senses and by interrogation (Usman Report 1923 Vol. 1, Appendix I: 50).[11]

[11] The attribution for this given by Dr Sen in the Usman Report is 'Sutrasthan – Chapter XI', but this passage appears to be from *Suśrutasaṃhitā* 1.10.3: 'Then he should enter into the patient's house with favourableness of messenger, sign, omen and other auspicious objects and having taken his seat should inspect, palpate and interrogate the patient. Some say – "generally diseases should be diagnosed by these

The most pervasive of these testimonies in the eyes of the committee was submitted by Drs Mabamabopadhyaya Kaviraj Gananath Sen and Yamini Bhushan Roy; both are quoted at length in the summary evidence. Dr Sen gives a compressed paraphrase of *Suśrutasaṃhitā* 1.10.4, which lists the six 'ways or agencies through which diseases can be definitely known' as follows:

(i) *Sravani Pareeksha* or auscultation (listening to the internal sounds of the body)
(ii) *Twachi Pareeksha* or touch and palpitation (including pulse diagnostics)
(iii) *Chakshushee Pareeksha* or (visual) inspection (focusing observation of bodily colour and movement)
(iv) *Ghrani Pareeksha* or examination by smell (especially smell of discharges)
(v) *Rasani Pareeksha* or examination by taste[12]
(vi) By questioning – interrogation

(Usman Report 1923, Vol. 1, Appendix I: 50)[13]

In the Usman Report, the centrality of experience based on a cultivated sensorium, or a training in sensibility, is further underlined by the written testimony of Janab Hakim Syed Mustafa Sahib Bahadur, who writes: 'This science is very closely connected to practice. A person's knowledge will grow according to the amount of experience he gathers' (translation by Datoo in Wujastyk and Barois 2022: 123).

Lisa Brooks has recently undertaken some groundbreaking epistemological reflections around the role of sensory diagnostics, particularly touch, with consideration of both the classical Ayurvedic textual authorities (traditional mode) and anthropological research on contemporary Ayurvedic practice in Kerala (Brooks 2018, 2020, and 2021). In regard to the classical textual emphasis on sensory experience, her work elucidates the way diagnostic observations in Ayurveda are tied to 'the physician's examination of the *guṇas*, such as "coldness, heat, stiffness, throbbing, softness, and roughness," particularly in reference to touch (*sparśa*)' but also explored indirectly through questioning (Brooks 2018: 115). In her work

three means of examination" but it is not correct, in fact, sixfold is the method of diagnosis of diseases such as by five sense organs ear etc. and interrogation' (Sharma 2011: 110).

[12] Dr Sen notes that this might be done by special instruments such as a speculum; other parts of the Usman Report explain that 'taste' can refer to second-hand use of this sense by observing the behaviour of flies and ants, e.g. ants are attracted to sweet discharges such as diabetic urine.

[13] *Suśrutasaṃhitā* 1.10.4: 'In disease, the items to be examined by hearing (auscultation) will be mentioned in the chapter on description of wound and its discharge such as – "there *vayu*, impelling frothy blood, comes out with sound (SU. 26.10) and so on; those to be examined by touch (palpation) are the qualities like cold, heat, smoothness, roughness, softness, hardness etc. in fever, inflammation etc.; those to be examined by vision (inspection) are development or otherwise of physique, signs of lifespan, strength, disorders of complexion etc.; those to be examined by gustatory sense organ are different tastes in *prameha* etc.; those to be examined by olfactory sense organ are different types of smell as signs of imminent death in relation to wounds and other cases; by interrogation one should elicit information about place, time, family or caste, suitability, onset of disease (etiology), aggravation of pain, strength, appetite and state of digestion; passing or otherwise of wind, urine and faeces duration etc. Other unmentioned diseases may be diagnosed on the basis of the symptoms of similar dosas" (Sharma 2011: 110–11).

with contemporary Ayurvedic *vaidya*s, Brooks describes complex negotiations between the authority of the classical texts, the ease and social and financial benefits of biomedical diagnostic tests, and the practice and ideals of a refined sensory sensibility achieved through personal instruction from a *guru*-practitioner, years of personal practice of the technique, as well as general sensory refinement of the physician through ascetic sensibility – for example, not consuming disturbing media, controlling the mind through meditation and having undisturbed digestion (2018: 126–31). The dynamic she describes focuses on the potential perfectibility of the physician as an instrument of diagnostic refinement, as negotiated with other types of diagnostics such as those found in laboratory or scanning technologies.

In exploring the possibility of giving more theoretical and practical attention to refining sensory sensibility (for both practitioners and 'patients') as an important aspect of health and healing, I don't want to suggest that Ayurveda or yoga traditions are unproblematic or more reliable than modern European models of medicine. Conversely, by calling for a re-emphasis on the experiential mode, I do not want to encourage blanket dismissals of the Indian indigenous medical traditions as 'non-rational'. The Indian traditions contain extremely nuanced articulations of logical principles and systemic reasoning that have a place of undisputed importance within theories of knowledge, such as Nyāya and Vaiśeṣika philosophical traditions (for introductions see O'Brien-Kop (this volume), Sharma 2011 and Hamilton 2001).

Rather, here I want to argue that the structures of epistemic capital in the modern period have created a lacuna in critical attention to the experiential mode and exploring its validity and reliability through systematic refinement of sensory sensibility. The converse tendency for European scientific authorities to use the epistemic capital of scientific rhetoric as a way of consolidating power and authority is also well established (e.g. Foucault 1974, 1980; Turner 1987; Deichmann and Müller-Hill 1998).

Parts of the Usman Report summary systematically addressed criticism of Ayurveda voiced by medical professionals. One of these appears to be that a basis in empiricism is 'unscientific'. This could explain the gap between science and empiricism as epistemic framings both at the time of the report and echoing into today. On this point the authors rebut:

> Similarly, it were well I think, if attempts had not been made to belittle the indigenous (or indeed any other) system of medicine on the ground that it is empirical. Sheer prudence, if nothing else, would require that people living in glass houses not throw stones at others. A perfect system may be free from empiricism, but the western system is admittedly not perfect and cannot at all afford to do away with empiricism.
> (Usman Report 1923, Vol 1, Appendix I: 70)

The Usman Report goes on to quote John Stuart Mill and 'Lectures on the Method of Science' by T. B. Strong of Oxford University, expanding the idea that there is a reciprocal relationship between reason and observable phenomena in the scientific method; the insights of valid logic and reason must be confirmed through observation of phenomena and observation of disconfirming phenomena necessitates reformulations of theory and logical arguments. With this insight into the privileged modes of epistemic capital at the time, it is understandable that the framing of the Usman Report did not explicitly explore the process of empirical discernment in which indigenous medical practitioners were trained, but instead sought to make the case for social capital and economic investment by deploying the rhetoric of using the most valued form of epistemic capital of the period.

Wishing to draw attention to the centrality of a physician's ability to provide accurate diagnostics by using sensory sensibility through years of experience, the Usman Report draws upon a recent publication by the esteemed Scottish cardiologist Sir James Mackenzie at length. In *The Future of Medicine* (1919), Mackenzie despairs on the over-reliance on laboratory analysis for medical diagnostics. This quote argues how the epistemic justification for a successful medical practice even in Europe likely relies quite extensively upon a sensory sensitivity refined by training and experience. Dr Mackenzie defends the importance of skilful questioning and intuition of the diagnostic significance according to specific sensory signals that are only developed out of long clinical experience: 'The laboratory worker obtains his results by a delicate mechanical contrivance. The physician has to train his senses, and this can only be done by a long process of education, only capable of being acquired by the constant contact with the patient'(Mackenzie 1919: 190 in Usman Report 1923, Vol. 1, Appendix I: 55). In the summary findings, the report points towards the centrality of developing a greater capacity and subtlety of sensory understanding through practice and experience:

> [I]n Modern Science, we seek to overcome the limitation, of our senses by equipping ourselves with various external aids like the microscope, telescope, the spectroscope, the crescograph, cardiograph and the like; the Hindus however sought to effect the same results, not by providing their senses with external aids, but by improving their own internal organs of sense ... that the acuteness of our senses could be appreciably increased is, of course, a matter of daily observation; by practice and effort, we train our ear to appreciate melodies to which we were dead before; certain hillmen, who live by hunting, are known to see and spot out their prey at distances, far too great for us to see or get a clear vision of; similarly, by practice and effort, we can appreciably increase the ranges of our other senses – smell, taste and touch That our senses, like muscles, grow by regulated exercise is a proposition to which few perhaps will be inclined to object; but, the Hindu view is that there is practically no limit to this growth, save the limitations of one's own capacity for exertion, and that it is possible for master-minds to perfect their 'senses' (in which term, they include the mind also – 'the sixth sense' as it was sometimes called) to so great a degree as to include, within their range, everything from the most microscopic to the most macroscopic – 'from the Paramanu to the Paramahatwa' as the scripture has it.
>
> (Usman Report 1923, Vol. 1, Appendix I: 21)

While some of the phrasing of this passage touches on claims of the potentials for developing sensory sensitivity that stretch credulity – for example, that the structure of atoms was directly perceived by ancient 'great seers' (although a theory often association with the principle of atoms, *paramāṇu*, is certainly present in Jainism and a central tenet of Vaiśeṣika philosophy) – the Usman Report immediately accepts that this is not an acceptable form of evidence for modern science where it could only be offered as a kind of hypothesis which would need to be verified by other means before becoming accepted (Usman Report 1923, Vol. 1: 21). The authors of the Usman Report saw a potential for mutual intellectual exchange and the growth of knowledge in such comparisons, even if many of the testimonials believed that there were fundamental differences between the indigenous systems of medicine and 'allopathy', which would make full synthesis impossible.[14]

While the Usman Report masters the style of epistemic capital necessary to challenge the hegemonic power of the European-trained 'allopathic' medical profession of 1923, a closer look at the evidence submitted to the report suggests that the epistemic knowledge of indigenous medical practices was very much based on forms of knowing – that is, epistemic modes, – which had less capital, or social prestige. The submitted testimony of the physicians very much relies upon knowledge gained through sensory observation and experience, as well as traditional knowledge, and in some cases knowledge that was 'channelled' or had a super-human origin (e.g. a narrative of medicine being a gift of the perfected Siddhars in the Siddha testimonials).[15] The centrality of 'training sensitivity' and the fundamental 'art' of successful medical practice runs through the report's narrative despite the attempt to firmly present a scientific rationale.

In the long term, the Usman Report's vociferous defiance of indigenous medicine using the rhetoric and epistemic capital of 'modern science' was largely successful in shoring up both popular and practical support for indigenous medicine.[16] In subsequent years there was greater investment in infrastructure and training for indigenous medical traditions within the Madras Presidency (Hausman 1996). In 1938 the Bombay Medical Practitioner Act established an official legal

[14] Here I am referring to the answers to Question 5 in the Usman Report's Questionnaire: '5) Do you agree with the view of the Calcutta University Commission that "There is an obvious and promising desire at the present moment among the numerous adherents of these (indigenous) systems for closer touch with modern scientific methods. In time, no doubt, they will be able to make available for the practitioners of Western medicine the traditional knowledge, which is of real value and will reject, as Western medicine continually rejects, those theories which are mere survivals, and cannot stand the test of experiments. The distinction between Indian and Western 'systems' of medicine will then disappear." If you agree that a unified system of medicine as indicated in the above passage is the ideal to be aimed at, what steps would you suggest for the fulfilment of such an ideal?' (Barois, Newcombe and Wujastyk 2022: xviii–xx and Usman Report 1923, Appendix II: 98).

[15] Also transliterated from the Tamil as *cittar* is a perfected person who has attained great spiritual powers (*siddhi*); it is believed that the medical system dominant in South India, i.e. Siddha medicine, was developed by Siddhars. Much of this tradition is recorded in dense, metaphorical verse and covers diverse topics, e.g. the *Tirumantiram* of Tirumūlar which can be dated broadly between the 6th and 12th centuries (see Kędzia 2017 and Sujatha in this volume). Siddha medicine has considerable overlap with, but also distinct features which differentiate it from, both the Ayurveda and Unani traditions.

[16] The phrase 'modern science' is used in the Usman Report Questionnaire itself (Usman Report 1923, Vol, 1, Appendix II: 97).

registrar for Ayurvedic and Unani practitioners (Wujastyk 2008: 47).[17] From 2014, the government of Prime Minister Narendra Modi invested strongly in indigenous medicine and yoga specifically. In creating an independent Ministry of AYUSH (Ayurveda, Unani, Siddha, Sowa Rigpa and Homeopathy), Modi signalled his commitment to Indian national self-reliance and traditional practices as well as promoting these as an exportable product and form of cultural capital abroad.

In the discussion above, I have noted that in many cases, the *vaidya*s and *hakim*s giving testimony in the Usman Report are claiming knowledge based in the modes of experience or tradition rather than 'directly demonstrable or observable facts … known to modern science' (Usman Report 1923, Vol. 1: 97). In so noting, I do not want to make any comment about the potential scientific basis or efficacy of any system of medicine or any treatment practice.

Rather, I want to argue that the lack of epistemic capital for knowledge gained through experience has meant our cultural ability to notice, understand and transmit this knowledge gained through the experiential mode has suffered. To date, we have largely missed an opportunity to develop our skill in observing, nuancing and analysing exactly what is observed and experienced, how this informs medical practice, and how this in turn may lead to both subject experiences of improved health and wellbeing as well as more objective 'cures' of identifiable and externally observable recognised conditions.

The Usman Report's erudite English makes as strong a case as possible that 'the Indian systems are strictly logical and scientific in their approach' by using the dominant scientific episteme explicitly and strategically (Usman Report 1923, Vol. 1: 14). Yet the importance of sensory skill gained through experience – skilled observation and interrogation of the patient and the environmental context – was a central part of epistemic explanations offered by the practitioners. I would argue that dominant global discourse has not sufficiently moved on from this early 20th-century framing of scientific epistemic capital. In other words, the attempt to justify other modes of knowledge with reference to scientific modes continues to be an issue today, obfuscating important aspects of knowledge production, particularly in the area of health and healing.

These rhetorical and conceptual gaps between personal experience, medical expertise and scientific epistemic justifications go some way towards explaining the varied and oppositional responses to public health directives during the public health crisis of Covid-19 between 2020 and 2022. The experiential episteme continues to be of vital importance to many people's personal experiences of health, wellbeing and decision-making. Both social scientists and medical professionals might find it fruitful to work on ways in which we can better articulate and analyse this episteme.

[17] The Indian Medical Degrees Act 1916 proscribed fines for 'assuming medical titles' other than those 'recognized by the General Council of Medical Education of the United Kingdom' throughout India, although The Madras Medical Registration Act of 1914 was already in effect for the Madras Presidency.

Now I'm going to jump back to the 21st century and the Covid-19 global pandemic experience, looking at the different role yogic interventions for health and wellbeing played in a particular pilot study on the experience of long Covid. I hope that this second example will further make the case for better understanding how senses can be deliberately trained, both for those offering health inventions, as well as by those suffering from ill health. Undoubtedly, in a time of epistemic crisis and uncertainty about the validity of all forms of knowledge, it is not enough to leave this mode of knowledge at 'it feels true' without further nuance or challenge. Feelings of 'truth' – and indeed our human experiences of health and wellbeing – can be cultivated and transformed through training. Human interpretation of sensations is always developed in a social context (what sensations are important, what can be ignored? what is the significance of the sensory data?) and can be refined and changed (at least to some extent) through training.

Nuanced experiential interventions: yoga for long Covid

By the summer of 2021, it became clear that up to one-third of those who were infected with Covid-19 continued to suffer from debilitating symptoms long after the acute phase of the virus ended. These lingering, sometimes debilitating, symptoms included extreme fatigue, dizziness, and memory and sleep problems, as well as lingering loss of smell, cough, headache and digestion problems (NIHR 2021). In response to this situation, the UK-based Iyengar Yoga organisation developed a working group to try to proactively do something helpful in response to these reported symptoms affecting a significant minority of the population. In the United Kingdom (as well as much of the rest of the world but specific to national contexts) there were a series of 'lockdowns' between March 2020 and December 2021 in which most of the population was required to stay in their own homes as much as possible, with those providing critical services still working outside the home; most of the population was instructed to stay in their homes except for essential shopping and an hour of outdoor exercise daily.[18]

During this period, most of the population's normal daily activities were severely disrupted. Many teacher-members of Iyengar Yoga (UK) were at home, not teaching their regular in-person classes, but were economically stable enough to have a quiet private room, fast internet access and high-quality computers. Born out of a desire to help those suffering from long Covid (which included some of the IY(UK) membership), IY(UK) ran an intervention for those suffering from long Covid (self-diagnosed) between October and December 2021. The pilot study was developed and organised by a working group of IY(UK) teachers and administered by IY(UK) staff with collaboration and research analysis provided

[18] A timeline of the UK lockdown measures can be found at the Institute for Government website (2022).

by a team based in the School of Health Sciences at York St John University (Shah 2022).[19]

The protocol for the intervention was based on a yoga sequence developed by Lois Steinberg, an experienced yoga teacher based in the US who has specialised in therapy work and trained directly under B. K. S. Iyengar for many years.[20] During the three-month pilot study, 115 qualified Iyengar Yoga teachers (and a pool of 19 cover teachers) based in the UK regularly volunteered their time in return for professional development training provided as part of the programme. This pool of teachers gave weekly yoga classes (held on Zoom) to 55 adults (ranging from 22–69 years of age) who self-identified as currently suffering from long Covid. The classes were offered for free, and the intervention involved each individual being taught by two yoga teachers (both teaching a single student online at the same time each week), supervised by a specialist therapy teacher (who was also often present in the online room during the class).

The protocol for the intervention is largely outlined in a booklet produced by IY(UK) and the interventions are illustrated in online video instructions (IYUK 2022; Steinberg 2024). In general, the sequence is largely based on 'prone' positions – where the abdomen, head and chest are all supported on a surface, usually a soft surface if possible. The justification for this is that this position 'allows the back body to broaden and lengthen and the diaphragm to soften', which in turn allows the back of the lungs to work more effectively and, by relaxing the diaphragm, stimulates the vagus nerve and parasympathetic nervous system (IY(UK) Therapy Committee 2022: 7). Some examples of the positions used in the programme are Figures 12.2, 12.3 and 12.4.

Although the postures are, effectively, a lot of 'lying around', the illustrations show that considerable and specific support is given to the body to enable relaxation. As part of the intervention, yoga props were sometimes donated and given to those participating. But a large part of the sessions, at least initially, consisted of the yoga teachers helping the student find an arrangement of household objects (e.g. tables, pillows, blankets) which would enable them to relax and feel comfortable in these positions. Moreover, the postures chosen for each session would vary in consultation between the student and the teachers, considering the most presenting symptoms and how the student was responding to the suggested positions. As the therapy booklet explains: 'Everyone's recovery needs are different and not all of

[19] The research team consisted of Vishal Shah (employed as student researcher), Dr Chris Boyes, Professor Alison Laver Fawcett, and Lynne Lacock from York St John University, working in partnership with Laura Potts, Ph.D. from Iyengar Yoga (UK) and Suzanne Newcombe (the author of this paper). I was involved in the discussions of research design, the supervision of the student researcher from York St John and contributed to writing the final report based on the qualitative interviews.

[20] The final programme, according to the credits on the Iyengar Yoga UK website, 'was compiled thanks to advice and guidance from Abhijata Iyengar, Lois Steinberg, Gulnaaz Dashti, Stephanie Quirk, the IY(UK) Therapy Committee, IY(UK) teachers who have experienced the virus themselves, and decades of work by BKS Iyengar and Dr Geeta S. Iyengar in medical classes at RIMYI in Pune' (IYUK 2022).

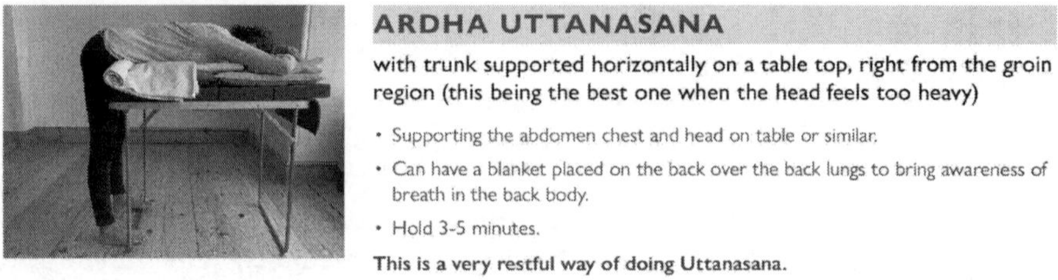

ARDHA UTTANASANA

with trunk supported horizontally on a table top, right from the groin region (this being the best one when the head feels too heavy)

- Supporting the abdomen chest and head on table or similar.
- Can have a blanket placed on the back over the back lungs to bring awareness of breath in the back body.
- Hold 3-5 minutes.

This is a very restful way of doing Uttanasana.

Figure 12.2 Ardha Uttanasana. Illustration and commentary from the booklet entitled *Covid-19 Recovery: A Suggested Yoga Programme* (IY(UK) Therapy Committee 2022: 14)

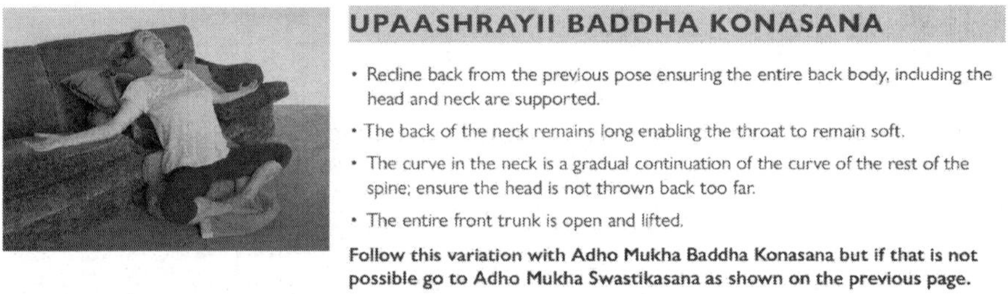

UPAASHRAYII BADDHA KONASANA

- Recline back from the previous pose ensuring the entire back body, including the head and neck are supported.
- The back of the neck remains long enabling the throat to remain soft.
- The curve in the neck is a gradual continuation of the curve of the rest of the spine; ensure the head is not thrown back too far.
- The entire front trunk is open and lifted.

Follow this variation with Adho Mukha Baddha Konasana but if that is not possible go to Adho Mukha Swastikasana as shown on the previous page.

Figure 12.3 Upaashrayii Baddha Konasana. Illustration and commentary from the booklet entitled *Covid-19 Recovery: A Suggested Yoga Programme* (IY(UK) Therapy Committee 2022: 21)

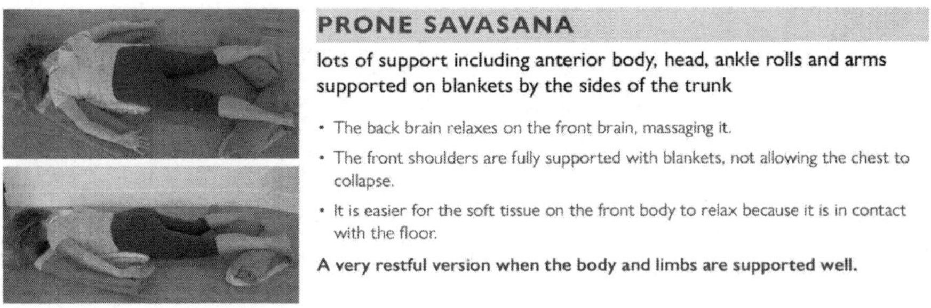

PRONE SAVASANA

lots of support including anterior body, head, ankle rolls and arms supported on blankets by the sides of the trunk

- The back brain relaxes on the front brain, massaging it.
- The front shoulders are fully supported with blankets, not allowing the chest to collapse.
- It is easier for the soft tissue on the front body to relax because it is in contact with the floor.

A very restful version when the body and limbs are supported well.

Figure 12.4 Prone Savasana. Illustration and commentary from the booklet entitled *Covid 19 Recovery: A Suggested Yoga Programme* (IY(UK) Therapy Committee 2022: 35)

the postures will be suitable' and the practice needs to be 'tailored to your needs' (IY(UK) Therapy Committee 2022: 7).

The original research evaluation protocol involved each participant filling out a self-reported checklist of symptoms before and after each session as well as taking part in follow-up qualitative interviews several months after the intervention with the paid student researcher at York St John University, Vishal Shah.[21] There were statistically significant improvements on general evaluation of both physical and mental wellbeing, as well as individual symptoms of fatigue and anxiety, and in reported cough, sore throat and phlegm from the beginning of the first session to the end of the last session. There were a variety of other reported measures that did not show any statistically significant improvement, such as headaches and ease of breathing (Shah *et al.* 2022: 4–10). Follow-up online interviews with a random selection of 11 students and 3 teachers were undertaken between March and June 2022. The interviews were transcribed and thematically coded using NVivo software by Vishal Shah under the supervision of the wider research team, which included the author of this chapter.

This data found that most of the participants were not regular yoga practitioners, but most had tried yoga in the past and had generally favourable impressions of yoga. The significant improvements described by the students in the qualitative interviews were reduced fatigue, greater ease in breathing, gaining muscle strength and better sleep. An improvement in the length and quality of sleep was a major theme described in the interviews and had not been part of the original quantitative survey design. The improved sleep undoubtably was related to improved fatigue and other aspects of participants' mood and recovery from illness in general.

Several of the interviews saw the participants expressing strong emotions, 'sharing how the programme made them feel special and looked after with the individual care and attention' (Shah *et al.* 2022: 12). This individual attention was often remarked upon in contrast to 'regular yoga sessions' (which sometimes made their symptoms worse) as well as many spontaneously complaining about the 'fatigue clinics' offered by the NHS (a subject that was not part of the interview schedule but repeatedly was brought up by participants). As one participant narrated:

> So, my GPs kind of said there's nothing, there's nothing they can do for fatigue. … it's around resting. It's around pacing. It's around, you know, keeping your body calm and learning to live with it. Not having anything to grasp, hold onto or help other than just being told that this was quite difficult.
>
> (Shah *et al.* 2022: 27)

This long Covid yoga intervention actively taught a method of *how* to rest and recover. It gave this population something specific and proactive to do which was manageable. Almost all participants spontaneously discussed how significant it was to them that the yoga teachers took their symptoms seriously and were giving focused attention towards exploring what specific positions and actions helped them feel better. Moreover, they could describe the process by which this feeling arose: through observation of the details of their experience, comfort and ability,

[21] Ethical approval was given by York St John's School of Science, Technology and Health Research Ethics Committee, reference STHEC0053 for the follow-up interviews; the first stage of the intervention was done completely by the IYUK team and the student participants were found through snowball sampling via both teacher and long Covid online networks.

and proactive and constructive responses to complaints and criticisms (both about physical symptoms and teaching methods). There was a specific process by which trust and communication was developed between students and teachers. This process of sensory observation – on the part of the teachers and the students – was identifiable, measurable and teachable.

Interestingly, a significant amount of sensory sensitivity that one might think was intimately bound to in-person observation was able to be applied successfully in the Zoom context. This could challenge some assumptions around sensation, sensory awareness and what facilitates the development of sensory sensitivity. However, it is important to remember that there were two to three instructors cross-checking their observations and collectively guiding each 'student' with long Covid; these instructors were relying on often decades of self-practice and instruction on developing this sensory sensitivity that was developed in face-to-face contexts. Therefore, the social context of the development of sensory sensitivity in the 'patients' relied upon a deep (in terms of years of face-to-face instruction) and broad (referring to the collaboration between those giving the intervention) resource base of those giving the intervention. The unique crisis of Covid-19 allowed for these human resources to become available for such a labour-intensive intervention that is not easily monetisable.

For the teachers, this process was an extension of normal yoga teaching practices for students without specific health conditions. The long Covid targeted therapy sessions offered the teachers an opportunity to further develop and refine their skills in observation and intervention when dealing with a specific health condition. For the students, trust in the expertise of the teacher and the ability of the student to feel better was built up, piece by piece, in each of the sessions through the movement of props and the adjustment of poses and timings in response to what symptoms and energy levels the student was presenting. Some of the participant comments highlighted in the summary study included:

> The degree of care and attention I just thought it was amazing actually. So, I wasn't expecting it to be so. Yes, so targeted to my specific needs.
>
> They would spot things like; I don't think you've got the blanket quite under your shoulders. Can you move it half an inch? Or can you fold the blanket neater? Can you have the other edge against your neck and not the ragged edge and you know just all these little things
>
> Sometimes they said we can see you are tired. Now we just want you to be in this pose, rest in this pose
>
> They make sure that I would have blanket, that I would be covered, I would not be cold while I was resting
>
> Really supportive and encouraging … kind of like praise and encouragement really helped me
>
> A little bit of switch in my eyes or anything they would ask me …
>
> (Shah *et al.* 2022: 23–4)

These statements suggest reasons why this particular yoga intervention was experienced as efficacious and healing. This intervention was essentially a process of sensory sensibility training for both the patients and the teacher-facilitators. Those suffering from long Covid were being taught to direct their attention to what positions and actions in their body could bring ease and relaxation, and learning what kind of supports their particular bodies needed to experience this ease. For the clients, this took their focus off the negative experience of chronic symptoms and opened the door to slowly building up different ways of the body being in the world.

At the same time, the involvement of several teachers actively being trained in 'therapy yoga' through dialogue and mentorship showed how this training in sensory sensibility was a dialogic process, involving considerable feedback and discussion as well as trial and error. Although results are not standardised in terms of the level and skill that was being developed in each participating yoga teacher, this intervention exemplified a recognisable and repeatable method of training yoga teachers to respond sensitively and creatively within a protocol and through application of principles of the method. The participating yoga teachers were offered certification of their time participating in this intervention as training in the therapeutic use of yoga within IY(UK). This example further demonstrates how considering in more analytical depth how the experiential mode of knowledge functions and can be actively transmitted to change the nature of experience can be extremely significant to experiences of health and healing. It is a mode of knowing that can be systematically refined from both the position of the client as well as that of the therapist.

Conclusion

The experiential episteme is crucial when it comes to evaluating health and wellbeing. How else can someone suffering judge their healing, if not through their own experience? But leaving cultural inquiry at the level of personal opinion and then quantifying it through surveys is not sufficient to critically evaluate interventions for health and healing. How can experience be actively trained to contribute to health and healing, such as being actively taught how to 'rest'? And how can medical and public health practitioners better interface with the experiential mode to achieve the most efficacious combination of evidence-based recommendations and effective communications?

A cultural lacuna in articulating epistemic competency has serious consequences for experiences of health and wellbeing more generally. Biomedical interventions, at their best, also depend upon the clinical skill of the practitioners involved in noticing and responding to sensory data presented by the patient. More systematic attention to empirical sensory experience could improve standard biomedical interventions wherever there is an interface between a patient and practitioner, as well as improve our understanding of how, when and why yoga and meditation interventions work, and when they might cause harm. This would be a specific advance in 'training sensibility' to counter epistemic injustice and promote better health and wellbeing.

It is possible to systematise, replicate and transmit traditions of promoting health and healing based on the experiential episteme. However, the cultural privileging of scientific and traditional epistemes has led to experiential knowledge being marginalised. Some empirical evidence is well integrated into the scientific mode, such as sensory evidence that can be approached by objective measures (e.g. quantifiable interviews and survey data as well as technologically measurable and verifiable observations of microorganisms under magnification). It was these measures by which the practitioners in the 1923 Usman Report were requested to justify the efficacy of their models of health and healing. However culturally prestigious they are, these epistemic methods cannot recreate the experience of 'feeling' more relaxed and healthier.

This chapter has presented an argument that there is a lack of cultural capacity in valuing, articulating, nuancing and discussing knowledge gained from sensory experience – that is, the experiential epistemic mode. It is postulated that this lacuna is one of several issues contributing to the epistemic crisis that has been developing over several decades in the postcolonial, 'post-truth' era of politics. It is an aspect of epistemic injustice at the hermeneutical level. More nuanced discussion in this area might help to avoid some of the oppositional polarisation found in the anti-lockdown protests during Covid-19, where some in Europe and the Americas felt their embodied experiences were not reflected in public health directives.

Furthermore, if we don't improve our competency in articulating, analysing and valuing the experiential mode, our understanding and messaging around embodied interventions will remain confused. This confusion makes it more difficult for suffering people to effectively and critically evaluate the most appropriate options for their own healthcare. In the healthcare context, there has been a gradual validation of the knowledge from lived experience since the late 20th century driven by feminist and disability critiques, which has led to self-help groups and patient participation models of healthcare provision.[22] What I am proposing in giving more attention to nuancing the development of skill and awareness in negotiating the experiential episteme is an extension of these developments.

Far from being irrational or just 'feeling true', yoga and meditation traditions have (at their best) systematic methods of transmitting and evaluating embodied traditions of experience. It is important to stop trying to articulate the healing experienced in experiential epistemes such as yoga with other categories such as quantitative-scientific measurements. This means that the focus on psychophysical measures of experiential interventions, such as heart rate variability (HRV), blood

[22] Notably, Patient Public Involvement (PPI) panels are increasingly a common feature of healthcare management decisions in the UK (see Rose 2014 as well as Harrett, Ryan and Hynes 2022 for a recent UK based critique of current practice and Marsolais *et al.* 2025 for a discussion on current US practice in this area).

pressure, respiration rate and oxygen consumption, are, at best, partial proxies for evaluating the efficacy of these kinds of experiential interventions. Although perhaps still relevant data in deciding a course or recommended therapy, these measurements provide no information about *how* the intervention was conducted or what adjustments were made by the expert providing the instruction/intervention in response to sensory information during the intervention to better ensure the desired psychophysical responses occurred. These psychophysical proxies occur in a social context of trained sensory sensitivity. The excessive focus on the 'scientific' metrics obscures the process by which these results are obtained. This impoverishes our ability to understand or critically evaluate the experiential episteme.

This habit is unhelpfully mystifying, obfuscating and ultimately furthers social divisions (i.e. 'we' understand this experience and 'they' do not). As a society we can do better. We can acknowledge experiential knowledge as a legitimate epistemic mode that is open to analytical evaluation, more refined training and intelligent, critical discussion. The cultivation and critical development of 'sensory sensitivity' within the experiential episteme is entirely possible.

Acknowledgements

The section on the Usman Report was made possible by Dagmar Wujastyk's generous leadership and funding from the European Union's Horizon 2020 research and innovation programme under grant agreement No. 639363. I would also like to express my gratitude to the Iyengar Yoga Long Covid Project team, especially Lara Potts for her comments on this chapter. I am also very grateful for conversation with Dominik Wujastyk during the May 2023 conference and his follow-up responses to further questions. Other individuals needing special acknowledgement as dialogue partners in the creation of this chapter are David G. Robertson, whose clarity, support and interest in ongoing dialogue on epistemic capital has been invaluable, and Lucy May Constantini for her deep understanding of embodied knowledge and persistence in attempting to articulate this type of knowledge in academic contexts.

References

Alavi, S. (2007), *Islam and Healing: Loss and Recovery of an Indo-Muslim Medical Tradition 1600–1900* (Delhi: Permanent Black).

Alpert, A., Evans, W. N., Lieber, E. M. J. and Powell, D. (2022), 'Origins of the Opioid Crisis and Its Enduring Impacts'. *Quarterly Journal of Economics* 137(2): 1139–79. https://doi.org/10.1093/qje/qjab043

Argentino, M. A. and Amarasingam, A. (2021), 'They Got It All Under Control: QAnon, Conspiracy Theories, and the New Threats to Canadian National Security' in L. West, T. Juneau and A. Amarasingam (eds) *Stress Tested: The COVID-19 Pandemic and Canadian National Security* (Calgary: University of Calgary Press), 15–32.

Arnold, D. (1993), *Colonising the Body: State Medicine and Epidemic Disease in Nineteenth-Century India* (London: University of California Press).

Attewell, G. (2007), *Refiguring Unani Tibb* (Hyderabad: Orient Longman).

Barois, C., Newcombe, S. and Wujastyk, D. (2022), 'Introduction to The Usman Report (1923): Translations of Regional Submissions' in D. Wujastyk and C. Barois (eds) *Usman Report (1923) – First Translations of Regional Submissions. eJournal of Indian Medicine*, Supplement 4: ix–xxxi. https://doi.org/10.21827/61e814114457b

Beer, F. A. and Hariman, R. (2020), 'Learning from the Pandemic: Catastrophic Epistemology'. *Social Epistemology Review and Reply Collective*, 9(5): 19–28. https://wp.me/P1Bfg0-4Wa

Beres, D., Remski, M., Walker, J. and DeMille, M. (2024), *Conspirituality: Dismantling New Age Cults, Wellness Grifters, and Conspiracy-Mad Yogis.* (New York: PublicAffairs).

Berger, M. (2013), *Ayurveda Made Modern: Political Histories of Indigenous Medicine in North India, 1900–1955* (London: Palgrave Macmillan).

Brooks, L. A. (2018), 'Epistemology and Embodiment: Diagnosis and the Senses in Classical Ayurvedic Medicine'. *Asian Review of World Histories*, 6(1): 98–135. https://doi.org/10.1163/22879811-12340027

Brooks, L. A. (2020), 'A Surgeon's Hand: Reflections on Surgical Tactility in Early Ayurveda'. *Asian Medicine*, 15: 30–62.

Brooks, L. A. (2021), *Translating Touch in Āyurveda: Medicine, Sense and Subjectivity in Early South Asia and Contemporary Kerala.* Ph.D. thesis, University of California, Berkeley.

Center for Tackling Digital Hate (CTDH). (2021), 'The Disinformation Dozen: Why Platforms Must Act on Twelve Leading Online Anti-vaxxers', 24 March. Available at: https://counterhate.com/research/the-disinformation-dozen/. Accessed 20 June 2024.

Crockford, S. (2023), 'That Which They Will Not See: Climate Denial as a Vector of Epistemological Crisis in the Contemporary United States'. *Ethnos*, 1–21. https://doi.org/10.1080/00141844.2023.2242599

Csordas, T. J. (2002), *Body / Meaning / Healing* (New York: Palgrave Macmillan).

Csordas, T. J. (2007), 'Transmutation of Sensibilities: Empathy, Intuition, Revelation' in A. McLean and A. Leibing (eds) *The Shadow Side of Fieldwork: Theorizing the Blurred Borders between Ethnography and Life* (Oxford: Blackwell), 106–16.

Deichmann, U. and Müller-Hill, B. (1998) 'The Fraud of Abderhalden's Enzymes'. *Nature*, 393: 109–11. https://doi.org/10.1038/30090

Foucault, M. (1974), *The Order of Things* (London: Tavistock).

Foucault, M. (1980), *Power/Knowledge, Selected Interviews and Other Writings 1972–1977* (Brighton: The Harvester Press).

Fricker, M. (2007). *Epistemic Injustice: Power and Ethics of Knowing* (Oxford: Oxford University Press).

Gayathri, V. (2012), *Coping with Diseases: Public Health and Medicine in Colonial South India, 1883–1925*. Ph.D. thesis, Pondicherry University. http://hdl.handle.net/10603/5235

Goldberg, J. (2020), 'Why Obama Fears for Our Democracy', *The Atlantic*, 16 November. Available at: https://www.theatlantic.com/ideas/archive/2020/11/why-obama-fears-for-our-democracy/617087/. Accessed 17 June 2025.

Guerin, C. (2021), 'The Yoga World Is Riddled with Anti-vaxxers and QAnon Believers', *Wired*, 28 January. Available at: https://www.wired.co.uk/article/yoga-disinformation-qanon-conspiracy-wellness. Accessed 17 June 2025.

Hamilton, S. (2001), *Indian Philosophy: A Very Short Introduction* (Oxford: Oxford University Press).

Harding, S. (ed.) (2004), *The Feminist Standpoint Theory Reader* (London: Routledge).

Harnett, C., Ryan, N. and Hynes, B. (2022), 'Protocol for Establishing and Evaluating a Public and Patient Panel for Organisation Science and Management Principles in Healthcare'. *British Medical Journal Open*, 12: e062196. https://doi.org/10.1136/bmjopen-2022-062196

Hausman, G. J. (1996), *Siddhars, Alchemy and the Abyss of Tradition: 'Traditional' Tamil Medical Knowledge in 'Modern' Practice*. Ph.D. thesis, The University of Michigan.

Honigberger, J. M. (1852), *Thirty-five Years in the East: Adventures, Discoveries, Experiments and Historical Sketches Relating to the Punjab and Cashmere in Connection with Medicine, Botany, Pharmacy and Together with an Original Materia Medica and a Medical Vocabulary in Four European and Five Eastern Languages* (London: H. Bailliere).

Indian Medical Degrees Act 1916. Act 7 of 1916 passed by the Indian Legislative Council. 16 March.

Institute for Government. (2022), 'Timeline of UK Government Coronavirus Lockdowns and Measures, March 2020 to December 2021', 9 December. Available at: https://www.instituteforgovernment.org.uk/sites/default/files/2022-12/timeline-coronavirus-lockdown-december-2021.pdf. Accessed 17 June 2025.

Iyengar Yoga UK (IYUK). (2022), 'Iyengar Yoga for Long Covid: Pilot Study Results', Iyengar Yoga UK website, 7 November. Available at: https://iyengaryoga.org.uk/iyengar-yoga-for-long-covid-pilot-study-results/. Accessed 17 June 2025.

Iyengar Yoga (UK) (IY (UK)) Therapy Committee. (2022), 'Covid 19 Recovery: A Suggested Programme'. Available at: https://iyengaryoga.org.uk/covid-19-a-suggested-recovery-programme/. Accessed 17 June 2025.

Kale, S. (2021), 'Chakras, Crystals and Conspiracy Theories: How the Wellness Industry Turned Its Back on Covid Science', *Guardian*, 11 November. Available at: https://www.theguardian.com/world/2021/nov/11/injecting-poison-will-never-make-you-healthy-how-the-wellness-industry-turned-its-back-on covid-science. Accessed 17 June 2025.

Kędzia, I. B. (2017), 'Mastering Deathlessness: Some Remarks on Kaṟpam Preparations in the Medico-Alchemical Literature of the Tamil Siddhas'. *History of Science in South Asia*, 5(2): 121–42. https://doi.org/10.18732/hssa.v5i2.16

Kuriyama, S. (1999), *The Expressiveness of the Body: And the Divergence of Greek and Chinese Medicine* (New York: Zone Books).

Leslie, C (ed.) (1976), *Asian Medical Systems* (London: University of California Press).

ListenNotes. (2024), 'Conspirituality'. Available at: https://www.listennotes.com/podcasts/conspirituality-derek-beres-matthew-remski-CeDtbd9O-85/. Accessed 17 June 2025.

Maas, P. and Verdon, N. (2018), 'On al-Bīrūnī's *Kitāb Pātangal* and the *Pātañjalayogaśastra*' in K. Baier, P. Maas and K. Preisendanz (eds) *Yoga in Transformation: Historical and Contemporary Perspectives* (Vienna: Vienna University Press), 283–334.

Mackenzie, J. (1919), *The Future of Medicine* (Oxford: Oxford University Press).

Marsolais, E., Anhang Price, R., Berdahl, C. T., Shenk, A., Schulson, L. and O'Hanlon, C. E. (2025), 'The Technical Expert/Clinical User/Patient Panel (TECUPP): Centering Patient and Family Perspectives in Patient-Reported Measure Development'. *Research Involvement Engagement*, 11(2). https://doi.org/10.1186/s40900-024-00661-4

Mbembe, A. (2021), 'Futures of Life and Futures of Reason'. *Public Culture*, 33(1): 11–33. https://doi.org/10.1215/08992363-8742136

Mukharji, P. (2011), 'Symptoms of Dis-Ease: New Trends in the Histories of "Indigenous" South Asian Medicines'. *History Compass*, 9: 887–99. https://doi.org/10.1111/j.1478-0542.2011.00813.x

Mukharji, P. (2016), *Doctoring Traditions: Ayurveda, Small Technologies and Braided Sciences* (London: University of Chicago Press).

National Institute for Health Care Research (NIHR). (2021), 'Up to One in Three People Who Have Had COVID-19 Report Long COVID Symptoms', 24 June. Available at: https://www.nihr.ac.uk/news/up-to-one-in-three-people-who-have-had-covid-19-report-long-covid-symptoms/27979. Accessed 17 June 2025.

Robertson, D. G. (2016), *Conspiracy Theories, UFOs and the New Age: Millennial Conspiracism* (London: Bloomsbury).

Robertson, D. G. (2018), 'The Counter-Elite: Strategies of Authority in Millennial Conspiracism' in A. Dyrendal, D. G. Robertson and E. Asprem (eds) *Brill Handbook of Conspiracy Theory and Contemporary Religion* (Leiden: Brill), 234–54.

Robertson, D. G. (2021), 'Legitimizing Claims of Special Knowledge: Towards an Epistemic Turn in Religious Studies'. *Temenos: Nordic Journal of Contemporary Religion*, 57: 17–34. https://doi.org/10.33356/temenos.107773

Robertson, D. G. (2025), *Religion and Conspiracy Theories: An Introduction* (London: Routledge).

Robertson, D. G. and Amarasingam, A. (2022), 'How Conspiracy Theorists Argue: Epistemic Capital in the QAnon Social Media Sphere'. *Popular Communication*, 20: 193–207. https://doi.org/10.1080/15405702.2022.2050238

Rose, D. (2014), 'Patient and Public Involvement in Health Research: Ethical Imperative and/or Radical Challenge?' *Journal of Health Psychology*, 19(1): 149–58. https://doi.org/10.1177/1359105313500249

Shah, V., Boyes, C., Laver Fawcett, A., Lacock, L., Potts, L. and Newcombe, S. (2022), *Iyengar Yoga for Long Covid: Pilot Study Results. Project Report*. Iyengar Yoga UK. Available at: https://ray.yorksj.ac.uk/id/eprint/7991/1/Iyengar-Yoga-UK-Long-Covid-Pilot-Study-Final-Report.pdf. Accessed 17 June 2025.

Sharma, D. (2011), *Classical Indian Philosophy: A Reader* (New York: Columbia University Press).

Singleton, M. (2010), *Yoga Body: The Origins of Modern Posture Practice* (New York: Oxford University Press).

Sivaramakrishnan, K. (2006), *Old Potions, New Bottles: Recasting Indigenous Medicine in Colonial Punjab (1850–1945)* (Hyderabad: Orient Longman).

Steinberg, L. (2024), 'Yoga for Long Covid with Lois Steinberg'. Recorded workshop, 2hr. 52 min. Available for rental at: https://www.union.fit/orgs/iyengar-yoga-therapeutics/videos/TgBkizDHywqNiqx2HaXkYMpV. Accessed 17 June 2025.

Sujatha, V. (2014), *Sociology of Health and Medicine: New Perspectives* (New Delhi: Oxford University Press).

Turner, B. S. (1987), *Medical Power and Social Knowledge* (London: Sage).

Usman, M. (1923), *The Report of the Committee on the Indigenous Systems of Medicine. Part I. The Report with Appendices. Part II. Written and Oral Evidence*. 2 vols (Madras: Presidency).

Wujastyk, D. (2008), 'The Evolution of Indian Government Policy on Ayurveda in the Twentieth Century' in D. Wujastyk and F. M. Smith (eds) *Modern and Global Ayurveda: Pluralism and Paradigms* (New York: SUNY Press), 43–76.

Wujastyk, D. (2011), 'The Path to Liberation Through Yogic Mindfulness in Early Ayurveda' in D. G. White (ed.) *Yoga in Practice*. (Princeton, NJ: Princeton University Press), 31–42.

Wujastyk, D. and Barois, C. (eds) (2022), 'The Usman Report (1923) Translations of Regional Submissions'. *Supplements to the eJournal of Indian Medicine*, 4. https://doi.org/10.21827/61e814114457b

Zysk, K. G. (2000), *Asceticism and Healing in Ancient India: Medicine in the Buddhist Monastery* (Delhi: Motilal Banarsidass).

13

Epistemes, Epistemologies and Public Health: Some Distinctions

CHAKRAVARTHI RAM-PRASAD

In thinking through this rich and varied collection of papers, one realises that interwoven issues underlie our sense of what is culturally complex about the global health challenges that were made so urgent and lethal by the Covid-19 pandemic. I would like to tease apart these issues through a series of seven distinctions, many of which are treated in this volume, if not always in the way I make them. Throughout, I help myself to the very useful distinction between an episteme and an epistemology that the editors make in the Introduction, Chapter 1 (and the relationship between which is explored in careful detail by Roussou in Chapter 3 of this volume): broadly, that an episteme is the situated expression of practices of knowledge, while an epistemology is a theory of knowledge.

The Eurocentric episteme and the globality of the biomedical

The first distinction I want to make is between (1) the Eurocentric episteme which claims, above all, to be grounded in a rational epistemology (Araújo and Maeso 2015), and (2) the knowledge processes of modern biomedicine followed in healthcare systems globally (Jansen and Roesch 2022). Of course, it is contingently the case that what we now call biomedicine evolved from the combination of the production of taxonomies of nature, anatomical investigation, radically new surgical and other techniques of intervention and the overarching governmentality of institutionalised treatment of individuated human beings that occurred in and characterised early European modernity (Petersen 2003). Early modern European society produced what we call 'medicine' now (Lindemann 2010). This very same European modernity also generated the brutal racial hierarchisation of humanity and the moral defence of the exploitation of the natural world, especially through the capitalist paradigm of the global market whose deleterious impact to this

Proceedings of the British Academy, **278**, 272–278, © Authors 2025.

day has made 'Eurocentricity' a potent and instantly recognisable concept even among states and people who have adopted its functionality (Sunar 2016). Now, as it happens – and it is futile to consider counterfactual histories – the tests and vaccines for the coronavirus were developed in the nexus of knowledge practices and institutional forces of this biomedicine. But it is worth considering whether the conception of modern biomedicine in the world is exhausted by the paradigm of the Eurocentric episteme. While a sharp critique of Eurocentricity as a still-potent historical force with specific hierarchical and exploitative modes is necessary when considering institutionalised health inequalities, I wonder whether that need be tantamount to a critique of biomedicine as an imposition upon a subaltern world. I suspect that the distinction between the Eurocentric episteme and the paradigm of biomedicine, while seldom explicated in this way by doctors around the globe, is one that implicitly informs their approach to health sciences.

This was evident in the way doctors around the world, deeply embedded in their traditional cultures and/or sensitive to the inequalities generated by Eurocentric paradigms, nonetheless were committed to a biomedical approach to the Covid-19 pandemic, in terms of tests, PPE, vaccines and the relationship between knowledge of transmission pathways and practices of safety (e.g. on South Africa see Bank and Nelly 2022). (That such responses might have been deeply hindered by infrastructural infirmities is a different point.)

Paradigms of biomedical treatment and institutional practices of treatment

The next distinction I want to suggest is between (1) the biomedical paradigm as an epistemology of evidence (double-blind, etc.) and drug development, and (2) institutional cultures of health treatment. On the one hand, it has proved extremely difficult for doctors in such systems as the UK National Health Service to challenge the scientific practices of the biomedical paradigm when practising in such systems: they are literally qualified only by virtue of their mastery of that paradigm, and have professional standing and can practise only if they can demonstrate such mastery. But even if doctors in some measure evinced such epistemic authority, many (especially from minority backgrounds) were and continue to be sharply critical of the institutional inequalities of treatment (Sowemimo 2023). What we have to keep in mind is the delicate balance doctors with such an approach must strike between mastering the biomedical paradigm's epistemology and not endorsing it. (One thinks of the place of acupuncture in Western medical services) (Cheung, Chapter 10 in this volume, and Cant 2020). Many doctors in the NHS from the Global South, even as they notice and resist inequalities of treatment for reasons they associate with the racialised episteme of Western healthcare systems, do not at all challenge the fundamental epistemological claims and methodologies of the biomedical paradigm (Keys *et al.* 2021). In short, it should not be assumed that criticism of the institutional structures and social assumptions of the biomedical episteme (in any case seldom articulated theoretically by practising medics) is tantamount to critique of biomedical epistemology by which diagnoses, tests and treatments are produced.

Saving lives and human flourishing

A third distinction that is worth keeping in mind is that between (1) merely supplementing the ostensibly core biomedical task of saving lives with religio-cultural therapies of human flourishing, and (2) focusing on the epistemology of religio-cultural therapies of human flourishing as a fundamental critique of the hegemonic biomedical episteme.

With regard to (1), for those with a commitment to exploring religio-cultural diversity, it is a difficult fact that there are life-endangering practices engendered by non- or anti-biomedical epistemes. It is difficult because there can be a variety of cultural and political motivations behind the demonisation of groups as being anti-biomedical in their faith practices. But from the perspective of simply saving lives – as doctors in healthcare systems mainly do – we should be mindful that it is legitimate to require that religio-cultural practices that claim to be therapies for human flourishing do not endanger the biomedical imperative to save lives. If saving lives is the *sine qua non* of cultural discussions of health, then it would seem right to require that religio-cultural practices with therapeutic claims only supplement – that is, minimally do not block – the task of saving lives. Even disadvantaged minorities should not have had community gatherings during the pandemic because their legitimate suspicions about public and political directives did not override the necessity for members of their community to not become superspreaders (Lee *et al.* 2022). (Note that this is consistent with the acknowledgement that groups with greater political capital – staff at the office and residence of a Head of Government, say – tended to escape blame for transmission in a way that those who behaved unwisely due to the epistemic pressures of their marginalised status did not.)

By contrast, the latter issue, (2), might seem to lack comparable urgency; but it is potentially important in contributing to the opening up of profound questions of philosophical anthropology that have significance for health epistemology, such as whether it is possible to go beyond the limitations of implicit dualist vocabulary in biomedical language (Sujatha, Chapter 5 in this volume). But it requires a more fine-grained understanding of critical reworkings – for example, about embodied medicine or the ecological brain – of biomedical paradigms too, reworkings that usually function within an episteme formed by European modernity (and not necessarily Eurocentric for that reason). It is an intricate problem to both call for an effective integration of biomedical and indigenous/alternative epistemologies that are founded on a variety of religio-cultural epistemes while also asking exactly how the latter can resist being subsumed by the former.[1]

The response to this problem, I suggest, is as follows: (1) on the critical side, to explore the deleterious impact on life saving by the institutional hegemony of biomedicine without resisting biomedical advances to life saving; and (2) on the constructive side, to focus on the larger ecology of flourishing offered by alternative epistemologies of healing without denying their shortcomings in life-saving technologies. The alterity can nonetheless be epistemologically complementary and therapeutically supplementary (see Steavu on psychedelic Daoism, Chapter 11 in this volume). But the individual and collective shift in the global episteme is going to be a long struggle.

External and internal contestations of the biomedical episteme

I would aso like to consider the distinction during the pandemic between (1) the resistance to biomedical approaches by those who saw their religio-cultural identity and practices as having been subordinated by a Eurocentric episteme behind biomedicine (especially protective measures and vaccines), and (2) the resistance by those – for example, the Christian Right in the US – who saw themselves as the true inheritors of the Eurocentric episteme and biomedicine as a global conspiracy against their political inheritance.

In other words, we do need to follow carefully the aetiology of resistance to the guidelines and practices of biomedical responses to the pandemic. Given the dreadful racialisation of medical tests in the United States over the centuries, for example, it was understandable why the American Black population had lower rates of vaccine acceptance (Jacobi and Vaidyanathan 2021). Similarly, due to a history of racial and religious discrimination, comparable differentials opened up in the UK (Hussain *et al.* 2022).

We need to contrast such resistance from the exploited margins with forms that drew on a long history of alternative pathways to biomedicine firmly within the modernist episteme of the West (Janik 2014). An even sharper contrast is with the resistance of those who simulate marginality through ideologies of alternative hegemony, such as QAnon, with its pervasive conspiracism (Deeley, Chapter 4 in this volume). We need to consider how the trope of marginality is a powerful element in the language of suspicion of and resistance to the full panoply of biomedicine's governmental and market power. It is no surprise that marginality is deployed by a Christian Right in America that has power in both government and private

[1] For an attempt that does not address the life-saving requirements of an 'anti-colonial' response to biomedicine, see Hollenberg and Muzzin (2010).

companies: it makes it that much more difficult for doctors and nurses on the ground to engage meaningfully and sensitively with those at risk through behaviours such as vaccine hesitancy born of genuine histories of exploitation and discrimination.

Western minorities and global majorities

Another complex relationship that we must distinguish is between (1) the situation of those who form minority religio-cultural communities in the West and (2) the situation of people in societies with ancestral religio-cultural epistemes of their own.

Particular and formidable challenges were faced during the pandemic by those whose identity lay with an episteme that placed them at odds with the biomedical presupposition of the apparatus of the state: an example was Black Pentecostalists (Ugba, Chapter 7 in this volume). Likewise, in a process typical of hostile stereotyping, Muslims in the UK during Covid-19 were distinguished in populist media between 'good' Muslims – those who were at the frontline of NHS services and had alarmingly high fatality rates – and 'bad' Muslims – particularly disadvantaged community clusters whose housing and community support practices could be castigated as vectors of spread. The religious values of Muslims made no difference; despite suffering disproportionately high infection and fatality rates in all cases, media 'othering' continued without regard to the relationship of cultural identity and medical practices (Poole and Williamson 2023). In short, the deeper issue was the religio-cultural identity of minorities rather than their adherence or resistance to biomedicine.

On the other hand, where people from such backgrounds belonged to the global majority in the South, there was a different situation, where the state backed using biomedical approaches to treat culturally complex communities, revealing different problems of power and politics. The religio-cultural attitude of communities towards biomedicine was not the salient factor here. Instead, existing political and social dynamics affected the relationship between biomedicine and religio-cultural narratives. This could take different forms: particular communities within a country could receive differential treatment (in a way that eerily mirrored the problems of minorities in the West); or there could be hypernationalist narratives about the exceptional capacities of a cultural paradigm to respond to the pandemic (Raveendran and Bazzul 2021; Chekar and Kim 2022).

Alternative alternatives: religious epistemes and medical epistemologies

A subtle distinction when we examine global experiences is between (1) the engagement with biomedical approaches by religio-cultural epistemes with a complex of bodily practices including healing (e.g. Bahia on Brazil, Chapter 8;

Sarfati on South Korea, Chapter 9 in this volume), and (2) the attempt to coordinate biomedical approaches with historically alternative medical epistemologies (e.g. Ebrahimnejad on Iran, Chapter 6; Sujatha on India, Chapter 5 in this volume).

I do not have much to say on what clearly requires further expert comparison; I admit that my distinction above is somewhat simplistic (although I do qualify it as 'subtle' …). It may be a better heuristic to think that different religio-cultural epistemologies map out the relationship between human life and human wellbeing in different ways. It may only be the hermeneutic prejudice of global modernity (and its privileging of at least some aspects of biomedicine) that makes one think of, say, the thematic of 'possession' (by spirits or ancestors to explain behavioural disturbances) as less 'medical' than a theoretically worked out discipline of pharmacopoeia; and yet, of course, they co-exist in āyurveda (Ram-Prasad 2018). Whatever the complexity of the matter, the location of a religio-cultural epistemology of human wellbeing within the narrative of a modern nation-state does affect how it is supposed to mediate between people's deeply held practices and the imperatives of biomedicine: whether the two are seen as hostile contrasts, as non-overlapping magisteria, as elements of a pluralistic medical service, or something else.

Biomedical treatment and therapies of experience

I think, it may be worthwhile in conclusion to say that there is (1) the issue of alternatives to specific biomedical interventions – especially vaccines themselves, and (2) the issue of alternatives to various aspects surrounding biomedical interventions; and that the wide-ranging and challenging papers in this volume should be taken as addressing the latter. In particular, I see these papers (as well as the rich discussions at the conference from which this volume arose) as addressing the growing literature on the multidimensional – communal, bodily, emotional – therapies of experience (Ernst 2002). The pandemic made clear the pressing need to rework the ecology of biomedicine through greater analytic as well as practical focus on experiences of wellbeing. Karen O'Brien Kop's 'lived religion' approach and Suzanne Newcombe's historical situation of yoga as a means to improve health are exemplary in this regard. As we move on in the coming years to bring religion to bear on biomedicine in a wide range of complementary, critical, conceptual and policy-driven ways, we may hope for an enduring shift in the paradigm of biomedicine itself when it comes to the pluralist teleology of human flourishing.

References

Araújo, M. and Maeso, S. R. (eds) (2015), *Eurocentrism, Racism and Knowledge: Debates on History and Power in Europe and the Americas* (London: Palgrave Macmillan).

Bank, L. and Nelly, S. (2022), *Covid and Custom in Rural South Africa: Culture, Healthcare and the State* (London: Hurst Publishers).

Cant, S. (2020), 'Medical Pluralism, Mainstream Marginality or Subaltern Therapeutics? Globalisation and the Integration of "Asian" Medicines and Biomedicine in the UK'. *Society and Culture in South Asia*, 6(1): 31–51. https://doi.org/10.1177/2393861719883064

Chekar, C. K. and Kim, H. (2022), 'COVID-19 Exceptionalism: Explaining South Korean Responses'. *East Asian Science, Technology and Society: An International Journal*, 16(1): 7–29. https://doi.org/10.1080/18752160.2021.2004355

Ernst, W. (2002), *Plural Medicine, Tradition and Modernity. Historical and Contemporary Perspectives: Views from Below and from Above* (London: Routledge).

Hollenberg, D. and Muzzin, L. (2010), 'Epistemological Challenges to Integrative Medicine: An Anti-colonial Perspective on the Combination of Complementary/Alternative Medicine with Biomedicine'. *Health Sociology Review*, 19(1): 34–56. https://doi.org/10.5172/hesr.2010.19.1.034

Hussain, B., Latif, A., Timmon, S., Nkhoma, K. and Nellums, L. B. (2022), 'Overcoming COVID-19 Vaccine Hesitancy Among Ethnic Minorities: A Systematic Review of UK Studies'. *Vaccine*, 40(25): 3413–32. https://doi.org/10.1016/j.vaccine.2022.04.030

Jacobi, J. J. and Vaidyanathan, B. (2021), 'Racial Differences in Anticipated COVID-19 Vaccine Acceptance Among Religious Populations in the US'. *Vaccine*, 39(43): 6351–5. https://doi.org/10.1016/j.vaccine.2021.09.005

Janik, E. (2014), *Marketplace of the Marvelous: The Strange Origins of Modern Medicine* (Boston, MA: Beacon Press).

Jansen, A. and Roesch, C. (2022), 'Introduction: Biomedicine in Contemporary History'. *Journal of Contemporary History*, 57(4): 843–58. https://doi.org/10.1177/00220094211039547

Keys, C., Nanayakkara, G., Onyejekwe, C., Sah, R. K. and Wright, T. (2021), 'Health Inequalities and Ethnic Vulnerabilities During COVID-19 in the UK: A Reflection on the PHE Reports'. *Feminist Legal Studies*, 29: 107–18. https://doi.org/10.1007/s10691-020-09446-y

Lee, M., Lim, H., Xavier, M. S. and Lee, E.-Y. (2022), '"A Divine Infection": A Systematic Review on the Roles of Religious Communities During the Early Stage of COVID-19'. *Journal of Religion and Health*, 61: 866–919. https://doi.org/10.1007/s10943-021-01364-w

Lindemann, M. (2010), *Medicine and Society in Early Modern Europe* (Cambridge: Cambridge University Press).

Petersen, A. (2003), 'Governmentality, Critical Scholarship, and the Medical Humanities'. *Journal of Medical Humanities*, 24: 187–201. https://doi.org/10.1023/A:1026002202396

Poole, E. and Williamson, M. (2023), 'Disrupting or Reconfiguring Racist Narratives About Muslims? The Representation of British Muslims During the Covid Crisis'. *Journalism*, 24(2): 262–79. https://doi.org/10.1177/14648849211030129

Ram-Prasad, C. (2018), 'The Body in Illness and Health: The *Caraka Saṃhitā*' in *Human Being, Bodily Being. Phenomenology from Classical India* (Oxford: Oxford University Press), 27–57.

Raveendran, A. and Bazzul, J. (2021), 'Socialized Medicine Has Always Been Political: COVID-19, Science and Biopower in India'. *Cultural Studies of Science Education*, 16: 995–1013. https://doi.org/10.1007/s11422-021-10093-1

Sowemimo, A. (2023), *Divided: Racism, Medicine and Why We Need to Decolonise Healthcare* (London: Profile Books).

Sunar, L. (ed.) (2016), *Eurocentrism at the Margins. Encounters, Critics and Going Beyond* (London: Routledge).

Index